The New Economic Role of American States

The New
Economic Role
of American States

*Strategies in
a Competitive World Economy*

EDITED BY

R. Scott Fosler

Committee for Economic Development

New York   Oxford
OXFORD UNIVERSITY PRESS
1988

Oxford University Press

Oxford   New York   Toronto
Delhi   Bombay   Calcutta   Madras   Karachi
Petaling Jaya   Singapore   Hong Kong   Tokyo
Nairobi   Dar es Salaam   Cape Town
Melbourne   Auckland

and associated companies in
Beirut   Berlin   Ibadan   Nicosia

Published by Oxford University Press, Inc.,
200 Madison Avenue, New York, New York 10016

Oxford is a registered trademark of Oxford University Press.

Library of Congress Cataloging-in-Publication Data
The New economic role of American states.
Bibliography: p.
Includes index.
1. United States—Economic policy—1981—
2. Industry and state—United States—States.
I. Fosler, R. Scott.   II. Committee for Economic Development.
HC106.8.N495   1988   338.973   87-12499
ISBN 0-19-505003-7

2 4 6 8 9 7 5 3 1

Printed in the United States of America
on acid-free paper

Acknowledgments

I want to thank each of the case study authors for his or her contribution. Their willingness to tackle so formidable a range of issues, their cooperation in comparing and contrasting the various cases, and their never-failing good humor made this enterprise not only possible, but enjoyable. The authors have acknowledged those who gave special assistance in the preparation of their individual cases, and I add my thanks for their assistance.

This research would not have been possible without the initiative and full support of the Committee for Economic Development's leadership. Edmund B. Fitzgerald, chairman and chief executive officer of Northern Telecom Limited and chairman of the Committee for Economic Development, supported the project from the start. William F. May, former chairman of American Can Company and currently chairman and chief executive officer of the Statue of Liberty-Ellis Island Foundation, Inc., initiated the state project as chairman of CED's Research and Policy Committee. William S. Edgerly, chairman of the State Street Bank and Trust Company, chaired the Subcommittee on State Economic Progress and provided intellectual leadership in framing the research and guiding it to conclusion. CED's president, Robert C. Holland, was involved in every stage of the project and contributed generously in the critical assessment of its findings.

The members of the subcommittee and its advisors participated in the selection of the cases, the framing of issues, and interpretation of the results. John J. Forrer, senior research associate, was an active partner in the design and management of the project. Carol Alvey, administrative assistant, gave steadfast and untiring effort in the monumental task of coordinating the research effort and preparing the manuscript. Claudia P. Feurey, CED vice president and director of information, has, as always, been indispensable in moving the research toward publication. She was ably assisted by the editorial skills of Benjamin Fulves. Gail Fosler, who at the time served as deputy director and chief economist for the United States Senate Budget Committee, gave of her personal time to provide invaluable perspective, analytic critique, and editorial advice.

I would also like to thank the people at Oxford University Press, in particular Herbert J. Addison, Vice President and Executive Editor, and Catherine Clements, Associate Editor, for their contribution and assistance in publishing this volume.

We are grateful for the financial support that was generously provided by the Ford Foundation and the Lilly Endowment, Inc. A special thanks is due David Arnold of the Ford Foundation for the substantive contributions he made both to this project and to a better understanding of the state role in the economy. We want also to thank the following organizations for their financial support: Aladdin Industries, Inc.; Alcoa Foundation; American General Life and Accident Insurance Company; J. C. Bradford & Company; Cherokee Equity; Commerce Union Bank; First American Corporation; The Hospital Corporation of America; Ingram Industries, Inc.; James Irvine Foundation; Eastman Kodak Charitable Trust; Monsanto Fund; Murray Ohio Manufacturing Co.; The Newhall Land & Farming Co.; Nissan Motor Manufacturing Corporation U.S.A.; Northern Telecom Inc.; Pacific Telesis Foundation; Peat, Marwick, Mitchell & Co.; Southern California Gas Company; Third National Corporation; and Transamerica Insurance Corporation of California.

To the many other people who contributed in some way to this effort, I express my thanks and apology for the absence of a personal mention.

Washington, D.C.   R. S. F.
April 1987

Foreword

The case studies in this volume cover a period of major change for the American economy and for economic policy at all levels of government. Many traditional industries have developed excess capacity; new technologies are creating new industries and transforming traditional industries; and the United States confronts an unprecedented degree of integration with the world economy. To the surprise of many, initiatives at the state level have been among the most creative and energetic of any American institutions in responding to this challenge. Here there is imagination, experimentation, and a valuable accumulation of practical experience with attempts to improve the basic economic assets of America: its workforce, physical infrastructure, technology, schools and universities, capital availability, small businesses, and entrepreneurship.

Especially encouraging has been the institutional flexibility shown by both public and private sector leaders in adjusting to these new circumstances. Public-private partnership, both to develop consensus on the appropriate state role and to mount effective action, has been a hallmark of the state economic initiatives.

The Committee for Economic Development traditionally has focused most of its research on national and international economic issues. But in addressing such pressing national concerns as competitiveness, productivity, education, health, labor adjustment, and product liability, we saw at every turn a strong regional dimension and important role for state leaders in both government and the private sector. States also have a major effect on the ability of local leaders to improve their economies. In our 1982 policy statement, *Public-Private Part-nership: An Opportunity for Urban Communities,* we stressed that effective local action in the years ahead could be sharply constrained or enhanced by state governments. We concluded, in sum, that the success of the U.S. economy as a whole depended increasingly on initiatives taken at the regional and local levels, and that states were critical to both.

In 1984, CED decided to examine more closely the growing economic role of states. A Subcommittee on State Economic Progress was established to bring together the best of practical experience and academic thinking on the role of states in the economy. The case studies presented in this volume were undertaken as part of the field research for that project. They provided a principal source of information for the CED policy statement, *Leadership for Dynamic State Economies,* which was issued in September 1986.

The case studies helped lead us to the conclusion that there is indeed an important role for states in today's competitive world economy. That role should not be oversold. The key to economic development remains, as it has always been, a market driven private sector. However, the states can play an important role in building such economic foundations as education, physical infrastructure, knowledge and technology, quality of life, and fiscal climate that are important to private sector success.

CED's principal conclusions about the state role are contained in the policy statement. However, we found the case studies of such value in understanding the evolution of regional economies and state economic policy that we decided they should be made available to practitioners and scholars.

In order to compete in the world economy, the United States will need to draw upon energies and capabilities from numerous sources. The experiences depicted in these case studies demonstrate the contribution that can be made by public and private sector leaders at the state level.

Boston, 1987   William S. Edgerly

Chairman, State Street Bank
and Trust Company

Chairman, CED Subcommittee
on State Economic Progress

Contents

Contributors

Timothy J. Bartik is Assistant Professor of Economics, Department of Economics and Business Administration, Vanderbilt University.

William A. Blazar is a consultant on economic development and tax policy in Minneapolis.

Ronald F. Ferguson is Assistant Professor of Public Policy, John F. Kennedy School of Government, Harvard University.

R. Scott Fosler is Vice President and Director of Government Studies for the Committee for Economic Development.

Douglas C. Henton is a Program Manager at SRI International.

John E. Jackson is Professor of Political Science and Director, Taubman Program in American Institutions, Institute for Social Research, The University of Michigan.

Ted Kolderie is a senior fellow in the Hubert H. Humphrey Institute of Public Affairs at the University of Minnesota.

Helen F. Ladd is Professor of Public Policy Studies, Institute of Policy Sciences and Public Affairs, Duke University.

Larry Landry is President of Landry & Associates, Phoenix, Arizona.

Steven A. Waldhorn is Director of the Center for Economic Competitiveness at SRI International.

Charles R. Warren is at Indiana University.

OVERVIEW

R. Scott Fosler

1

Introduction

States have become leaders in confronting the global challenge to American competitiveness. Considered by some people to be Constitutional anachronisms not too many years ago, states have reasserted their traditional roles as experimenters and first-line managers in regional governance. In today's interdependent world economy, they are not so much the traditional "laboratories of democracy" as fifty bubbling crucibles in an American national laboratory that is seeking a new formula for global economic success.

The key to American competitiveness is, as it always has been, a dynamic, innovative, market-driven private sector. The responsibility for achieving it belongs principally to the private sector itself. But the private sector will be successful only through partnership with government at all levels. Some states are well advanced in holding up their end of the bargain.

The New State Activism

Until the 1970s, the few states that had formal economic development programs focused them on efforts to attract business to the state. In response to the economic turbulence of the 1970s and, especially, since the severe recessions of the early 1980s, many states have broadened their efforts to include creation, expansion, and retention, as well as attraction of business. They have rediscovered the economic importance of such traditional state services as education and trans-

3

portation. And, they have established new programs in numerous areas: for example, to provide new sources of capital, to promote new technology, to support small business and entrepreneurship, and to expand export markets. This surge of activity has intensified throughout the 1980s and shows no signs of abating.

Is this new activism by the states significant? The case studies presented in this book found that it is. They conclude that while the state economic role is limited, it is increasingly important and in certain instances may be decisive. The initiatives described in the case studies reflect an emerging state economic role that is substantially different from the conventional one in three important ways:

- In the conventional role, economic development is viewed as a government function (similar to police or health) whose principal mission is to recruit industry to the state. In the new role, *economic development is conceived as a process* that occurs predominantly in the market driven private sector, but is affected in all its phases—creation, expansion, relocation, contraction, and regeneration—by a wide range of state actions, which cut across traditional functional lines.

- In the conventional role, the state passively accepts prevailing economic forces (at most attempting to influence business location decisions), on the implicit assumption that national economic growth is more or less inevitable and, in any case, could be influenced only by federal policy. In the new role, the state employs *an active strategy to improve its competitiveness* by confronting and taking advantage of prevailing economic forces.

- In the conventional role, institutional responsibility for economic policy is consigned to a line agency of the state government, typically a department of economic development or commerce, whose principal mission is to recruit industry. In the new role, a fundamentally different set of institutional arrangements—involving numerous organizations in both the public and private sectors and at various levels of government—is used to accommodate the new strategic orientation, *institutions that are more versatile and flexible* in permitting the state to anticipate, specialize, experiment, integrate, evaluate, and adjust in dealing with new and changing economic forces.

The essence of the new role lies in the states' consciously striving to adapt to an environment that is more complex, competitive, and uncertain. The purpose of the case studies presented in this book is to examine the role of the state within that changing environment and to consider the implications of that role for economic policy in the future.

The Focus of Study: State Political Economies

The case studies that make up this book were intended to provide practical guidance to those concerned with improving state economic performance. Early in our study, it was clear that no single program or set of policies would provide a simple prescription for state economic success. The temptation to rely on quick fixes and simple "how to's" undeniably is strong, and there remains today, even after more than a decade of experience with a seemingly endless flow of the "latest" economic development programs, a tendency to vest unrealistic hopes in the fad of the moment.

But, the sober reality is that success most likely lies in addressing numerous issues with individually small but cumulatively significant economic impact. By the end of the period covered by the case studies (the mid-1980s), a vast array of new economic programs had been introduced, covering virtually every arena of state action. Most of the tools, it appeared, were on the table. The real question was how to use them effectively.

For this reason, our case studies focused on the role of state *institutions* and the *process* by which they diagnose economic problems, formulate strategies, put those strategies into effect, evaluate the consequences, and make adjustments as warranted. State institutions are defined here to include not only the government and political institutions associated with the public sector (including local government) but also distinctive private sector organizations that play a major role in determining the direction of the state economy.

State institutions are geographically circumscribed by state political boundaries that rarely correspond to the contours of regional economies. The definition of a *state economy,* therefore, can be a contrived statistical shorthand. In reality, the economic activity in any given state is the aggregation of all or part of the various regional economies encompassed within its borders. It is the vitality of those regions that matters. And in the American federal system, the state defines key power centers where public action is taken that affects that regional vitality.

In the past, American regions have traded and competed almost exclusively with one another. The important competition has not been in the highly publicized "smokestack chasing," designed to attract plants with financial incentives, but in building internal economic dynamism that fosters growth organically from within. A loss of comparative advantage by one region meant a gain in comparative advantage by another, with the country as a whole usually ending up the winner. Today, by contrast, the regions of America are trading and competing not only with one another but with the regions of the world.

The central issue is how state institutions can shape regional economies to make them more competitive in the new world economy. To address that issue, the case studies ask three basic questions: How have regional economies evolved? What has been the impact of actions by state institutions on regional economies in the course of that evolution? And, what are the implications of those findings for the future economic role of states?

Our interest, in short, has been to understand the dynamics of state political economies, the better to improve their performance.

Four states were selected for comprehensive study: Massachusetts, Michigan, Tennessee, and California. The four provide a reasonable representation of distinct regions: the Northeast, Midwest, South, and West. Taken together, their evolution sharply depicts regional variations and changing state roles. They also generally reflect the wide range of economic conditions and recent policy experience among states.

In addition, three other states—Arizona, Indiana, and Minnesota—were selected for narrower study because each had attacked the problem of state economic policy with a distinctive strategy. These three narrower studies supplement the more comprehensive analyses of Massachusetts, Michigan, Tennessee, and California.

The cases are not limited to formally designated economic development programs but examine a range of actions that have important economic content. These encompass such areas as human resource development, physical infrastructure, natural resource management, technological development, capital markets, regulation, and fiscal policy. The intent was to determine what state actions affect the economy, not just what actions policy makers believe have an effect.

The case studies also benefit from a range of perspectives, which vary according to the academic discipline and professional experience of the authors. The Massachusetts study was prepared by Ronald Ferguson and Helen Ladd, who are professors of public policy. The author of the Michigan study, John Jackson, is a professor of political science with a special interest in institutions of economic consequence. The Tennessee study was prepared by a professor of economics, Timothy Bartik. The California study authors are public policy analysts and consultants Douglas Henton and Steven Waldhorn. The Arizona case study was authored by Larry Landry, a business and public policy consultant, who from 1979 to 1983 directed the Arizona Office of Economic Planning and Development. The Indiana study was prepared by Charles Warren, a policy analyst with a background in intergovernmental institutions, who has returned to academia as a political scientist. The Minnesota case study was prepared by Ted Kolderie, a professor of public policy, who from 1967 to 1980 was executive director of the Citizens League of St. Paul/Minneapolis, and Bill Blazar, a policy analyst and consultant.

Organization of the Book

Chapter 2 establishes a general context for the case studies. It describes the way in which economic regions have evolved individually and interacted with one another; the role that states have played in that development; and the changing distribution of economic responsibilities at the federal, state, and local levels. The way we think about the states and regions has been heavily conditioned by the predominance of the federal government and the nearly exclusive focus on the national economy over the past half century. With a broader perspective, we can see many of today's seemingly novel and perplexing regional changes as familiar historical patterns that had been obscured by their own glacial progression and our own hardened habits of mind.

The four principal case studies are presented in a sequence that generally reflects their historical emergence and industrialization within the American economic landscape.

Massachusetts, one of the earliest colonies, was also the first state to industrialize, in the nineteenth century. Michigan nurtured its industrial base throughout the latter nineteenth century and then stole the initiative from New England in the early twentieth. Tennessee's frontier economy expanded into a prosperous plantation economy that was destroyed by the Civil War, and then struggled with its neighboring southern states for a century to catch up with the industrialized Northeast and Midwest. California began its entrepreneurial tradition with the gold rush of 1849 and benefited from successive waves of natural resource based industries until transformed by defense industries in the 1940s.

Not coincidentally, the four states have followed a roughly similar sequence in responding to the economic turbulence of the 1970s and 1980s.

Massachusetts' leaders actively began seeking ways to strengthen their economy when the economic shocks of the early 1970s exposed the decrepitude of the state's traditional apparel industries and when the scaling down of the Vietnam War cut back activity in the state defense industry. Leaders in Michigan ignored repeated danger signals as to the vulnerability of the automotive industry until the sustained depression level unemployment of the late 1970s and early 1980s made it clear that the state economy was suffering not just a cyclical downturn but a major restructuring. The turbulence of the late 1970s persuaded Tennessee not only to intensify its traditional strategy of recruiting branch plants, in part by looking to Japanese manufacturers, but to give greater attention to the important economic foundations of the state. California's economic complacency was jolted in 1977 when the Dow Chemical Company cancelled plans to construct a $500 million plant in the state, purportedly due to overly restrictive environmental regulations.

In each of the cases, the authors provide a context for understanding these events, describe the institutional and strategic responses to them, and consider the implications for the future.

The three more narrowly focused case studies each explore a distinctive theme. In Arizona, state leaders attempted to transform an economy that had relied heavily on natural resources into a more diverse economy that would benefit from new growth industries, especially in high technology. Indiana, following a period of intense self-examination (which included consideration of the economic policies and institutions of other states), designed a novel institutional structure for economic strategy. In Minnesota, state leaders saw the quality of life in general and the quality of public service systems more specifically as integral to the state's economic development.

The concluding chapter compares and contrasts the seven cases, suggesting how the experiences more generally define a new economic role that is applicable to all the states. It constructs a composite agenda from the numerous actions deemed economically important in the various states, discusses the types of strategies employed, and analyzes the key institutional changes being made to accommodate the more expansive and strategically oriented state role. The chapter, and the volume, conclude with a discussion of the national implications of the new state role.

2

The State Economic Role
in Perspective

The new state economic role is more than a package of economic development programs. It embraces the capacity of state institutions to correctly read prevailing economic forces and reorient state economic strategy accordingly. To understand the scope of that role requires placing it in a broader historical context.

Three important factors have created the context for recent state actions: the dynamics of regional change; political and economic developments over the past half century that have shaped the conventional state role and conditioned thinking about it; and world and national forces that are transforming the economy, the regions, and public responsibilities for economic policy.

States and the Dynamics of Regional Change

Economic differences among the American regions today are widely depicted in the popular media as a novel development. In fact, throughout its history, the United States has been a nation of diverse regional economies whose relative fortunes have fluctuated over time. The patterns and cycles reflected in the case studies have long been apparent to students of regional dynamics, but during the past several decades, they largely have been ignored by macro economists and policy makers preoccupied with national economic issues.

8

A Continent of Regions

Since colonial times, the prosperity and hardship of individual regions have fluctuated with the fortunes of specific industries as they began, expanded, and
matured, and relocated, modernized, and declined.

Massachusetts prospered from the industrialization and sustained growth of
its textile and apparel industries throughout the nineteenth century. Michigan's
economy, meanwhile, remained primarily dependent on natural resources, principally agriculture and timber. But the furniture-making and chemical industries
evolving out of the timber industry, along with the railroads and shipping used
to haul farm goods and lumber to eastern markets, were laying the base for
industrialization in Michigan.

In contrast to its industrializing counterparts in New England and the Midwest, Tennessee pursued the agricultural path of its regional neighbors in the
South. As late as 1860, all the southern states combined had less manufacturing
than the state of Massachusetts alone. Tennessee's per capita income fell from
80 percent of the U.S. average before the Civil War to 55 percent after the Civil
War, in part because of the fall of cotton prices. But, unlike Massachusetts,
which could develop its manufacturing skills slowly and without overwhelming
competition, and unlike Michigan, where the combination of a diverse economic base and favorable timing produced industrial growth, Tennessee had
virtually no manufacturing base to turn to for immediate relief and no industrial
tradition upon which to rebuild. Rather than evolve its own homegrown industrial base, Tennessee sought to attract manufacturing branch plants whose technologies and processes had already been developed in the North, a zealous
preoccupation of Tennessee that continues to the present time.

Changes in one region have affected conditions in others. In the late nineteenth and early twentieth centuries, both Massachusetts and Michigan were losing manufacturing jobs to lower wage states like Tennessee in the South. But, in
Michigan, the booming new automobile industry more than compensated for its
losses in the furniture industry. Massachusetts, by contrast, having failed to
develop a major new growth industry, was unable to replace the jobs lost as its
textile and shoe industries relocated. The Massachusetts economy, overly
dependent on industries with limited growth potential and plants unable to compete for existing markets, throughout the 1920s sank into the depression that did
not hit the booming Michigan economy until the 1930s.

The predominantly low-wage manufacturing jobs that flowed out of the
Northeast and Midwest into the South did little to raise Tennessee's share of
national per capita income, which continued to hover around 55 percent until
World War II. Such manufacturing growth as Tennessee enjoyed was concentrated in industries such as textiles and food processing, which had already
reached a point of mass standardized production, employing relatively low-
wage labor. The manufacturing branch plants reduced dependence on agriculture, but not enough to prevent Tennessee, with other farming states, from
suffering the depression in agriculture that, like the contraction of traditional

manufacturing in Massachusetts, continued its downward spiral throughout the 1920s.

It was not until after World War II that a second wave of durable goods manufacturing from the North and Midwest helped to raise Tennessee's relative per capita income, a trend Tennessee officials sought to encourage through the creation, in 1945, of an Industrial Development Division in the State Planning Commission.

Dynamics of Change Within Regions

Each regional economy has evolved in its own particular fashion, building mainly on the assets of labor, capital, organization, and natural resources already in place. New industries have been spun off from existing industries as entrepreneurs and investors sought new opportunities and adjusted to changing markets. Adaptable businesses sometimes regenerated themselves by improving their productivity or developing new products or marketing strategies. Uncompetitive enterprise was sloughed off, with salvageable assets—labor, skills, physical stock, managerial know-how, capital—channeled into more productive uses or relocated to other regions.

The seeds of change, for both growth and decline, have tended to be sown by the prevailing industries and economic climate of the day. Sustained prosperity often has created dependencies and rigidities in habits and institutions that impeded the transition to new technologies and new industries. Decline, on the other hand, has tended eventually to loosen rigidities, curb costs, and compel experimentation with new approaches. Strong trends in either direction have tended to obscure the signs of change that could reverse fortunes. Prosperity has masked forces of decay; hardship has obscured the potential for renewal.

By the turn of the century, Massachusetts was a mature industrial state with a skilled work force, an extensive network of modern textile and shoe plants, a growing energy capability, a strong machine tool industry, a core of highly motivated and capable inventors, and substantial venture capital. But despite its apparent comparative advantage, Massachusetts proved incapable of capturing the next major surge of industrial growth, the automotive industry, which took root in Detroit.

The reasons Michigan stole the initiative from Massachusetts in commercializing the automobile are complex. But, instructively for our age, the key seems to have been the inclination of most New England entrepreneurs and financiers to rely on the steam and electric power technologies common in their industrial processes to produce a commercially successful automobile, while Michiganders more aggressively pursued the gasoline internal combustion engine, which was familiar to them through its use in marine transportation.

The industrial decline of Massachusetts was slow and obscure. Net employment losses in cities like Lowell and New Bedford, as early as 1910, were overshadowed by continued overall growth in New England's shoe and textile employment until 1923. But, during the remainder of the 1920s, Massachusetts suffered a net job loss in cotton goods and shoes, as these industries accelerated their relocation to the West and South. Textile and shoe manufacturing capacity throughout the United States had expanded to the point that the older, higher wage factories in New England were at a comparative disadvantage with the newer, lower-wage plants in states like Tennessee. As jobs were lost and threatened, there was an increase in the labor militancy that in part had prompted manufacturers to shift investment outside the state in the first place, thereby reinforcing the trend. The textile industry enjoyed a brief surge during World War II but employment fell by two-thirds between 1947–64, and by 1975, Massachusetts' employment in the textile and shoe industries had plunged to pre-Civil War levels.

Michigan prospered from seventy years of growth in the automotive industry. Since the late 1970s, however, the state has paid for its dependence on an industry that now faces limited growth potential and stiff foreign competition. Michiganders were slow to acknowledge the trouble signs and today are confronting the difficulties of adjusting to a more competitive environment.

In Massachusetts, meanwhile, just as signals of decline went largely unheeded during its long years of prosperity, so the signs of new growth potential were obscured during its long, relative decline. As early as the 1920s, the seeds of new enterprise were germinating in the form of a nascent electronics industry, university research increasingly linked to product commercialization, business services, and a new generation of defense contracting. These were to fuel Massachusetts' resurgence in the late 1970s.

California's economy over the years has benefited from successive surges in new industries: gold, agriculture, oil, entertainment, and defense production. The state's economy was radically transformed by World War II. Defense production increased the manufacturing work force two and one-half times between 1940–43 and generated a major aircraft industry in Southern California. Many of the 7 million service men who passed through the state returned to live there after the war.

Defense contracting continued to play a major role in California during the postwar expansion, spurring the development and eventual commerical production of integrated circuits. Microprocessors and semiconductors stimulated a further revolution in microelectronics in the 1970s, accelerating the growth of "Silicon Valley" in the San Francisco Bay Area.

Silicon Valley's development over several decades is attributable mainly to the presence and active involvement of Stanford University, effective venture capitalists, and the particular talents and tastes of a few individuals who developed and applied the new technology. The Defense Department provided the principal incentive and initial financing for the development of integrated circuits and the microprocessor. Key inventors and entrepreneurs chose the Bay Area in part for personal reasons, including the pleasant climate and their personal familiarity with the area, and in part because of the technical and financial resources available. But even Silicon Valley appears to be subject to historic patterns of regional evolution. Once hailed as the high technology region of the future, by the 1980s, the area was suffering from a severe slide in the American semiconductor industry.

Role of the Public Sector

Regional economic growth has resulted principally from the initiatives of private enterprise driven by market pressures and opportunities. Only in rare (although at times important) instances have government or public institutions led in promoting new economic endeavors or in prompting the private sector toward a more innovative or energetic response to changing market forces. On the other hand, from the beginning, public institutions have been an essential part of the process of regional growth. Responding to political pressures or practical need, they have established the institutional framework, provided essential support services, and influenced the incentive for investment and change. The two sectors have been so integral to one another that it is difficult to separate the endeavors of private individuals and organizations from their common public foundations.

We are accustomed today to thinking of the federal government as inherently prominent in public economic policy, because it has been so for the past fifty years. But this has not always been the case. The relative prominence of federal, state, and local governments in economic affairs has varied over time. State institutions over the years have become so thoroughly integrated with regional economies that their influence is pervasive, if frequently unrecognized, and often difficult to assess.

In colonial times, the political and religious institutions of Puritan Massachusetts actively supported individual enterprise but in a strictly defined commonwealth of interests. The colonial government provided a militia for the common defense and a physical infrastructure, such as highways, roads, and ferries. The first corporations chartered by the commonwealth of Massachusetts were expressly for community purposes: churches, hospitals, schools and colleges, municipalities, and poorhouses.

The adoption of the U.S. Constitution provided a solid political and legal basis for open commerce among the states, but economic initiative continued to rest with individual enterprise and the states and localities, as it had during colonial times. Whereas Alexander Hamilton's plan to promote manufacturing was abandoned by the federal government, the Massachusetts state government actively encouraged local manufacturing to reduce dependence on British imports. Massachusetts chartered 379 manufacturing corporations (mainly mills) between 1810–35, deeming them to have a quasi public character.

During the early nineteenth century, the states led the way in promoting growth by building canals and highways, financing business ventures, chartering banks and corporations, and sometimes taking equity positions in private enterprises. The feverish investment by state governments, in fact, may have contributed to the financial crisis of 1837.

In the late nineteenth century, the states limited their direct involvement in enterprise development, although they were active along with their local governments in providing transportation, water supply, and other utilities to accommodate urban growth and industrialization. State bonds in Michigan helped to finance the railroads that moved lumber and agricultural products to eastern markets. The Southern Pacific Railroad and California state government were so closely intertwined through political and financial dealings that the two were considered by many to be one and the same. Agricultural expansion in California required the construction of major water supply facilities with government support to nurture California's soil-rich but parched farm regions.

The states have responded to economic change differently over the years. In some instances, they have been innovators and experimenters. For example, in the late nineteenth century, Massachusetts established a State Board of Arbitration to mediate the increasing number of labor management conflicts, and opened state employment offices in key urban centers to help laid-off textile workers find jobs. In other instances, they have been followers, even laggards. The effectiveness of response depended at least in part on the quality of civic leadership. Over time, all of the states have tended to adopt the policies and institutions forged by the leaders, and thus, the basic economic role maintained a certain similarity from state to state.

The National Eclipse of States and Regions

Beginning with the depression of the 1930s, the economic role of states and regions was eclipsed by the expanding power of the federal government. It is instructive that the nation's collective memory recalls the Great Depression as an economic calamity that hit the country as a whole with sudden force, following the stock market crash of 1929. As noted earlier, in reality, states like Massachusetts and Tennessee sank slowly into depression throughout the 1920s because of an inability to generate new growth to compensate for the declining industries on which they depended so heavily. When, in the early 1930s, the more robust industries in other regions faced a sharp drop in demand, no region was able to act as an engine of growth and a general depression descended upon the entire national economy.

In their battle against the depression, the New Deal experimenters drew liberally on such economic and social programs of the states and cities as unemployment insurance, workmen's compensation, and old age income security. The federal government also began a series of efforts to address regional economic problems. The Tennessee Valley Authority, for example, was established in the 1930s to spur economic development in Tennessee and neighboring states by controlling floods and providing cheap electricity.

Massive federal spending associated with World War II finally brought the United States out of the depression and laid the base for an economic expansion that benefited every state. The war effort also reinforced the predominance of the federal government in the American federal system. Federal taxing and spending surpassed that of the states and localities; economic theory and policy became preoccupied almost exclusively with national, macroeconomic issues; and virtually all policy initiatives thereafter appeared to come from the federal government, including those specifically designed to promote economic development.

The states, nonetheless, played an important role in providing key public services to accommodate the postwar expansion. Nowhere was that role more monumental than in California, which used a large surplus accumulated during the boom years of World War II to build new highways, schools, colleges, hospitals, prisons, and water projects. In the 1950s, California's capital spending grew at twice the rate of the population. Between 1958–66, the state constructed 1000 miles of freeways, a $1.75 billion water project, three new university campuses, and six state colleges. The massive investment in modern public facilities helped California accommodate a population surge from 16 million in 1960 to 20 million in 1970, when it surpassed New York as the most populous state in the nation.

But, while the states played a major part in accommodating the economic growth associated with the postwar expansion, their role was largely reactive. State leaders generally assumed that national economic prosperity was inevitable (with occasional cyclical downturns) and that economic management was the exclusive realm of the federal government. Similarly, today's competing economic theories—Keynesian, monetarist, neo-classicist, supply side—have disagreed on many things, but on two points there has been implicit consensus: The basic unit of aggregate economic analysis is the nation, and it is the federal government whose policies affect that unit. Certainly, there can be no dispute over the predominance of the federal economic role during the past fifty years. But as the case studies reveal, the historical patterns of regional dynamics and state involvement have persisted, even if they have been overlooked.

The Reemergence of the States

In the 1970s, a combination of three powerful forces began to alter fundamentally the conventional state role: transformations in technology and economic factors that have affected nearly all industries and regions; the increasing vulnerability of the U.S. economy to foreign competition; and a major political change in the relative responsibilities in the federal system of government.

Economic Transformation

Two hundred years of national economic growth has affected every region of the country and, in important ways, has made them very similar. All of the states are now predominantly urban, and their employment is primarily in services, secondarily in goods production, and (with a few exceptions) fractionally in agriculture. For example, whereas a century ago Massachusetts was predominantly a manufacturing economy and Tennessee an agricultural economy, in 1983 about 70 percent of earnings in both states were generated by industries other than manufacturing and agriculture. In both states, manufacturing is less than 30 percent and agriculture less than 2 percent of earnings.

Every region has shared in the wealth generated by national economic growth. What is more, the disparities of income among them have been diminished dramatically. In 1930, California and Massachusetts were two of six states with per capita income above 130 percent of the national average, while Tennessee was one of sixteen states with income below 70 percent. By 1980, per capita income in all three was, like Michigan's, between 80 and 120 percent of the national average; now, Alaska is the only state above 130 percent and Mississippi is the only state below 70 percent of the national average.

The contrasts in economic structure within states in some ways are now more striking than the differences among them. In Tennessee, for example, per capita income in 1980 was 4 percent above the national average in Nashville/Davidson County but less than one-half the national average in ten rural counties. In all four states, urban service-oriented economies flourish alongside depressed rural areas whose economic base is concentrated in agriculture, natural resources, or low-wage manufacturing. Within urban areas, some older core cities decline, while robust and frenetic growth is transforming the periphery.

These new realities have yet to change greatly the conventional stereotypes of the American regions. But, even before the popular images have been able to catch up with the current reality, new economic forces are already changing the regional picture again. These forces include the following:

- In industries such as durable goods manufacturing, agriculture, and natural resource extraction, productive capacity has outpaced market growth, creating a highly competitive environment and causing stress in regions where those industries are concentrated.
- New technologies in information processing, robotics, biotechnology, and ceramics and composite materials have spawned new industries in specialized regions and are affecting other industries throughout the country.
- Relative shares of employment have shifted from manufacturing to services as overall manufacturing employment has remained more or less constant while service jobs have increased; meanwhile, employment losses in some manufacturing industries have been substantial with corresponding declines in employment in the regions where they were concentrated.

The regional implications of these recent trends are significant: losses in manufacturing employment in the Northeast and Midwest with gains in the South and West; the substantial growth of service based employment in the Northeast; geographical pockets of growth based on the new technologies; loss of employment in the resource based economies; and shifts in population associated with all of these changes. But, perhaps the most important implication for regions is that competitive advantage among places increasingly depends upon the better use of technology, human resources, and organization. This reality has not been lost on America's trading partners.

Foreign Competition

Competition from abroad has challenged American industries nearly across the board. The oil shocks of the 1970s dramatized the extent to which the U.S. economy had become vulnerable to foreign influences. Surging imports, sluggishness in exports, and a consequently widening trade deficit, even as the dollar declined in 1986, have underscored the magnitude and strength of the competition.

The American economy has always been subject to the forces of world economic change. Colonial America became prosperous by trading with Europe and drawing on European technology and institutions, which themselves were in the throes of the industrial revolution. The continental nation then added its own assets: vast natural resources; the appeal to waves of ambitious immigrants eager to work and improve their lives; huge markets with few artificial barriers; relative isolation from foreign competition during a critical period of industrialization; and political and social institutions that encouraged change and, in the main, rewarded performance. In the nineteenth century, the American economy placed its own mark on the European economic revolution and, by the early twentieth century, was leading it. By the final quarter of the twentieth century, however, that lead was being challenged by vibrant and aggressive foreign economies.

Americans today face the sobering question of whether, in the perspective of history, their economic leadership will turn out to have been a relatively brief period of less than one century, during which world economic leadership passed through North America from one group of economic giants in Europe to another in Asia. Each American state is inescapably a part of that national story and the worldwide forces that have molded it.

The new international realities have affected every region. Foreign competition in the automotive industry has severely strained the Michigan economy. Industries such as footwear, textiles, and apparel that had moved to Tennessee from the North in search of low-wage labor have sought even lower-wage labor in Asia and Latin America. California's semiconductor industry was being battered by Japanese competition soon after it was established, challenging the precept that America can always compete in world markets by being first in research and innovation.

Some global trends have been beneficial for Massachusetts, in large part because Boston is a major international financial and business services center. Massachusetts also benefited from increases in federal defense spending, which itself is affected by international events. But even Massachusetts, which in the mid-1980s boasted one of the strongest and most well-positioned economies among all the states, continued to be concerned about the potential foreign threat to its high technology industries.

Under the relatively closed national economy of the past, the loss of comparative advantage in one American region would be compensated by a gain in comparative advantage in another American region. Today, losses in one American region may as well mean gains for a foreign country.

The experience of Silicon Valley demonstrates how the combination of changing technology and foreign competition are affecting regional dynamics. Contrast the development of Silicon Valley's electronics based economy with that of southeast Michigan's automobile based economy. There are important similarities. In the early days of both, numerous firms were designing and marketing new and competing products based on a common new technology. Competition thinned the ranks, and a few large firms soon prevailed. Meanwhile, a multitude of firms and industries developed to provide support services in design, manufacturing of parts, sales, and distribution. In time, both industries expanded beyond their regional base of origin.

But, there also are important differences that highlight the new economic realities. One is that the production technology of microprocessing equipment, once having stabilized, is not nearly as labor intensive as traditional automobile manufacturing, while the software component continues to provide abundant commercial opportunities and is highly labor intensive, albeit at a high level of skill and training. Another important difference is the rapidity with which the microelectronics technology has become vulnerable to foreign competition. The American automobile industry enjoyed fifty years of unchallenged domestic growth, while the American semiconductor industry was under seige in its home market less than a decade after it took root. By the mid-1980s, Silicon Valley had already lost its lead in semiconductors to the Japanese.

The New Economic Federalism

Economic transformation compounded by foreign competition would have been challenge enough for the states. But, in addition, they have had to shoulder major new political and government responsibilities within the federal system.

The federal retrenchment in domestic policy, begun in the Carter Administration and accelerated in the Reagan Administration, has not so much given economic powers back to the states as revealed the substantial power states already had to affect economic performance.

State governments provide key public services, such as education and physical infrastructure, on which the private sector depends. They also regulate business activity and the management of natural resources.

State tax and spending levels are substantial. In 1986, for example, estimated state and local personal income, sales, and property tax receipts were $406 billion, greater than federal personal income taxes of $361.8 billion; state and local purchases of goods and services were $498.1 billion, or 85 percent of all nondefense purchases by all levels of government.

States are a critical link in the American federal system. They have major responsibilities for implementing federal programs. Local governments, meanwhile, depend upon states for their legal, structural, and financial capabilities.

State boundaries more narrowly encompass economic regions than the nation as a whole, yet more comprehensively cover metropolitan and rural economies than most fragmented local jurisdictions. The cooperation among government, business, labor, universities, and community groups that can influence economic growth in many cases is best undertaken at the state level. State governments can bring together tax, regulatory, financial and technical assistance elements to pursue joint ventures, become their own land developers for economic projects, tailor assistance programs to the needs of different kinds of firms, or generally to foster an entrepreneurial climate. This is especially important at a time when the economy is characterized by the creation of so many new and small firms.

The more energetic exercise of state economic powers does not necessarily imply a diminished federal economic role. The magnitude of the federal government's spending alone assures it will continue to have a major effect on the economy. The globalization of U.S. economy, moreover, increases the importance of federal trade and exchange rate policies. Federal fiscal and monetary policies may be more problematic in their ability to regulate national economic forces, given the influence of international financial flows, but they remain critical nonetheless.

Federal policies, while supposedly neutral, can have widely uneven effects on particular industries and consequently on the regions where those industries are concentrated. The automotive industry, for example, is highly sensitive to interest rates, and thus states like Michigan and Tennessee, which have concentrations in automotive manufacturing, are more likely to respond quickly to changes in monetary policy than Massachusetts or California. Cutbacks in defense spending, on the other hand, could more seriously affect the latter two states, both of which get a substantial proportion of defense contracts. Federal trade policy can be even more particular in its regional impact. Michigan benefited substantially if temporarily from quotas on foreign auto imports, and California stands to benefit similarly from recent agreements to limit the sale of Japanese semiconductors in the United States. These and related actions in taxation, regulation, and lending constitute an implicit "industrial policy" of the federal government.

Whatever its strengths and potential, however, the federal government's ability to initiate new programs has been constrained by massive debt and budget deficits. Having accepted that they could expect little help from Washington, state leaders began to recognize and test the potential of their own substantial powers.

The States Respond

The timing and nature of the state response generally has corresponded to the degree of economic pain they have felt. Massachusetts was among the first to venture forward into the new role in the 1970s. Michigan, Tennessee, and California later joined the experiment, as did Arizona, Indiana, and Minnesota in the late 1970s and early 1980s. The conversion continued into the mid-1980s, as the once flush agricultural and energy states confronted the forces molding the new state economic role. No state has been left unaffected.

The case studies that follow describe numerous new programs and techniques designed to improve a state's economy. And these are important. But a far more important critical dimension of the new state role is the capacity to understand the context of state actions, including the internal and external forces that are transforming regional economies, and to reorient state strategies accordingly. It is in analyzing this dimension, as much as in describing the programs and techniques of economic development, that the case studies contribute to our understanding of the new economic role.

MASSACHUSETTS

Ronald F. Ferguson
Helen F. Ladd

3

State Economic Renaissance

Two special achievements in Massachusetts have attracted growing national attention. First, the state's economic performance has been outstanding when measured in terms of the unemployment rate; joblessness has fallen from over 12 percent of the labor force in 1975 to under 4 percent in 1985. Second, innovative civic and political leadership has made the state a national leader in creating new roles for states to play in economic policy. Public officials from around the country, indeed from around the world, are trying to learn from the "Massachusetts miracle."

They must be careful, however, what lessons they draw. The Massachusetts experience shows that the short-term impact of state economic policy can be positive on the firms and geographic areas directly affected. With time, these effects may diffuse through the state's economy and accumulate. But state sponsored economic initiatives are neither quick fixes for weak economies nor certified elixirs for healthy ones. Neither the scope nor the timing of recent policy initiatives in Massachusetts supports the view that they were an important catalyst in the remarkable economic turnaround of the past decade; the turnaround in the unemployment rate reflects slow labor force growth and the capacity of the state's private sector to respond to growing worldwide demand for certain goods and services. At the same time, state initiatives helped to attract growth to some depressed central cities and slow overheated growth in some regions, and may have helped at the margin to sustain the state's revival once it began.

Massachusetts, like other states, is a small open economy for which a sub-

21

stantial share of the goods and services produced are sold to nonresidents. In the short run, a state's economic base is relatively fixed and the state's economic performance reflects the ability of its economic base to respond to national and international changes in the demand for goods and services. Gradually, innovation and investment enhance and expand a state's economic capacities. In this dynamic process, state policies are among the many factors that have small but cumulative effects on innovation and investment by communities, firms, and households. The slow cumulative nature of economic development and the stronger role of broader economic forces imply that the host of economic development policies introduced in Massachusetts between 1975–86 probably exerted their most significant initial impacts on the location, as distinct from the aggregate level, of state economic growth. At the same time, most of the new programs and policies are well formulated, and their impacts are likely to expand over time.

The Economic History of Massachusetts

The current Massachusetts economy has roots that extend back to the beginning of the nineteenth century. Broad economic and social forces have driven the state's economic development, but state government has actively participated in economic affairs and has repeatedly adjusted its role in response to changing social, political, and economic conditions.[1]

Merchants and the Transition to Manufacturing

Many of the colonists in Massachusetts before the American Revolution were farmers, even though Massachusetts had poor agricultural resources relative to the other colonies. Other colonists worked in small scale manufacturing, which has existed in Massachusetts since the seventeenth century when, as records show, the colony granted patents to make agricultural tools. Skilled artisans working in small mills used water or animal driven machinery to produce tools, nails, furniture, farm implements, textiles, and other goods. The common skills developed in the construction of machinery and the production of wood and metal products provided a strong base for the subsequent development of the state's machine tool industry.[2]

Merchants also were an important group. Boston was the most important port in the colonies and the merchants increasingly grew wealthy with trade to Virginia, the West Indies, and England. By 1771, the richest 5 percent of Boston merchants owned 44 percent of the city's taxable property. As Boston developed a wealthy merchant class and established trading institutions, its comparative advantage became grounded on these assets and on its convenient location as a stopover point for transoceanic voyages.

The wealth of the merchant class and the early machine tools industry were among the special factors that helped forge New England as the birthplace of modern manufacturing in America. The embargo of 1807, the 1810 Non-Intercourse Act, and the War of 1812 restricted trade and forced the merchants to look for investment opportunities beyond those linked to trade and shipping. These events also led the state to promote the commonwealth's economic independence from Great Britain. "Manufacturing thus became a political instrument ... against England, and self-sufficiency in industry acquired a patriotic quality."[3] Significant progress toward these goals occurred in 1813, the year a group of merchants established the Boston Manufacturing Company in Waltham, a suburb of Boston. Using a water powered loom, this textile mill was the first fully integrated factory in which all steps in the production process, from the collection of raw materials to assembling the finished product, were located under one roof. The mill's success influenced other merchants to invest in additional mills along other water power sites in northern Massachusetts. The growing complex of tool makers, financiers, production workers, and mill operators formed industrial agglomerations in the original centers of production in eastern Massachusetts. From 1810–35, the state chartered 379 manufacturing corporations, many of which were mills.[4]

Even as merchants became the financiers of manufacturing enterprises, transportation links with western New York and the Midwest were opening up new opportunities to expand Boston's role as a transportation node and a center for mercantile activity. These links included the Erie Canal in New York and state sponsored railroads in Massachusetts. As part of the same process, the opening up of fertile farmland in western New York and the Midwest put Massachusetts farmers at a competitive disadvantage. Many farmers were induced to move to the emerging urban centers and join the manufacturing work force.

As the number of mills grew, new cities such as Lowell, Chicopee, and Lawrence developed around the mill sites. Boston exploded in size from 16,000 in the eighteenth century to 60,000 in 1830 and 180,000 in 1860. Urbanization increased specialization and expanded the demand for shoes, furniture, clothing, and construction.

Industrial Massachusetts

By the time of the Civil War, the largest industries in Massachusetts were shoes and leather goods, textiles, machine building, and metalworking. Shoemaking had begun as a small cottage industry in the eighteenth century and had grown with urbanization to be the largest industry in the state. In 1860, 60,000 people representing 28 percent of the work force worked in the shoe industry in Massachusetts, while the second largest industry, textiles, employed 50,000. By this time, the state's economic base had developed from traditional crafts to industry, marked by the creation of a permanent urban factory class and clear lines between labor, management, and owners.

As during other wars, the Civil War stimulated innovation and caused a shift forward in the scope and sophistication of the state's and the nation's technology. The demand for weapons with interchangeable parts stimulated important advances in toolmaking that reduced the need for tool makers and their customers to locate close to one another. These advances presumably carried over into the production of machinery used for other tools and consumer goods.[5]

Steam power also was developed at this time. Together, interchangeable parts and steam power enabled production to move away from the tool makers and the best sources of water power. At first this movement was slow, but as labor militancy increased and old plants became obsolete, the shoe and textile industries migrated south, where labor had less of an industrial history and class consciousness. Relative to their New England counterparts, southern workers were content with lower wages, were less militant and more nonunion, and offered little resistance to the introduction of new technology and production methods that used cheaper, less skilled labor. According to one study, capital invested in the southern states increased by 400 percent from 1880 to 1894, while the comparable figure for New England was 75 percent.[6]

From 1873 until the mid-1890s, the nation went through economic hard times. Failing companies were taken over by growing financial empires. Between 1886–1905, the size of the one hundred largest firms in the country quadrupled. Boston financiers were in the forefront of this reorganization and concentration of industry. Conglomerates developed in the textile industry. As concentration increased, larger and more efficient mills were built, forcing smaller mills out of business. The pace of change was swift, disrupting workers and their communities to the point of provocation.

By the end of the nineteenth century, industrial strife was commonplace. Productivity was rising while wages were falling. Workers organized to demand higher wages and equal pay for women. State and local governments became increasingly involved. From the 1870s on, many reports and government hearings deplored the conditions in the factories. In the late 1880s, a Massachusetts State Board of Arbitration was set up to mediate labor management conflicts and, by 1906, state employment offices were organized in Worcester, Springfield, and Boston.

This period of industrialization and urbanization found state and local governments intervening increasingly to alleviate the worst aspects of the living conditions of the urban work force. After the turn of the century, the state intervened to encourage suburbanization and private home ownership. In 1911, the Massachusetts legislature appointed a Homestead Commission to help redirect workers from cities to suburbs and rural areas. The nature of government involvement was no longer to facilitate industrial development, as in the early ninteenth century, but rather to mitigate and reform the excesses of the factories and urban slums.

The Corporate Economy

By the end of World War I, the foundation of modern American industry, the corporation, was in place. The most healthy sectors of the national corporate economy were the technologically advanced industries of oil, steel, autos, electrical engineering, and chemicals. Rapid growth of financial and banking institutions accompanied these developments.

The Massachusetts economy still depended largely on the traditional mill-based industries. The shoe industry had been given a boost by the war, as had the textile industries. Between 1919–29, however, the state lost 2035 industrial establishments and 157,000 jobs. In 1921, Massachusetts ranked fifth among the states in the value of industrial production. By 1935, it had slipped to eighth. The economy recovered somewhat in 1936, but the underlying decline in manufacturing continued until World War II.[7]

Just as before World War I, labor-management conflict continued during the period between World War I and World War II. In the textile industry, workers continued to resist owners' attempts to introduce labor saving devices, speed-ups, and wage cuts. Employers tried to break the unions with a program of selected shutdowns. In an attempt to quell labor militancy, the state cracked down on labor leaders, charging them with un-American activities. The most important employer strategy continued to be the movement of capital out of the state.

World War II gave a brief boost to the textile and footwear industries, but after the war the decline that began in the 1920s accelerated.[8] The decline in footwear and leather goods has continued uninterrupted through to the present. In 1983, textile and leather goods employment in Massachusetts were 17 and 22 percent, respectively, of their 1950 levels.[9]

The high technology sector, however, was developing at the same time that traditional mill-based employment was beginning to decline in the early 1920s. In 1923, the electrical machinery industry was already the commonwealth's third largest employer and MIT had become an integral part of the science and technology landscape in Massachusetts. "As early as the 1920s the institute had established a division of industrial cooperation to handle institute wide contracts with industrial companies. In addition, MIT professors have always moonlighted for industry with the school's blessing and encouragement."[10]

Route 128, a circumferential state highway outside of Boston started in 1951, had a profound effect on the economic geography of the state.[11] By 1961, 306 companies had located adjacent to the highway. Firms producing electronics and instruments predominated, but distribution and warehousing operations located there, too. New housing developments, shopping centers, and general suburbanization followed. Workers for these new establishments were either highly qualified professionals or semiskilled, mostly female, assembly workers in modern production environments.

Defense spending has always been vital to the Massachusetts economy, dating back to the contracts for development of interchangeable parts for rifles before the Civil War.[12] During World War II, the federal government placed major military contracts with metalworking firms, electronics firms, and research organizations, including MIT. Numerous authors cite the pivotal role of government contracts and research institutions in the development of the high technology sector in Massachusetts. But other manufacturing sectors also were affected by military spending on such items as jet engines and machine tools. Thus, as spending for the Vietman War declined in the early 1970s, Massachusetts was hit harder than most states. The decline in military spending, plus a dramatic increase in the price of oil on which the state was highly dependent, made a national recession in 1973–74 into a depression in Massachusetts.

State government spending had increased dramatically in the 1960s, particularly on public welfare. Between 1962–73, state and local expenditures increased from 10 to 16 percent of gross state product. Massachusetts apportioned a larger percentage of state personal income to public welfare, over 2 percent, than any other state. State and local taxes increased between 1963–73 from 9.6 to 14.8 percent of personal income, 15 percent above the national average. Between 1959–71, elected officials made fourteen changes in the tax laws, including thirteen tax rate increases and the enactment of a sales tax.[13] Yet, with the 1974–75 recession, the state government was near bankruptcy in 1975 when newly elected Governor Dukakis called for the biggest tax increase in the commonwealth's history.

The State Economy in 1975

Manufacturing wages in Massachusetts had been lower and unemployment higher than the national average for most of the twentieth century. By 1975 the unemployment rate in Massachusetts was 12 percent compared to the 8.5 percent national rate. Manufacturing wages were 93 percent of the U.S. average. Per capita income had been 131 percent of the national average in 1940; by 1975, it had fallen to 106 percent.[14]

The structure of the Massachusetts economy had changed radically in the postwar period. By 1975, the state economy was quite well diversified, with private sector employment divided relatively evenly among manufacturing, services, and wholesale and retail trade. The postwar decline in manufacturing was offset in part by a rise in nonmanufacturing employment. Between 1947–75, nonmanufacturing private sector jobs nearly doubled to 1.4 million jobs. Electronics was the largest single manufacturing industry and, along with the production of instruments, accounted for 6 percent of total private employment. But, traditional engineering industries, such as nonelectrical machinery (only one-quarter of which was office equipment and computer production in 1975) and transportation equipment, had survived and, in 1975, were still somewhat larger relative to the Massachusetts economy than they were to the national economy. The financial and service sectors, dominated by health and education, accounted for 34 percent of private employment, exceeding the U.S. average of 32 percent. Employment in wholesale and retail trade accounted for 26 percent of the state's private sector jobs, slightly less than the 27 percent comparable national share.

The potential for growth of this more diversified economy, however, was not well understood in 1975. Instead, with high unemployment, state government near bankruptcy, rising oil prices, and declining defense spending, the economic future of Massachusetts looked bleak.

The 1975–85 Economic Renaissance

According to two common measures of economic welfare, the unemployment rate and per capita income, the Massachusetts economy took off during the

1975–85 period. By 1985, the Massachusetts unemployment rate had dropped to 3.9 percent—the lowest of any state in the nation and substantially below the national rate of 7.2 percent. Similarly, per capita income, which had been falling relative to the U.S. average during the early 1970s turned upward in 1979 and, by 1985, exceeded the national average by 15 percent.

Many observers of the Massachusetts economy, and particularly elected state officials, have claimed that enlightened state economic policy was a major cause of the state's economic revival.[15] The timing of the turnaround, however, suggests a more complex story. The upturn had clearly begun by 1979 and, in terms of unemployment, can be dated as early as 1975, the year in which unemployment began falling relative to the U.S. average. Most of the initiatives of the first Dukakis administration were too late to be given credit for the initial turnaround. Moreover, the state's stringent property tax limitation measure, Proposition 2½, often cited for its favorable impact on the state's tax and business climate, passed in 1980, well after the state's unemployment rate started dropping and a year after per capita income began to rise relative to the U.S. average. This suggests that policies initiated during the 1975–85 period probably contributed little to the initial turnaround of the economy. The strong performance of the economy after 1979, however, leaves open the possibility that policy initiatives may have helped sustain growth once it began.

Another plausible explanation of the economic turnaround lies in the dynamics of the state's population and labor force trends. Total jobs in Massachusetts increased 16.2 percent between 1975 and 1983 and another 5.9 percent in 1984. This represents a dramatic change from the 1967–75 period, when jobs increased by only 4 percent. But job growth is not the whole story behind the drop in the state's unemployment rate relative to the U.S. average. Between 1975 and 1983, Massachusetts' population remained virtually constant while total U.S. population increased 8.6 percent. A rising labor force participation rate and demographic changes led to more than a 10 percent increase in the state's labor force, but this, too, was well below the 19 percent growth in the national labor force.

Low in-migration of people into Massachusetts is the key to understanding the state's lack of population growth.[16] Out-migration was about the same for all regions in the country between 1975 and 1980, but the state's in-migration rate was 7 percent compared to the national average of 9.7 percent. In-migration rates for the South and West were 11.9 and 13.4 percent. Observers have attributed the state's low in-migration rate to low wages and the high cost of living, particulary high housing costs. Thus, ironically, the improvement in the economic welfare of Massachusetts' residents during this period is attributable in part to the relative unattractiveness of the state for in-migration.

Job growth, though not the only contributor to the fall in the state's unemployment rate, is still the key element that distinguishes state economic performance before and after 1975. The state's employment performance in the 1975–83 period improved dramatically both relative to its own performance in the 1967–75 period and relative to the national average.

Two conclusions emerge from an analysis of Massachusetts' job growth.

First, the state was well positioned, in terms of its industry mix, for the economic changes experienced by the nation during the 1975–83 period.[17] Hence, the initial turnaround in the state's economy appears to have little to do with specific policy initiatives taken to get the economy going.

A second conclusion is that industry mix alone cannot account for the sustained and accelerated growth after 1979, a period in which many Massachusetts sectors including computer related and electronics industries, significantly outperformed their national counterparts. The state's disproportionate share of federal-defense related spending, the special attractiveness of Massachusetts for high technology industries and exportable business services, and the increased spending associated with rising income probably account for the bulk of the above average performance of key Massachusetts sectors during this latter period.

The state's particular mix of industries in 1975 accounts for a large part of the state's net job growth relative to the national average during the 1975–83 period. Industries or economic sectors with above average national growth rates, such as electronics and the service sector, were over-represented in the state's economy, while industries that were declining nationally were under-represented. Thus, although Massachusetts continued to rely heavily on manufacturing employment in 1975, the state was well positioned to benefit relative to other states from changes in the national economy. Importantly, the state's favorable position in 1975 largely reflected the long process of economic adjustment described earlier, a process that gradually and often painfully reduced the state's reliance on textiles and other mill based manufactured goods and increased its reliance on high technology products and consumer and business services.

Table 3-1 lists the Massachusetts sectors with the highest absolute growth rates between 1975–83 and the net new jobs created in each sector. The indus-

Table 3-1. Fastest Growing Sectors in Massachusetts Economy, 1975–83

	Growth Rate (Percent)	Job Growth (000s of jobs)
High Technology Sectors		
Nonelectrical Machinery	38	27.8
Electrical and Electronics	34	28.8
Instruments	31	13.6
		70.2
Services		
Business Services	95	62.8
Health Services	33	56.6
Legal Services	61	6.4
Other Noneducation Services	28	56.9
Financial, Insurance, and Real Estate	28	38.0
		220.7

Source: Constructed with data obtained from Bureau of Economic Analysis (BEA) Regional Economics Information System.

tries are grouped into two categories: financial and business services and high technology manufacturing.

Financial and Business Services

Employment in high technology manufacturing is not the only engine of the state's growth. Rapid growth in financial and business related services also played an important wealth generating role between 1975–83. Not only did these service sectors grow fast, but, like high technology manufacturing, they also contributed to the state's economic base by bringing new resources into the state. One study estimates that more than 44 percent of all financial services employees in the state are engaged in exporting services to—and importing wealth from—outside the state.[18] Employment in business services grew 95 percent during this period. The other fast-growing service and financial sectors grew at rates ranging from 28–61 percent. These categories generated 221,000 new jobs, many more than those generated in high technology manufacturing industries.

A large part of this growth reflects national trends. With changing modes of production and technological advances in communication and data processing, business and financial services have grown in importance. Throughout the twentieth century, and particularly after World War II, manufacturing firms moved many of their production facilities out of cities to suburban areas and to more rural sites in the South and West, thereby reducing the manufacturing employment base of many New England cities. It is no coincidence that the redevelopment of older cities like Boston and New York happened in the late 1970's and coincided with the changing organization of production to more globally integrated operations. By the late 1970's, many of the major urban centers once again had become expanding production centers, with production now consisting of the information, communication, and coordination functions necessary for firms to compete in the world economy. Boston, the heart of the Massachusetts and New England economies, was well positioned in 1975 to exploit these broad economic forces and has now emerged as a national center of financial and business services.

High Technology Manufacturing

National trends clearly play an important role in explaining the rapid growth of high technology manufacturing. We focus here on explanations of the rapid growth that are specific to Massachusetts.

The first and most important explanation is defense spending. Massachusetts typically does well in terms of federal procurement but, like other states in the Northeast and Midwest, fares less well in terms of such components of defense spending as personnel, construction, and operation. Between 1960–80, the state experienced severe reductions in military and civilian personnel with the closing of several of the state's military bases. But, the commonwealth typically receives more than 5 percent of all prime contracts, a percentage that is double its share of the U.S. population. Large procurement increases in the early

1980s raised prime defense contracts as a percentage of state personal income from 5.7 in 1977 to almost 8.2 percent in 1984. This substantial growth in defense contracts was probably an important factor in Massachusetts' superior economic performance relative to the nation during the 1980–81 recession. In addition, recent reports indicate that the state received a total of $7.7 billion in such contracts in 1985, a larger amount than any other state except California, Texas, and New York, all of which are much larger than Massachusetts.

A logical inference is that these defense contacts have provided, and continue to provide, a major stimulus to high technology manufacturing in the state; estimates for the U.S. indicate that defense oriented private sector employment represents substantial proportions of nonelectrical machinery, electronics, and instruments, precisely the three manufacturing sectors that have grown most rapidly in Massachusetts.[19] Defense contracts also generate indirect effects on the economy in the form of spin-off enterprises that apply the newly developed technology to new circumstances or ventures. One study lists forty-eight spin-off companies generated from the research and development efforts at Draper Labs.[20]

A second factor in the growth of the high technology sector in Massachusetts is the agglomeration of research and training institutions in the Boston metropolitan area. This agglomeration is centered around MIT and secondarily Harvard but also involves other schools that produce a large share of the area's engineering graduates. Thirty-seven institutions of higher education in New England have engineering programs, and Massachusetts ranks among the top five states in granting engineering degrees. Defense procurement interacted with this academic base to broaden and deepen the research base of the high technology sector.[21] Since World War II, when MIT Professor Vannevar Bush was the government's leading science advisor and helped direct seventy-five wartime contracts totalling $117 million to MIT, Massachusetts universities have continued to benefit from government research contracts. In 1983, MIT was the state's fifth largest prime defense contractor, receiving $245 million for research on radar and communications.[22] In addition, the state received substantially more than its proportionate share of federal research grants for nonmilitary purposes.

A third factor in the growth of the state's high technology sector is the availability of risk capital. Venture capital firms provide equity capital and business development advice to young high-risk, high-potential, and typically technology based enterprises. The industry is geographically concentrated. In 1981, according to one report, California, Massachusetts, and New York accounted for nearly 60 percent of the nation's venture capital disbursements, and Massachusetts accounted for nearly a quarter of this 60 percent.[23] Presumably, risk capital is more plentiful in Massachusetts because of the abundance of potentially marketable ideas. This has become part of a self-reinforcing feedback loop, where high tech entrepreneurs find it easier to start their businesses here because of the abundance of risk capital.

American Research and Development (ARD), founded in Boston in 1946, was the first important venture capital firm in the United States. General Georges Doriot, a Harvard Business School professor, and Karl T. Compton, then president of MIT, were two of its three principal founders. Compton brought in some of MIT's best minds as technical consultants. ARD is said to have been "instrumental in stimulating the high technology boom" in Massachusetts.[24] Its most famous and lucrative investment was $72,000 in the late 1950s to Ken Olson, who worked at MIT's Lincoln Lab, to start the Digital Equipment Corporation (DEC). DEC was the first and most successful minicomputer firm in the nation.[25] By 1983, DEC had sales of over $4 billion and, by one account, was directly responsible for 10 percent of high tech employment in the state.[26] DEC's basic story, an entrepreneur spun off from MIT or a large successful firm, funded and shepherded through the early years by enterprising financiers, has since been repeated in Massachusetts many times.

The Bank of Boston has also played a key role in financing the state's economic growth. Lloyd Brace, its chairman in the 1950s, along with other influential figures such as James Killian, the president of MIT, made a commitment to help promote the growth of knowledge based firms in Massachusetts.[27] While Killian supported the affiliation of MIT scientists with private business, as MIT officials did before him, Brace led the bank to high risk finance. In the 1960s, any Massachusetts firm with a federal contract was guaranteed financing from the Bank of Boston, and the bank actively courted researchers who held patents for marketable technology applications.

A fourth factor is the cost, quality, and attitude of the labor force. For much of the twentieth century, manufacturing wages in Massachusetts have been lower than the national average. In 1975, average hourly wage rates in machinery were 95 percent and in electronics 96 percent of the U.S. average; in instruments, however, they exceeded the national average by 10 percent.[28] The existence of a well-educated work force available at below average wages along with the availability of cheap production sites in the old mills made Massachusetts a profitable site for high technology manufacturing. Only since 1985 have there been growing concerns that the booming economy will significantly raise relative wage rates.

Secular declines in traditional industries and the relative weakness of the state's economy for much of the century left other legacies for the 1970s. Female labor force participation rates exceeded the national average and labor organizations were weakened; since World War II, unions in the state have been weaker and less militant than at any time during the previous hundred years. Massachusetts high tech firms have been especially effective at resisting unions. In 117 high tech union representation elections in Massachusetts between 1961–81, unions were victorious in only 33 elections.[29] These labor market conditions probably do not explain the existence of research, innovation, and early stage production in Massachusetts. They may, however, have induced some companies to keep a significant share of their production capacity in the state after the start up stage. Low wage rates have led one observer to argue, in addition, that the production processes used by the state's high tech firms are significantly more labor intensive than in other states and, consequently, that employment is higher than it would be had wage rates been higher.[30]

An alternative or perhaps complementary explanation for the surge in high

technology employment in the past decade is the role of state economic policy.
The outstanding performance of the high tech sector relative to national trends
after 1979 could possibly reflect a positive response of the business community
to the pro-business attitude of Edward King's governorship, an attitude that carried over into the Dukakis administration that followed King's. We argue in
subsequent chapters that state policy, in fact, has exerted a positive impact on
the state's overall business climate and perhaps on economic performance, not
so much as a result of specific policy initiatives but rather as a result of the process through which state policy decisions are now being made. The importance
of the factors just discussed suggests, however, that state policy probably played
at most a marginal role in stimulating the state's recent economic growth.

Geographic Variation Within the State

The Massachusetts economic "miracle" of the past decade reflects primarily the
effects of market forces external to the state and the legacy of over two centuries
of economic development. By 1975, the diversified economic base that
remained after fifty years of painful economic adjustment was well suited to benefit from national and international economic trends that increased the demand
for technology based goods and business and financial services. New state policies implemented after 1975 played a marginal and generally supportive role in
sustaining the recovery but, as subsequent chapters show, were too late and too
limited to have much impact on the initial turnaround. Today, in 1986, the Massachusetts economy is the strongest among the industrial states and shows few
signs of faltering.

The trends just described have left the state in excellent economic condition. The transformation of the state's economy away from mill based production toward high technology manufacturing and services, however, has exacer-
bated regional differences. The changes have especially helped the Boston
metropolitan area and other regions north of Boston. But, at the same time that
unemployment rates were falling relative to the state average in most regions of
the state, unemployment rates in the New Bedford and Fall River regions in the
southeastern part of the state rose substantially between 1975 and 1982.[31] Since
then, the situation has improved somewhat; between 1982–85 unemployment
rates in these two regions have steadily declined both absolutely and relative to
the state average but still remain well above the average.

The differential patterns of the regional unemployment rates reflect largely
variations in the composition of employment across regions. New Bedford and
Fall River had the highest proportions of their employment in manufacturing
in 1981. Moreover, 1981 manufacturing employment in both regions was still
heavily concentrated in traditional industries such as apparel.[32] There is a clear
negative correlation between a region's unemployment rate and the proportion
of its manufacturing employment in high technology manufacturing. Business
services have a similar association with low unemployment.

4

Pioneering State Economic Strategy

Starting with the state's economic crisis in 1975, innovative civic and political leadership in Massachusetts has made the state a national leader in creating new roles for states to play in economic policy. For the most part, the new roles do not represent an explicit and coherent state strategy of economic development. Instead, many represent the outcome of a complicated process through which "policy entrepreneurs" and leaders in government, labor, and business interact to make public policy. Hence, as policy makers from around the nation seek lessons from the Massachusetts example, they need to examine the policy process as carefully as they review the state's new policies.

Case studies of Massachusetts policy innovations since 1975 show that the state shaped its economic initiatives through an open and creative policy process not excessively influenced by narrow special interests. Initiatives for nontraditional state policies were often spearheaded by public-minded "policy entrepreneurs" in commissions or state line agencies. Their work centered around four normative policy ideas that for the most part exerted little influence on Massachusetts policy before 1975: that the state should foster geographically balanced growth, fill bottlenecks or "gaps" in capital and labor markets, promote a good business climate, and actively foster the interstate and international competitiveness of the state's economy. Legislative leaders provided only token resistance to most of the new proposals; they generally agreed with basic aims and considered the budgetary requests modest, given the priority accorded to job creation in Massachusetts after 1975.

33

Extensive use of federal financial resources has limited the burden of Massachusetts' economic strategies on the state's resources. Thus, while Massachusetts policy makers can correctly claim that they are in a better position than federal officials to determine the needs of their state and to implement specific policies, their capacity to do so in the past ten years was strengthened by federal resources.

Another theme of the Massachusetts experience is the growth in sensitivity of elected officials, especially governors, to business perspectives. To the limited degree that state policy can have short-term effects on the size and location of private economic development decisions, the tone of the policy process may be even more important than the content of particular programs. Business representatives in Massachusetts report, for example, that firms planning to expand elsewhere decided to remain once the tone of the state's relationship with business interests improved in 1979. Although the claim itself is difficult to document, its plausibility comes from the centrality of expectations to private investment decisions, the outcomes of which occur in an uncertain future.

The First Dukakis Administration

Michael S. Dukakis became governor of Massachusetts in January 1975, amid a state fiscal crisis and a deep recession.[33] By any measure of economic performance, Massachusetts was in poor condition and getting worse. Two years earlier, in 1973, when the national unemployment rate of 4.8 percent was the lowest since 1970, the lack of jobs in Massachusetts led organized engineers from towns north of Boston to lobby the state legislature for funds to retrain them for other professions. By November 1974, the national unemployment rate had risen to over 6 percent, while the rate in Massachusetts had grown to 9 percent and was rising. With long-term structural changes continuing to erode the state's manufacturing base, lower federal spending for national defense and the space program, and the onset of "stagflation," conditions were ripe for a new conception of state government's role in the Massachusetts economy.

When Dukakis took office in January 1975, the official deficit projection for fiscal 1975 was $350 million. In his budget message that month, he announced, "Massachusetts today faces the most serious budgetary crisis in memory—the largest current budget deficit of any state in the nation and an economic base that is stagnant and eroding."

A year later, the budget deficit was $550 million. By the middle of fiscal 1976, the state's unemployment compensation system, which had boasted a surplus reserve of $377 million in 1970, was deeply in deficit and the state had to borrow $265 million from the federal government to keep it solvent. Toughly bargained negotiations with the federal government about a loan to the state's major banks to restructure the state's debt forced Governor Dukakis and the legislature to impose a 7.5 percent surcharge on the state's income tax, to make deep cuts in the budget, especially in social welfare programs, and to remove voluntary quits from eligibility for unemployment compensation. The change in unemployment compensation eligibility rules and cuts in social welfare programs earned praise from the business community but bitter condemnation from vocal members of the political coalition that had helped elect the governor to office.

While the governor's critics on the left accused him of selling out to the business community, various members of the business community complained that the 7.5 percent income tax surcharge worsened the state's already dismal business climate. By the middle of his second year in office, Dukakis also had managed to alienate much of the legislature by giving the impression on several occasions that he did not care about legislators' opinions. Though his popularity gradually improved from its low point in 1976, Dukakis' political support never fully recovered from the enmity and disappointments of his first year and one-half in office.

Perception of a poor business climate in Massachusetts was well established even before Dukakis took office. In the early 1970s, during the Sargent administration, various segments of the business community and well-organized consumer and environmentalist groups waged heated political battles. These latter groups gained passage of new consumer and environmental legislation that made Massachusetts one of the national leaders in legislation to protect the natural environment. Further government interference with business decisions came in the form of anti-redlining legislation that forced banks to increase mortgage lending in minority and declining neighborhoods. In addition, the state's tax burden as a percentage of income rose from 97 percent of the national average in 1970 to 107 percent by the last year of the Sargent administration and 109 percent at the midpoint of the first Dukakis administration, making the state unattractive to highly skilled workers.[34] A national plant location consulting firm, the Fantus Company, ranked the Massachusetts business climate forty-sixth among the forty-eight contiguous states in 1975. This ranking remained a standard statistic in the debate over the state's business climate for the next four years.

By the end of 1976, the governor's relationship with the business community and the legislature had improved. A concerted outreach program coordinated by the much maligned Department of Commerce, in which the governor met regularly with business people and attended openings of new plants, contributed to the improvement. In addition, some credit must be given to a document released on August 11, 1976, "An Economic Development Program for Massachusetts." It served two political purposes. It fulfilled the governor's campaign promise to produce an economic plan for the state, and it assured members of the business community that the governor's office was thinking seriously about how to improve the state's business climate. The report was produced by the governor's Office of State Planning and the Development Cabinet, in consultation with labor representatives, business people, and representatives of local governments.

Frank Keefe, the director of the Office of State Planning, was the Chairman of the Development Cabinet and was responsible for coordinating economic policy and implementation of the report's recommendations. The Development

Cabinet comprised the Lieutenant Governor and the line agency Secretaries of Economic and Manpower Affairs, Transportation, Environmental Affairs, Communities and Development, and Consumer Affairs. Although people we interviewed report that the Development Cabinet system worked fairly well, largely because of Keefe and the exceptional quality of his staff, full realization of the development program was difficult because the program had to be carried out with existing agency staffs, which were too small, underqualified, or uncooperative.

Despite its commitment to improving the state's business climate, the Dukakis administration remained more devoted to social welfare and consumer interests than to business interests. The governor allowed free reign to his aggressive young pro-consumer and regulatory activist Banking Commissioner Carol Greenwald and Insurance Commissioner Jim Stone. In speeches about the need for the growth, the governor seldom failed to suggest that growth is not an end to itself, but rather a means for achieving social goals. He supported the graduated income tax that would have shifted more of the tax burden onto the incomes of the well to do. He supported rent control. He seemed deaf to the demands of certain segments of the business community, especially high technology entrepreneurs, that personal taxes should be reduced to make it easier to attract and keep engineers in the state. Although Dukakis considered himself to be very attentive to the concerns of business people, business representatives report that "He listened but he did not hear."

According to John Crosier, Commissioner of Commerce during this period, the governor's main problem was that he sent the business community mixed signals. One day he would take a pro-business position and the next day, on another issue, he would take an anti-business position or allow a member of his administration to do so. This lack of predictability sustained the uneasiness and the continual complaints about the business climate, even when the governor took pro-business positions.

One legacy of the 1975–79 Dukakis administration is the less aloof, politically more sensitive style that Dukakis adopted in his second term, a new style that has significant implications for how Dukakis currently deals with the business community. Two other legacies from his first term form the core of a new, more active approach to economic development policy. The first is the establishment of a set of new financial institutions to promote economic development and the second is the governor's strategy of geographic targeting.

State Sponsored Institutions for Financing Development

Massachusetts currently has the most sophisticated and complete network of publicly created development finance institutions in the nation.[35] Most of them were created or funded in a set of legislative proposals passed in 1978. A common perception is that these proposals were shaped largely through the work of the Massachusetts Task Force on Capital Formation, which was formed in April 1976 and issued its final report on January 14, 1977. In fact, the process that shaped the proposals began in 1972 and was largely complete by the end of 1975. That process is reviewed in some detail in the following pages.

The idea that private sector capital markets might work only imperfectly, thereby leaving a gap to be filled by publicly created institutions, played an important role in the establishment of the state's new financial institutions. At the same time, however, most of the relevant actors clearly had few illusions about the direct significance of the new institutions to the state's economy. Instead, support for the new institutions stemmed more from a desire to provide a symbol of the ability of the public and private sectors to cooperate creatively. The Capital Formation Task Force, hence, served to develop a formal consensus among business, labor, and politicians that these new finance institutions should exist, and that their functions are legitimate activities for state government to perform.

The Genesis of New Finance Institutions

Two sets of activities and development goals eventually led to the formation of the Capital Formation Task Force. The first is the work of the so-called Wednesday Morning Breakfast Group, with its concern about community economic development. The other is the work of the New England Regional Commission, with its concern about gaps in private-sector capital markets.

The Wednesday Morning Breakfast Group. The first discussions of a state development finance institution that link directly to the eventual formation of the Capital Formation Task Force took place in the autumn of 1972 in the office of State Representative Mel King. A veteran activist-leader in Boston's black and progressive communities, King also ran (and still runs) a program in the Department of Urban Studies and Planning at MIT, the Community Fellows Program, whose mission is to enhance the community and economic development skills of community leaders. The discussions took place at 7:30 every Wednesday morning over breakfast at MIT. The group continued to meet on Wednesday mornings throughout the remainder of the 1970s and became known as the Wednesday Morning Breakfast Group (WMBG).

The initial members of WMBG were Mel King, Elbert Bishop, Beldon Daniels, and David Smith. Mel King and Elbert Bishop were seeking a mechanism to rebuild a section of Boston's Southwest Corridor, demolished in anticipation of a downtown highway link to Interstate Highway 95 that was cancelled by Governor Sargent in 1972, after years of bitter protest from communities along the proposed route. Elbert Bishop, a young black lawyer, was president of the Southwest Corridor Coordinating Committee.

David Smith and Beldon Daniels, both consultants with backgrounds in finance and community development, worked closely with the Center for Community Economic Development (CCED). This organization was funded by the federal Office of Economic Opportunity (OEO) to publish a newsletter and to examine the Title VII Special Impact Program, which channeled federal funds to neighborhood-based community-development corporations (CDCs). Increasingly frustrated with the federal administration of the Special Impact Program, in 1972, the Center asked Daniels to examine the potential role of state government in community economic development finance.

WMBG's agenda was to design a state mechanism, such as an independent authority, that could finance the development of the Southwest Corridor. Meetings had no clear leader. Initial discussions were organized around the work Daniels and Smith were doing for the Center for Community Economic Development. Memos by Bishop show that he struggled with Smith and Daniels to keep the focus of the group narrow enough to produce something that would not arouse too many powerful opponents.

Early in 1973, Mel King asked Governor Sargent and the legislative leadership to establish a joint gubernatorial-legislative commission on community development. This would give the WMBG's ideas greater visibility and would begin to develop a place for them on the state's agenda. The commission, which was set up without a budget, was called, impressively, the Massachusetts Special Commission on Development Banking. Daniels acted as staff to the commission, having persuaded CCED that the work of the commission was a continuation of the work he already was doing for CCED and that, perhaps, a community development model for other states could be created in Massachusetts. This could help break the stultifying dependence of community development corporations on restrictively administered one-year grants doled out through the OEO Special Impact Program.

Mel King and Allan McKinnon became the House and Senate chairmen of the commission. McKinnon was a committed liberal and chairman of the Senate Committee on Commerce and Labor. A slightly expanded WMBG became the forum for conducting much of the commission's business. In a memorandum to the commission dated May 8, 1974, the "Development Bank Study Group," as the expanded WMBG now called itself, issued a set of proposals to form a community development finance system. It included a state sponsored High Risk Equity Corporation, a state funded Special Impact Program to fund CDCs, and a Municipal Bond Bank patterned after Vermont's. Each was to target resources to low-income communities. No legislative action was ever taken on these proposals, but the WMBG continued to meet and to formulate ideas.

Two weeks before the gubernatorial election of 1974, Michael Dukakis accepted an invitation to address the WMBG. Dukakis told them that he believed in what they were trying to do and would support them. The election of Dukakis gave the group hope that it might succeed, so its efforts intensified.

Within a few months they had designed the Community Development Finance Corporation (CDFC). The Corporation was to provide loan and equity finance to firms in low-income areas, where financing from conventional sources was often unavailable. Firms could apply only through local CDCs, and CDCF could share its financial participation in a deal with the sponsoring CDC. Any business granted assistance would have to convince CDFC that it was financially viable and that it had made a good faith effort to secure funding from other sources. CDFC would be financed with a $10 million general obligation bond that the state would use to buy CDFC's shares.

The CDFC bill was sponsored in the House of Representatives by Mel King and in the Senate by Allan McKinnon. It developed a surprising amount of support in the legislature. This was partly due to McKinnon's power as a committee chairman in the Senate and partly due to Mel King's close relationship with the Speaker of the House, Thomas McGee. The main political opposition was led by Representative Richard Demers from Chicopee. Demers was McKinnon's counterpart in the House, the House Chairman of the Committee on Commerce and Labor.

It was 1975 and the economy was in the middle of a deep recession. Business failures were high. Demers, who had a record of actively trying to respond to the state's economic difficulties, believed that state government needed to send business people a signal that the state was trying to do something to help them. But, he believed that CDFC was targeted toward too narrow a constituency and that businesses would be unwilling to apply through CDCs. He preferred a bill sponsored through his committee that would establish the Massachusetts Industrial Mortgage Insurance Agency (MIMIA). MIMIA would provide loan guarantees on industrial mortgages to manufacturing firms.

Demers had originally tried to sell MIMIA as a better use of the state's resources than CDFC, and the two bills came to be seen as an either-or choice. When Demers discovered that CDFC had more support than MIMIA, though perhaps not enough to pass, he suggested that the two be presented as a package, and the sponsors of CDFC agreed. Very late in the legislative session in December 1975, both bills passed. However, no money was appropriated for either program. The state was still in the midst of financial crisis; inclusion of money at that time probably would have killed the package.

The New England Regional Commission Task Force. While CDFC and MIMIA were making their way through the legislature in Massachusetts, the New England governors and the New England Regional Commission (NERCOM) sponsored the New England Regional Commission Task Force on Capital and Labor Markets. Established in April 1975, it issued its final report in November. The job of the NERCOM Task Force was to suggest policies designed to alleviate bottlenecks in the region's capital and labor markets. The major recommendation of the task force was that NERCOM should investigate the possibility of setting up a Regional Development Bank. Few of the proposals from the NERCOM Task Force were ever implemented. Nevertheless, it played a central role in shaping development finance in Massachusetts.

The NERCOM Task Force was important in three ways for the Massachusetts effort that was to follow. First, the studies commissioned after the task force, to follow up on its recommendation concerning a development bank, called attention to the possibility that profitable investment opportunites in New England might be going unexploited because of gaps in the region's capital market. Beldon Daniels, who coauthored a background study for the task force with Martin Katzman of Harvard's Department of City and Regional Planning, was given greater visibility and a more mainstream affiliation than he had with the WMBG. His involvement with the task force moved him into the inner circle in the discussion about whether there should be a regional development bank and what shape it should take. The task force paper also afforded Daniels an opportunity to publicize the proposed Massachusetts Technology Development Corporation (MTDC), discussed later. Third, the regional bank models examined by NERCOM inspired insurance industry leaders in Massachusetts to consider setting up such a bank in Massachusetts in exchange for the removal of a 1 percent gross investment tax. This proposal laid the groundwork for the Massachusetts Capital Resources Corporation, also discussed later.

The Massachusetts Task Force on Capital Formation

By the final months of 1975, when the NERCOM Task Force Report was issued and CDFC was on its way to passage, the idea that the state needed to be more organized and systematic in its approach to development finance had become a dominant theme in the WMBG's discussions. Beldon Daniels explained the WMBG perspective to John Moreno, the Massachusetts Commissioner of Commerce and Development, and suggested the establishment of a gubernatorial task force. Moreno took the idea to his immediate superior, Howard Smith, Secretary of Economic Affairs, and the two of them presented the idea to the governor. The governor agreed and the Task Force on Capital Formation was established. A small amount of money was allocated for staff, and Daniels was appointed the executive director.

Membership. The task force members were selected by Daniels, Moreno, Smith, and Richard Geiser, the former Dukakis campaign advisor who had become an undersecretary of Economic Affairs. Thirty-four regular and seven ex-officio members were appointed. Representation was broad. Bennett Harrison, professor of Urban and Regional Planning at MIT, and Sandra Kantor, Senator McKinnon's aide, were appointed representatives of the WMBG, but they resigned when they learned that most task force members had little interest in development for low-income communities. Chief executives from the state's large commercial banks, thrift banks, venture capital firms, manufacturing firms, high tech firms, land developers, insurance companies, department stores, community groups, and local chambers of commerce were included. The building trades and the AFL-CIO were represented. The president of the state's only (at that time) well-organized and vocal statewide business organization, the manufacturers' Associated Industries of Massachusetts, was also included, as was Howard P. Foley, president of Jobs for Massachusetts.

Jobs for Massachusetts (JFM) is an organization of the state's top power brokers from business, labor, and government. Started in 1972 to coordinate an effort to bring more jobs to Massachusetts, it usurped the primary role of the state's Department of Commerce and Development by independently running an extensive campaign financed by the private sector to recruit firms to Massachusetts. JFM experienced a few successes but, for the most part, its efforts failed. By 1975, JFM had decided to shift away from recruitment toward the promotion and facilitation of growth within the state. Thus, in 1976, when the task force was formed, a consensus had already emerged among the state's leadership that it was time to try something new.

The Shaping of the Task Force Report. In a memorandum presented to the task force at its first meeting, Daniels pointed out the existence of conditions in state and regional capital markets that could be ameliorated by new quasi-public financial institutions. At the time of the meeting, none of these institutions was actually functioning, even though some of them, such as CDFC and MIMIA, legally authorized and preliminary models for the others, existed on paper. The institutions described and endorsed in the task force's final report can be traced directly back to Daniel's initial memo.

The final report of the task force rejected the notion that there was a capital shortage, saying: "Supply and demand will always intersect at a certain price, and capital will be available to those who can pay for it." The report went on to acknowledge that "the costs and availability of capital may limit the creation or expansion of certain kinds of firms—and therefore, of jobs and tax revenue." Brief descriptions of capital gaps are included in the report, based in large part on work that venture capitalist Peter Brooke did for the New England Regional Commission Task Force. The relationship between a capital gap and a capital shortage, in all likelihood, was left vague purposefully, so that all members would be willing to endorse the report. The final paragraph before the summary of recommendations cautions that the task force was not able "to quantify the gaps through the use of a tight experimental design, or determine the precise depth of the need. It is, therefore, essential that all the proposals of the Task Force be designed to grow only in response to demand, and subject to ten year 'sunset laws'."

The task force proposed that the new institutions be placed under an umbrella organization, the Massachusetts Industrial Development Authority (MIDA), which would have a board of directors appointed by the governor and would set general policy for its subsidiaries. MIDA was already on the books, quietly passed into law without funding in 1975 as a favor to a state legislator who needed it for his congressional campaign. According to the 1977 Capital Formation Task Force Report, the revived MIDA was to have three subsidiaries:

- *The Massachusetts Technology Development Corporation (MTDC),* a venture capital agency to work with the financial community, high technology industry, and Massachusetts universities in the creation of new technologies and industries.
- *The Massachusetts Industrial Finance Agency (MIFA),* to house the industrial mortgage insurance program, MIMIA; serve as the only statewide institution empowered to issue industrial revenue bonds; package industrial revenue bonds to finance pollution control facilities for small businesses; and engage in secondary marketing of various types of federally insured loans.
- *The Community Development Finance Corporation (CDFC),* to provide loan and equity finance to firms in low-income areas.

MIFA, MTDC, and CDFC were all funded and implemented in 1977 and 1978. All had been conceived before the task force, but with the task force's endorsement, they were more easily embraced by the political establishment. Several other programs that were not products of the task force were inserted into the same legislative package. These included the Commercial Area Revitalization District (CARD) Program, created to restrict the commercial use of industrial revenue bonds (IRBs) to commercial districts in distressed areas. The brainchild of Frank Keefe in the Office of Economic Planning, the CARD program was part of a broader strategy to target economic development to distressed urban areas. In addition, the Community Economic Development Assistance Corporation (CEDAC) was created to help CDCs package deals to present to CDFC, and the Community Enterprise Economic Development (CEED) program was created to help fund technical and management assistance for CDCs. These were both proposed by the WMBG as part of their strategy to strengthen community development corporations. MIFA (including funding of MIMIA), MTDC, CARD, CEDAC, CEED, and funding for CDFC were all shepherded through the legislature by Representative Demers, who three years earlier had resisted the creation of CDFC.

The umbrella, MIDA, was never set up. The constituencies for MIFA, MTDC, and CDFC, lobbied strongly against it. Also, MIDA would have threatened the power of the Office of State Planning and the Executive Office of Economic Affairs to make state economic development policy. MIDA had no constituency beyond its proponents on the Capital Formation Task Force, most of whom tuned out when the task force ended.

Motivation of Task Force Members. Members of the task force expected that the net effect of these new institutions would be positive though small. The report emphasized that the most serious impediment to strong growth and recovery in the state was high taxes: "The Task Force is *emphatic* in stating that these short term recommendations are limited in their long-run capability to stimulate jobs and revenue creation, *unless* there is fundamental tax reform and expenditure control." By "short term recommendations," the task force referred to the development finance institutions that in contrast to the tax and expenditure control recommendations, could be implemented immediately. The emphasis on fiscal reform in the final report was part of a deal struck within the task force between the advocates of short-term actions and the advocates of tax reform. Under this agreement, all members agreed to unanimously support all of the report's recommendations—those relating to the quasi-public state sponsored finance institutions and those relating to fiscal reform and expenditure control.

Since everyone involved knew that fiscal reform was unlikely to be implemented and since the new finance institutions were expected, at best, to have only a marginal effect on the state's economic vitality, one must look further to understand why labor, business, and political leaders worked for ten months to refine their proposals and arrive at a consensus.

For some participants, the task force report may have been viewed as a good podium from which to deliver a clear statement about the need for fiscal reform. This appears to be the motivation, for example, of some of the high tech entre- preneurs, who vehemently argued that the state's high personal taxes made it difficult to recruit engineers and middle managers.

Other participants appear to have been motivated by the mostly unspoken understanding that it was important in 1976 to come together and agree about something. Proving to themselves and to one another that agreement was pos- sible, apparently for some, was as important as the substance of what was agreed upon. Endorsing and creating the new finance institutions therefore were impor- tant not only because of the economic activity the institutions might eventually generate but, also, and perhaps more importantly, because in 1976–77 they were much needed symbols of the ability of the public and private sectors to coop- erate creatively. No one was happy with the level of discord in the state. Both public and private sector actors maintain that good working relationships are an important element of the business climate and that now, in 1986, they are part of what makes Massachusetts a special place in which to live and do business. Further, because the development finance institutions are not line agencies, but quasi-public authorities with members from both public and private sectors on their boards of directors, they continue to be forums for public-private cooperation.

Massachusetts Capital Resources Corporation

While the task force was in operation, a parallel process was initiated by the insurance industry. Desiring a tax cut, the industry agreed in exchange to create the Massachusetts Capital Resources Corporation (MCRC). Daniels reports that MCRC was kept out of the formal task force package because it was more con- troversial than the other pieces and, conceivably, could have "blown the package up." The only allusion to MCRC in the task force report is an endorsement of the proposition that the state should remove the 1 percent gross investment tax on insurance companies. As stated earlier, the idea for MCRC and the rationale for it grew directly out of the New England Regional Commission Task Force. Peter Brooke used cases from the paper he wrote for NERCOM to testify in the Massachusetts legislature that MCRC was needed.

After a hotly contested political struggle, in which some of the most vocal opposition came from the then highly politicized WMBG (Daniels was no longer a regular member), the state granted the tax cut in exchange for a $100 million investment fund (MCRC) to be owned and operated by the state's insurance industry. The fund was legally empowered to make unsecured loans to busi- nesses that could demonstrate an inability to get money elsewhere on affordable terms and that could demonstrate that they would create jobs. The job creation impact was to be monitored by the Secretary of Economic Affairs. If it ever could be shown that the industry had not lived up to the terms of the deal, the tax cut would be rescinded and insurance firms would have to pay all back taxes, as though the tax cut had never taken place. For a lack of a better deal, the insur- ance companies agreed. They expected that the $100 million was simply the price of the tax break; they were subsequently surprised by the financial success of MCRC.

Massachusetts High Technology Council

An inadvertent outgrowth of the process creating the new state finance institutions was the birth of the Massachusetts High Technology Council.

Governor Dukakis was invited to attend the final meeting of the Capital Formation Task Force in January 1977, at which the final report was to be presented to him and the significance of the recommendations discussed. On the day of the task force meeting, the governor attended a morning funeral, was detained, and arrived at the meeting about an hour late. He stayed for a few minutes, then left. Several members of the task force were furious. Among them were high tech entrepreneurs Edison de Castro of Data General and Raymond Stata of Analogue Devices, who were already rather disgusted with the outcome of the task force. De Castro says, "I think what the governor wanted out of the task force was totally different from what a lot of the members wanted out of it. Some, particularly those from the high technology sector, were convinced that the real problem with capital development in Massachusetts was that the business climate was so bad that nobody wanted to invest in the state. The governor's view was that more bureaucracy was necessary to finance tax exempt bonds and put *financing* packages together. There was a feeling by myself and Ray and perhaps some others that the whole problem was being swept under the rug. . . . Fundamentally, I think he had no interest in hearing our view. . . . And businessmen had been unwilling to stand up and be counted."[36]

De Castro and Stata, assisted by Howard Foley, decided to set up their own forum to discuss economic problems in the state. Most of those invited were high tech entrepreneurs, and the eventual outcome was the Massachusetts High Technology Council (MHTC), formally established in October 1977. Howard Foley became its executive director. MHTC figured prominently in the events that followed.

Impacts and Performance of the New Development Finance Institutions

In 1976, the year the Capital Formation Task Force was formed, the net new private capital committed to venture capital firms in the U.S. was $50 million—down two-thirds from 1969, when Congress increased the maximum tax rate on capital gains. This $50 million augmented a total investment pool of slightly under $3 billion. In 1978, the year Massachusetts finished the legislation for its new finance agencies, Congress reduced the maximum tax rate on capital gains and removed restrictions that had previously prevented the use of pension funds for venture capital. This had a dramatic impact: The net new capital committed to venture capital funds rose from $39 million in 1977 to $600 million in 1978. By 1983, the first year of the current Dukakis administration, the total pool of venture capital in the U.S. had risen to $12 billion, with $4.5 billion added in 1983 alone. Between 12–15 percent of the venture capital invested in the United

States is invested in Massachusetts firms.[37] Hence, a case might be made that whatever need existed for the new Massachusetts institutions in the late 1970s no longer remains in the 1980s.

But, a growing body of literature supports the view that structural features of private financial markets sometimes inhibit the full exploitation of worthwhile opportunities.[38] Hence, we believe that while the Massachusetts institutions are not absolutely necessary to the state's economy, they are still useful. They increase the supply of jobs and economic diversity created by certain types of projects. For a majority of the projects, the entrepreneur's lack of personal equity or collateral, rather than low expected returns or high uncertainty, is the reason for the private sector's reluctance to provide full funding. All of the agencies provide primarily "gap financing": They coinvest with private banks and venture capitalists and, using equity or subordinated loans, make up the portion not provided by the private sector.[39]

It must be acknowledged, however, that the experience in Massachusetts is not necessarily a sign that similar institutions will do as well in other states.[40] Thus far, the success in Massachusetts appears to be built on effective insulation from pressure to finance politically popular but financially unsound projects, easy access to expert technical and financial advice from other institutions in the state, a good supply of marketable business ideas from smart aggressive entrepreneurs, institutional flexibility to change in response to market and institutional needs, and talented experienced managers and board members who have the savvy, with appropriate outside help, to recognize good entrepreneurs and good projects. These conditions may be more difficult to meet in other states than they are in Massachusetts with its concentration of sophisticated financial firms, universities and entrepreneurs in the Boston metropolitan area.

The fact that these institutions appear to be successfully managed is important but says little about how significant these agencies have been to the state's economic performance. It is impossible to know what fraction of the jobs that they take credit for would have been lost in the absence of agency investments, but the agencies' claims provide a reasonable upper bound. In the most recent annual reports, the following numbers of jobs are listed as created or retained through 1985: 9000 by the Massachusetts Capital Resources Corporation, 1109 by the Community Development Finance Corporation, 1300 by the Massachusetts Technology Development Corporation, and 74,529 from industrial revenue bonds (IRBs) for industrial and environmental uses by the Massachusetts Industrial Finance Agency (MIFA).[41] MIFA does not give a job creation number for its commerical IRBs because it says this number would be too speculative.[42]

The first three figures listed total 11,409. Although hardly trivial, this represents less than 0.5 percent of statewide employment. The picture changes with the addition of the 74,529 jobs claimed by MIFA; these jobs represent 10 percent of the state's manufacturing workforce and about 2.5 percent of the state's total employment. We strongly suspect, however, with all due respect to officials at MIFA, that this number significantly overstates the jobs that would not exist without industrial revenue bonds.[43]

In conclusion, these agencies have probably performed better than many on the Task Force on Capital Formation anticipated, and their long-term impact in

Massachusetts may prove to be worth much more than the value of public resources invested. At the same time, it is difficult to argue that they were a major force in the state's economic turnaround or that their contribution to sustaining it was very substantial. The precedent set by the task force for business-government collaboration in policy innovation and the creation of the Massachusetts High Technology Council were probably at least as important as the direct investment impact of the new agencies in shaping the political economy of Massachusetts after 1978.

Geographic Targeting

The second economic legacy of Governor Dukakis' first term is the policy of geographic targeting. Governor Dukakis has stated his belief that private market decisions, by themselves, do not always produce socially optimal outcomes.[44] The economic development philosophy through both Dukakis administrations has been that the resources of government should be used to target growth toward areas that need it most—places with high unemployment and declining economic bases—and away from places where it produces undesirable side effects. Through both administrations, Dukakis and his economic policy advisors have shown the greatest commitment to the revitalization of cities and declining regions.

Credit for initiating geographically targeted development in Massachusetts belongs to Dukakis and the people he brought into his first administration to implement it through the Office of State Planning (OSP). Before 1975, Massachusetts had no urban policy. Most urban policy in the United States at that time emanated from the federal government, through programs like Model Cities and Urban Renewal, both created by federal legislation. The urban focus that the Dukakis administration brought to state governments was radically new. What makes it especially interesting and noteworthy is that it was launched through purely administrative maneuvers, with no new legislation. Most of the associated legislation was passed in 1978. By that time, targeted development had been the state's policy for three years.

As Dukakis' first term proceeded, the policy of targeted development acquired a broad statewide constituency developed through a twenty-month process culminating in a 1977 report, "City and Town Centers: A Program for Growth." As with the Capital Formation Task Force, the "growth policy process" was a participatory exercise guided by documents that were presented to participants when the process began. In this case, the documents were produced by Frank Keefe and the OSP.

The Growth Policy Process

Hundreds of organizations and over 5000 members of Local Growth Policy Committees in 331 of the state's 351 cities and towns participated in the growth policy process. A massive effort by staffers at the OSP distilled thousands of pages of local committee reports down to the ninety-page final report. Meetings held around the state after the final report was issued praised the OSP for their accuracy in representing the views expressed in the local reports.

The consensus in the local reports was that the state's policy should be to support and encourage growth in the state's older cities and towns rather than in the suburbs and outlying areas. Central cities supported this policy because it offered hope that the unemployed might find jobs and the tax rolls might grow; suburbanites liked it because it would help to preserve the quality of life in their communities; and environmentalists favored it because it lessened pressure to develop in farming and forest areas. Statewide business interests did not play an active role. To the extent that business representatives were involved, it was through their towns and cities. Developers who favored continued expansion into undeveloped areas had no effective voice.

The initial impetus for the process came during the Sargent administration. Spurred by the constant tension between environmental protection groups and economic development interests, a number of state legislators became concerned about the lack of coordinated planning in the executive branch. In 1973, the state passed a bill that established a "Special Commission Relative to the Effect of Present Growth Patterns on the Quality of Life in Massachusetts." The commission became operational in 1974.

In the first months of the Dukakis administration, the land use committee of the commission, chaired by Senator Saltonstall, was nearly stalemated because of conflicts among environmentalists, economic development advocates, defenders of home rule for cities and towns, regional planning agencies, and state bureaucrats. Saltonstall had recruited a staff for the committee, led by Professor Lawrence Susskind of the Department of Urban Studies and Planning at MIT. Susskind was convinced that the only way to make progress was to go through a "bottom up" process involving local communities and regional planning agencies in setting priorities and articulating goals.

Initially, Keefe and Dukakis were both opposed to having the OSP take an active role in the work of the commission and to the prospect of new land use or planning legislation. They believed that the state had passed enough legislation over the previous decade and that much of what needed to be done could be done administratively. In the summer of 1975 Susskind convinced Keefe that a "bottom up" process involving OSP would be useful in developing a constituency for the governor's program for cities and towns.

Hence, the Massachusetts Growth Policy Development Act, supported by the commission and the governor, passed in the final days of the 1975 legislative session. It provided for (but did not require) the establishment of Local Growth Policy Committees in all cities and towns. These committees would hold open meetings and prepare local growth policy statements. Statements from the towns would be reviewed by the regional planning authorities in the respective regions and summarized along with the governor's own policy recommendations in a final report. In practice, Keefe and OSP significantly influenced the outcome of this bottom-up process by circulating a preliminary draft of the final report early in the process and by writing the handbook to guide the local committees.

From the perspective of its participants, the process worked well. First, it provided a context for discussion in the cities and towns that, in several places, led to direct action to solve local problems or take advantage of previously unexploited opportunities. Second, people who were active participants developed an understanding of, and a commitment to, the targeted development strategy. One of these was Byron Matthews, a Republican mayor who later became the Secretary of Communities and Development in the King administration. As secretary, Matthews hired a number of people from Frank Keefe's staff from OSP and expanded the work begun by OSP under Keefe. Third, seventeen bills were passed in response to the report's recommendations.

State and Targeted Development

The Dukakis administration began implementing its policy of targeted development long before the Economic Development Program was published. The implementation plan put into effect in early 1975 was simply to employ the state's resources in any way imaginable to revitalize urban centers. At one point in 1976, Keefe's office even worked on a plan to block the construction of suburban shopping malls, but Dukakis became persuaded that politically it was a bad idea and called it off. Dukakis' approach was not to block private development in suburbs but rather to encourage it to go to central cities. The result, the administration expected, would not be an end to suburban expansion but a more even pattern of vitality and a greater number of jobs in central cities, where fiscal pressures, unemployment, and blight were greatest. Further, the administration believed that economically and culturally strong central cities were necessary preconditions for reviving the state's declining regions.

OSP and Frank Keefe were audaciously creative. In fact, Keefe's creativity as city planning director of the city of Lowell first attracted Dukakis' attention to him. Keefe and the director of the Lowell Model Cities Program, Pat Mogan, produced a concept paper for a state "Heritage Park," a historic theme park to preserve the historic canals and other structures that tell the story of the development of the textile industry in downtown Lowell. After a guided tour during the gubernatorial campaign of 1974, Governor Sargent replied that though it was a brilliant idea, the state had no money to give cities for parks. After reading Sargent's response in the newspaper, Alden Raine, Dukakis' campaign advisor for economic issues, sent Dukakis to Lowell to give the "right answer." By 1980, the Lowell Heritage Park had received over $10 million in state funds and a larger amount from the federal government and had been designated a national historic park. Today, the state's system of Heritage Parks is one of its most highly promoted tourist attractions, and the Lowell Heritage Park is a centerpiece in the cultural and economic revival of the city.

Keefe's creativity, along with that of his "brain trust" at OSP, produced a number of innovative changes in the rules that guided public investment. It was through changes in rules that the Dukakis strategy of targeted development was implemented. Executive Order 134, issued in 1975, established the requirement that all moves and expansions of state office facilities had to be into existing structures in city centers. This angered many bureaucrats, but it reversed the emerging trend whereby motor vehicle registries and offices of the Department of Education were tending to follow commercial activity into shopping centers and surburban locations. With the formation of regional transit authorities under federal legislation, OSP made a big deal of the decision that all new bus terminals in Massachusetts would be in downtown areas. Through Lieutenant Governor O'Neill's Office of Federal State Relations, the state successfully pressured the Federal Urban Systems Highway Program to do more projects involving benches, trees, and sidewalks, rather than just wider streets and computerized traffic lights. Federal highway and sewer funds were targeted to places that were already developed or to carefully chosen locations for new development. According to Alden Raine, now director of the governor's Office of Economic Development, "We did everything we could to retard the use of that money for purposes that would encourage sprawl."

The state developed a reputation for expertise in urban development that seemed to enhance its competitive advantage in winning federal grants. In 1978 Massachusetts won over $40 million in Urban Development Action Grants (UDAGs) for ten projects in eight cities. This represented 10 percent of the funds distributed nationally, far larger than Massachusetts' 2 percent share of the nation's population. Overall, the state ranked seventeenth in 1977 and twelfth in 1978 in the receipt of federal funds per capita.

Even where the state had no formal authority to make location decisions, they intervened "informally." For example, when the towns of Pittsfield, Chicopee, and Lawrence were planning to build new high schools on the outskirts of town, OSP persuaded them to renovate their existing downtown high schools. Provisions in the state reimbursement formula that discouraged renovation of existing schools were changed. In Lowell, the city renovated a high school that sits next to the main canal in the Heritage Park and built a footbridge over the canal connecting the renovated section with a new addition. In another example, the administration "broke arms" to get the North Shore Community College to locate its new campus in downtown Lynn, rather than adjacent to a highway interchange along Route 128 and to get Roxbury Community College placed in Boston's Southwest Corridor.

Today, Raine points to numerous places around the state where public investments during Dukakis' first term were the catalysts for private investment and center city renewal. The most dramatic and the most famous is Lowell, where the overwhelming majority of the investment now occurring in downtown Lowell is private and the unemployment rate is 3 percent.[45] But there are less well known examples as well. Downtown Fitchburg boasts two new parking garages, three blocks of totally redone commercial space, an expansion of General Electric's downtown plant, three major housing developments, a new transit terminal, and a park for runners along the river. Raine reports that, "Now you go to Fitchburg and the mayor stands there with you and says, 'Mike Dukakis helped us do all this stuff and it was really his vision.'"

The King Administration, 1979–83

In a surprise upset, Edward J. King defeated Michael S. Dukakis in the Democratic primary election for the governorship of Massachusetts in September 1978 by a margin of 51 to 42 percent. In the heavily Democratic state, he then easily won the election itself.

From Ed King's perspective, the proper role of state government in economic policy was quite straightforward. The bottom line was that people needed jobs. He summarized his perspective in an interview: "A person's frame of mind is affected by whether he or she is working or not, and by whether he is working at a job that is consistent with his or her abilities. This affects everything in a person's life." Businesses create jobs, so, "If you are anti-business you are anti-people." During the 1978 election campaign, King promised to end the hostilities between state government and the business community. The signals he sent to the business community were quite clear. His administration, he promised, would listen to the business community, learn what its needs were, and do everything within the power of the executive branch to fulfill them. Further, during his first year in office he promised to cut the burden of state and local taxes by $500 million.

Because his values were unbashedly pro-business, King's relationships with interest groups were much less muddled and ambivalent than Dukakis's. If organizations clearly were working to create jobs or to eliminate barriers to creating jobs, then he was their ally and they had his ear. If, on the other hand, they were working for social welfare causes that King believed might reduce people's incentives to work or causes that could dampen business' enthusiasm to expand in Massachusetts, then King had no use for them and they had none for him. Hence, King's relationships with human services providers and industrial labor unions were never very good. His reputation for being staunchly pro-growth was well known from his fights with the Sargent administration when King was the director of the quasi-public Massachusetts Port Authority (MassPort). Because of King's pro-growth reputation, the construction unions were among his strongest supporters.

Ed King's economic development strategy was to break down any barrier that stood in the way of job creation. The lion's share of the rhetoric coming from businesses in 1978, when King ran for governor, was that the state's high tax burden and bad business climate were driving firms to expand out of state, many into New Hampshire, just north of the Massachusetts border. King did not come into office with novel theories about how to organize state government to achieve his goals or an activist plan for new programs or regulatory reforms. What he had was an objective—build a better business climate in order to create jobs.

King approached governing by hiring people with whom he was ideologically compatible and then turning them loose to perform the duties inherent in their job titles. His main economic policy appointees clearly understood the governor's values and their instincts were compatible with his. The freedom to operate extended to discretion in hiring staffers. As already noted, Byron Matthews, King's Secretary of Communities and Development, hired several of Keefe's staff from the Office of State Planning (OSP). Similarly, George Kariotis, Secretary of Economic Affairs, reports that he kept on most of Howard Smith's staff because he felt that he "did not know enough about that business to throw everybody out and start over." Both Kariotis and Matthews were criticized by King's supporters for keeping so much of Dukakis's staff. Still, neither was asked by King to change his decision, despite King's feeling that the Dukakis administration's approach was wrong.

Consistent with his belief that Dukakis' methods were misdirected, one of King's first acts was to abolish the Office of State Planning. During his transition period, two or three of Dukakis' cabinet secretaries reported to King that the OSP was an intrusive layer over their heads, which made it difficult for them to manage their responsibilities. This, combined with King's distrust at the time for anything called *planning*—he once said "Planners are those who plan to see that nothing is done"—killed the OSP. When pushed, King agreed that state government should do planning to be sure that problems and opportunities are not overlooked but that it should take place inside the individual secretariats, with conflicts among the secretariats refereed by the governor.

King replaced the Office of State Planning with the governor's Development Office, headed by Michael Daley. Just as with his cabinet secretaries, King gave Daley no clear mandate. In contrast to the secretariats, however, the job had no natural turf. As one person put it, "He'd enter other people's turf and be told to get the hell out. He didn't have the wherewithal politically to move around." While acknowledging that "Daley was no Frank Keefe," another King appointee says that "Matthews, [James] Carlin [Commissioner of Commerce], and Kariotis were very strong personalities and cut the legs out from under him." After a good deal of confusion, Kariotis went to King and asked to have Daley report to him rather than King. King agreed. Daley finally left the King administration when offered a private sector job by a member of the governor's Commission to Simplify Rules and Regulations.

This commission represents both a high point and a low point of the King administration. As part of his promise to improve the business climate, King instructed the commission to come up with ways to ease the burden of regulation. Its membership included all of the cabinet secretaries and five of the state's most respected business leaders. With Daley serving as Staff Director, the commission produced a number of administrative and legislative proposals for significant changes in regulatory procedures. It was a high point in the work of the King administraton because of the quantity and quality of the work done. It was a low point because almost none of the proposals were given a serious hearing in the legislature.

Part of the King administration's efforts toward economic development involved carrying on programs initiated during the preceding Dukakis administration. Much of the success of Dukakis initiatives is due to the efforts of Byron Matthews. Matthews was the chairman of his local growth policy committee during the Dukakis administration, when he was the mayor of Newburyport, and was a member of the twenty-member state policy board that oversaw the growth policy process. He developed an understanding and commitment to the state's urban development policy that carried over into his term as Secretary of the Executive Office of Communities and Development (EOCD) in the King Administration. As mentioned, Matthews, to the dismay of many people, hired several of Keefe's staff. To a large degree, the work of the OSP, which King abolished, was carried on in EOCD.

Most of the legislative initiatives dealing with economic development, most significantly the Commercial Area Revitalization District (CARD) program, were just coming on line in 1978, at the end of the first Dukakis administration, and were barely implemented before Dukakis left office. The CARD program restricted commercial use of Industrial Revenue Bonds (IRBs) to specially designated commercial revitalization districts. The CARD legislation gave to EOCD the authority to approve CARD districts. Matthews says that some of his toughest battles were to maintain the integrity of the CARD program. Pressure was often exerted—although never by Governor King—to designate CARD districts in places that obviously were not eligible. One of the few battles that he lost involved the designation of a CARD district around Fenway Park, home of the Boston Red Sox, where the owners used an IRB to renovate luxury sky-boxes in the stadium. Though some critics say that precise and unambiguous guidelines should have been written that would have resulted in designation of fewer CARD districts, Matthews made an honest and, for the most part, successful effort to protect and maintain the program.

Due to the efforts of Matthews and other officials in the King administration, several new programs were legislated that used CARD boundaries to define eligibility. These included programs with various levels of state support for parking garages, sewers, and convention centers. Other new programs that did not rely on CARD boundaries included the Community Development Action Grant Program (CDAG), a program similar to the federal UDAG program (but only for local public improvements to support job creation), created for cities that barely missed qualifying for federal UDAGs. Matthews' office, in partnership with the Department of Environmental Quality Management, also managed most of the contact with cities to implement the Heritage Park Program, which was just beginning to take shape as a statewide program at the end of Dukakis' first term.

While Matthews was still mayor of Newburyport in 1977, he and the mayor of Washington, Pennsylvania, were instrumental in convincing the Congressional Housing and Urban Development Committee not to abandon the Small Cities Block Grant Program. As the state's Secretary of Communities and Development, he was an active member of the national organization of state secretaries of community affairs that played an important role in the federal government's decision to have the Small Cities Block Grant Program administered by the states. John Judge, who worked in OSP under Keefe, was Matthews' right-hand man and Raine's deputy in the governor's Office of Economic Development in Dukakis's second term. Judge wrote the state's regulation for distribution of the Small Cities Block Grant funds. Massachusetts became one of the first states to receive and distribute the block grant funds, and its system of distribution became a national model.

It is impossible to know which of the numerous policy events of the King years will have the most impact on the state's economy. The programs and policies managed by Matthews at EOCD may have the most lasting effect. Alternatively, there were achievements in education, in the form of the reorganization of state higher education under a single Board of Regents, and in environmental and hazardous waste regulation, transportation policy, and management reform. Governor King and his administration deserve credit for all of these. Two developments of the King years have received more attention from around the nation than most others and continue to affect current policy debates and options. The first is tax reform and Proposition 2½ and the second is manpower training through the Bay State Skills Corporation and the Massachusetts Technology Park Corporation.

Proposition 2½ and Its Legacy

Proposition 2½ is the tax limitation measure passed by Massachusetts voters in November 1980, which forced local property taxes down to 2.5 percent of market value. The lively campaign that preceded it and the 60–40 percent confirmation by the voters were the most contentious and reform provoking events of the King administration. This initiative law had three major effects: First, it substantially reduced the local property tax on which Massachusetts had relied to a much greater degree than most other states. This reduced the total state and local tax burden in Massachusetts by enough to diminish significantly the ranks of those who complained about the state's business climate. Simultaneously, however, it also forced cutbacks in services at both the state and local levels. Second, it substantially increased the amount of state aid to local governments and made local governments more dependent on the health of the state economy. And third, its overwhelming success at the polls sent a strong message to elected public officials, thereby setting the tone for a more conservative fiscal policy in Massachusetts for the 1980s.[46]

Proposition 2½ also is important because its success at the polls enhanced the political power of the Massachusetts High Technology Council (MHTC). Members of the MHTC paid over half the campaign expenses of the Citizens for Limited Taxation (CLT) in the drive to pass Proposition 2½ and were considered in many circles to be the movement's real sponsors.

Background

Tax reform was a major preoccupation of activists of all ideological perspectives within the state throughout the 1970s. The business community maintained adamantly that high state taxes resulted in a poor business climate. Individual businessmen and business organizations like the MHTC and the Associated Industries of Massachusetts (AIM) continually threatened that businesses would leave the state and expand elsewhere if the state's tax burden was not reduced. The first response from the state came in 1970, when AIM succeeded in winning a 1 percent investment tax credit. The credit was "temporarily" increased to 3 percent in 1973 and periodically has been renewed ever since. AIM and their friends in the legislature call the tax credit the cornerpiece of the state's industrial policy.

Citizens' groups tried twice to amend the constitution to allow a graduated income tax, first in 1972 and then again in 1976. The business community, particularly those who later broke from AIM to form the MHTC, argued that higher rates on high-income households would make it difficult to recruit high-paid senior executives and engineers to the state. Moreover, many people feared that a graduated income tax would give the state a license to spend, especially in an inflationary environment where tax revenues would rise automatically with inflation. With AIM playing a lead role in the opposition, the graduated tax was defeated by a 2 to 1 margin in 1972. By 1976, a decision by a Massachusetts court, which was later overturned, had ruled out direct business contributions to influence outcomes of public referenda. This set the stage for the growth of Citizens for Limited Taxation (CLT), a fledgling tax limitation group that became the vehicle through which segments of the business community exerted political pressure on tax issues. Its role in the 3 to 1 defeat of the 1976 graduated tax proposal put CLT on the map and was the beginning of a growing movement for tax limitation within the state.

In response to rising pressure to reduce local property taxes and to make the state more competitive, gubernatorial candidate King promised to reduce property taxes by $500 million. Then, in February 1979, his second month in office, he agreed to a highly touted "Social Contract" with the MHTC to lower total state and local taxes to the average in seventeen competitive industrial states. In return, MHTC promised to created 60,000 new jobs in Massachusetts over the next four years, and this, they said, would indirectly generate an additional 90,000 new jobs in manufacturing and support services. Both the job creation and the tax reduction goals of the social contract were achieved.

How much job growth would have occurred without the social contract is hard to determine, however, durable manufacturing, which includes the high technology sector, grew faster in Massachusetts than in the rest of the nation between 1979–83. This provides some, albeit weak, support for the view that the social contract may have led to more job creation than otherwise would have occurred. Even so, the social contract is not taken seriously by many outside of the high tech business community. Those who were part of the agreement, however, still discuss it with pride, recalling the strong ideological commitment of the MHTC.

Governor King started the tax reduction ball moving but ended up playing a minor role in the achievement of his part of the social contract. Early in 1979, Governor King proposed a 0 percent growth cap on local property taxes, combined with an increase in local aid. The legislature, however, passed a less stringent 4 percent cap with an easy override provision. Thanks to the cap and the new local aid, property taxes declined in 1979 for the first time in several decades. The following year, however, they increased by the largest amount in four years, as communities took advantage of the override position to offset stable aid, rising state assessments, and depleted reserves.

During the fall of 1979, CLT collaborated with AIM and MHTC to get signatures for two petitions to put a variety of tax limitation measures on the 1980 ballot, with CLT providing the volunteers and the business groups providing the resources. One petitition was an initiative law sponsored by CLT to reduce property taxes to 2½ percent of market value (commonly called *Proposition 2½*). After the legislature vetoed the Proposition 2½ petition in May 1980 by a vote of 173 to 5, CLT quickly gathered enough additional signatures to put Proposition 2½ on the November 1980 ballot.

The other petition, sponsored by AIM and MHTC, was an initiative constitutional amendment to reduce property taxes and limit total state and local taxes. On July 3, 1980, a special session of the legislature was convened as a constitutional convention to consider the AIM-MHTC amendment. At 5:30 P.M., the legislature voted 97 to 91 to adjourn, signifying an unfavorable vote on the proposed amendment. In a memorandum written the next day to his board of directors, MHTC president Foley wrote, "We expected a tough fight—and we were ready for it—but we never expected to be denied a vote!" MHTC soon announced its full support for Proposition 2½, backed by a $250,000 contribution to CLT. Thus was born the partnership between CLT and MHTC that led to the large popular vote for Proposition 2½ in November.

Much has been written about the variety of concerns that led to the popular support for Proposition 2½. Concern about the state's business climate was not the dominant issue for most voters. At the same time, however, survey research shows that three out of four Massachusetts voters expected Proposition 2½ to make the state more attractive to industry and that those voting yes were substantially more likely than those voting no to hold this view.[47]

Legacy of Proposition 2½

Massachusetts voters spoke loudly and clearly for tax restraint in passing Proposition 2½. This message plus the strong state economy has changed Massachusetts from a state with above average tax burdens to one with below average burdens. By 1984, Massachusetts state and local taxes and fees as a percent of personal income were 10 percent below the national average.

The rollback of local taxes forced a major restructuring of state-local fiscal relations. Governor King's first response was to offer local governments a paltry $38 million in additional local aid, an amount that was based on the flawed argument that Proposition 2½ was a vote against local government alone and did not obligate the state in any way. But the legislature pressed him to increase aid to $265 million, an amount that required substantial cuts in state government agencies and employees, given the absence of a state budget surplus. In response to continuing pressure from cities and towns who were struggling to meet rising service demands out of limited revenues, the state responded generously in subsequent years as well. Thus, state government ended up sharing the pain of adjusting to Proposition 2½.

Two longer-term effects clearly have emerged from the tax limitation measure. First, local governments now have a much bigger stake in the growth of the state economy than they did before. This reflects Governor Dukakis' pledge in 1983 to give local governments 40 percent of the revenues each year from the state's major growth taxes: the personal income tax, the corporate income tax, and the sales tax. State government policies to encourage economic growth or to cut business taxes now have direct implications for the revenues available to local governments. Second, Proposition 2½ has radically altered the tax climate within the legislature. The clearness with which the voters spoke in favor of lower taxes makes legislators extremely reluctant to support tax increases and, thereby, has made it difficult for the state government to enact major new programs.

Financial support from the High Tech Council played a key role in the electoral success of Proposition 2½. Five years later, in 1985, events dramatically illustrated that Governor Dukakis and the legislature were acutely aware of the combined power of MHTC and CLT.

As part of its continuing campaign to reduce state and local taxes, CLT filed two initiative petitions in 1985. One would curb state revenues by repealing the 7.5 percent "temporary" surcharge on state income taxes imposed during the 1975 fiscal crisis. The same CLT petition would limit the growth rate of state taxes to the growth rate of wages and salaries. The second petition would phase out the surtax and reduce from 10 to 5 percent the tax on unearned income. (Massachusetts currently taxes earned income at 5 percent and unearned income at 10 percent.) The MHTC also was working on an initiative petition. It was well understood that the MHTC and CLT would join forces in the upcoming political battle; much of the work on shaping the petitions was done jointly by the two organizations. The estimated loss from the MHTC proposal would have been about $300 million per year, a revenue loss that might have limited the governor's ability to achieve his "opportunity for all" agenda.

In what the media described as an impressive political coup, Governor Dukakis convinced the MHTC to drop its petition plans. The agreement was that MHTC would work with the governor for tax reform through the legislative process. A number of considerations may have influenced the MHTC's decision: concerns expressed by the governor and the Massachusetts congressional delegation about the effect of potential cutbacks in federal aid, polling results showing that high tech employees were more concerned about education and public safety than about taxes, threats by the legislative leadership that it might push for tax reforms opposed by businesses, and probably most important, the governor's assertion that MHTC had a good chance of achieving many of its goals through the legislative process. Thus, wishing to avoid the confrontational politics and polarization that comes from the referendum process, Governor Dukakis explicitly agreed to work with the council to develop a compromise tax reduction package. One result has already occurred: In the fall of 1985, the legislature voted to repeal the 7.5 percent surcharge. The fact that MHTC can always change its mind, however, and at a later stage, support the ongoing work of the CLT to pass a state tax cap, significantly enhances its bargaining power in the current Massachusetts debate on tax policy.

High Tech Manpower Training

The involvement of high technology entrepreneurs during the King administration extended beyond tax reform. King's Secretary of Economic Affairs, George

Kariotis, belonged to MHTC before he joined the King administration and remains a member today. Secretary Kariotis fathered the Bay State Skills Corporation and the Massachusetts Technology Park Corporation, two innovative new programs intended to unclog bottlenecks in labor supply for the state's high growth industries.[48]

The Bay State Skills Corporation

The story of the Bay State Skills Corporation demonstrates how the focus of public policy can change, depending on the allegiances of those in office. In addition, it shows how political and practical forces can distort (and sometimes improve) the original conception of a program as it makes its way through the legislative process. Finally, it illustrates the frequently observed mismatch between the lifespans of problems and the time it takes to design and implement solutions.

The Bay State Skills Corporation (BSSC) grew out of the difficulty of science based firms in Massachusetts to find engineers and technicians in the late 1970s. The shortage was cited often by high tech executives in the 1970s as the motivation for their vigorous attempts to lower state taxes. Lower taxes on households, they argued, would make it easier to attract engineers to the state. Many government officials believed that if the high tech community wanted more engineers to come to Massachusetts, they should simply pay higher wages.

In 1978 Howard Smith, Kariotis' predecessor, commissioned a Cambridge research firm called Technical Marketing Associates to determine whether there was an engineering shortage in Massachusetts. The study was completed after the Dukakis administration left office and was delivered to Kariotis in 1979. The study is reported to have found that indeed there was an engineering shortage, and that it was severe enough to pose a bottleneck for private sector research and new product development. Lowering the state's personal tax burden would not be enough; the state needed to do something to augment the level of training available, and the report made several suggestions.

Based on the report, Kariotis decided that something had to be done. He readily admits that his affiliation with the high tech community affected his concern, although no alternative location would have provided a more favorable supply, so that the high tech firms were unlikely to move in any case. Thus, the potential problem was not so much the likelihood of a mass exodus as rising wage rates and lost opportunities.

Kariotis had the president of Northeastern University convene a group of college and university presidents to find out what could be done. All said they would like to help but that tight budgets kept them from expanding their engineering programs. This posed a problem because the legislature was unlikely to approve additional funds for state schools and would never give money to private schools. They proposed instead a public-private partnership arrangement in which firms that could not find workers with required skills would pay 50 percent of the cost of training and the state would pay the other 50 percent. For their share of the match, firms could donate either equipment or money. These resources would help financially strained education institutions develop state of the art training programs, thereby augmenting the educational establishment's ability to provide people with skills that were in demand. The proposed Bay State Skills Corporation would be a quasi-public instrument of the state with public and private members on its board of directors, similar to the development finance agencies.

A bill was written and submitted to the legislature. When it didn't pass, Governor King gave $500,000 from the governor's emergency fund to start the program.

Kariotis appointed a board of directors with representation from public and private sectors, then proceeded to solicit proposals and award contracts. Technical training lasting years rather than months would have required more time and money than was available for the pilot program. The board chose to use the pilot program for occupations, such as machinists, whose training could be completed in months. The plan was to take the successful pilot program back to the legislature to obtain funds and time to teach more technical and high level skills. Companies received the program enthusiastically.

Kariotis took the program back to the legislature in 1981. Aware of resentment in the legislature against the high tech community because of Proposition 2½, the framers of the bill went out of their way to make it look as if the program would target not just high tech occupations but "growth industries." Firms would apply through educational institutions, which would bring the proposals to the BSSC for consideration. The bill was successful in the legislature.

By the time the BSSC was up and running, the engineering shortage had begun to abate.[49] Salaries of engineers rose relative to other professionals in the late 1970s, and a study sponsored by the National Science Foundation estimated that the supply of engineers for the remainder of the 1980s was likely to be sufficient, except for computer specialists and aeronautical engineers.[50] The same study reports an outside chance of a shortage of electrical engineers.

BSSC now differs from what its founders intended it to be. The absence of an engineer shortage renders this appropriate. Today, BSSC more closely resembles the broadly targeted institution that its founders described to get it through the legislature. The continuing need for state subsidized training to fill skill bottlenecks is not clear, however. Nor is it clear that the skills BSSC targets are in short supply. The primary criteria used for funding seems to be that skills be in occupations for which there is a growing demand. Most of its activities remain associated with occupations less advanced than those for which the corporation was first envisioned. Literature from BSSC reports that it funds programs in a variety of occupation areas including machine operation, precision machining, nuclear medicine technology, respiratory therapy, word processing, microwave engineering, computer aided design, electronics, advanced automation, and robotics. The few evaluations of the Bay State Skills Corporation have concluded that, for the most part, it is running well and serving a valuable purpose.

Shortly after it was set up, Senator Chester Atkins, chairman of the Committee on Ways and Means, persuaded BSSC to take on the additional assignment of target populations, such as displaced homemakers, the mentally retarded, and other groups more traditionally identified with federal training programs. BSSC pays a larger share of the training expense when target populations are involved. The BSSC experience with these groups has been successful: It has high placement rates and less of a stigma than is traditionally associated with government training programs. The staff report that their ability to operate outside of the state's line agency structure allows them to respond quickly and professionally to private sector requirements, and to pay their bills on time. Because they "look, act, and talk" like the private sector they can sustain relationships with the private sector that otherwise would not be possible. BSSC's budget is usually $2–3 million each for 50/50 match and targeted 20/80 match programs. Planned enrollment for all training projects that BSSC set up in 1985 was 4500, with 2700 from targeted populations. An average of around 1200 public dollars per trainee seems fairly uniform across projects in both targeted and untargeted categories.[51]

Like several other projects discussed here, BSSC is not an essential state program. Nevertheless, at least two rationalizations for the programs are possible. First, to the extent that the training has both general and job specific components, public-private sector cost sharing makes sense. Second, though it may not be serving a critical function in the current economic environment, it may prove so when future labor bottlenecks arise. The story of its introduction clearly illustrates the difficulty of setting up new institutions of this sort in a timely manner. Also, the collaboration between educational and private sector institutions in setting the content of training programs increases the probability that skills will be applicable to the marketplace and produces a more appropriate level of training than would either a fully public or a fully private training system.

In 1985, BSSC received a demonstration grant from the U.S. Department of Labor to help Massachusetts apply the Bay State Skills model to the federal Job Training Partnership Act (JTPA). Twelve training projects across the state, expected to train about 300 clients, generated $500,000 (in cash or in-kind contributions) from the private sector to complement a similar contribution from the demonstration grant. Although in its early states, the effort indicates another possible benefit of state-sponsored programs of this type, namely, that their existence helps the state take full advantage of federal programs, especially those that leave a lot of discretion to state and local governments.

Finally, potentially the most far reaching activity of BSSC began in 1985 in conjunction with the state's Centers of Excellence program (discussed in later chapters). Eleven special institutes allowed 300 faculty members from Massachusetts educational institutions to share information with industrial experts on emerging technologies and then incorporate the updated information in their curricula to better prepare students for employment in Massachusetts companies. Funding was through a 50/50 private match, much of it through in-kind contributions and donated employee time. Topics of the institutes included microcomputer software applications, computer applications in biology and biochemistry, marine science technology, computerized hospital database applications, computer integrated manufacturing, and biotechnology. While these institutes do not necessarily respond to existing skill bottlenecks, the potential number of students reached by faculty who participate in these and similar programs in the future could conceivably affect the production options of the state's firms in important ways.

The Massachusetts Technology Park Corporation

The Massachusetts Technology Park Corporation (MTPC), is another quasi-public instrument of the state with a board of directors comprising members from academia, the public sector, and high technology firms. Its goal is to establish a semiconductor training capacity on the East Coast to compete with the one in California.

Semiconductor technology was invented in Massachusetts but made its way to the West Coast because Raytheon chose not to fund the idea and lost the initiative to Hewlett and Packard. In 1982, when Kariotis decided to push the idea of developing a training capacity on the East Coast, none of the schools in Massachusetts, not even MIT, had a strong program in semiconductor technology. Similarly, few Massachusetts firms were active in semiconductor production; most procured and continue to procure their semi-conductor components from the West Coast. Wang and Prime in Massachusetts had considered doing in-house production but decided not to, and Data General did its production on the West Coast. It was unlikely that this potentially lucrative market would open in Massachusetts without a concerted cooperative effort.

MTPC was easier to sell to the legislature than BSSC. Kariotis harped on the idea that Massachusetts already had lost semiconductors to California and did not have to lose again to North Carolina, which, under Governor Hunt, had recently decided to try a similar program. Kariotis asked for a $20 million bond issue from the state that would be matched by at least $20 million from the private sector. The legislature was swayed by Kariotis' warnings and passed the bill unanimously on a suspension of the rules at the close of the legislative session in 1982.

MTPC has three main projects. The first was to set up a network of machines for computer aided design in the state's public and private universities, so that students could have hands-on experience in school. The second was to provide the schools with half a dozen semiconductor and processing labs, so that students can get their hands "dirty" actually making semiconductor components. The third was to provide a major "clean room" facility in a central location, where students can come to manufacture state-of-the-art integrated circuits. Implementation has begun on the first two projects and the clean room facility is under construction. Some schools have jumped the gun; they hired new faculty members and are complaining about the slow progress on the clean room facility. Pledges from private firms exceed the promised $20 million match.

Training and employment will not be linked directly. Kariotis said, "We are doing it on faith," expecting that students trained through the new system will remain to work in Massachusetts. This is probably a riskier project than any one institution would have undertaken alone.

MTPC is now presented in promotional materials with the state's new Centers of Excellence program, discussed later.

Conclusion

Dukakis' strategy of geographic targeting and the initiatives of the Task Force on Capital Formation aimed at modifying structural features of the state's economy that seemed in part responsible for the state's high unemployment and fiscal crisis. Similarly, the perception that the economy was recovering too slowly played a role in the success of Proposition 2½ and other initiatives during the King administration. As new policies were adopted to address the economy's ailments, however, subtle changes crept into the state's political culture. The process through which new ideas often were debated and refined outside the legislature, and eventually adopted into law, moved the state toward a political culture in which negotiation and compromise among interested groups would play an expanding role in shaping state policy. This style of politics and policy-making became a central characteristic of the second Dukakis administration and helps explain the continued acceptance in Massachusetts of the active role of state government in economic policy.

5

Creating the Future

In 1983, newly reelected Governor Dukakis began his second term with a thriving economy. This presented him with challenges of a very different sort from those he faced in 1975. Given his activist approach to state economic policy, the returning governor faced two key questions: How could state government help those sectors of the economy or regions of the state that were lagging behind? And what new public actions were needed to sustain and promote the state's economic growth?

The Second Dukakis Administration: 1983–Present

In contrast to the crisis atmosphere of 1975, the first year of Mike Dukakis' second term was relatively calm. To be sure, politically volatile and emotionally charged issues had to be resolved, but nothing major had to be decided immediately—and nothing like the tax hike of 1975 had to be forced down the throat of the political establishment to avert a fiscal collapse. In 1983, the issues on the agenda could be addressed without forcing the governor to take politically unpopular positions.

Another big difference between 1975 and 1983 was that Mike Dukakis was eight years older and wiser. With only a few notable exceptions, Dukakis had learned to deflect attention away from himself on controversial issues. On several of the most sensitive political issues that it has had to face, the administration has chosen to seek negotiated settlements between the opposing constituencies. This approach has produced a new right to know law on hazardous chemicals in the workplace, another law on workers' compensation, and successful legislation on early notification of plant closings, including compensation for workers who lose their jobs. The negotiated approach has met with less success in the areas of pension reform and the creation of a new statewide infrastructure bank, called *MassBank*. Dukakis declared that improvement of public education was a high priority of his second term and sponsored an initial version of an education reform bill. The legislature took responsibility for managing public debate of the bill and shaping it into final form, however, and put the governor back out front only when it was time for the bill to be signed.

Responsibility for the coordination of economic development policy in this administration is centered in the Governor's Office of Economic Development (GOED), directed by Alden Raine. Raine is the governor's screen for new ideas and often the governor's voice on matters of economic development policy. The cabinet secretaries of Communities and Development, Transportation, Labor, Environmental Affairs, and Economic Affairs report, in effect, to Alden Raine. All are members of the Economic Development Cabinet, which Raine chairs.

Raine, as introduced earlier, was Dukakis' campaign advisor for economic issues in the 1974 election and was a leading member of the Office of State Planning under Keefe. Keefe is now the state's Secretary of Administration and Finance, directly responsible for designing the governor's budget recommendations and overseeing revenue collection and other financial dealings of the state. The three people who control policy in the field of economic affairs, thus, are Dukakis, Raine, and Keefe. Their relationship is one of complete trust and mutual respect.

The climate of cooperation during this term and the absence of major crises have allowed the state to make progress on designing approaches to less urgent, longer-term problems and opportunities. These include efforts to rethink the state's methods of managing primary and secondary education, pensions, workers' compensation, infrastructure finance, plant closings, emerging industries, welfare dependency, waste disposal, and subsidized housing construction. An Employment and Training Choices Program, which offers work and training incentives to women with children on public assistance, and an unbelievably successful tax amnesty program that helped raise the possibility of a similar federal effort are among the administration's more publicized achievements. Serious efforts have gone into all of these. Interested parties were given access to deliberations and were allowed to contribute their ideas and defend their points of view. Most issues, even those on which there has been new legislation, are still under active discussion and can be expected to undergo further revision and renegotiation. There seems to be a growing sense in the state that opposing groups can make progress in a spirit of amicable cooperation and compromise.

Many of the second Dukakis administration's economic development activities continue initiatives begun during his first term. These include the geographic targeting programs, now coordinated by Alden Raine. The view that growth and development should be shared across the state remains the central idea that guides the state's development activities. It is increasingly augmented, however, by the idea that the state should consciously prepare to remain competitive in an international "knowledge based economy." The special attention to city and town centers continues but has been expanded to cover five regions of the state called *targets for opportunity.*

A story from one of the Targets of Opportunity, Southeastern Massachusetts, has received much media attention.[52] It is the story of the Miles Standish Industrial Park in the city of Taunton. The park was a World War II prisoner of war camp that became the site of a mental hospital and, in 1976, was turned over from the state to the city of Taunton for an industrial park. At that time, the state also helped the city to get a federal Economic Development Administration grant for the park's sewers and roads. The site covers 325 acres along a stretch of interstate highway whose completion held a high priority in the first Dukakis administration, partly because of its proximity to the park. Raine, then a member of Keefe's staff at OSP, went with the Secretary of Transportation to Taunton in 1977 to help design an off-ramp so that traffic would flow easily into the park from the highway. The off-ramp opened in 1982.

Among Dukakis' priorities early in the current administration was to persuade the Board of Directors of the state chartered, quasi-public Massachusetts Technology Park Corporation to build its new microelectronics center in the Miles Standish Industrial Park. This would give the park the visibility and prestige it needed to attract larger employers. The governor failed to convince the board to put the microelectronics center in the park but his efforts attracted a great deal of attention in the state's newspapers. This alerted businesses throughout the state to the new industrial park, the governor's commitment to it, and its convenient location. The state and the city have worked closely together to capitalize on this new found notoriety.

Today, Taunton's mayor credits the state for helping to create 2000 new jobs in and around the city and for the fact that the park, now nearly full, attracted major employers like the GTE Corporation. Taunton now is a centerpiece of the state's effort to promote revitalization in Southeastern Massachusetts. State officials express hope that slow-growing Targets of Opportunity in other parts of the state similarly will begin to attract a larger share of the state's job growth away from areas like Route 128 near Boston, where unemployment is extremely low and traffic congestion high.

As in the first term, the present Dukakis geographic targeting strategy is not spelled out in a detailed plan, but is a loosely structured initiative by which the five regional Targets of Opportunity receive preference for state resources, the personal attention of Raine and the governor, and are specifically promoted to business people as places where the state would like more development. Though it is difficult to argue that the strategy has attracted many new jobs to the state and though its effects cannot always be firmly distinguished from what might have happened without state intervention, it seems clear from the details of specific examples that state efforts have fostered improvements in the geographic distribution of business activity and have brought the hope of a better quality of life for people in the state's economically distressed communities.

Three episodes in the story of Dukakis' second administration deserve special attention. First is the governor's Commission on the Future of Mature Industries. The commission's ability to reach a compromise on mandatory prenotification of plant closings prevented sure deterioration in the political relationship among government, business, and labor leaders, thereby preserving the potential for subsequent resolution of other issues. The second episode is the administration's unsuccessful attempt to set up MassBank, a new financing authority for development related infrastructure projects. Among other things, this case demonstrates the limitations of cooperation and compromise. The third case covers the Centers of Excellence program, which represents the adoption of a new policy "idea" in Massachusetts, that the state should take an active role in shaping its future industrial competitiveness, even to the point of targeting industries.

The Governor's Commission on the Future of Mature Industries

Massachusetts is home to service and high technology sectors that are the envy of most other states.[53] At the same time, its mature industrial sector employs one-half million people. The state's older industries have been losing firms and jobs for several decades and the trend is continuing. Nevertheless, many of these older firms are modernizing, reinvesting, and restructuring. Firms in mature industries such as manufacturers of hand tools, industrial machines, paper, shoes, apparel, plastics, abrasives, and other basic industrial products are more concentrated in the southeastern and western parts of the state, where growth is slower and unemployment higher than in the Boston metropolitan area. A declared high priority of the Governor's Office of Economic Development this term is to initiate revitalization in five older industrial sections of the state, the so-called Targets of Opportunity. As a first step, the governor formed a Commission on the Future of Mature Industries in June 1983, his first year back in office.

Political Background

Stabilizing mature industries in Massachusetts has never been on the agenda of any organized business lobby. Rather, this problem belongs to organized labor and its allies in academia, government, and citizens' groups like Massachusetts Fair Share.

The Commission on the Future of Mature Industries was formed for three interrelated reasons. First, Dukakis and Raine saw it as an opportunity to develop a framework for revitalizing regions in which mature industries dominate the economic base. Second, it was needed to head off a divisive showdown over plant closing prenotification bills in the legislature. Third, it partially fulfilled a campaign promise. In 1980, Dukakis promised organized labor an early notification plant closing law in return for their help in reelecting him. He also promised labor a right to know bill for workers dealing with hazardous chemicals in the workplace, and support for the creation of a new cabinet agency for labor, the Executive Office of Labor.

These three items had been on the AFL-CIO's legislative agenda during the King administration but were not pushed. Tim Bassett, chairman of the House Committee on Commerce and Labor, said that he repeatedly sent early notification bills out to be "researched" because he was told by House Speaker McGee not to let them reach the floor of the house, since they would be too divisive. The new Executive Office of Labor was passed almost surreptitiously, at the last minute of the last legislative session before King left office, and King signed it into law. However, early notification and right to know legislation were waiting when Dukakis came into office.

The Dukakis team would not support any of the legislation that was under consideration on these issues. Nonetheless, Bassett reported to Dukakis that legislation on prenotification had to be faced. Dukakis surely was concerned that he would be seriously damaged by the negative message sent the losers in any right to know or prenotification legislation that favored excessively either business or labor. He decided, instead, to seek negotiated agreements between business and labor. For the prenotification issue, he appointed the Commission on the Future of Mature Industries.

The commission was composed of thirty-eight people from business, labor, government, and academia. The business people on the commission were members, but not officers, of the Associated Industries of Massachusetts (AIM) and the Massachusetts High Technology Council (MHTC). Representatives from MHTC were appointed to stem criticism from MHTC and to generate ideas about how advanced technology might assist in the renewal of mature industries. Reportedly, the leaders of the Associated Industries of Massachusetts were disturbed about being excluded but could not complain too loudly because they were represented by some of their members.

As indicated earlier, the immediate political purpose of the commission was to fulfill a campaign promise and defuse the early notification plant closing issue. However, the commission's mandate (to "develop a comprehensive and cooperative strategy among leaders from business, labor, and government for supporting and strengthening the Commonwealth's mature industries") indicates that the governor wanted more than a narrow solution to this issue. Despite the efforts of a high quality professional research staff, commission members were not very interested in finding a "comprehensive and cooperative strategy" for strengthening mature industries. Instead, they focused on narrower issues.

Two Agendas: Prenotification Versus a Strategy for Mature Industries

Because the business and labor members of the commission were preoccupied with whether there should be mandatory early notification of plant closings and major layoffs, the primary focus of the commission was diverted from the broader realm of mature industries policy to the narrow but politically more important task of finding a middle ground on which business and labor could agree. The governor had received high marks from the business community for negotiating a right to know compromise in 1983 and coming to an early agreement with the legislature on the 1984 budget and local aid allocations. But, as time passed with no agreement within the commission, pro-business op-ed pieces in the state's major newspapers warned that the Mature Industries Commission was "beginning to look like a Trojan Horse for mandatory prenotification." They threatened that the verdict on this issue would "provide either positive or negative signals . . .that [would] affect job growth for years to come." Threats from the left counter balanced the pro-business threats. Labor and social welfare groups led by Massachusetts Fair Share warned that Dukakis would make a big mistake if he abandoned them the way he had during his first term. Raine and Ben Kincannon, Raine's deputy in GOED and executive director of the commission, had to find a way out.

The breakthrough came six months into the commission's term, on January 31, 1984, when Kincannon called an off the record meeting in the office of Commerce Commissioner, Ronald Ansin. It was the first meeting held away from the full membership. The meeting was attended by Charles McKay, of the high tech Foxboro Company; George Carpenter, Secretary-Treasurer of the AFL-CIO; Professor Barry Bluestone, Carpenter's advisor; Ansin; Raine; Kincannon; Secretary Evelyn Murphy, of the Executive Office of Economic Affairs; and Secretary Paul Eustace, of the Executive Office of Labor.

Businessman McKay came up with the compromise. He agreed that the plight of dislocated workers deserved attention but he still insisted that mandatory prenotification was untenable. He suggested that business might agree to "voluntary appropriate action," by which he meant voluntary prenotification and voluntary severance benefits. Displaced workers would be guaranteed a package of benefits from their employers or from the state if their employers were unwilling or unable to comply. These benefits included a combination of 90 days notification and supplemental employment benefits, extension of health care for ninety days beyond termination, and extension of state job training and relocation programs. This package was more than Carpenter had hoped for. It was a defeat only insofar as it did not punish firms that refused to give notification. It was a good compromise.

From then on the commission mainly fleshed out the details of the compromise proposal. Though Kincannon disagrees, others report that the governor's representatives seemed to lose their commitment to finding a comprehensive approach to the problems of mature industries. Their energies appeared to be focused on making sure that the agreement on the prenotification of workers' benefits issues hung together.

The push to come up with a comprehensive mature industries policy remained strongest among the commission's staff, an ancillary group that called themselves the Labor Caucus, and Representative Bassett and his staff from the Commerce and Labor Committee. Most of the mature industries proposals emanated from the Labor Caucus. One piece, the Product Development Corporation, a quasi-public agency to help finance residual capital requirements for firms attempting to diversify their product lines, was modeled after the Connecticut Product Development Corporation by a member of Bassett's staff. The feeling among some members of the commission's staff, the Labor Caucus, and Bassett's staff was that the formulation of a mature industries policy had become merely a sideshow for the commission members. An additional problem was that the staff did not complete the industry studies until it was too late for their findings to influence the commission's recommendations.

The governor's Commission on Mature Industries issued its final report in June 1984, as scheduled. All its recommendations were adopted in the legislation. The governor's office chose not to put the Product Development Corporation in the legislation, but agreed not to object if Bassett added it in committee. Bassett not only added the Product Development Corporation but also appropriations for each of the bill's major components. These appropriations ranged from $2 million for the Product Development Corporation to $5 million for reemployment assistance benefits. Bassett "ran the bill through behind the budget process," and the $13.5 million bill passed with little opposition.

The recommendations of the commission represented a compromise but, unlike those of the Task Force on Capital Formation in 1977, not a consensus. Members agreed to disagree and to include dissenting opinions in the report. The least ideological dissenting letter was from Lynn Browne, a commission member from the Federal Reserve Bank of Boston, who expressed two legitimate concerns. First, the supplemental unemployment insurance benefit is available only to people who become unemployed through plant closings or large layoffs and, therefore, discriminates among unemployed people in essentially similar circumstances. It is not directly related to the difficulty of finding another job. Second, a perverse incentive in the law may induce employers not to give early notification. Because the law promises benefits for ninety days beginning on the day of notification, the later the time of notification in any given layoff, the longer is the period after leaving the firm in which laid-off workers will be entitled to supplemental benefits. These benefits will be paid by the state if the employer is unwilling or unable to pay. A financially strained employer who cares about the welfare of his employees has a perverse incentive not to give early notice, because with no prenotification, his layed-off employees will receive supplemental benefits from the state for a longer period of time.

Implementation began in early 1985 and is overseen jointly by the Secretaries of Economic Affairs and Labor, as specified in the legislation. The director of the program believes it makes sense for her program to straddle both secretariats because the problems of mature industries clearly involve both business and labor issues. The Industrial Services Program (ISP) is the umbrella over all the business assistance, worker assistance, and economic monitoring programs (other than the Product Development Corporation) that were created to the legislation. ISP is the only jointly administered agency in Massachusetts government.[54] Current plans make ISP the lead agency in refining and coordinating the state's policies toward mature industries including, ultimately, a more systematic effort to encourage plant modernizations.

Evaluation

The experiment in joint administration between the Executive Office of Labor and the Executive Office of Economic Affairs clearly was worth trying. It supported a stronger positive relationship between labor representatives and state government, and it increased the likelihood that valuable ideas from the labor community to help mature industries would be heard and taken seriously by senior line-agency staff members. In contrast to the period before 1983, when there was no Executive Office of Labor, labor representatives now felt that they had inside access to state government in the same way that business has through the Executive Office of Economic Affairs and the Department of Commerce. This sense of inclusion resulted in concrete programs. For example, the Assistant Secretary of Labor is the architect and coordinator of a program called *Cooperative Regional Industrial Laboratories* (CRIL), one of the new reemployment assistance programs addressed by the commission. CRIL brings skilled workers directly into the discussion of plant closings and major layoffs. All concerned parties in a local area work together to find solutions. As with other state initiatives, CRIL relies largely on federal funding; much of its funding is from the Displaced Worker Funds of the federal Job Training Partnership Act.

The work of the mature industries commission and the changes in public policy it produced are not easy to evaluate. By creating the commission and its agenda, the governor successfully defused a volatile issue. In addition, he improved the state's ability to ease the transition of workers out of declining industries and to provide assistance to employers that, without help, were in danger of closing. Although market forces limit what the state can do practically on behalf of laid-off workers and failing businesses, the results of the commission were positive, especially with respect to the coordination of worker assistance.

The Massachusetts compromise compares well to plant closing notification laws in other states. Its acceptance in the business community reflects largely the fact that it is voluntary; if the employer refuses to pay, the law transfers to the general taxpayers the burden of supplementary benefits even when the firm can afford to pay. This, however, creates problems of horizontal inequity among firms. Similar inequities apply among workers, where only those unemployed by plant closings or major layoffs are eligible. Hence, for its achievements in the political art of shifting the burden to the general taxpayer and from the interests seated at the table, the Commission on the Future of Mature Industries in Massachusetts deserves high marks, but clear inequities and perverse incentives remain.

Massachusetts Development Bank (MassBank)

Touted as the most important initiative of the Dukakis administration in fiscal year 1985, the Massachusetts Development Bank, commonly called MassBank, was designed to provide substantial new funding for roads, bridges, sewers, and water systems in the commonwealth.[55] As described in the governor's budget message, MassBank was not really a bank but an independent authority that would channel substantial amounts of new funds into infrastructure projects by tapping the market for non-general obligation bonds. As details of the MassBank proposal began to leak out, it soon became apparent that the final package involved more than the establishment of a new independent authority; part of the package was a complicated set of tax changes, which were included to garner business support for the proposal.

The legislature did not pass MassBank in 1984 despite heavy lobbying by the administration and its advocates nor did it pass a revised package submitted in 1985. Nonetheless, MassBank serves as an important case study of the state role in economic development policy in Massachusetts. The scale of the proposal was vast; had it passed and had the dreams of its proposers been achieved, it would have produced huge amounts of new spending on development related infrastructure projects in Massachusetts and might have served as a model for other states nationwide. In addition, the process through which the administration tried to develop support for the MassBank package illustrates the limitations of the governor's negotiation and consensus building strategy and the dangers inherent in not bringing all interested parties to the bargaining table.

How MassBank Got on the Agenda

MassBank was put on the agenda directly by the administration, particularly Governor Dukakis, Frank Keefe, and Frederick Salvucci, the Secretary of Transportation. The time seemed ripe for such a proposal. Concern at the national level about the nation's crumbling infrastructure had led to a major congressional study of the problem and talk of setting up a national development bank to help finance state and local infrastructure projects. Per capita capital spending in Massachusetts was below the national average, local communities were apparently cutting back on maintenance and capital spending in response to the fiscal pressures of Proposition 2½, and the congressional study indicated a large shortfall between projected infrastructure needs and available revenues in Massachusetts unless some action was taken. Vividly brought to the attention of the general public by the collapse of a bridge in nearby Connecticut, the problem seemed relatively clear. Moreover, the timing was propitious. The strength of the state's economy made it feasible to devote substantial resources to infrastructure projects. In addition, to provide the base for continued economic growth, old infrastructure systems would have to be repaired and new ones built.

Though the desirability of more capital spending was relatively clear, the need for a separate new authority was less obvious. The administration maintained that the state had a serious problem with the structure of its debt. Compared to other states, Massachusetts relied too heavily on general obligation bonds. Though ranked twenty-third nationally in terms of total per capita debt, Massachusetts ranked ninth in terms of general obligation debt. The administration argued that this, along with other factors such as failure to use generally accepted accounting principles (GAAP) and a large unfunded pension liability, contributed to a bond rating from Moody's of A1, that was low, given the health of the state's economy. Hence, it was important to set up MassBank to provide a mechanism through which the state could shift some of its debt financing to revenue or limited obligation bonds. As opponents of MassBank continually pointed out, however, the authority to issue revenue bonds already existed in the Treasurer's Office.

Thus, the true debt-structure related justification for a separate authority was a bit more complex and reflected the administration's desire to quickly channel huge amounts of new money into infrastructure development. Because sufficient user charge revenues would not be available to support each of the following three years, a new dedicated revenue source was needed to get MassBank going.

The proposed solution was to dedicate certain business taxes to cover debt service on the bonds to be issued during the first three years of MassBank operation. Issuing the new bonds through a separate authority, it was argued, would help the market distinguish these limited obligation bonds, backed by the dedicated revenue source, from the general obligation bonds issued by the commonwealth. Without this distinction, the shift to the new bonds would do little to improve the rating on the state's bond issues for nondevelopment purposes.

The legacy of Proposition 2½ provided a second, even more compelling justification for a separate authority. Stung by the criticism of his need to raise taxes at the beginning of his first term and fully aware of the antagonism of the legislature toward raising taxes following Proposition 2½, Governor Dukakis understood that the only hope for getting substantial new funds for infrastructure projects was to develop a funding mechanism that did not involve raising broad-based taxes. This concern was especially strong because 1984 was an election year for legislators. A new authority with its own dedicated revenue stream seemed to be a logical way around the problem. New revenues dedicated to a problem about which there was widespread agreement, he hoped, would be palatable to the legislature and, at the same time, free up existing revenues for other spending on the governor's agenda.

Developing Support for MassBank

As first presented in the budget, the MassBank proposal included only a vague reference to start-up financing, with emphasis placed on user charge financing. Thus, a major component of the process of developing support for the new agency involved working out a financing mechanism that would maximize support for the proposal.

The administration argued that some form of business tax was a logical choice for a dedicated revenue stream for MassBank because business would benefit directly from the types of infrastructure that MassBank would support. Moreover there was widespread publicity about the declining share of business taxes within the state and the perception that business was not paying its fair share of taxes.[56] Thus, the political problem became one of how to get business first to agree to pay for MassBank and then to support the package within the legislature.

The administration's strategy was to make a deal with business. Certain possible concessions by the government were relatively obvious, such as the reduction of taxes for unemployment compensation and a three-year extension of the state's investment tax credit. Both were valued highly by business and were easy for the administration to agree to, since they were likely to occur in any case. Discussions between the administration and key business leaders, especially representatives of the Associated Industries of Massachusetts (AIM) and the Massachusetts High Tech Council (MHTC), soon made it clear what concession business wanted most: full repeal of the state's worldwide unitary approach to corporate taxation.

Background on the Unitary Tax Issue. Relying on a 1932 law, the Department of Revenue under the King administration started selectively using worldwide unitary accounting as the basis for assessing corporate taxes. With reference to the same law, Ira Jackson, the Commissioner of Revenue during Dukakis' second term, in early 1984 announced that he planned to implement full worldwide unitary accounting. He estimated that additional revenues would amount to about $50 million per year. Multinational firms within the state were outraged and argued that worldwide unitary accounting would force them to leave the state or to expand elsewhere. The president of the Mass High Tech Council asserted that forty of the seventy-five members planning expansions were delaying their plans until decisions were reached on unitary taxation and plant closing legislation. To dramatize its displeasure, one electronics firm, Augat, Inc., announced with great fanfare that its decision to expand in southern Maine was directly related to the administration's decision to implement worldwide unitary accounting. (The rhetoric was inconsistent with reality, however; the firm's decision to move had been made the previous summer. Moreover, when the firm had initially announced the move, in November, it blamed plant closing legislation rather than unitary taxation, despite Maine's position as one of only a few states with *mandatory* plant closing prenotification laws.)

Somewhat fortuitously, the two issues came together at the same time. Business opposition to unitary accounting played right into the hands of the administration, which was struggling to develop support for MassBank. Clearly, there was room for a deal. The administration could back off the unitary tax issues in return for business support of MassBank.

The Deal-Making Process. The administration started holding secret meetings with key business groups, primarily AIM and MHTC. The proposal hammered out in these early meetings included an outright repeal of unitary accounting in return for business support for MassBank, with the debt service on the initial bonds to be financed by a payroll tax on business.

When the *Boston Herald* publicized this deal in February 1984, there was a loud outcry. Even the response of the business community was mixed. AIM and

MHTC were strongly behind it, but many business groups, including those representing the financial community and small in-state firms, recognized that they would be burdened by the payroll tax yet receive none of the benefits from the repeal of worldwide unitary accounting. Non-business groups were appalled both by the secret dealings themselves, in which they played no role, and the sellout to business through the substitution of the regressive payroll tax for the unitary tax, widely perceived to be a fair tax. Many of these groups, including labor groups, Massachusetts Fair Share, and the Human Services Coalition, had testified in support of unitary taxation in hearings held by the Department of Revenue.

Continuing negotiations between the administration and the business groups led to a compromise solution. Instead of repealing completely the unitary tax, the administration proposed limiting the reach of Massachusetts taxes to the "water's edge"; that is, to profits of Massachusetts firms earned within the United States excluding Puerto Rico and other U.S. territories.[57] The dedicated revenue stream under the new proposal was to be a tax on business profits. Officially called an *infrastructure development assessment* rather than a *tax,* this in fact was a group of taxes that applied to various types of firms in Massachusetts, with rates set to produce assessments in line with each type's share of total business taxes. Thus, the administration ended up with a revenue source that it could claim was fair and nonregressive, while business gained a limitation on the hated worldwide unitary tax and the potential for substantial improvement in the state's infrastructure in return for higher profits taxes.

Strength of Support. The governor officially unveiled the deal on March 22 with great fanfare and surrounded by representatives of many of the large business groups. He emphasized the significance of the business support; if the groups that were footing the bill were in favor of it, MassBank must be a sound proposal. Further support for the proposal appeared in a long list of official endorsements and in subsequent favorable editorials in major newspapers throughout the state.

But the support was much shakier than it first appeared. Even within the business community, support was not wholehearted. AIM was strongly behind the package, having won a major concession on the unitary tax, the exclusion of U.S. territories from the definition of water's edge. The High Tech Council was much more circumspect. Officially, it endorsed the concept of MassBank but opposed the specifics of the funding. Unlike AIM, it was not satisfied with the compromise on the unitary tax, and wanted its outright repeal. Individual high tech firms took differing positions. An Wang of Wang Laboratories came out in support, but the CEO of Augat, Inc., strongly opposed it. The Business Roundtable gave it a vague endorsement, but the Massachusetts Taxpayers Foundation opposed the idea of new taxes and believed that a new state agency was not needed. Savings banks and associations of small businesses endorsed MassBank, but commercial banks were opposed, in part because they thought their assessment was too high.

There was little support among the legislative leadership. They tended to view the package as simply a way for the governor to raise new taxes, an act that simply would not fly, especially during an election year. In addition, some feared the development of a large new bureaucracy and viewed the package as an attempt by the executive branch to centralize its power over capital spending. These legislators typically argued that the goals of MassBank could be achieved through existing administrative arrangements. In addition, many legislators believed that the complex issue of unitary taxation should be determined on its own merits and not as part of the controversial MassBank package. The administration made it clear, however, that a vote to decouple the unitary tax from MassBank was a vote against MassBank. Clearly, the compromise on the unitary tax was a critical part of the administration's deal with business.

Most painful and shocking to the administration was the opposition from the non-business groups that traditionally supported the governor. Labor groups were generally opposed, given the stance of labor at the national level in favor of worldwide unitary taxation. The Human Services Coalition believed that the package just restructured business taxes, earmarking a portion of the overall amount for infrastructure. Thus, their concern was that the package would reduce the funds available for human services. The group representing Massachusetts cities and towns originally endorsed the package but became concerned about the loss of revenues from the compromise on unitary taxation. Their concern was more than just academic. A reduction of $35 million in corporate taxes translates into a loss of $14 million to local governments based on the governor's promise that 40 percent of all growth revenues would be used for local aid.

Despite heavy lobbying by key members of the administration, delaying tactics by a coalition called the *Tax Reform Group* (led by staffers from the Senate Taxation Committee), which sided with social service interests and opposed MassBank, kept the bill from being passed in 1984. By the time the legislature was ready to consider it again in the 1985 session, a state supreme court decision in a case brought by Polaroid had knocked the winds out of the MassBank sails.

Polaroid successfully argued that the 1932 law, under which first the King and then the Dukakis administration applied worldwide unitary accounting, did not provide valid statutory authorization for the practice. The decision in Polaroid's favor immediately removed worldwide unitary accounting as a bargaining chip for the administration. This was devastating in terms of garnering business support for the proposal. After the decision, the business community viewed the water's edge compromise on the unitary tax as a $15 million increase rather than a $35 million reduction in corporate taxes.

In 1985, the administration submitted a modified version of MassBank to reflect the new reality. The new proposal specified that existing taxes on business be dedicated to MassBank, with the loss of general fund revenues made up by the imposition of the water's edge unitary accounting and by restricting the use of accelerated depreciation. This new funding package was more acceptable to the governor's non-business supporters but, in contrast to the earlier version, was opposed by both AIM and MHTC. It failed to pass in 1985.

Why MassBank Was Not Enacted. Lack of executive leadership and commitment can easily be ruled out as an explanation of the legislature's failure to enact MassBank. The administration devoted its top talent and clout to lobbying for the proposal in the legislature and around the state, with Frank Keefe, Secretary of Administration and Finance, playing the lead role. The package represented many hours of negotiation with AIM and MHTC initially, then with a multitude of other interest groups, legislators, and editorial writers throughout the spring. In addition, the administration backed off at least one other revenue proposal, a proposal to raise state fees as part of the fiscal year 1985 budget, in order to avoid diverting attention from MassBank. Though somewhat mixed signals came from the Revenue Department's apparent commitment to worldwide unitary accounting at the same time that Frank Keefe was using it as a bargaining chip, there was little doubt about the depth of the administration's commitment to MassBank.

A case can be made, however, that the administration made some mistakes and miscalculations in the process of building a coalition. First, it apparently underestimated the importance of the diversity of the business community, focusing too much attention on the concerns of AIM and MHTC and ignoring the concerns of small firms and the financial community. Second, it miscalculated the interests of the non-business groups. The administration apparently expected these groups to fall in line once they learned that the main effect of the infrastructure package would be to remove the pressure of funding development from the regular budget, thereby freeing funds for other programs. Instead, the groups looked closely at the various pieces in the complex package and concluded that, in fact, business would end up paying no more taxes than before; business taxes would simply be diverted from the general fund to infrastructure projects. Moreover, the administration underestimated the strength of the antagonism toward its proposal to back down on the unitary tax issue. The administration seemed to ignore the evidence from the February hearings at the Revenue Department, at which representatives from many groups testified strongly in favor of worldwide unitary taxation.

Finally, and perhaps most critically, the initial package and all of the revisions it underwent may have been too complicated. It represented a very fragile deal, which has been described by journalist Robert Kutner as a Calder mobile with the weights too delicately balanced.

Even the best marketing job might have failed, however, given the view of state legislators toward new state taxes. Citizens for Limited Taxation, the group that led the successful drive for Proposition 2½, came out strongly against MassBank, arguing that if infrastructure development has such a high priority, it should be able to compete successfully for additional funds through the regular political process and that the establishment of a separate authority represents an undesirable override of the traditional democratic process. Others, such as the head of the House Taxation Committee argued for using existing taxes, such as the gas tax, instead of the new earmarked business taxes proposed by the administration. A rising state surplus also bolstered the case against new state taxes.

As evident from the discussion of the proposals to repeal the 7.5 percent surtax, the legacy of Proposition 2½ and the tax limitation spirit lived on in Massachusetts.

Would MassBank Have Worked? We believe that, had it passed, MassBank clearly would have achieved its major short-term goal, the injection of large amounts of new funding for bridges, roads, sewers, and water systems, and would have been a good example of how government and business can work together to achieve mutual interests. It is debatable, however, whether the dedicated revenue stream would have achieved MassBank's other short-run goal, serving as a vehicle to help the state make the transition to revenue bonds. How the market would have treated bonds backed by a dedicated stream of business taxes is unclear.

The longer-run outlook for the agency was even less clear. The Dukakis administration was vague about the specifics of the user charge financing that would pay the debt service on the bonds issued by the agency after the first three years. Yet, these user charges were crucial both for the success of the shift away from general obligation bonds and for the state to reap the managerial benefits of insulating infrastructure project financing from the political process. Although long-term benefits were possible, the danger was that the establishment of a new bureaucracy might be unnecessary and wasteful and that, in the long run, it might exert undue pressure to channel scarce resources to physical infrastructure projects and away from other purposes, such as human services.

Centers of Excellence

In fall 1985, Governor Dukakis led a series of visits to innovative companies in six regions of the state. In January 1986, he inserted a presentation of slides from these visits into the State of the State Address and expressed great optimism about the future health of the state's economy based on the many applications of new technology he had seen. Soon after the State of the State Address, he sponsored an all-day conference at the State House, entitled "Creating the Future." The conference's 200 invited participants represented business organizations, organized labor, individual businesses, the state legislature, and public and private universities.

The proper role of the state government in shaping the state's economic future is a topic on which informed citizens often disagree. One perspective is that state government should simply do a better job at the roles it has played for most of the twentieth century. These include providing education, infrastructure, and social services, and regulating and taxing the private sector. The importance of these for sound economic development is well established and the emerging consensus is that they should be carried out with a more careful eye to their strategic importance. When these roles are not performed adequately, the foundation of the state's economy is weakened and private market activities are less efficiently conducted. Though the Massachusetts economy currently is thriving, the potential threat from insufficient attention to the state's infrastructural and regulatory environment should be taken seriously in any vision of the state's role in creating the future.

A more expansive conception of state government's role in creating the future is that states should not only improve their performance in traditional roles but reach beyond these roles and assume a more active function. An important legacy of the past ten years of economic development policy in Massachusetts is that the private sector has grown accustomed to an expanding role by state government. Geographic targeting, state sponsored development finance agencies, partnerships with the private sector for training workers in specific vocational skills, special services and benefits for workers unemployed through plant closings or major layoffs are all new roles in which the public and private sectors have worked closely together.

According to a still broader conception, government should try to understand the impact of its policy on specific industries and should consciously support the interstate and international competitiveness of strategically important sectors. Some would call this conception industrial policy.[58] In the past three years, Massachusetts has planted the seeds of an industrial policy but has been careful not to call it this. A central component is the Massachusetts Centers of Excellence Program, the topic of the remainder of this section.

Except for geographic targeting, the state's strategy for targeted business assistance is not well developed. The administration has tended to avoid overt hints of favoritism toward specific industries. Indeed, the state has made no sustained or successful effort to understand its industrial structure and the implications for tax, regulatory, or geographic targeting policy. In this, Massachusetts is no different from most other states. An effort to implement a program of economic monitoring was mandated by the legislation that followed the Commission on the Future of Mature Industries and has begun on a modest scale. So far, however, senior officials in state government apparently have not thought much about how to use the information in policy making.

Even so, a state industrial policy is developing in the Executive Office of Economic Affairs. Early in 1983, as the second Dukakis administration got underway, Secretary of Economic Affairs Evelyn Murphy began looking for a mechanism by which her office could work with others to help sustain the state's economic preeminence into the twenty-first century. She proposed a Commission on the Knowledge Based Economy to consider the state's future in a comprehensive fashion, but the business community expressed little interest and the state legislature was more interested in reform for primary and secondary education.

Failing to gain support for a commission, Murphy turned instead to the Centers of Excellence Program. A small staff in her office and in the Executive Office of Energy began designing and implementing the program in 1983; legislation passed in January 1985. The centers provide partial funding for partnerships between businesses and universities leading to new commercial products in polymers (plastics), biotechnology, marine sciences, and photovoltaics (solar energy), and new production processes in these as well as more mature industrial sectors. The first round of grants came in 1986 and awarded about $100,000 to each of twenty projects from an applicant pool of 150. Partnerships for each technology are concentrated in four regions of the state: western, central, southeastern, and northeastern Massachusetts. An illustrative list of forms that collaborative efforts might take includes

- support for university-based research projects;
- establishment of on-campus shared business incubator facilities;
- purchase or shared use of state-of-the-art equipment;
- development of academic-industrial liaison programs;
- hosting of major technical conferences;
- sponsorship of distinguished professorships;
- establishment of export marketing facilities;
- creation of technical education centers.

By law, all must be guided by the needs of the private sector and involve private sector financial or in-kind support.

The Centers of Excellence program has two sets of goals. The first is to create the conditions that will induce sustained growth of industrial clusters in the four targeted technologies and regions. Each of the regions is already home to small concentrations of firms and research institutions in the respective technologies. This is especially true of photovoltaics and marine sciences, which are located almost exclusively in the northeast and southeast corners of the state. Polymer production is more evenly distributed, with about half of it within an hour's drive of the University of Massachusetts at Amherst. In biotechnology, the most visible center of activity in the state is around MIT and Harvard, in Cambridge and Boston, and 40 miles east of the city at Worcester, where a Center of Excellence Biotechnology Park is being developed in the central region. Worcester is home to a second cluster of respected academic and research institutions in Massachusetts, which has formed a consortium to coordinate their research activities and manage the Biotechnology Park. The other major goal of the Centers of Excellence initiative is to build the state universities in these regions into integral components of their regional economies.

What will it take for this agenda to succeed and what is the state's proper role? A current study of a number of regional industrial clusters reveals that several conditions typically characterize growing clusters of high technology industries. These are listed and briefly explained in Exhibit 5-1.

By far the most essential requirement for these clusters is the presence in the region of incubator institutions in which potential entrepreneurs learn their trade, develop their ideas, and make useful contacts. These incubators have to be strong research oriented firms and universities that are special enough to attract talented students and researchers from both inside and outside of the region. These talented people become not only the entrepreneurs but also the skilled workers of infant firms that are spun off. The history of microelectronics in Massachusetts is rife with stories of firms spawned by institutions like Raytheon and the various laboratories associated with MIT. Similar stories abound for high tech clusters in other places. Parent institutions perform other functions listed in Exhibit 5-1 as well, such as being initial customers, serving as models of success, and providing managerial advice.

All of the conditions listed in Exhibit 5-1 for successful industrial clusters, including the availability of risk capital, are present in Massachusetts for photovoltaics, polymers, biotechnology, and marine science. The potential role of

---

Exhibit 5-1. Conditions for Self-Sustaining
High Technology Industrial Clusters

Incubator Institutions

These can be established firms or research universities. As incubators, these institutions train potential entrepreneurs and skilled labor and expose them to the knowledge that leads to ideas for new products and businesses. In most established high technology clusters, there are identifiable incubators and many of the firms in the cluster have clear geneological links.

Initial Customers

The established firms in a cluster often serve as the initial customers for new firms by subcontracting work to them and offering them consulting opportunities to smooth their cash flow. Officials of established firms also introduce new entrepreneurs to potential customers.

Models of Success

Models of success reduce the perceived risk of new ventures. Lower risk attracts more entrepreneurs into an industry than would enter otherwise. It also makes potential clients, partners, suppliers, distributors, and financiers less reluctant to enter into business relationships.

Risk Capital

Few entrepreneurs have all the money they need to finance their businesses. Hence, there must be investors and financial institutions that are willing to take chances on new ideas.

Management Advice

The most important sources of management advice are established firms and financiers. Financiers who work in risk finance, especially venture capitalists, have experience working with new firms and often insist on a management role during the start-up phase as a precondition to their financial participation.

Experts to Screen Ideas and Entrepreneurial Talent

Financiers and their technical advisors select people in or out of the entrepreneurial pool. Venture capitalists frequently have technical expertise as well as experience identifying people who have high potential as entrepreneurs. Because they have this expertise, they also serve as professional intermediaries for less expert investors.

Note: This exhibit draws on work in progress by Roger Miller and is based on observed patterns. Also see Roger Miller and Marcel Côté, "Growing the Next Silicon Valley," *Harvard Business Review* 4 (July–August, 1985), pp. 114–123.

state government is catalytic, to provide information and resources for coordination that individual firms and others may be reluctant or unable to provide entirely on their own and to help train the required work force. Most fundamentally, the state needs to secure the cooperation of the key incubator institutions. This will include short-run costs to the institutions, as some of their best and brightest employees are encouraged to leave and start new ventures or to spend time in supportive roles like helping screen proposals for university-industry partnerships. The four centers currently are well structured to foster this sense of commitment. Executive officers of the state's top research and business institutions from the relevant disciplines are on each center's seven-member board of directors. The level of private sector commitment given to these endeavors will depend in large measure on how steadfast state political leaders seem in their commitment to the program's success.

The principal role of the state university system in support of these new industrial clusters is, as it should be, to train students from their home regions in the skills necessary for basic research and production. Only the University of Massachusetts at Amherst is likely to develop the research capacity to consistently generate significant innovations in commercial applications in the foreseeable future. To argue otherwise strains credibility and could dampen private sector commitment to the basic goals of the program. In our view, a successful Centers of Excellence program should be structured so that each of the state's institutions is relied on to do what it does best, while building capacity to do more later. This capacity can be built through research and training partnerships with private firms and universities that have historically served as incubators.

Although it is too early to evaluate this program, we believe the Centers of Excellence initiative has the potential to play a useful catalytic role. It can speed the expansion and thickening of professional networks along which ideas will move from the lab to the market and it can facilitate the discovery of new knowledge and applications. In addition, the program can be used to coordinate the targeted use of existing state training and financial assistance agencies and serve as the vehicle for submitting applications in partnership with other states for special research and institution-building funds from the federal government. Finally, the governor and the state's political leadership can use it as a symbol of the state's commitment to remain a national leader and, hence, to inspire and motivate the state's citizens in ways that will contribute to both the present and the future quality of life in Massachusetts.

Themes of State Economic Policy Since 1975

Our discussions of gubernatorial administrations and policies show that many ideas for state participation in fostering economic development have made it to the agenda and into policy since 1975. Programs and institutions have proliferated. The staffs of agencies and programs created over the period have developed working relationships and often cooperate on projects. When quick action is needed or the necessary level of coordination is high, the Governor's Office of Economic Development, or the governor, often steps in to help.

Our examination of gubernatorial administrations and policy initiatives shows that most economic development policy in Massachusetts since 1975 has been guided by four distinguishable policy ideas. First is the idea that state government should promote geographically balanced urban and regional growth. Second is the idea that government should intervene to make investments in private human and physical capital that are in the public interest but missed by the private market. This is the view, in other words, that government should fill "gaps" in capital and labor markets. Third is the idea that government should support a good "business climate." A fourth and more recent idea is that government should actively support the future interstate and international competitiveness of the state's economy.

Geographic Targeting

Uneven and inefficient geographic patterns of growth, at first, were an issue specific to Michael Dukakis and his director of state planning, Frank Keefe. They shared a geographically defined conception of economic development that combined the objectives of helping people and helping places. Keefe and several of his staff members had backgrounds in urban economics and planning. This field focuses on spatial relationships and emphasizes the role of externalities, that is, the positive or negative effects of the decisions of firms and households on others. It may be in the public interest for new development to be nudged by public policy directives or incentives to locate away from places where its "external" effects would reduce the welfare of others.

Externalities played an important role in the thinking of the Dukakis administration, especially the crowding and straining of suburban infrastructure facilities caused by the movement of households and firms to the suburbs from central cities. At the same time, the exodus from the central cities left urban infrastructure facilities operating below capacity and smaller tax bases to support central city services. Firms that left the city, it was believed, did not take into account the increased commuting and information costs imposed on current and potential employees who remained behind. The new governor began to apply these ideas in 1975, when the state was desperate for a way out of its economic malaise, a malaise that was most severe in the central cities. Initiated by the grass-roots Growth Policy Committees, targeting city and town centers to attract growth from suburban and rural areas began at this time and was carried on during the King administration.

The second Dukakis administration continued to direct resources to city and town centers but also focused attention on five regions that lagged behind the rest of the state economically, with a new strategy called *Targets of Opportunity*. This initiative, conducted by Alden Raine and the Governor's Economic Development Cabinet, appears to have contributed to the current economic renaissance in the southeastern region of Massachusetts.

How much geographic targeting has increased the aggregate level of economic activity in the state, as opposed to redirecting growth that would have occurred anyway, is an open question. In our view, its dominant short-run impact has been to redirect growth. However, to the extent that the strategy represents a response to significant negative externalities, in principle, it could also exert a positive effect on aggregate economic indicators.

Gaps in Capital and Labor Markets

The second set of perceived problems involves gaps, or alternatively bottle-necks, that inhibit economic expansion either in the state as a whole or in certain targeted communities. Policy responses in Massachusetts include the establish-ment of new institutions to fill gaps in capital and labor markets. In the time it took to get the new institutions running, however, much of the worry about labor and capital gaps abated. The small amount of money involved relative to the billions of dollars invested by the private market make it difficult to argue that the absence of these institutions would seriously damage the state's econ-omy. Nevertheless, both the Bay State Skills Corporation and the institutions created to fill gaps in capital markets have probably produced some net benefits by reducing the probability that important opportunities would be missed.

State sponsored development finance agencies in Massachusetts are devel-oping institutional capacities that can be called upon to aid current and future state economic strategies. Hence, their potential importance cannot be measured simply by examining their budgets and the number of clients they have pro-cessed. Neither, however, can their future impact be known with any degree of certainty or used as an argument for their adoption by other states. A former director of the Massachusetts Technology Development Corporation (MTDC), who now runs his own venture capital firm, said that the factors critical for the success of MTDC are an abundance of potential deals, expert advice from area businesses and academic institutions, and private sector financial institutions that support entrepreneurialism. Other conditions, such as insulation from political manipulation, must be maintained as well. In states where these con-ditions cannot be met, publicly sponsored development finance institutions may be a waste of public money.

Maintaining a Good Business Climate

In the mid-1970s, Massachusetts was reputed to have a bad business climate, which discouraged firms from locating and expanding in the state. The most frequent complaints from business people focused on tax burdens and some sup-port of the Proposition 2½ initiative petition was based on the belief that lower taxes would attract more businesses and jobs. Even beyond taxes, business lead-ers complained that they did not feel welcome in Massachusetts, and they pointed to what they thought was an excessive list of environmental and con-sumer oriented legislation passed during the previous decade. When Michael Dukakis reached out to business during his first term, his overtures were incon-sistent and earned mixed reviews. Edward King's pro-business style and rheto-ric, combined with the tax reductions mandated by Proposition 2½ and other lesser tax changes, essentially ended complaints about excessive taxes in Massachusetts. In his second term, Dukakis has changed his style and, for the most part, the business community is pleased. These, along with broader improvements in the state's political culture, make complaints of a poor business climate in Massachusetts a thing of the past.

The link between business climate and economic development, however, remains a point on which business people and others disagree. The preponderance of evidence in available studies is that the business costs imposed by state government have little impact on investment and hiring decisions.[59]

This is especially true when it comes to taxes. Economic theory suggests that the effects of tax policy depend in complicated ways on the tax structure as well as on the level of taxes, but theory alone cannot give the magnitudes (nor even the direction, sometimes) of the effects. The empirical literature on state and local taxes and business location decisions uniformly shows a small or negligible effect of state and local taxes on business decisions. Business location and investment decisions, the literature finds, are likely to be dominated by market demand, the tone of labor-management relations, access to specialized inputs, and major costs like labor and energy.[60] On the other hand, the claim among business people that taxes affect their decisions is nearly as unanimous. Methodological problems such as the inability to control for differences in public service levels and the quality of life plague many of the studies, and as economists, we agree with business representatives that the incentive effects of the tax structure should be better understood and consciously calibrated to avoid unnecessary inequities or inefficiencies. But, in general, the empirical literature is quite convincing that reducing broad based taxes to affect business location or expansion decisions is probably misdirected policy, especially if lower taxes lead to lower public services that affect the ease of doing business or the quality of life.

Though they continually strive to reduce state-imposed costs, business representatives interviewed for this study pointed to stability and predictability in the political and economic environment as the most important aspect of the business climate. Entrepreneurs want assurance that once they have committed resources to a given location, conditions will not deteriorate through unexpected changes in regulation, taxes, or labor-management relations. They also want government to be a willing and able partner when they have problems with which government can be of assistance. On all of these counts, Massachusetts has improved its business climate.

The business climate has changed in other ways as well. Many of the legacies of the economic crisis of the mid-1970s involve new laws, new programs, and new institutions. In addition, however, there has been an important change in the relationship between government and business: New organizations to represent business interests have multiplied.

Through the mid-1970s, the most vocal representative of business interests in Massachusetts was the Associated Industries of Massachusetts (AIM).[61] Since 1975, however, several important statewide business organizations either have formed or reconstituted themselves. The first new organization was the Massachusetts High Technology Council (MHTC), formed in 1977. MHTC was followed, in 1979, by the Massachusetts Business Roundtable, which organized to provide a unified voice for business interests around the state. Its membership includes the state's sixty largest employers and initially included representatives from the state's other major business organizations, until it became clear that the interests and political styles of the large employers were not well matched to those of other business organizations. The High Tech Council, the Roundtable, and AIM all have had ready access to the state's political leaders.

Recognizing the receptivity of political leaders to business interests, several other business organizations and publications have emerged in Massachusetts more recently. These include, among others, EMERGE (representing small high tech firms), the Massachusetts Software Council, the International Coordinating Council (to promote international trade and competitiveness), the Defense Technology Council, and the Massachusetts Biotechnology Council (formed in February 1986). The Small Business Association of New England, formed in the 1930s, is also an active organization with a membership of over 2000. Dukakis attended the inaugural dinner of the Biotechnology Council and promised help with land acquisition, training, and finance. The council asked for a coordinated system of regulation, help with training, and help to increase public awareness in order to calm fears. This relationship of the governor to new business organizations is typical. Besides the new organizations, new magazines like *New England Business* and tabloids like the *Boston Business Journal* quickly have become features of the state's economic culture. This proliferation of new voices for business interests is most obviously a manifestation of the state's economic fecundity. However, it also is a manifestation of a state political climate in which business people expect that organizations tailored to represent their narrowly segmented interests can make a difference.

Representatives of the state's larger businesses now play a much more active role, than before 1975, in helping to shape policies that, in the past, were less accessible to direct business influence. The Massachusetts Business Roundtable and the Massachusetts Taxpayers' Foundation have participated actively in designing policies for containing health care costs, public pension reform, public education, local aid formulas, and other public management problems that are important to the state's long-run fiscal health and, consequently, to the business climate. Some of the business leaders active in these organizations are also part of Jobs for Massachusetts, reconstituted since its industrial recruitment drives in the early 1970s. Through Jobs for Massachusetts, the governor meets once a month with the state's top legislative, labor, and business leaders to discuss current issues. Jobs for Massachusetts has been functioning in this way since the late 1970s. Dukakis praises the usefulness of the organization as the only forum where he and the state's legislative leaders can speak clearly together and directly to leaders of the labor and business communities.

None of these groups claim to have been pivotal in any of the important policy developments of the past ten years, including those that address issues of fiscal management. This modesty may be warranted, since theirs is a quieter style and the issues on which they tend to focus are basic problems of public management, but it is always difficult to determine the forces critical in affecting particular outcomes. Nevertheless, their developing role as a voice in the policy process, particularly on matters of fiscal management, is an element of change that may be very significant to long-term trends in the state.

Fostering Interstate and International Competitiveness

In Massachusetts, as in many other states, state economic policies are becoming focused less on attracting and retaining firms *per se* than on maintaining and expanding the state's share in world markets. Part of this reorientation reflects the national concern about declining competitiveness and fear of a long-term threat from Japan.[62] The state's new focus on market competition is reminiscent of the early nineteenth century, when politicians desired to help the state develop quickly in order to break free from a risky overdependency on England. A primary policy focus then, as it is becoming now, was on innovation and the commerical application of knowledge.

Officials now recognize rather clearly that competitive advantage is not static and they believe that state policies affect the state's position in the international economy of the future. In the past three years alone, this new perspective has shown up in discussions of educational reform, mature industries policy, the Centers of Excellence Program, Secretary Murphy's call (albeit unheeded) in 1983 for a Commission on the Knowledge Based Economy, a Massachusetts Office of International Trade and Investment created in 1984, and a Legislative Commission on Quality of Worklife Issues in 1986.

Conclusion

The turnaround in the Massachusetts economy began in 1975 and accelerated around 1979, when many sectors of the state's economy began to outperform their national counterparts. Our analysis of job growth in Massachusetts suggests that statewide economic indicators in Massachusetts are not very different today from what they would have been in the absence of many new state programs and agencies. Specific policy initiatives have improved the quality of life for people and places directly affected but were too limited and too late to be important explanations of the turnaround.

At the same time, political processes that fashioned the initiatives helped foster a political culture that currently allows for smoother resolution of political-economic issues. This new political culture in turn, may help business people feel more secure about placing new investments in the state. The extent to which changes in business attitudes and expectations actually influenced business location and investment decisions during the past ten years is impossible to measure. The range of other considerations determining business location choices suggests, at most, a limited role for state policy. Still, in 1986, entrepreneurs feel good about expanding in Massachusetts and say so publicly. Debates about economic policy are perceptibly more civil and productive today than in the past because of the increased interaction among government, business, and labor. The credit for this improved climate goes largely to the personal styles of Governors King and Dukakis (during his second administration) and to the new business organizations established during the period. Clearly, the strength of the economy helped as well.

Compared to other states, Massachusetts has been remarkably open to policy innovations directed toward economic development. While we acknowledge that some of the new programs that emerged from this environment might not pass a rigorous cost benefit test or for various reasons should not be directly transferred to other states, we believe that other states might do well to try to nurture creative policy environments of the type found in Massachusetts. Several salient characteristics of the state's political culture and policy process emerge from the case studies and help explain why policy entrepreneurialism is so prevalent in Massachusetts.

First, elected officials generally welcome new ideas for approaching problems and seizing opportunities. Broad access is relatively easy to achieve in Massachusetts because most of the state's leaders and major institutions are concentrated in the Boston metropolitan area, the home of roughly half of the state's population. Second, the process of shaping legislative proposals is often conducted outside of the legislature, generally through commissions and task forces and within line agencies. Ideally, this process provides the consensus and quality control required by the legislative process. The greater the fiscal importance or the interest-group conflict, however, the more the legislature is likely to play an active role, as in the case of MassBank. Third, there is a willingness to take prudent financial risks. Massachusetts has avoided excessive funding of new initiatives and, thereby, the mistake of placing too much money at risk. Instead, most of the new initiatives were regarded as experimental and given only enough early funding to get started. Other initiatives, such as geographic targeting, make little use of new state funds, instead relying heavily on federal expenditures and the funds of existing state programs.

The cases also illustrate that Massachusetts has organized itself effectively for policy implementation. The Governor's Office of Economic Development coordinates projects across agencies and has substantially enhanced the state's ability to implement its strategy of geographic targeting. Backed by the authority of the governor, this office speeds regulatory approvals when needed and helps package assistance from several state agencies. Its multiple successes in facilitating development projects in Massachusetts makes it worthy of imitation by other states.

In addition, Massachusetts has addressed the common criticism that government lacks the expertise to make sound investment decisions by explicitly drawing on the expertise of the private sector. The Capital Formation Task Force, in 1977, wisely recommended that quasi-public agencies with public-private boards of directors should implement gap-financing assistance for business development. This structure minimizes the likelihood of bad decisions while serving public purposes. Similarly, the public-private boards of the Bay State Skills Corporation and the Centers of Excellence program help mix the expertise of the private sector with the goals of the public sector. Placing public resources in authorities beyond the easy reach of politics seems appropriate and appears to work for these programs.

In our view, the state government's expanding involvement in the Massachusetts economy now requires a larger and more structured capacity for analysis. Just because several of the new agencies have survived their start-up periods does not mean that they could not be improved. Furthermore, analysis is needed to determine which programs should be expanded and which cut back. Anticipated reductions in federal resources only intensify this need for analysis. No longer should programs be justified on the basis of positive benefits alone; instead the benefits need to be weighed against the costs of state-generated resources. Thus, the Massachusetts state government needs to expand its capacity to ask tough analytical questions and to use the results of analytical studies. Not all of the analysis needs to be done internally, however. Just as people from inside and outside of government contributed creatively to the design of economic policies between 1975–85, the process of analysis and evaluation may benefit from similar openness.

The political history of economic development policy during the ten years, 1975–85, has provided a firm foundation for an ongoing activist role for state government in Massachusetts. Dukakis' phrase "creating the future" is an appropriate theme for spreading a more strategic long-term perspective that recognizes the value of efficiency, creativity, and broad based opportunity across a wide range of public and private sector activities. The large number of ideas collected from participants at the governor's January 1986 State House Conference and from citizens around the state during his "innovation tours" suggests that many in Massachusetts believe that state policy matters and are willing to help shape the vision. Despite their number and variety, most of the suggestions are already within the mandates of existing institutions or could be accomplished within them.

Hence, the creation of still more agencies is not what the state needs now. Instead, the current challenge is to better understand the impact of existing policies, to set priorities across current options, to match priorities with the duties and capacities of existing agencies, and to identify where the mandates of relevant institutions need to be modified, capacities enhanced, budgets adjusted, regulations changed, or procedures improved. In other words, after ten prolific years of expanding government's role through new programs and agencies, the state should redirect its creative energies toward effective implementation across both traditional and nontraditional state roles. Here, states still have much to learn and Massachusetts is likely to remain a leading laboratory.

MICHIGAN

John E. Jackson

6

The Mature Industrial State

Birmingham, England, has come to symbolize both the height and depth of Britain's industrial revolution and the rise and fall of an industrial empire. Some contend that the United States is close to emulating Britain, and that Michigan will be the next Birmingham. Lack of innovation in basic industries, loss of manufacturing jobs and market share to foreign competition, and an apparent shift to a service economy are cited as evidence for this comparison. If this analogy to Great Britain is valid, a bleak picture can be projected for durable goods manufacturing and for the people, regions, and institutions dependent on those industries. This gloomy projection is not shared by all, though few will disagree that it is a possible outcome.

Discussions of Michigan's economy inevitably begin with the automotive industry. While this is an important and in many ways a dominant feature of the state's economy, it is far from being the state's only industry. Michigan is a center for the production of office furniture, chemicals, processed food, appliances, computers, and computer software. The development of this extensive, highly productive economy is a true economic development success story. Look at the progress. Barely 100 years before some began pronouncing the death of the state's current economy, Michigan's primary sources of income were agriculture, mining, and lumber, sectors typically associated with less developed countries.

Tracing Michigan's growth from the early extraction sectors helps explain the dynamics of industrial evolution and the uneven and simultaneous progressions of growth and decline. New industries emerge from existing activities in a manner that, over time, makes economic history resemble biological evolution and genetic mutation. As new industries develop and old ones decline or are transformed, some regions, workers, and organizations will experience enviable growth while others will suffer serious losses. Thus, there are perpetual, simultaneous winners and losers in the economic development process. Two examples from Michigan's history illustrate these points.

Evolution of the Natural Resource Industries

One very unlikely genealogy begins with timber and lumber in the 1870s and 1880s and ends with the current office furniture, tourist, and chemical industries. During this period, lumber was the state's second largest industry, following agriculture, and Michigan was the nation's largest lumber producer.[1] How this industry led to things as diverse as tourism and chemicals is an impressive story of economic change.

At the height of the lumbering boom, railroads expanded extensively throughout the state to haul felled trees and cut lumber to markets in both the East and West. The challenge for the railroads came at the end of the nineteenth century, when most of the trees had been cut and the lumber industry was dying out. The railroads, faced with the obvious loss of business, first, and unsuccessfully, tried to promote farm settlement by offering cheap land in the areas that had been cleared. In a more successful venture, the railroads financed large resort hotels in the Upper Peninsula and the northern Lower Peninsula, giving tourism a major boost. The most prominent of these was the Grand Hotel on Mackinac Island, which was financed by the Grand Rapids and Indiana and Michigan Central Railroads and the Detroit and Cleveland Navigation Company. Similar projects were undertaken all along the Lake Michigan coast and some of the inland lakes. Tourism, recreation, and second homes are still major industries in parts of the state. Areas that could not make the transition from lumbering to tourism or some other business quickly became ghost towns.

A second spin off from the lumber industry was the development of major furniture manufacturers. The southern Lower Peninsula was heavily forested with hardwoods, in contrast to the northern pine forests, encouraging the manufacture of flooring, veneer, and furniture. The subsequent invention of the dry kiln seasoning process in Grand Rapids substantially reduced the time required to season lumber before it could be worked into furniture, as natural seasoning took three or four years. This innovation significantly cut manufacturer's inventory costs and was accompanied by the growth of several large firms in the Grand Rapids area. The dry kiln is only one example of a technological innovation that became the basis for a major state industry.

Following the pattern of manufacturing development, the companies involved in the mass production of standardized, low-cost furniture began leaving Michigan for lower wage areas in the South near the end of World War I. This was not the end of the state's furniture industry, however. There remained a set of innovative, very specialized firms dependent upon highly skilled labor to produce scientifically designed office work stations and high quality home furnishings.

A more remarkable outgrowth of lumbering was the creation of a large salt producing industry, which evolved into the currently prominent chemical industry, typified by the Dow Chemical Company. Sawmill operators discovered they could use the scrap wood left from the saw mill as fuel to evaporate the brine drawn from salt wells. Water was pumped through the salt formations and the brine brought to the surface was evaporated to produce salt. This method evolved into a strong alkali business in which the byproducts, including soap, paints, and varnishes, soon dominated. The most important byproducts proved to be bromine, calcium, and magnesium, which supported the growth of Michigan's chemical industry.[2]

The evolution of lumbering into a series of very successful and diverse industries illustrates that economic progress is a continual process of invention, innovation, and transformation. Wealth was and is created continually by new industries not just by the continued operation and expansion of existing ones. Areas that could not develop or support new industries, at least during the late 1800s and early 1900s, were simply vacated. A related lesson is the fact that the new industries arose from innovations that evolved from the opportunities and resources of existing and, at times, declining industries.

Transformation in Transportation

The transformation of the state's early transportation manufacturing activities was more monumental, though not as diverse as that of the lumbering industry. These changes reinforce some of the previous lessons as well as provide new insights into the developmental process and the conditions that encourage growth.

Michigan's location on the "western frontier" with no natural rivers flowing to potential markets made accessible, cheaply powered transportation vital to the state's early economy. The need to reach eastern markets with furs, lumber, iron and copper ore, and agricultural products reliably and cheaply made transportation alternatives essential.

Early transportation was by ship, across Lakes Huron and Erie to eastern markets and from the Upper Peninsula via Lakes Michigan and Superior. Great Lakes shipping, by creating access to Michigan's hardwood forests, led to the development of shipbuilding firms. The rapid growth of lumbering after the Civil War spurred the expansion of the railroad network throughout Michigan. Aided by state bonds and federal land grants this network was completed by the late nineteenth century. The railroads promoted the creation of heavy manufacturing industries, the most prominent of which was the manufacture of railroad cars. Michigan also became home to an important set of carriage builders located close to the lumber industry.

The presence and influence of these transportation manufacturing activities are important because each, in its own way, became an important piece in the creation of the automobile industry.[3] The early development of the automobile industry evolved from these industries in much the same fashion that new industries evolved from the lumber industry and its derivatives. In contrast to what might be expected, the first automobiles were not made in Michigan. The Duryea Company of Springfield, Massachusetts, had already begun commercial production of a gasoline powered vehicle in 1896, before the first one even appeared in Michigan. Massachusetts was a natural place for the industry to develop because of its extensive manufacturing base and machine tool industry. And yet, Ransom Olds, Michigan's pioneer producer, began commercial production in 1899 and, within five years, the state was producing 42 percent of the nation's cars. By 1914, Michigan accounted for 78 percent of the national output.[4]

The industry's development in Michigan was due to a simultaneous combination of factors: the presence of entrepreneurs in the marine engine business who were looking for new and expanding markets, existing industries, skilled manufacturing workers, and available local venture capital. Together, these factors produced the critical mass for the agglomeration and continued innovation that was difficult for any other geographic area to match or surpass. This process is remarkably similar to that which built the computer industry in northern California.

The shipbuilding industry, more than the carriage industry, was central to the creation of the automobile industry in Michigan. Great Lakes shipbuilding led to considerable investment in steam and gasoline marine engine production and in related machine shops and foundries. Internal combustion gasoline engines were particularly important in shipping on Michigan's rivers and lakes, in contrast to ocean-going vessels which relied more on steam. The internal combustion engine proved to be far better suited to personal vehicles than steam or electricity. The two cars produced most often in 1902 were the steam powered Locomobile built in New England and the gas powered Oldsmobile in Michigan. Each company produced over two-thirds more cars than any other manufacturer that year.[5] Clearly, the Oldsmobile had a longer, more successful history than the Locomobile.

Many of the automobile pioneers had been producers of marine engines (Olds), had provided machined parts for these engines (Leland), or had worked repairing them (Dodge and Ford). These people wanted to refine and expand this technology to convert their engines for use on land, enabling them to tap the enormous potential market for personal transportation. The development of the auto industry illustrates the economic process by which entrepreneurs exploit a technology developed in one sector to create a new industry.

The presence of other industries, such as the carriage makers, wheelwrights, and machine shops provided the base for other necessary supplies, once the basic engine technology had been determined. Although in some cases these related firms produced the precise items needed, in most instances their value was their ability to design and build new equipment required by the auto manufacturers. As Eckstein claims, "What Detroit, Lansing, Flint, Jackson, and Pontiac represented to Olds and the later pioneers was not so much a set of relevant industries as a set of relevant skills that could be adapted to automotive use."[6] These secondary industries are still a vital part of the Michigan economy. The skills and advantages provided by this existing base included a work force accustomed to manufacturing processes and possessing skills with relevant tools and machinery acquired from making carriages, ships, railroad cars, and engines.

The final, and critical, ingredient in Michigan's development and dominance of the automobile industry was a ready supply of local venture capital. Michigan entrepreneurs had amassed considerable fortunes in the lumber and mining industries during the preceding thirty years and needed investment opportunities. Their investments in the new auto firms permitted Olds, Ford, and the others to maintain their fledgling companies during the early precarious years. Those who did not receive such funds failed. In most instances, the location of these venture funds dictated the location of firms. Some firms followed funding away from Michigan, as in the case of Maxwell-Briscoe; some stayed in Michigan; while still other firms, such as Packard, relocated to Michigan to obtain financing.

The creation and growth of the automobile industry illustrates the importance of three fundamental ingredients in the economic growth process: aggressive, innovative entrepreneurs; a skilled, adaptable work force; and venture capital. These factors, combined with a successful product, create what Eckstein calls an "innovative contagion," in which the development of ideas, products, and markets acquires its own momentum and energy, continuing until the industry matures. This process continued in Michigan until well after World War II, with the ultimate emergence of three major automobile producers, one marginal firm, and only a few small speciality operations.

Economic Development: The Industrial Evolution

The evolution of lumbering and the early development of automobile manufacturing illustrate the necessary contributors to continued economic growth and its consequences. Economic growth is a continual, though not necessarily smooth, process, hence the title "The Industrial Evolution." New firms and industries evolve from the creative activity of people within industries, who take advantage of opportunities presented by that industry's resources, markets, and technologies. Simultaneously, existing industries fade as raw materials are depleted, as new products create obsolescence, and as lower-wage areas perform the routine, standardized manufacturing at lower cost. These declines, as seen in lumbering, mining, and furniture, leave workers, cities, and local businesses in a depressed state. Historically, the salvation of these people was migration to growing areas or the creation of new industries, as exemplified by tourism and chemicals.

Several conditions must be present for this evolution to occur and to create the wealth required to keep the system moving. As the declining areas reveal, the process must be ongoing for economic survival. Technological innovators were at the root of Michigan's new industries, from the kiln drying of wood for furniture to chemicals and to the conversion of marine engines into automobile engines. These innovators needed financial backers and support from those who wanted to create a marketable product not just another innovation. Both groups are characterized by people willing to take risks, albeit of different kinds. The first group is risking its time and the possibility of a secure job, while the financier is risking savings. In many instances, the same individual may share both risks by playing both roles. In the case of the automobile industry, there were many financial entrepreneurs who played only the second role. Finally, the presence of a skilled work force was a necessity. These skills apply to both the manufacturing and the management aspects of the industry. Eckstein points out that one of the important innovations in the Michigan auto industry was the development of mass production, which was accomplished by Olds and Leland prior to Henry Ford. As we continue our analysis of the Michigan economy and of the strategies of public and private organizations to continue the evolution that yields growth and development, it is vital that we keep these lessons in mind.

The Michigan Economy of the 1980s

As the auto and other durable goods industries grew throughout the 1950s and 1960s, hundreds of thousands of Michigan residents found good jobs, high wages, and generous benefits. In short, Michigan was seen as a good place to work and live, a place that offered the prospect of a comfortable life for many people. These feelings were shattered by the recurring recessions of the 1970s, the two massive escalations in oil prices, increased foreign competition, the impact of hasty government regulations, and the general belief that America was losing its manufacturing base and becoming a service economy at best.[7] This general pessimism culminated with the 1979–82 recession, which drove the state's unemployment rate over 17 percent, the highest level in almost half a century. Almost daily, residents were bombarded with stories of firms and people leaving Michigan for the Sun Belt. Most can still recall the news media's pictures of Michigan residents buying out the *Houston Chronicle* in Detroit, Flint, and elsewhere in the search for jobs. Michigan came to be seen as the heart of the Rust Belt, projecting the image of crumbling factories and decaying cities. Many were writing off Michigan as the Birmingham of the twenty-first century. Before addressing the question of how Michigan citizens and organizations began to counter this prediction, we want to give a clear analytical picture of the structure and recent performance of Michigan's economy. There is far more variation and even potential sources of optimism than common wisdom implies.

Michigan's Economic Engine

Manufacturing and related business services, often referred to as the *base economy,* constitute the engine that powers Michigan's economy. These sectors provide the wealth and jobs that support an extensive array of local service jobs, frequently called the *local economy,* ranging from retail to government to legal and medical services.[8] These base sectors are particularly important in Michigan, given its economic history and structure. Our discussion focuses on the recent changes and current composition in manufacturing and business services. To understand these sectors is to understand Michigan's economy.

Michigan's economic base is dominated by durable goods manufacturing. This is true even after excluding automobile manufacturing and its related suppliers. The proportion of all Michigan employment in durable manufacturing, excluding automobile manufacturing, is still a percent higher than in the rest of the United States.

Two important facts emerge when we examine manufacturing earnings in Michigan over the past twenty years compared to the rest of the United States, both attributable to the concentration in durable manufacturing. Michigan's economy is much more susceptible to swings in the business cycle than the rest of the country; thus, the adage, "When the U.S. economy has sniffles, Michigan gets pneumonia." Second, between 1957–79 Michigan maintained its share of national earnings in manufacturing. Thus, when we average over the business cycle, Michigan did not lose the ground in manufacturing that many people perceived. In this sense, some of the serious difficulties in 1979–83 are attributable to the severe impact of aggregate U.S. economic conditions on Michigan's durable goods industries.

The ability of a state government to directly affect the location decisions for those few firms that move is marginal at best. Cost variations associated with wages, transportation costs, energy availability, and access to raw materials and related firms dominate variations in state controlled costs in location decisions. The second reason why the diversification strategy was not effective was that, by the time the blue ribbon commission made its report, the issue was discussed, and a set of actions selected, the national economy was already recovering and the need for diversification could be and was ignored.

The Condition of Michigan's Base Economy in 1984

To many people, the overall strength of manufacturing in Michigan relative to the nation as a whole confirmed their view that the early 1980s were just another recession, albeit much more severe than normal. The facts and the warning signs from various economic sectors suggested this was not so. At the most visible level, one could see the inroads of foreign competition in industries such as automobiles, machine tools, and primary metals. One could also hear repeated statements from different industry groups that Michigan had a poor business climate: The cost of doing business in the state was too high relative to other states. These high costs included state controlled costs such as workers' compensation, unemployment insurance, and state and local taxes; high wages; high energy costs; and an overly bureaucratized, insensitive government regulatory system. These advocates of lower costs claimed that Michigan was losing jobs to areas such as Indiana, the South, and foreign countries because of these excessive costs.

Other more analytical studies supported the claims that Michigan was losing its competitive position in various manufacturing sectors. In a shift-share
analysis of the growth of manufacturing earnings 1969–79 for different industries, Michigan's growth rate lagged in thirteen of the twenty industries that constitute manufacturing.[9] The sectors that fell furthest below the national growth
rate were nonelectrical machinery, motor vehicles, and fabricated and primary
metals, the traditional core of Michigan's economy. The most successful sectors
were electrical machinery, fabricated textiles, and furniture and fixtures.

The ability of Michigan's manufacturing sector to retain its *relative* share of
U.S. manufacturing earnings was due to the greater growth in the industries
where Michigan's economy is concentrated than in other industries nationwide.
Thus, Michigan was blessed with a mix of the "right" industries but was losing
ground in those "right" industries. Such a process, were it to continue, promised
a bleak future for Michigan's economy and the state's residents. Regardless of
whether the United States as a nation was losing its manufacturing base, Michigan was losing its traditional advantage over the rest of the nation in its basic
industries.

This bleak analysis does not tell the whole story nor does it reveal a true
picture of Michigan's base economy. Between 1979–84, despite the most severe
recession in Michigan's recent history, many new firms were created and survived and a significant proportion of the existing firms increased their employment. A firm by firm analysis that identified employment change in new, failed,
and continuing firms, revealed some significant and possibly startling results.[10]

In manufacturing alone, births nearly equaled failures, 2960 to 3176.[11]
Among firms existing in 1978 and 1984, 51 percent showed employment
increases, and these increases averaged 50 percent. The new and growing firms
added 137,000 new manufacturing jobs between 1978 and 1984. The jobs lost
in declining and failed firms exceeded these gains and were extremely costly to
Michigan's well being. These losses were concentrated in the state's largest firms,
suggesting the possibility of long-term difficulties. However, these circumstances
should not totally dominate one's perception of the changing structure of the
state's economy. In spite of very troubled times, a significant set of firms showed
substantial growth and vitality.

The machine tool industry, which is central to Michigan's economy and
which epitomizes the troubled economy, offers some important insights about
the nature of change and why some firms grow and others do not. In this industry between 1978–84, even though total employment declined by 2900 jobs, 53
percent of the continuing firms grew in size, adding nearly 10,000 new jobs. Over
400 new firms added another 5000 jobs. This vital industry, then, has a significant number of robust, successful firms.

We can further explore some of the characteristics of these growing firms
with data from a study of the financing of Michigan machine tool firms.[12] This
study asked firms to report their age, size, and their employment and revenue
changes over the 1980–83 period. The firms also were asked if they used computer numerically controlled machines (CNC machines), which are some of the
most technologically advanced production devices, or numerically controlled

machines (NC machines), which are an older technology. These data reveal that the firms relying on CNC machines are newer and smaller than other firms. These younger, smaller CNC firms also were the fastest growing firms. A statistical analysis indicated that the firms using CNC machines grew about 15 percent more than firms of the same age and size that did not employ CNC technology. The successful firms, then, are the ones most dependent upon and taking the most advantage of technological change. This detailed examination shows the beginnings of the same process that historically has nurtured and enhanced Michigan's economy—the innovation of new methods and products within existing industries, even at times when many firms in the industry were threatened by a changing economic environment.

The Michigan economy also reflects the nationwide growth of the service sector. Financial and business services that contribute to the base economy, such as banks, computer services, consulting firms, etc. had a net job increase of 38,000 jobs between 1978–84. The firm by firm analysis of new and existing firms reveals even more dramatic change here than in manufacturing. Births outpaced failures by 3 to 2 and 60 percent of the continuing firms grew in size by an average of nearly 60 percent. A total of 83,000 *new* jobs were created in this sector. These data exclude personal services and local business services, such as janitorial and temporary employment services. Thus, in terms of employment, basic business services are becoming a substantial part of the state economy, and generally we are talking about higher skill and higher status jobs, not fast food.

The challenge to Michigan industry, government, and nonprofit organizations is to promote and enhance these evolutionary changes within and between sectors, while at the same time dealing with the consequences of decline in some existing sectors and firms. Before examining what various individuals and organizations are doing to confront this challenge, we want to provide some conceptual arguments about the political economy of economic change. Although this may be seen as digression, it will help provide some insight and perspective on the various activities going on within Michigan, better organize the description of these activities, and provide some way of evaluating them.

7

The Political Economy of Development in Mature Economies

Economic progress is not inevitable. Selection and implementation of an economic development strategy requires decisions by individuals working within a set of public and private organizations. These choices and decisions are not simply matters of economics but are laden with conflict, uncertainty, risk, and minimal information. How societies are organized to make and implement these choices has a considerable effect on their economic future. Issues of institutional design are central to building a future.

The challenge facing private and government organizations during periods of economic stress has evolved considerably since the late 1800s and early 1900s, when Michigan began to reach economic maturity. As illustrated by lumbering, furniture making, and mining in the Upper Peninsula, when an industry declined, the people, governments, and businesses dependent upon that industry had three choices. They could adapt by creating new ventures, they could migrate, or they could live with a greatly reduced standard of living: the "get smart, get out, and get poor" strategies. Choices were dependent upon specific circumstances and individual motivation. There was very little role for government involvement in this process and virtually no demands for an "economic development strategy."[13]

The Government Role in Economic Development

Circumstances and expectations have changed dramatically since the early 1900s. A lesson learned from the Great Depression, embodied in the Full

Employment Act of 1946, was that government was responsible for ensuring jobs for those who wanted to work and supplemental income for those who could not find jobs. The tangible changes wrought by these responsibilities, combined with altered expectations about the proper role of government in economic and social affairs, now has placed federal, state, and even local governments in a central and at times conflicting role during periods of economic stress and evolution. The important question is: How well equipped are governments to manage resources during such periods and to make and implement the strategic choices required for long-run growth?

The answer to this question depends upon the way the government is organized, the structure of the state's economic and social interest groups, and how well the leaders in the public and private sectors understand the economic development process. As seen in Michigan's history, the initiatives for continued economic innovation and growth must come from the private sector. State government is a classic "local industry" and its efforts to create jobs directly in the public sector simply substitute for jobs in other industries.[14] The state government's role is a very limited but critical one.

State and local governments have necessary and important functions beyond questions of development. How governments fulfill these obligations affects economic development and significantly biases the choice and implementation of a development strategy. The most direct conventional functions of state governments derive from the presence of public goods and market failures. The public works infrastructure, such as transportation, water and sewage, and flood control are classic public goods, required for the public well-being and unable to be provided by private initiative. Regulation to overcome market failures, such as with utilities, transportation companies, and financial institutions, is an important and widespread public function. Other market failures emanate from activities where the prices faced by individuals and private organizations do not fully reflect social costs and benefits, as with education at all levels, land use, basic research, and environmental quality and safety. We can add the maintenance of public order, the enforcement of contracts, and the administration of justice to this list of public goods the government must provide. Effective government interventions, in the form of taxing and spending, regulations, and restrictions are widely accepted in these areas and, if done properly, can achieve their stated public objectives at the same time that they promote economic growth.

Promoters of technology based growth strategies have identified what they believe to be a substantial market failure in the research, development, and marketing process.[15] Their argument is that basic and applied research are social and economic necessities but not profitable for private investors, hence the need for public support. The federal government has traditionally supported basic research. Historically, applied research, designed to take the results of basic research and convert them to marketable products and to new businesses, has been left to the private sector. However, given the magnitude of the risks, the time required to market new technologies, and the benefits that cannot be captured by the individual firm, private investment in applied research has lagged behind the level needed for maximum technology transfer and growth. Individuals subscribing to this view advocate the creation of centers for applied research and development and government grants to entrepreneurs to overcome this deficiency. Frequently, governments are expected to play a role, at times a major role, in initiating and funding these centers.

The other side of state and local fiscal policy is how governments fund these activities when they choose to perform them. State governments can favor explicitly those sectors that are sources of economic growth and innovation in setting tax policy. For example, the state government can tax consumption rather than the return on capital investments; it can adopt more or less progressive individual taxes; it can effectively tax various industries, businesses, and even firms at different rates; and it can tax differentially labor and capital. These choices depend upon how the tax code, with its many detailed provisions, is written, and they have strong implications for economic growth. State governments also can be more or less efficient and prudent in how they accomplish their specified functions, which will affect the private sector's ability to create and to expand firms.

The altered expectations about government responsibilities to provide jobs and transfer payments to the unemployed and to protect people against economic adversity have created a third, and poorly understood, role for state government in the economic development process. These expectations evolved from a static economic theory focused primarily on business cycles rather than on industrial evolution and transition. Deviations from full employment supposedly were cyclical in nature and correctable either by better use of fiscal and monetary instruments or by the natural progression of the business cycle. The federal government had the primary responsibility for regulating the macro-economy in a counter-cyclical fashion through its economic policies. States' responsibilities were confined to perfecting local labor market conditions. They administered unemployment insurance programs, which could not be done privately, provided information about job openings, and tried to establish a balance between the powers of large corporations relative to those of individual workers. In the latter role, states either intervened directly to ensure the rights of workers who were injured, laid off, or otherwise discriminated against or they gave additional leverage and power to unions to represent workers. Thus, state governments are now seen as having a responsibility to protect and support people adversely affected by economic conditions and they have created a set of policies and institutions designed for that purpose. Unfortunately, many of the measures properly taken to protect and support workers in a cyclical but otherwise static economy, to protect workers from the hazards of an industrial society, and to give greater political influence to those adversely affected by economic conditions function differently in periods of structural economic decline and evolution. For example, unemployment insurance functions quite differently in a period of longer-term structural unemployment than during the ups and downs of the business cycle.

In considering whether and how state governments can promote economic development, both explicitly and in their proper roles as public service providers, we must examine the many interests associated with fiscal, developmental, regulatory, and economic security decisions. It is very important that we consider how governments respond to the demands of these many varied interests, with particular attention to the demands for protection from economic adversity. Can governments be responsive to these needs and simultaneously take positions that support long-term economic change and development?

A number of important interests are created by a declining economy, by demands to counter the effects of that decline, and by the efforts to promote long-term growth. The first, and most obvious, set of interests will be those workers, firms, and localities hardest hit by the decline. These interests will demand some form of government assistance and can be expected to be most supportive of actions to retain and protect current jobs and industries. With the many programs already in place to assist workers harmed by the business cycle and by the other negative externalities of industrialization and with the set of formally organized groups representing these interests, these demands are readily and influentially expressed. The basic characterization of these demands is that they desire to maintain existing industries, production methods, and local economic bases—the economic status quo.

A second set of interests are those associated with whatever new industries might emerge through the continued evolution of the present economy. As should be clear from the discussion so far, the continued growth of an economy requires continual innovation in the form of new products, production methods, and markets. In periods when such innovations are vitally important, as is currently the case in Michigan and the United States as a whole, these are very important interests to have represented in any government decisions. Yet, there is an obvious "Catch-22" in creating new firms and industries: There are few obvious organizations to directly represent those interests in advocating policies that will spur the creation of these enterprises, or at least to oppose policies that create barriers to new businesses. To offer one example, governments are frequently confronted with proposals that will direct capital towards existing but declining firms or that will reduce their taxes. Such policies are likely to make capital more difficult to obtain and more expensive for other growing firms or effectively raise taxes on these other firms, thus retarding the evolutionary process. This argument suggests there is a potential inherent conservatism, meaning bias towards the status quo, in government economic development activities, unless a set of existing organizations has a strong incentive to act as proxies for the unborn firms.

Any state or regional economy has several groups with a strong stake in a vibrant economy but no particular economic stake in the existing industries and firms. There are actually many organizations that fit this definition, though they are seldom politically organized and active. In a rough way, these interests can be found in the local economic sector, with the possible exception of state and local governments. These entities would include the public utilities, such as Michigan Bell, Detroit Edison, and Consumer's Power, retail and other local service establishments, and public colleges and universities. None of these entities are very mobile, and some cannot be moved at all: The University of Mich-

igan and Michigan Bell cannot relocate to Indiana, Texas, or Korea. These organizations are dependent on a healthy state economy but can be relatively
indifferent to what industries form the basis for this health. Finally, there will
be specific individuals and organizations, such as foundations, who are tied to
the regional area because of past business, family, or historical associations.
These individuals may have the option of moving, but they have no compelling
reason to do so and, because of personal commitments and vision, may join the
effort to effect an economic transition.

The financial industry could be an important political force promoting
regional economic development and change. Banks and other financial organizations obviously are dependent on the economic health of their area for depos-
its and loan opportunities, whether commercial, personal, or real estate. Until
recently, the area served by most banks was limited at least to the state and often
to counties, in some states. This gave the financial industry an exceptionally
strong stake in the local economy and in policies that affected the future of that
economy. However, the regional deregulation of the financial industry and the
creation of virtually national financial markets is eliminating these regional
stakes and reducing the role of banks in trying to influence local development
policies.[16]

The political strength of the various interests will vary with their organizational structure and their internal resources and will depend upon what government body they need to influence. Obviously, larger business firms are well organized and are likely to have considerable resources with which to "play politics,"
and we should expect to see a number of state policies reflect that fact. It is also
a well-established fact, since the early days of elite political studies, that corporate leaders in any area, and even the country for that matter, cooperate extensively to promote their view of the public interest. Thus, we should expect civic
groups of this type to be active in promoting economic development. The issues
they push, and how those issues relate to economic change or to maintaining the
viability of the existing economy, will depend upon the part of the economy
from which they come and how that experience shapes their perception of the
problem and its likely solutions.

Beyond the organized corporate groups, a fact of life in the late twentieth
century is that virtually all political interests are organized, though some are
better organized and have more resources. Most of the existing manufacturing
firms are part of industry trade groups organized around that industry's needs
and of broader business groups such as the Chamber of Commerce and Associations of Manufacturers. These groups can be expected to represent the interests of the existing industries, as reflected in their memberships. Workers also
may be organized, particularly in the currently industrialized states such as
Michigan. As organizations, unions have strong needs to represent the interests
of their members in keeping their current jobs, in maintaining wage and benefit
levels, and in maintaining the union as a viable organization.

Business associations and unions have a considerable common interest in
finding ways to subsidize and protect the current economy but will differ sharply
on proposals that will reduce labor related costs, be they wages or public pro-

grams. Historically, both these groups are experienced in political behavior. Unions, going back to the 1930s, have been dependent upon public policies in order to organize and have maintained extensive and influential political action groups. The increasing presence of government intervention in market decisions has led the business sector to recognize its need for political action at the level of both the individual firm and the broad industry. This recognition has prompted the creation of powerful political action committees to promote the views and programs of business groups. Together, the union and business groups constitute an exceptionally strong lobby for protective measures, as we have seen with textiles, automobiles, steel, and even computer chips.

The local sector, with its interest in a strong area economy, is not without substantial organizations, though these organizations may be less visible and not as experienced in forming effective political coalitions. The public utilities have all the advantages of large businesses just mentioned, plus considerable political experience, given their regulated status. Retailers and local service businesses frequently are organized into associations, such as the Chamber of Commerce, the Federations of Independent Business, etc. The largest barriers to the political actions of these organizations is their small size and dispersed and independent character, which easily leads to the free rider dilemma facing all efforts at collective action. The fact that frequently many of these firms do not see their long-run stake in a growing economy as separate from their connections to current manufacturing activities further reduces their likelihood of pushing for change.

People in different sectors of the economy and in different organizations will have quite different views about the nature of the state's economic problems and the strategies that will solve them. This is the point at which honest differences arise in perceptions about the nature of the problem and about the efficacy of various policies. These differences render decision making difficult and make it "political." The issue becomes how these politics affect the choice and implementation of any strategy and determine the long-term implications of these decisions.

Economic Development Strategies

There are three basic strategies for maintaining or expanding a state economy threatened by evolving competitive forces:

1. Maintain existing industries and firms, with their current technologies, products and markets;
2. Recruit to the state firms from other areas or induce out of state firms to build branch plants within the state;
3. Create new industries and enterprises, either through the birth of new firms or by the transformation of existing firms.

These strategies are not mutually exclusive. However, they have some internal inconsistencies, require different policies, and have substantially different long-term implications for the state's social and economic structure.

Maintenance Strategies

The maintenance strategy focuses on the survival needs of the existing firms faced with increasing competition. Policies to meet these survival needs generally involve some combination of three components: protection, subsidy, and cost reduction.

Protection. Protection routinely takes the form of tariffs, quotas, boycotts, and domestic content laws intended to aid industries threatened by foreign competitors with lower costs or better products. Forcing higher costs on competitors through unionization, stringent labor standards, regulations, or minimum wage legislation accomplishes the same objectives and is another form of protection practiced within the United States. These policies clearly are designed to insulate existing firms, employees, and suppliers from change. They also deny consumers the advantages created by lower costs and new products.

Subsidies. People dependent upon threatened industries frequently seek subsidies of some form to maintain their cost competitiveness. Subsidies may be in the form of cheaper capital, relief from taxes, or public expenditures that directly aid existing firms. In theory, subsidies will be used to reduce prices, thus keeping the firms competitive. Those seeking such subsidies frequently justify them by arguing that the public costs of reduced production and employment in existing firms (for example, those arising from income maintenance and social service programs and from reduced tax revenue) will exceed the cost of the subsidies. Frequently, these subsidies substitute long-term for short-term costs and their net effect is simply to impose higher costs on other sectors of society, who pay for the subsidies.

Cost Reduction. The most visibly painful maintenance option is cost reduction, which epitomizes the get poor strategy. Unfortunately, this is the only way to retain threatened production jobs using existing production methods. Labor costs are the dominant production expense, and truly effective cost reduction must begin by lowering wages and reducing staff in order to compete with the newer producers with access to cheap labor. (Wage reduction and staff cuts, to be effective, must apply to white collar and executive employees as well as to production workers.) This is an obviously difficult process, as it lowers the living standard of workers in the threatened firms and of enterprises dependent upon these workers, such as local services and governments.

Individual firms, and even coalitions of firms, generally find it very difficult to reduce wages. This resistance is part psychological and institutional, individuals and unions strongly resist such moves, and part a consequence of the larger labor market. Few individual firms or even whole industries, with the possible exception of automobile manufacturers in Michigan, can exert a significant influence on wages in an entire region or state. Attempts to reduce wages will simply reduce the size and quality of the work force available to the firm or industry as other industries hire the better workers. Thus, efforts to reduce costs through wage reduction face considerable individual, organizational, and market resistance, and we can expect to see rare use of this strategy, though it is by far the most direct way to challenge low-cost competitors. Wage reduction also is difficult to implement as a public policy option. Governments have little or no control over wages, though they can influence the power of unions, which in turn affects wages and work rules.

Most of the public discussion about cost reduction concerns governmentally imposed or controlled costs, such as state and local taxes and unemployment and workers' compensation insurance rates. Although economists argue that these costs are only a small portion of a firm's total costs and that firm location decisions are not very sensitive to variations in these costs, reducing government imposed costs can be very important to existing, threatened firms. In the first place, any reduction in these costs has an immediate and direct effect on a firm's profitability and cash flow. For a marginal firm seriously threatened by competition, this increase in profits and cash flow may significantly aid its survival. In this case, the value of the cost reduction is not measured relative to other costs but in relation to current profits or losses. Second, it is likely easier, particularly with the aid of trade associations and similar lobbying organizations, to force governments to reduce their costs than to obtain wage reductions. Finally, these reductions are far less disruptive to a firm's internal relations than are wage concessions. For these various reasons, we are likely to see considerable efforts by threatened firms and industries to reduce governmentally controlled costs.

Maintenance Strategies in the Long Run

The net long-run effect of these maintenance programs is likely to be small and possibly negative. These efforts are designed to lower costs by simply reducing living standards, services, and worker protections. This get poor strategy leaves the aggregate economy worse off and reduces the region's living standard. Such policies also effectively redistribute the share of remaining income, leaving some individuals better off in that they gain a larger share of a smaller pie. More important, none of these efforts addresses the basic cause of the distress, the continual industrial evolution, where economic activity perpetually expands to less developed areas once production methods and technologies become routine and commonplace and labor cost differences become a major determinant of competitive advantage. Most maintenance activities may help in the short-run by extending the life of marginal firms, but they have little long-run benefit unless they increase productivity or promote innovation in products and markets. (Obviously, reforms that improve labor and public sector efficiency are valuable in the long run, but this is not the issue being addressed here.)

Recruitment

Some states and localities aggressively pursue a strategy of attracting existing firms from other areas or of getting these firms to locate branch plants locally.

Often, this strategy closely resembles a maintenance policy, only now actions are being adopted by areas recruiting businesses, rather than by areas attempting to hold onto these same enterprises. The recruiting state frequently advertises its low wages, taxes, and state imposed costs and its hospitable business climate. The latter usually means that business leaders are listened to by government officials, are not likely to be harassed by regulators, and do not have to confront organized labor and rigid work rules. These recruitment efforts by lower-wage areas are mostly speeding the natural industrial evolution process by publicizing their cost advantages.

Recruitment efforts by more developed states with high wages and high levels of public service and taxes frequently concentrate on offers to offset these costs. Offers to locating firms usually include tax abatements and/or promises of specific services, ranging from dedicated public works, such as water and sewer service and highways, to specific job training programs for company workers. On a pure cost basis, the more developed states are at a considerable disadvantage in this competition. Wage rates are the largest determinant of relative costs, and governments can do little about wages. Governments, and their citizens, have the unenviable choice of admitting their disadvantage and not competing or of making exceptionally large concessions on tax abatements and services provided. These efforts impose higher costs on present firms in order to fund the subsidies.

Leaders in some developed areas aggressively publicize "natural" attributes that will offset high wages. These include the presence of a highly skilled and technically proficient labor force, a substantial infrastructure of public works, access to scarce resources or large markets, knowledgeable financial institutions, a comfortable climate, and/or a critical mass of related businesses and services. Proximity to any of these attributes can convey a competitive advantage to the locating firm. In California and Massachusetts, for example, access to progressive research universities, venture capital, and expanding related businesses is a prime attraction for many firms.

Most significantly, what a locality emphasizes in a recruitment effort determines the types of firms it attracts. Stress on low wages and costs attracts relatively footloose industries dependent upon low production costs for a competitive advantage. By contrast, emphasis on access to research and educational resources attracts firms dependent upon innovation and an educated labor force and employees who value education for their families.

The recruitment strategy has one implicit, but erroneous, assumption as perceived by most observers. The notion that one region builds its economic base by attracting firms and plants from other regions fosters the view that there is a fixed amount of economic activity and jobs in the country, or the world, and that states and countries are engaged in a zero sum competition to attract those jobs. The very names *smokestack stealing* or *chip chasing* promote such a perception. This perception, however, leads to considerable competition and conflict among various localities and, at times, decisions that do not promote collective well being.

The facts contradict this perception in two ways. It is economically efficient for firms to seek out the most competitively advantageous locations. This searching leads to lower costs and better products for consumers, to a more efficient global economy, and to a higher living standard in newly developing areas. Second, real aggregate economic growth and development requires the creation of new industries, new production methods, and new markets, not just the search for lower-cost production sites by existing firms. Most recruitment focused on cost subsidies for mobile firms and regional competition often blinds policy makers to these important facts and promotes socially undesirable policies.

Industry Creation

The third job creation strategy is explicitly based on the concept that economic growth derives from innovation and entrepreneurship. Just as Michigan's growth in the nineteenth and twentieth centuries required the creation of the tourist, furniture, salt, chemical, and auto industries (and others not included in the historical narrative), the economic future of any region depends upon this process. In newly developing areas, this strategy means the creation of new firms. In more developed areas the industry creation strategy may mean new firms, but it also means adaptation and innovation within existing firms. These are not competing alternatives and both must be followed for mature regions to grow and even to survive.

Several factors are critical for the success of the creation process:

1. Institutions that support basic research and innovation *and* that promote the transfer of these innovations into marketable products;
2. A pool of entrepreneurs willing to risk their time and resources to market these products;
3. Sources of venture capital managed by individuals who understand and are committed to the entrepreneurial process;
4. A skilled, adaptable labor force who can meet the needs of the emerging industry.

The creation strategy contains considerable risk and a great deal of uncertainty. The risks for the individual entrepreneurs and investors are pretty well understood, if poorly practiced. There also are considerable risks for public and private leaders who advocate and adopt this strategy. There is no well-defined constituency to articulate the benefits of and champion this strategy. Furthermore, government and business leaders have few short-run, tangible benefits they can hold out to voters and other critics to bind them to the strategy. Demonstrated successes are less noticeable and more intangible than cutting ribbons on new plants about to employ thousands of workers.

The creation strategy is gambling on a process that few understand, so it is easy for critics to argue against its possible success and hard for the masses of people to identify with what is being done. It is exceptionally difficult to get people to bet on an industry and products that do not yet exist. It is hard enough to get sophisticated investors to make such commitments in most areas, let alone the less experienced and knowledgeable public, who psychologists indicate generally avoid risk and uncertainty.

The maintenance, recruitment, and creation strategies are not mutually exclusive; in fact, many states and countries pursue a mixture of all three. There is one point at which the maintenance and creation strategies become complimentary. That is the effort to retain existing enterprises by transforming them. This can be done if firms create new products, expand markets, and develop technologies that raise productivity and that require a highly skilled labor force not likely to be found in less developed areas.

A major source of innovation and potential growth can be the improved management of existing firms. There is no "iron law" of private bureaucracy that says mature firms cannot innovate, experiment, and act entrepreneurially. Much of the current discussion about "entrepreneurship" is focused on precisely this question. We also have examples of major corporations that continually create new products, markets, and production methods. Witness IBM and Hewlett-Packard in the computer field, Dupont in chemicals, Steelcase and Herman Miller in office furnishings, and Upjohn in pharmaceuticals. With the proper education and experience, more managers may come to understand these dynamic processes, at which point we will need to be less concerned about an economic development strategy or the conflict between the economic status quo and change—change will be the status quo.

A second form of transformation lies in the fact that in large corporations, mass production activities will always be mobile, but headquarters, communication, and research and development functions are generally not footloose. A region may lose some of its routine production, but if it houses the headquarters of many companies, rather than simply branch plants of out of state companies, these headquarters are likely to remain. As the corporation expands, so will its office activities, creating additional employment. Furthermore, in many industries these are the activities that become the engine for future innovation and new enterprises. States with advanced economies should recognize that they may lose traditional production jobs and concentrate on keeping the nonproduction activities of local firms. For Michigan, such a dual maintenance-transformation strategy has an added advantage in that these headquarters functions tend to be less cyclically sensitive than production jobs in durable goods industries.

A difficulty with this creation and maintenance strategy is that it leaves many production workers without their traditional jobs. The expanded corporate jobs are likely to be in a variety of service occupations, many of which pay high wages but demand quite different skills than those possessed by production workers. These changes in labor demand present both economic and political problems. The obvious economic problem is to provide training for new workers and retraining for present workers to facilitate these occupational shifts and to meet the occupational demands. The political problem is to get individuals and organizations to recognize, accept, and hasten these transitions and not try to retard this evolution. Political organizations must also resolve differences over who will pay for training and education programs and over how much money will go into income maintenance for those whose jobs are lost permanently. The inability to resolve these political issues and to gain acceptance of the transition may prevent its occurrence, leading to the worst of all worlds.

At some points the various strategies conflict or at least require careful balancing of resources and policies. The maintenance and recruitment strategies clearly conflict if states subsidize heavily recruited firms and plants, who then use the cost advantage to compete with existing enterprises, whose taxes increase to pay for the subsidies.

Industry creation and recruitment strategies are dependent upon high-quality public services or on environmental amenities regulated by government conflict with maintenance and recruitment policies based on maintaining low public-sector costs. Frequently desired services include things such as education, job training, transportation, water and sewer services, while amenities include items such as water creation, clean air, and freedom from fear of toxic wastes. Each of these attributes requires a more active, more expensive public sector, which conflicts with any maintenance and recruitment strategy based on reduced costs and less regulation. Conflicts between policies require that government and other public leaders make some choice about which development strategy to follow. It is in these choices, both in an overall strategic sense and in the tactical realm of specific programmatic decisions, that we confront the true political economy of economic development and the questions of institutional organization.

8

Initiation and Implementation
of a Creation Strategy

The unfortunate circumstances of the early 1980s in Michigan brought into focus many of the issues and strategic choices just described. Increasingly, people doubted that the next swing in the business cycle would return the state to its previous prosperity. However, even among those who agreed on that pessimistic forecast, there was considerable divergence about the causes of and the remedies for Michigan's long-term difficulties. Some blamed the unions for overly rigid work rules and high wages. Others accused management, particularly in the automotive industry, of being uncreative, of not making proper investments in new products and technology, or of being insensitive to changes in the world and domestic economies during the 1970s. State government was blamed for creating a bad business climate through high taxes and excessive workers' compensation and unemployment insurance costs. The proposed remedies often followed one's perception of the causes and generally fit the "get poor, get out, or get smart" options that Michigan has historically faced in times of economic change.

Michigan has continued to adopt, in different ways, all three development strategies just described. Over the six years, 1979–85, and across two administrations, the creation strategy, focused on new and existing firms, has become dominant, with less but continuing attention paid to maintenance and recruitment. The last years of William Milliken's administration mark the beginning of the evolution in state policy from a focus on maintenance to one of creation. Efforts during this evolution combined the skills and energy of the private and public sectors, sometimes conflictually but frequently cooperatively.

The Initial Response—A Maintenance Approach

The earliest explanation for Michigan's economic difficulties was a bad business climate. Studies comparing wage rates, taxes, employment related costs (such as unemployment insurance and workers' compensation), and energy costs among the fifty states consistently ranked Michigan poorly. Michigan's workers' compensation costs in 1978, for example, were 40 percent above costs in other Great Lakes states. The annual Alexander Grant rankings of state business climates, the most often cited of these studies, routinely placed Michigan at the bottom of their scale. Relatively higher costs in Michigan were used to explain bankruptcies, a purported exodus of firms from Michigan to states with lower costs, such as Indiana and the southern states, and the shifting of production by Michigan firms to foreign countries. The proposed solutions were to reduce costs and to protect existing firms.

Government Imposed Costs

Traditional business interest groups with strong representation from durable goods manufacturing firms focused on workers' compensation and unemployment insurance costs, demanding reforms in requirements and eligibility, administration, and financing. Initially, most of the proposals presented a version of the "get poor" strategy, with labor giving up most of the benefits, and were met with strong opposition. Labor leaders had fought hard for these gains and felt they were required to protect their members from a harsh, cyclical economic environment. The Milliken administration successfully reduced both of these costs.

The unemployment insurance changes increased the unemployment insurance tax in order to meet the state's obligations and to repay the federal government for loans during past recessions but set the stage for reduced costs in the long run. Rates were increased proportionally more for negative than for positive balance employers. The former were those whose workers collected more in benefits than the firms paid into the fund, largely the cyclically sensitive durable goods manufacturers. The positive balance firms were service and nondurable goods firms such as K-Mart, Kellogg, etc. The Milliken administration also was able to engineer a compromise on the workers' compensation issue. Benefits for eligible workers were increased but procedures were initiated to reduce claims, to coordinate with other benefits (such as retirement funds, unemployment insurance, and social security), and to require competitive bidding among insurance companies. The legislature also mandated an immediate 20 percent rate decrease. These changes substantially reduced Michigan's cost disadvantage but did not resolve complaints or remove this issue from the agenda.

The story behind these cost reductions provides insights into the interest group politics associated with the maintenance strategy. The driving force behind these efforts was the Michigan Manufacturers Association (the MMA). The MMA is an association of about 3500 manufacturing firms, whose principal activity is to lobby for legislation favoring manufacturers. Historically, their agenda focused on reducing state imposed costs and promoting support for member firms. The MMA wanted to reduce workers' compensation costs by limiting benefits and eligibility and coordinating benefits with those from other sources. They achieved a degree of success with the Milliken administration changes.

A group important in working out the compromise unemployment insurance plan was the Economic Alliance. The alliance, formed in early 1982 under the leadership of Fred Secrest, a retired Ford executive vice president, and Irving Bluestone, a former UAW vice president, includes a very large number of union and business leaders, representing all areas of the state and many different industrial sectors. It is a private initiative to bring together industrial and labor leaders to discuss and propose remedies for Michigan's problems. The alliance participants were able to obtain agreement on and push the unemployment insurance reforms in large part because of their diverse interests. Union leaders agreed with the rate increase required to maintain benefits and the positive balance employers supported the differential rate increase. General Motors, however, opposed the alliance's plan and promoted its own proposal.

The alliance was much less successful in advancing proposals on other cost questions, demonstrating the limitations of this type of heterogeneous interest group. The divisions on workers' compensation were both too intense and too clearly seen as "win-lose" for the alliance to be effective. The alliance also tried, unsuccessfully, to confront the health cost issue, as it potentially offered benefits to both labor and management. If health costs were contained, fringe benefit costs would be reduced, and labor and management could bargain over the residual to each's potential gain. This potential coalition broke down, however, whenever reduced benefits or coverage or increased copayments were proposed as a way to reduce employer costs. The topic on which alliance paticipants achieved some consensus was plant closings, which obviously served both management and labor interests. They embarked on an effort to identify potential closings and to find ways to obtain assistance and subsidies for these plants in hopes of retaining them in Michigan, a classic version of the maintenance strategy.

Wage Reduction

A second aspect of the effort to be more cost competitive was totally confined to the private sector. Beginning with the negotiations over the federal loan guarantees for Chrysler in 1979, labor increasingly was asked to "give back" wage benefits gained in earlier contracts. This was part of a national effort to lower labor costs, reduce inflation, and meet foreign competition. In their negotiations with the big three automakers, the United Auto Workers accepted give backs and agreed to profit-sharing plans as a means to lower unit manufacturing costs.

Protection

The area of greatest cooperation between government, labor, and business has been in seeking import restrictions, particularly on Japanese automobiles. On

March 16, 1981, Governor Milliken led a delegation of governors to meet with President Reagan to promote financial subsidies for the auto industry and import restrictions on the Japanese. These efforts were strongly supported by labor and management and by Michigan's congressional delegation and eventually led to import restrictions. Similar cases have been pressed for steel and machine tools in recent years, though without as much success. This is obviously a strategy that can appeal to all parties in a specific region. The conflicts created by these proposals are between consumers, who are widely dispersed and poorly organized, and all the parties in the affected industry, who are concentrated and usually well organized. The political cooperation between management and labor subsequently decreased as domestic auto assemblers entered into joint production arrangements with Japanese firms and as unions promoted domestic content legislation.

Initiation of the Creation Strategy

Governor William Milliken, in his State of the State Address in January 1981, proposed a strategy to promote innovation and new high technology business in the state. In his speech, Milliken proposed "major initiatives to expand high growth, technology based industry through a joint effort of Michigan universities, industries and state government . . . a special group to help develop an accelerated action plan, and . . . establishment of a technology based innovation fund and an Innovation and New Product Center." The genesis of these proposals and their implementation over two administrations is an important story in private-public partnership and an illustration of how different interests can coalesce to promote economic change.

The original, and strongest, arguments for this initiative started outside the government. The concept of high technology research centers and an advisory group on technology based innovation was pushed by Ted Doan and Harold Shapiro. Doan is the former chairman of Dow Chemical, a former member of the National Science Board, and currently the chairman of Doan Resources, the largest private venture capital firm in Michigan. Harold Shapiro is president of The University of Michigan, a nationally respected economist who surely saw Michigan's recovery as an important public policy issue and as vital to his university's future.[17] As president of Michigan's most prominent public university, he also had a strong interest in putting the university in a position to play an important role in shaping the state's economic policy.

Both Doan and Shapiro fit the earlier description of people with a large stake in a growing economy but no particular tie to existing industries and firms, because of their personal backgrounds and/or their organizations. Both men knew each other well, were used to collaborating, and had served together on several boards and committees. They proposed to Milliken that he appoint a group that would, in a low key manner, advise and help establish centers for applied research in specific areas and quietly promote the creation of technology based businesses in Michigan. Milliken accepted the idea and created the Governor's High Technology Task Force.

The original task force membership, announced three days after the State of the State address, consisted of leading figures from academia, finance, and Michigan's more entrepreneurial and scientifically based firms. Executives from the automobile and targeted industries were noticeably absent from the task force. (Milliken, in the 1981 address promoting an innovation strategy, also promised help for the auto, agricultural, forestry and tourism industries.)

On September 17, 1981, in a "Special Message to the Legislature on Economic Development," Milliken presented his new initiatives in the area of technology based industry. He coupled this presentation with his proposals to reduce business costs through changes in the workers' compensation and unemployment insurance programs and in the single business tax.[18] The centerpiece of Milliken's initiatives was a brief outline for state and private investments to expand Michigan's high technology industries. Milliken proposed expenditures of $200 million over the next ten years to promote the development of new technologies, specifically in robotics and molecular biology. This money would be raised from public and private sources. Milliken also proposed the creation of an economic development fund to provide capital for business expansion and the investment of public pension funds in ways that would create new jobs.

Milliken's proposed development fund and the public funding for the research centers was accomplished through the Michigan Economic Development Authority (MEDA). MEDA's $25 million allocation was an off budget appropriation from oil and gas revenues. The money was diverted to MEDA before going to the state treasury and was not subject to annual appropriations decisions. If legislative review had occurred, funding for the centers and the development fund would have been unlikely, given cuts forced throughout the state budget. The legislature was willing to authorize this procedure because of its relative invisibility. In addition to state funding, a vast majority of the money for the institutes came from Michigan foundations, primarily Kellogg, Dow, and Mott. These foundations initially pledged, with various contingencies, more than $50 million over a ten year period. The plan was for the centers to become financially self-sufficient within that time, financed through grants and contracts from industry and government.

The largest and most advanced of the centers is the Industrial Technology Institute in Ann Arbor. This center concentrates on the development of computer integrated and computer aided manufacturing: robotics. This initiative was seen as a natural way to extend Michigan's manufacturing base into the technology frontier.[19] Smaller centers were created for biotechnology (the Michigan Biotechnology Institute, now located in East Lansing) and for urban development (the Metropolitan Center for High Technology in Detroit). The latter is designed as an urban incubation center rather than assigned a particular substantive topic. Baba and Hart suggest the mix and location of the three centers constituted an acceptable political coalition based on geographical, industrial, and university interests within the state. (Each center is located close to a major public university, though university-institute relations have tended to be weak or even strained at times.)

The second part of the task force's recommendation and Milliken's proposal was the creation of more financing for technology based businesses. Implemented in 1982, this legislation authorized the state to invest up to 5 percent of public employee retirement funds, about $400 million, in growth firms. The state used this money to create several venture capital funds and to attract out of state venture capital firms to the state. According to task force estimates, the amount of private venture capital in Michigan has increased from $10 million in 1978 to $250 million in 1984.[20]

Milliken's initiatives in high technology marked a significant departure from conventional economic development strategies and earlier task force recommendations.[21] Previous task forces and blue ribbon commissions have recommended that Michigan diversify its economy and become less sensitive to the repeated cyclical fluctuations of a durable goods manufacturing economy. There are no blueprints for implementing such a strategy, although it was usually interpreted as a call for increased firm recruitment. Milliken's proposals abandoned this recruitment strategy in favor of reducing costs for firms presently in Michigan and providing initiatives to create new industries in the state.

The creation process would flow primarily from innovations within existing firms and the creation of new firms. The government's role would be to support research centers, to aid the innovation process, and to help assure the availability of capital for new firms, which are perceived to have difficulty in the financial markets.

Organizing for Development: A New Administration

James Blanchard's election as governor, in November 1982, ended the Milliken period and meant new individuals and a new party for the first time in two decades. Blanchard won on a campaign that stressed three priorities—Jobs, Jobs, Jobs. The most remarkable aspect of this transition, taken in its larger context, is the continuity between the two administrations in economic development strategies and policies. The continuity of private and public sector actions establishes an important point in Michigan's economic development.

The major, and ultimately very significant, difference between the administrations was their approach to the state's budgetary situation. Milliken tried to balance the budget through short-term funding cuts, often directed at education, and creative bookkeeping. His administration felt that getting an adequate tax increase through the legislature was impossible, given the emotion surrounding that issue in 1980 and 1981. The administration's hope was that the state's economy would recover, thus avoiding the need for explicit long-term cuts and tax increases and permitting restoration of some of the education cuts later in the fiscal year. Unfortunately, the recession was longer and more severe than anticipated, necessitating continued cuts, preventing any restoration, and leading to ways to disguise the real deficit.

The result of these fiscal actions was that Blanchard faced a significant real debt immediately upon taking office. (The debt had been estimated to be as high as $1.7 billion.) He decided it had to be eliminated if the state was to have credibility in national financial circles. Blanchard achieved his objective through a temporary increase in the state income tax. His tax proposal, which passed on a straight partisan vote, stabilized fiscal policies, paid off the debt, and raised the state's bond ratings. This cost Blanchard considerable political capital and his Democratic majority in the state Senate. Two freshman senators were recalled and replaced with Republican senators. Uncertainty and divisions were created by the successful recalls and, in turn, delayed several Blanchard initiatives and clouded his ability to work with the Senate. It also strengthened the conservative bloc within the Republican party, which had important ramifications for how Michigan dealt with questions of economic development and change.

Blanchard's initial economic development decisions were procedural rather than substantive. His political experience was in Washington, not Michigan, and his top appointments to positions most concerned with development were from outside the state.[22] Furthermore, the Milliken administration had been in office for fourteen years, so the relevant departments were staffed with entrenched bureaucrats unlikely to support Blanchard's initiatives; in fact, some had been unresponsive to Milliken's creation efforts. Consequently, the incoming administration had relatively little detailed knowledge of Michigan's economy and politics and few political resources with which to build and implement a program. Blanchard's initial efforts created internal and external organizations that would compensate for these deficiencies and permit the creation and implementation of an economic development strategy.

The Cabinet Council

Internally, Blanchard created the Cabinet Council for Jobs and Economic Development. The council consisted of seven department heads and three other officials whose actions most affected economic development.[23] The council's primary missions were to form an economic development strategy, to coordinate the economic development activities of these departments, to resolve turf and bureaucratic conflicts, and to ensure adherence to the governor's priorities. The council also selected a large number of special projects that cut across agencies, such as reducing paperwork and business reporting requirements, creating a summer youth employment program, and confronting the business climate issue.

The council was staffed by departmental people, selected and directed by an executive director, Peter Plastrik. The staff did not have to be selected from a political list and were independent of their agencies while on the council. One person said this independence was a key to the council's success. Plastrik rotated staff members through the council and back to their respective agencies, where they would implement projects developed during their tenure on the council. This procedure created a cadre of middle level executives in some key departments who understood and supported the governor's objectives and who knew appropriate people in other departments. During its early days, the council also relied heavily on outside consultants from Washington, D.C., who had experience with state economic development.

The council's first task was to develop a strategy to guide Blanchard's public statements and actions in the development area. The council felt it needed to act quickly and visibly to demonstrate the new governor's commitment to his campaign pledge to revitalize the state economy and to provide jobs. Early, visible actions would buy time for a longer-term strategy and allow the new administration to deal with older, conflict-laden issues, such as workers' compensation, taxes, and other business costs. Working with the outside consultants, the council identified several high priority areas, including infrastructure maintenance and regulation, and several target industries on which to focus attention. The target industries were forestry, food products, and automobile suppliers—identical to Milliken's targeted industries. Subcommittees drawing on the council staff and representatives from relevant departments set to work identifying and implementing specific actions in each area, though one person admitted they had little idea of what could actually make a difference in some of these areas.

The council functioned as a strong force within the Blanchard administration, fulfilling its mission to develop, coordinate, and promote the governor's economic priorities. It initiated and completed a number of successful projects. Its major contribution seemed to be as coordinator and enforcer of the administration's agenda. At times, it undoubtedly deserved its reputation for "bureaucrat bashing," given the entrenched and undynamic nature of many of the departmental bureaucracies. However, as one staff member put it, the coordination was somewhat easier when the priorities were as clearly stated as Jobs, Jobs, Jobs. The council was disbanded in December 1985, as called for in its initial charter. The various projects and activities initiated by the council were distributed to the appropriate departments.

The Governor's Commission on Jobs and Economic Development

The first external group Blanchard organized was the Governor's Commission on Jobs and Economic Development. The commission, chaired by Lee Iacocca, president of Chrysler, and Douglas Fraser, then president of the United Auto Workers, was composed of major figures from industry, labor, finance, and academia. The commission was designed to review proposals coming from the administration and to function as an advisory panel. It was not intended to initiate policies or actions. Operationally, the commission worked to build supporting coalitions and to legitimize proposals before they were subjected to the formal political process. Many of the subcommittees formed within the commission paralleled the working groups on the council staff.

The commission tended to deal with traditional economic development questions, such as business costs. Its work frequently reflected the private agendas of the individual members. At an early stage, a working group on automobile suppliers was created and chaired by representatives from General Motors. Its role was to parallel the administration's actions to stimulate that industry through its targeting efforts. The administration hoped this group would help develop and implement plans to promote innovation, raise productivity, and more effectively compete with the Japanese. Instead, the group's report concentrated on traditional ways to reduce business costs. The experience of this commission suggests that such a partnership functions well as a public forum for debating issues and managing some of the conflicts associated with traditional labor-management issues. It can help build consensus around proposed policies better than it can formulate innovative policies.

The Governor's Entrepreneurial and Small Business Commission

In late 1983, Blanchard, through an executive order, created the Entrepreneurial and Small Business Commission. The ESBC was chaired by David Bing, president of Bing Steel, and Alan Suits, president of Recomtex. The ESBC's mission was to represent entrepreneurial and small business in the executive and legislative branches of government and to promote the state's small business climate. Composition of the ESBC ranged from local service businesses to high tech businesses. A majority of the activities have been directed at cost reduction, either directly by cutting taxes and workers' compensation costs or indirectly through reduced red tape, paperwork reform, and regulatory changes. The ESBC has also promoted more basic changes designed to promote entrepreneurial activity. These changes include securities deregulation, the development of a Strategic Fund and Small Business Lending Corporation, and the creation of small business incubation centers. Similar to the Jobs and Economic Development Commission, the purpose of the ESBC was largely to advise, build coalitions, and coopt a variety of interests into the policy process. Together, the Iacocca-Fraser commission and the Entrepreneurial and Small Business Commission provided representation and access for both the large and small business constituencies in Michigan.

The Task Force for a Long-Term Economic Strategy for Michigan

A number of the members of the cabinet council were concerned that the Blanchard administration lacked a long-term development strategy. They recognized the need for short-term actions but felt a long-term strategy was required to guide policy for an entire term, and possibly through a second term. Some council members also had reservations about the targeted industry policies that had been announced early in the administration and wanted more analysis of how public policy could affect a state's economy. The result was the appointment, in late 1983, of Doug Ross to chair a task force to create such a strategy. Ross, former leader of the Citizen's Lobby and state senator, successfully managed several new, short-term programs for Blanchard during the administration's first year and was appointed Director of Commerce in November 1984. In contrast to previous task forces, this one was created quietly, kept small, and composed primarily of academic researchers rather than corporate, labor, and academic leaders.

The task force's mission was to diagnose the structure and recent changes in the Michigan economy and to assess what was known about how states can affect regional economic change. Based on that diagnosis and assessment, the task force was to design a strategy for future state action. Created without a single public announcement and working well away from the spotlight of public attention, in a basement room at the Institute for Social Research at The University of Michigan, the task force delivered a report, *The Path to Prosperity*. Their report outlined several basic themes:

- Any economic development strategy must concentrate on the economic base, which in Michigan is primarily manufacturing and related business services;
- Michigan's future depends upon having innovative firms developing new products and production technologies;
- Private industry must take the lead in investing in these new technologies as government can only play a supportive role;
- State investments should be in education and research and in assistance to workers displaced by changing manufacturing technologies;
- State policies should concentrate more on the services valued by new and expanding businesses than on financial subsidies to relocating or failing firms;
- Reduced state related business costs are not a quick fix solution to the development problem, but costs should be comparable to those of other states in the region.

The task force report was released in late 1984. It has been widely circulated and well received by a wide range of economic groups, with no loud objections from any sector of the economy. General comments have criticized the emphasis on the economic base concept and on manufacturing specifically. People associated with other sectors pointed to their importance in creating jobs and the difficulty in distinguishing export from import activities. Praise generally has been received for the emphasis on innovation and on the need to transform the state's economy and for rejection of the assumption that a cyclical recovery would remedy the state's problems. Overall, the report continues the emphasis on the creation strategy begun by the Milliken administration. (One former Milliken advisor commented that he agreed with all but some small sections of the task force report.)

The Path to Prosperity had a substantial impact on the Blanchard administration's actions. Many of the initiatives that will be discussed were derived from the strategy laid out by the task force. Three factors distinguished this task force from previous ones and help account for its greater impact on state policy. The first is its academic composition. This firmly established that the effort would be an objective examination of the state's economy and of how state actions might alter that economy. Members began with perceptions of Michigan's economy and of what state actions might improve it, but these perceptions were readily altered by the analysis and evidence produced by the task force. Earlier commissions were composed of prominent corporate, labor, and political leaders who arrived with strong, preconceived agendas for altering the state's economy. These preconceptions meant that much of the effort went into mediating and searching for acceptable recommendations rather than weighing evidence and creating a strategy based on that evidence.

A second factor in the task force's effectiveness was anonymity, both of the task force itself and its members. With no trumpets announcing its creation, the group was free to work without pressure from the media. This absence of media pressure and of previously publicized and organizationally determined viewpoints permitted the task force to examine evidence carefully, to freely debate alternatives, and to substantially alter initial views and ideas. Ross explicitly acknowledges this process and its importance in the report's preface.

The final factor is Ross himself. He had Blanchard's trust, confidence, and attention. His selection as Commerce Director clearly indicates their relationship and demonstrates that Ross was able to persuade the governor to adopt the task force report. Several task force members commented on Ross' openness, energy, and overall ability as a major factor in the task force's success.

The task force success is a result of the interaction of all these factors. No one single item determined its success. However, it is also likely that the absence of any one of them would have severely limited its role.

Implementation of a Development Strategy: The First Steps

Implementation of the task force's strategy, which Ross continually enunciated in talks around the state, was the real challenge facing the Blanchard administration. This multifaceted challenge required the invention, selection, and execution of specific actions to promote creation, the building of a constituency for change, and the management of many conflicts resulting from economic decline and change. Much can be learned from the Blanchard administration's experiences in meeting this challenge, which required short-term as well as long-term actions.

Governor Blanchard and his advisors felt they had to confront the highly salient maintenance demands of existing firms and workers and achieve some highly visible economic success given the state's economic condition and his compaign pledges. This need became imperative after Blanchard suffered a serious loss of public support and his Democratic majority in the state Senate, due to recalls after he pushed through a tax increase to pay off the state's $1.7 billion deficit. These initial efforts would provide time and political leverage to formulate and begin the longer-term creation strategy. In pursuing these short-run goals, the administration relied on maintenance and recruitment but not in their traditional forms.

Cost Reduction and Maintenance Efforts

The Blanchard administration, and increasingly the private sector as well, has reduced the emphasis on pure cost reduction as a means to compete domestically and internationally. However, in early 1983, this was still a very symbolic, emotional issue on which Blanchard felt he had to make some visible progress. The actions taken helped convince the business community that Blanchard was sensitive to their concerns and responsive to their needs. Michigan, at that time, still ranked high, even relative to northern industrial states, on two cost items: workers' compensation and local property taxes. Michigan's unemployment insurance costs, corporate taxes, and personal and sales taxes were quite favorable, particularly for new businesses, when compared to these same states.[24] Blanchard departed from the previous, highly conflictual options, however. Rather than accepting that the only way to reduce costs was to commensurately reduce benefits or services, most of his cost reduction actions were intended to reduce costs through increased efficiency without reducing benefits. Debate and action focused on three areas: workers' compensation, paperwork costs, and property taxes.

Workers' Compensation. In spite of the workers' compensation reforms passed during the Milliken administration, costs to Michigan firms remained above the regional average, though the differential had decreased significantly. Needless to say there was a continued demand from manufacturing companies and their trade associations to reduce these costs. These demands were made all the more salient by reports that benefits paid in Michigan were not higher than those in states with lower costs.[25] The explanation for this result was a combination of poor administration, loose eligibility requirements, and excessive litigation. Blanchard's response was to appoint Theodore St. Antoine as a special counselor to undertake a detailed study of the workers' compensation system and present recommendations for ways to reduce costs. (St. Antoine was a former dean of The University of Michigan Law School and a recognized authority on workers' compensation.) Blanchard's hope was that ways could be found to reduce costs but not benefits and that St. Antoine's appointment would restrict debate on the issue and buy time. The appointment was received well by all parties.

St. Antoine's report, released in December 1984, made several significant points:

> • The 1980–81 reforms had saved Michigan firms $500 million, mostly through rate reductions attributable to competition and public pressure ($400 million) and some due to reduced eligibility ($100 million);
> • There had been a dramatic drop in numbers of claims and in the number of contested claims;
> • The cost gap between Michigan and other states had been reduced and comparisons with Indiana should be ignored as Indiana's benefits were so meager that they did not even approach the poverty level for disabled workers;
> • Changes should be made in the appeals process to make appeal possible only in cases where errors of fact were involved;
> • The number of administrative law judges should be reduced and their work monitored more closely to increase efficiency.

There was general support for St. Antoine's recommendations, the state Chamber of Commerce being an exception. The chamber, representing a large number of small businesses, wanted tighter eligibility standards and reduced costs, so that Michigan's costs became comparable to those in other states. Blanchard eventually got most of what he hoped for, namely changes in the administrative structure that would reduce costs but not benefits. At this point, the major opposition came from the judges and members of the workers' compensation bureaucracy rather than the business community.

Paperwork Costs. One important project undertaken by the cabinet council was a study of ways to reduce the amount of state paperwork imposed on business. This project required departments to examine and reduce the number of forms they used and that they required businesses to file. The outcome of this study was a substantial reduction in costs, which was hailed by business as both a true cost savings and an important signal that Blanchard was serious about listening to business concerns. Again, it was a cost reduction achieved without a commensurate reduction in public benefits.

Property Taxes. The Blanchard administration had not addressed the question of business property taxes, though they have made extensive and continued recommendations to lower residential property taxes through expanded use of the state personal income tax credit for local property taxes. (This credit goes to homeowners and renters but not to commercial and industrial property owners.) General Motors, however, initiated a large scale attack on its local property taxes by challenging local assessments in tax court. The consequence of these challenges, if successful, would be to seriously and substantially reduce revenues for a large number of local communities where GM plants are located. It also would mean a substantial saving for GM. GM's contention was that its property is over-assessed relative to its true worth, and it was simply trying to end excessive taxation, which it must stop to remain competitive.

Interestingly, in an important speech in May 1986 to local developers, John Thodis, president of the Michigan Manufacturers Association, argued against local property tax abatements. He said they were not effective development tools and discriminated against the larger number of firms who had to pay higher taxes to cover the revenue lost from abatements.

In general, tension has lessened over the issues of relative business costs. Obviously, these issues will not ever be resolved. Firms facing an increasingly competitive environment will always see reductions in the benefits and costs of workers' compensation and unemployment insurance and in state and local tax rates as a way for them to remain viable. The tensions could easily return if the national economy declines, threatening many firms. It is also true that Michigan governments have not done all they could to improve their efficiency, so it will be possible to reduce costs without reducing services. However, the extent to which the salience and priority of cost issues have been reduced is evidenced by the comments of John Thodis to the local developers. He strongly criticized the Alexander Grant ratings, which continually rank Michigan last in their index of business costs, as being largely irrelevant in predicting and promoting long-term economic growth. This is a substantial change in position from the early 1980s and indicates increasing agreement on Michigan's long-term development strategy.

Recruitment as a Benefit/Cost Decision

Recruitment in the traditional sense of competing for branch plants and relocating firms has played a reduced role in the Blanchard strategy. A few highly
promoted competitions have attracted considerable national press coverage and
generated a response by the state government. One location decision was
recorded as a Michigan victory by the media scorekeepers, while the other two
were considered partial victories by Michigan officials. The acknowledged victory was the decision by Mazda to open its U.S. facility in Flat Rock, Michigan,
on the site of a former Ford engine plant. The partial victories were the decision
by Saturn, the highly touted GM entry into the high tech small car field, to locate
its headquarters and R & D facilities in Troy, Michigan, while the first production plant was placed in Spring Hill, Tennessee, and the decision by Mitsubushi
to locate in Illinois. The reason for viewing the latter as a partial victory will
explain much about why the use of subsidies for recruitment has become a secondary strategy in Michigan.

The Blanchard administration took a well defined benefit/cost approach to
the question of recruitment while concentrating on ways to support the Michigan firms that gave clear evidence of being competitive. The benefit/cost
approach was designed to ensure that Michigan, both workers and the government, did not give away more in subsidies to a recruited plant than were
returned in state and local taxes. The state hired a group at the Institute for
Labor and Industrial Relations at The University of Michigan to develop an
input-output model of the state's economy. This model was used to trace the
expected multiplier effects of any new, large facility located within the state and
to estimate the total earnings, jobs, and state and local tax revenues it would
produce. On this basis, Blanchard, with the advice of the cabinet council, would
decide what, if any, subsidies the state would offer to attract the facility.

Mazda. Mazda's decision to locate its North American plant in Flat Rock
received considerable attention and was the result of considerable effort by the
state government, the Ford Motor Company, and the UAW to recruit the plant.
Officials made numerous trips to Japan and entertained frequent Japanese del-
egations to Michigan. The state promised Mazda subsidies in the form of lower
taxes, worker training, and investments in infrastructure developments after
determining that, in the long run, the benefits from the Flat Rock plant would
exceed the cost of the subsidies. Flat Rock is located in an area of high unemployment with many failed or declining firms. The location of the Mazda plant
on the site of this former Ford engine plant promised significant jobs and
income for an area badly in need of new economic activity.

Saturn. One of the big media events of the year was General Motors' staging of
the decision of where to locate its first Saturn assembly plant. Saturn was promoted as an entirely new venture by GM designed to use new production and
automotive technology and innovative management and labor relations to com-

pete with the Japanese in the small car market. The decision on locating the first production facility became a highly symbolic event, even making the Phil Donahue show. Michigan made a strong bid for the plant. In addition to the traditional cost subsidies authorized in state legislation, Saturn was offered an innovative package of incentives related to worker training, technical support, and community development. Roger Smith, the GM president, called the Michigan package very innovative and a landmark in plant recruitment efforts, but the site eventually was located in Spring Hill, Tennessee.

General Motors' decision to place Saturn's headquarters and research and development center in Michigan has equal or greater significance for the state's economy. These centers would employ nearly as many people as the assembly plant, though many of the new jobs will require highly skilled technicians, professionals, and office workers, rather than traditional line workers. These jobs, though formally in manufacturing, will further the transition of Michigan's economy from traditional manufacturing to service jobs.

The headquarters and R & D facilities provide Michigan with several advantages the assembly plant would not. Employment in these service units usually is less cyclically variable than production work, thus helping to reduce the state's sensitivity to fluctuations in the national economy. In addition, in many industries, headquarters and research facilities become the source of innovation for spin-off firms and industries. Thus, for a state attempting to implement a creation strategy, these Saturn units may contribute more to long-run development than the assembly plant, which is seldom the source of new enterprise. Michigan clearly wanted and would have benefited from having both the central units and the assembly plant. But, it was still a winner in the Saturn contest, even though Tennessee reaped all the publicity.

Mitsubushi. The Mitsubushi case is a simple one. Analysis indicated that the potential gains if the plant was located in Michigan did not offset the cost of the subsidies being requested, so the state withdrew. The plant ultimately went to Illinois. Mitsubushi's demands, had they been accepted, constituted a bad precedent and were unfair to existing Michigan firms, in addition to presenting a bad benefit/cost ratio. The Mitsubushi case demonstrates there is a definite limit to how far the state would go in subsidizing a recruitment effort, particularly since, in the long run, subsidies must be financed by existing businesses.

Promotion. Extensive effort and resources are going into a promotional campaign, both within and outside Michigan, to publicize the technological and economic changes taking place in the state and the advantages they offer to certain types of firms. The obvious intent is to attract the attention of entrepreneurs, investors, and workers who can further these changes. This is not the traditional recruitment strategy. The state government is not seeking to attract branch plants and mobile firms looking for a cheaper place to do business or even simply to attract firms that are similar to the *average* industrial firm in the state. To the extent the campaign is trying to attract the relocating firm, the state is trying to lure the technologically advanced firm that will contribute to the creation strategy. More likely, the campaign will appeal to investors, to those looking to sell to Michigan's new firms, and to people within the state itself.

A Nonrecruitment Strategy. A significant change in development strategy under Ross was that the Department of Commerce altered the activities of the traditional economic development field agents. Historically, these individuals called on firms around the country, trying to recruit new firms and plants to Michigan. However, since 1985 these individuals have been assigned responsibility for contacting and servicing growing firms in Michigan in hopes of promoting the further growth and retaining the successful firms, already in the state. The Department of Commerce used the Economic Development and Job Creation Database developed at the Institute for Social Research at The University of Michigan to identify the fastest growing firms in different industrial sectors. An agent was assigned responsibility for a specific list of firms and his or her performance was evaluated on the basis of how well the assigned firms did. This marks a dramatic shift away from the traditional recruitment strategy. Unfortunately, it is too early to assess the results of this shift.

In summary, the state has only selectively followed a subsidy based recruitment strategy in the past several years. When cost effective opportunities are available the state will compete seriously. For the most part, the state has directed its efforts at promoting and retaining its existing growing firms.

Implementation of a Creation Strategy: The Long-Run Policies

Michigan's dominant strategy is now one of innovation and creation, both in new industries and in older sectors. A two part effort is implicit in the actions of both state and private sector officials. One effort is directed at making existing firms more competitive by increasing productivity through the adoption of new production technologies and by the creation of new products. This expansion and retention effort will assist the transition of the existing Michigan economy from one dependent upon large scale, traditional manufacturing to one founded on specialized and technologically advanced methods and products. The second effort is intended to promote the creation of new firms and industries based on the emerging needs of existing, but changing, industries and on the scientific research capabilities within the state. This increasingly dominant strategy is the evolution of the strategic shift first begun under the Milliken administration and enthusiastically embraced by Blanchard and his key officials.

A basic premise of *The Path to Prosperity* was that industrial innovation is a process beginning with basic research and ending with the marketing and production of products.[26] This process has five stages:

1. Basic research in the sciences, engineering, and social sciences;
2. Applied research, which is quite specialized and interdisciplinary;
3. Product development;

4. Commercialization, which includes capitalization and organization creation;

5. Marketing, which includes managing the production and delivery of the product.

A combination of public and private sector actions are required for this process to succeed. Government policy is vital for the early stages while private initiatives are needed to complete the process.

Basic Research

Basic research is done at the nation's major universities and must be funded by the government because of its public goods nature, its uncertainty, and its extraordinarily long payback period. The federal government is the largest supporter of basic research, though an ever increasing share of federal research funds are going to the military, where they have the smallest benefits for industrial development. The Blanchard administration, recognizing the critical role of universities in basic research has increased the funding for higher education in the state, relative to other public programs. The administration also proposed a special $25 million research excellence fund to be allocated to the four major research universities: The University of Michigan, Michigan State University, Wayne State University, and Michigan Technological University. The research excellence funds were to be spent for research that would promote economic development.

The subsequent history of Blanchard's higher education funding proposals indicates the difficulty the political process has in making decisions that transfer and concentrate resources, altering the status quo. Basic research is expensive, requires a critical mass of scarce talent in one place, and must have a solid infrastructure that only a few universities can provide. Governments, however, like to do things inexpensively and to spread money and programs around so that everyone shares in the activity. These political imperatives, at times initiated by Blanchard himself, severely diluted the administration's plans for increased basic research. For two consecutive years, Blanchard strongly pressured state universities not to raise in-state undergraduate tuition. The pressure meant a very small increase in total revenues and operating deficits for the larger research universities, in spite of increased state funding, because state general funds constitute a smaller portion of their budgets. These deficits, following immediately after the budgetary crises of the early 1980s, left the major universities with a severely deteriorated physical and human infrastructure.

The research fund was treated as an educational pork barrel by the legislature and about half the funds were redistributed to all state supported colleges and universities, with minimal controls on whether the money was used for research related to economic development. Supplemental appropriations recommended by Blanchard and approved by the legislature subsequently restored some of the money originally intended for the larger research institutions.

Applied Research

Efforts to increase and promote organizations doing applied research were a central part of the Milliken and Blanchard strategies. The High Technology Task Force has remained a strong force promoting the three original institutes and starting a fourth center. In addition, the state has done what it could to encourage and financially support the new institutes and other applied research centers, such as the Environmental Research Institute of Michigan.

The Michigan High Technology Task Force. The High Technology Task Force became a privately chartered organization after Milliken left office, chaired by the former governor and the succeeding lieutenant governor, Martha Griffiths. The membership and agenda remained essentially unchanged. In addition to the first three institutes, the task force submitted a proposal for a Software Engineering Institute (eventually located in Pittsburgh, Pennsylvania) to the federal government and has initiated, with state support, a fourth center focused on materials and materials processing. It also functions as a clearinghouse processing information for firms with problems related to high technology and matching organizations with research resources and needs with appropriate research centers. The task force remains outside the political process, except in a promotional way.

The Applied Research Centers. The state's applied research centers continued to flourish, with help from foundations and state and national governments. The Industrial Technology Institute received most of the publicity and funding. Its impact to date has been mostly symbolic, as it is too early to measure its performance. The Michigan Biotechnology Institute and the Metro Center are still in the embryonic stage and have been less visible.

Michigan's most prominent success in the applied research field was the Environmental Research Institute of Michigan (ERIM), formerly the Willow Run Laboratories at The University of Michigan. Most of Willow Run's funding came from the Department of Defense for electronic surveillance, remote sensing, and radar. The WRL became ERIM in the early 1970s, when the university was pressured to abandon military and classified research. ERIM is now a private nonprofit research center funded primarily by DOD research grants.

ERIM's state support comes primarily from a state statute that exempts research organizations from local property taxes. (ERIM has made an in lieu payment to Ann Arbor each year, whose amount is far less than a full property tax assessment would require.) The city of Ann Arbor, faced with declining federal revenues and increased demands by Democrats for social expenditures, has challenged the application of this statute to ERIM. The city contends that ERIM increasingly is engaged in commercial activities, as it spins off its innovations into successful firms but retains an equity or royalty interest in the progeny. State officials have lobbied and testified on ERIM's behalf in this contest. So far, the challenge has resulted in increased contributions to the city, but court action is still threatened.[27]

ERIM's success as an incubator for new technologies and firms is substantial. At one count, over fifty firms, most of whom have stayed in Michigan, evolved from either ERIM or WRL. These numbers are disputed and ERIM remains in an ongoing conflict with some of its progeny. The further ERIM gets into licensing and commercializing its activities, the more the private firms see a competitor. They contend that ERIM is greatly advantaged by its tax exempt status and its government contracts. (It is alleged that some of these firms are supporting Ann Arbor's efforts to remove ERIM tax exemption.) The private firms want ERIM to stay out of the applications area. Despite these conflicts, ERIM is an economic development success. Its record is cited as evidence of the power of applied research centers and as justification for the investments in the applied research centers promoted by the High Technology Task Force and those funded by the state at its public universities.

Private Industry Activities. A number of the large corporations in Michigan support considerable applied research on their own. For example, a recent article stated that General Motors had the largest research and development budget of any company in the country. Other Michigan firms, such as those in chemicals, pharmaceuticals, and scientific instruments in addition to the automobile industry, have also invested heavily in applied research.

Product Development and Commercialization

There is less state activity to discuss in these areas, as increasingly we are discussing topics that can, and should, be effectively done by the private sector. State government activities have been directed at technology transfer or the ability to move innovations from the basic and applied research stages to commercialization.

The Michigan Industrial Technology Deployment Service. The MITDS, begun in late 1985, provides technical assistance and support for firms adopting and adapting to computer based manufacturing technology. The service gives special attention to the needs of small businesses trying to alter their structures in order to compete. MITDS draws on experts from around the state, such as those at ITI, to advise in a number of areas, such as finance, job training, and scientific and technical information. This service grew directly from an extensive study of the automobile industry in Michigan directed by Jack Russell of the Department of Commerce and Dan Lurea of ITI. This study interviewed a sample of auto supply firms to determine their future and their needs, given the technological changes in automobile manufacturing. The study concluded that considerable assistance in learning about, in adopting, and in using computer based production methods was needed and could be provided effectively by the state.

The Technology Transfer Network. A second effort to enhance the transfer of technology from Michigan universities to the private sector is the Technology Transfer Network (TTN). This project is a joint effort between Wayne State University, The University of Michigan, Michigan State University, Western Michigan University, and Michigan Technological University. It is an outgrowth of an ambitious study of industry-university relations conducted by researchers at the five universities. The network is a database of resources at the five universities available to assist firms in adopting new technologies. In some ways, it parallels the MITDS, though the TNN concentrates on university based resources. With funding from the Department of Commerce, the universities' databases are linked together and provide firms access to each university's resources through a single entry point.

Marketing

The state has little activity in the marketing of new products. State activities have been largely promotional. Michigan's overseas offices aid firms in international marketing efforts. Paula Blanchard, the governor's spouse, heads an extensive campaign promoting Made in Michigan products, though it is not clear how large an impact, beyond its symbolic value, this effort has on job and wealth creation.

Financial Assistance

The importance of risk oriented, equity based financing, frequently referred to as venture capital, in creating new businesses had been recognized increasingly in this country.[28] There was a sense among state leaders that Michigan lacked a venture capital base, particularly for a state of its size, wealth, and industrial activity.[29] There also was clear evidence that commercial banks within the state were not an important factor in financing small manufacturing firms. A study by the Institute for Social Research at The University of Michigan estimated that fewer than 7 percent of the metal working firms in the state had received loans from commercial banks and only 11 percent had received funds from *any* financial institution in 1983. In contrast, over half had obtained funds from the owner or the owner's friends.[30]

The state began a series of initiatives to increase the availability of capital to new and small firms. The first of these came under the Milliken administration with the authorization to invest up to 5 percent of the state public employees pension fund as a venture capital fund. The Blanchard administration continued and expanded these efforts.

The Michigan Venture Capital Program. The provision that Michigan could invest up to 5 percent of the public pension funds in small business and venture capital firms led to the creation of the Venture Capital Division within the state Treasury in 1982. It makes direct investments in some firms and acts as a limited partner investing in other funds. The program's directors have both a fiduciary responsibility to obtain a high return and maintain the solvency of the retirement fund. They also understand the objectives of promoting economic growth in Michigan. What is not clear at this point is how these potentially competing roles will be balanced. So far, it has led to placements in more mature enterprises and not in seed or start-up ventures. Two-thirds of the money has been invested through the limited partnership route. This leaves more of the decision making to distant third parties. It also attracts more out of state capital to Michigan, as these outside venture capital firms are attracted by the state financing.[31]

The Michigan Strategic Fund. This fund will provide a wide range of investment capital for Michigan firms by combining public and private efforts. The conditions of the fund require private participation and spread the risk among the private and public partners. The intent is to pyramid state funds through these partnerships and capture private sector expertise and judgment. The fund is administered by a nine member board of directors, which includes individuals from the private sector, the Treasurer, and the Director of Commerce. The fund may issue bonds and notes, make grants, loans, and investments, and may claim royalties and revenues from these investments in return. The fund was formally organized in late 1985, with Peter Plastrik as the director. Obviously, it is too early to examine the fund's activities and assess their impact on Michigan's economy.

Private Financial Institutions. Michigan has had little success at convincing major financial institutions to begin funding new and higher risk firms. Both Michigan National and Comerica, two of the state's larger banks, started capital investment companies during the early 1980s. However, both banks have closed or will close these operations. The increased competition arising from deregulation and the uncertainty in the banking sector has led both banks to avoid long-term risky investment programs. This is both an economic and a symbolic blow to the state's development efforts but strongly reinforces the decision of the state to enter the area of financing. Michigan also does not have any large insurance companies that might be a source of industry financing, as they have been in other states.

Private Sector Initiatives

The ultimate test of Michigan's strategies is what happens to the state's industries. Only if the mature firms become technologically innovative, thereby raising their productivity and creating new products and markets, and only if new firms and industries develop and grow can these programs be considered successful. Innovation and change must occur in the private sector for the economic development strategy to succeed. There is clear evidence that Michigan's major industries are moving in that direction.

The Auto Industry. Some of the most visible, far reaching innovations are newly designed products and the new, highly automated plants being built by the automobile companies in this country, and specifically in Michigan. More dramatic evidence is the automobile manufacturers' purchases of interests in machine vision firms and other small firms in the automated manufacturing sector. Ford's successful new models, GM's acquisitions of Electronic Data Systems and Hughes Aircraft, and Chrysler's takeover of AMC are representative of changes taking place in all three major car producers. These actions are having profound impacts on Michigan's economy. EDS alone adds several thousand high-skill jobs in programming, information processing, and business services, furthering the transition from a production to a service economy. The auto companies also are trying to diversify away from automobiles and even from transportation. Ford and GM are exploiting the deregulation of financial institutions to turn their consumer credit organizations into broad based nationwide financial institutions, which will further diversify both the firms and the Michigan economy.

Innovations in automobile production policies are also having a major impact on employment in Michigan. Increasingly, the big three firms want their suppliers close to the assembly plants as they shift to a "just in time" inventory system. This system reduces inventory costs and gives the large firms more control over the supplier for things such as quality and delivery time. The consequence of these production changes is to greatly increase the auto related employment, outside the big three firms, and has led to an increase of new firms in auto supply sectors.

Other Industries. Auto assembly is far from Michigan's only evolving manufacturing industry. Other sectors are making major innovations in products, production methods, and markets that are increasing substantially the jobs in the state. The large office furniture manufacturers are expanding their facilities in Michigan. Steelcase, for example, announced plans for major new plants to produce its new and very innovative lines of office furnishings. Upjohn announced a new product that may help cure baldness that, if successful, will surely expand that firm's market. As a last example, a substantial computer software industry is developing in Washtenaw County, taking advantage of the resources at The University of Michigan, the Industrial Technology Institute, and the increasing automation of Michigan's manufacturing firms. To complement this resource, EDS and The University of Michigan have announced plans for a major Center for Machine Intelligence, which will further add to the technology bases and to the process of innovation in that region.

Short-Run Success and an Unknown Future

The private sector innovations and investments chronicled throughout this chapter are having substantial positive impacts on Michigan's economy. They are evidence that Michigan industry is beginning the process of innovation and entrepreneurship that created the industrial state in the first place and that have been central to other successful economies. Unfortunately, it is too early to assess the creation strategy as a long-term strategy. It is likely to be a decade, at least, before such an evaluation can be made.

In the short run, however, Michigan is doing well. It has been favored by external economic events. The national recovery, declining interest rates, the Japanese import quotas, and recently, the decrease in petroleum prices have produced a period of relative prosperity for the state, which eases the political pressure on the Blanchard administration and gives the creation strategy time to work. The consequences of large scale structural change are still present, however. For example, the automobile companies had record profits and sales in 1984 and 1985 and are well on the road to recovery, at least in the short term. Employment, however, has not and will not return to pre-1980 levels, given the increased investment in automation. The obvious consequence of making older industries competitive is lower employment levels. "Get smart" is preferable to "get poor" or "get out," but it means that fewer workers are required to achieve previous output levels, as the obvious alternative to lowering wages to compete is to raise productivity to match the wage differential. Michigan's unemployment rate is still above the national average, in spite of the recovery. The removal of automobile import restrictions and any softening of the national economy will be the acid test for Michigan's strategy.

Choosing an Economic Future

Economies, whether they be state, regional, or national, must continually create new industries and transform existing ones to maintain their economic well-being. Change must be the status quo. The industrial evolution assures us that production, once it becomes routine, will seek the area of the world with the lowest wages and other costs. The only salvation for well developed, mature regions is to continually invest their wealth, talent, and energy in creating new industries, which add wealth to the local economy before they too begin to expand globally—the "get smart" strategy. The alternative is to attempt to maintain the existing industrial structure, even as it declines in the face of innovation and competition from elsewhere—the "get poor" option. The specter of Birmingham, England, should haunt those contemplating this latter choice.

Michigan's economic history and the recent experiences of reindustrializing states demonstrate that innovation and entrepreneurship are the sources of economic growth. What would Michigan be today if not for the transformation of lumbering into furniture and then into office systems; had sawmills not become the basis for the salt industry, which in turn led to the chemical and soap industries; and if a few industrial pioneers had not turned the marine engine, carriage, and few other manufacturing sectors into the automobile industry? We would certainly not now be worrying about deindustrialization but underdevelopment.

The creation, or innovation, strategy is not an easy one to follow, for an individual, a company, or a government. It entails risk, uncertainty, flexibility, and a long-term perspective, none of which are common individual or organizational traits. The current story of economic development in Michigan is the efforts by a number of individuals and organizations, both private and public, to implement the creation strategy within their respective organizations. A number of Michigan companies, large and small, are addressing this challenge. History will record their success and their success will determine Michigan's future. As pointed out in *The Path to Prosperity* and noted here, it is the private sector that creates the wealth and jobs required for long-run growth. The public sector plays a vital role in encouraging, or restricting, this needed innovation and change, but what happens in the private sector is critical.

The task of promoting innovation and change is more difficult for leaders in the public sector than those in the private sector. The task requires that resources be shifted from one sector, region, or organization to others and frequently requires that resources be concentrated in one place to achieve a critical mass. Simultaneously, the competitive threats that make innovation and change imperative reduce the wealth of some older, mature economic entities, which are more likely to be the larger and more politically influential groups. Not suprisingly, these groups want and demand support and protection, making the case that their decline would mean economic disaster.

The difficulties facing public leaders are compounded by the structure of America's public institutions. Our system is better designed to prevent governments from pursuing policies that harm large segments of society, to offer aid to those harmed by industrial change, and to avoid a concentration of resources than they are to promote economic change.[32] It becomes an exceptional exercise in leadership for public officials to forego traditional maintenance and recruitment strategies and embark on a creation strategy. As traditionally practiced, the two former strategies are more clearly designed to aid and protect existing industries. Arguments for protection are the extreme case. The creation strategy, by contrast, does not have any obvious, ready-made constituencies. Political leadership is required to build these constituencies.

The political obstacles to public policies that promote economic change are evident at several points in Michigan's recent history:

- The early demands, led by business trade associations and some large manufacturing firms, for a maintenance strategy based upon reductions in business costs through reduced workers' compensation and unemployment insurance benefits;
- The inability of some traditional business-labor coalitions to pursue issues other than business costs and plant closures and their difficulty in making recommendations on anything where labor and business leaders disagreed;
- The demands of some organized sectors in Michigan for import quotas on automobiles, machine tools, and steel, which have been repeatedly pressed in Washington by politicians from both parties as well as by business and labor leaders;
- The recommendations of the governor's commission on how to promote the auto supplier sector of the economy, which focused on the question of business costs and not technological change;
- The legislature's initial conversion of Governor Blanchard's proposed $25 million research excellence fund into an educational pork barrel and Blanchard's demands that all universities freeze tuition;
- The comments by people in both administrations that visible action had

to be taken on issues of business costs in order to have the time and the opportunity to develop and pursue a creation strategy, which implies that there is not
a constituency for innovation and change per se.

The interesting and important story is not these impediments but how a constituency for innovation and change was fashioned in a relatively short time by
two administrations from different political parties.

The political strategies of the two administrations were fairly similar in their
broad concepts. These strategies relied on one of the propositions put forth earlier, the mobilization of elites dependent upon a strong economy but not necessarily on existing industries. Both governors also relied on an approach not
mentioned earlier but that has always been central to American politics, to shift
the focus of the conflict and debate if possible.

The influence of the groups expected to have a larger stake in change was
quite evident throughout the study, and continues so. The High Technology
Task Force was largely the initiative of Ted Doan and Harold Shapiro, heads,
respectively, of a venture capital firm and The University of Michigan and consisted of leaders from high growth, technology based companies, higher education, finance, and the law. No one on the task force was from the industries
targeted for growth by Milliken and Blanchard. Also, Michigan foundations
became a major source of funds for the first institutes proposed by the task force.

The major utilities have begun extensive programs directed at economic
development. These programs are directed increasingly at providing services
needed by growing firms and at promoting technological change rather than simply lobbying for a better business climate. The most ambitious of these efforts is
by Michigan Bell. Michigan Bell is working with local communities to study
their manufacturing sectors to ascertain what assistance can be provided to promote new growth. Michigan Bell also is collaborating with researchers at The
University of Michigan to further analyze the data being collected to assist in
planning economic policies, both locally and statewide. The other commercial
groups hypothesized to be dependent upon the long-term health of the economy
and that might push for change, such as retail and service firms, have not been
particularly visible in the economic development effort. This sector's traditional
difficulty in organizing for political purposes, given their diversity, diffuseness,
and relative smallness, may explain their absence.

One aspect of both the Milliken and Blanchard development strategies that
greatly aided their efforts to develop and then implement a creation strategy was
their ability to shift the traditional conflicts over the business climate to other
questions. As members of both administrations mentioned, these issues had to
be dealt with because of their high salience and the strong constituencies
involved. Both administrations, however, managed to shift the debate to a
search for ways to reduce costs without necessarily reducing benefits, thus
diminishing previous conflicts and stalemates.

This tactic was particularly evident in achieving changes in the workers'
compensation system. Efforts to promote competition among the providers of
workers' compensation insurance, to eliminate the appeals process except for

factual errors, and to increase the efficiency of administrative law judges politically changed the structure of the conflict. No longer was it exclusively a business-labor conflict, which easily paralyzes the state and inhibits progress. After the shift of focus, the opposition became the worker's compensation bureaucracy itself: the insurance funds, the judges, and the lawyers filing appeals. These are less sympathetic and influential groups, easing implementation of the new policies, which reduce costs but not benefits by a corresponding amount. This is a "get smart" rather than a "get poor" strategy for the public sector, in that it improves the productivity of the system as a means to reduce costs.

Governor Blanchard turned the traditional industry promotion campaign into a means to build a constituency for economic change. Under Blanchard and Ross, this campaign has been directed at promoting the technological and economic changes taking place within the state, as discussed earlier. This campaign, by airing very effective spots within the state, also builds a constituency for the creation strategy by indicating that innovation and change are happening in the state and are a positive force for growth. The spots featured industrialists and researchers, touting Michigan as a place for advanced technologically based manufacturing and business services. One cannot measure the impact of these promotions, but they certainly help broadcast the basic message of the state strategy and reduce the attention paid to more conventional cost reduction and recruitment strategies.

It is premature to assess the success of the Milliken and Blanchard economic and political strategies. As mentioned earlier, the national recovery has helped the state economy. Michigan's unemployment rate is no longer the highest in the nation, 1984 and 1985 were very profitable years for many firms, and new enterprises have been created at a record pace.[33] Whether these events signal a reversal of the state's long-term structural decline is unknown, but the short-term recovery, even if only cyclical, is buying precious time for the long-term strategy to begin to work. The long-term effects may take a decade to measure accurately.[34]

The long-term political success of the creation strategy cannot be ascertained yet. The short-term success is impressive. Blanchard's popularity, as measured by the *Detroit News Michigan Poll,* has been very high after recovering from the serious decline following passage of the needed income tax increase in 1983. More significantly, he won reelection in 1986 by the largest margin ever for a Democrat. William Lucas, the Republican challenger, campaigned on the traditional business climate and cost and tax reduction issues. Thus, in the short run Michiganders are choosing the creation strategy, though a number of factors, ranging from differences in personality to campaign funding, also contributed to Blanchard's victory. Whether this strategy will continue to be the choice as the necessary economic transition leads to further loss of traditional manufacturing activity and jobs is unknown. It remains a major challenge to the leaders of the state's public and private institutions.

TENNESSEE

Timothy J. Bartik

9

The Emergence of
an Industrial State Economy

Tennessee has made enormous progress in the past forty years. Per capita income has grown much more rapidly than the U.S. average. Increasingly, the state has become a center of sophisticated manufacturing as well as of traditional low-wage industries. The state's capital, Nashville, is one of the true boom towns of the South.

Tennessee's success is based largely on strong economic fundamentals. Powerful economic forces, such as central location, good transportation, low wages and unionization, and a traditional work ethic, attract new industry to the state. State policy makers, however, also point to a vigorous industrial recruitment effort as a self-generated force that has helped Tennessee's economy. This recruitment effort relies not on heavy subsidies to new industry but on providing information and hospitality to prospective new plants. Tennessee's industrial recruiters probably exaggerate their influence. Still, this study concludes that Tennessee's recruitment effort has affected positively the state's economy, although its impact is secondary to that of more fundamental economic forces.

Many Tennessee business and political leaders also believe Governor Lamar Alexander (1979–87) positively influenced the state's economic development. Alexander's economic development role took two forms: personal involvement in industrial recruitment and the formation of new initiatives to improve the basic public infrastructure, such as education and transportation.

Although Alexander's efforts to improve Tennessee's public infrastructure cannot be fully evaluated as yet because of their long-run nature, this report concludes that the governor's personal intervention has made some difference in attracting new branch plants.

Despite these successes, Tennessee faces major economic problems. Nashville's boom is not matched in other Tennessee cities. Many rural counties face double-digit unemployment and serious poverty problems. While Tennessee's per capita income continues to grow, in recent years this growth has only kept pace with that of the rest of the United States. Moreover, despite recent growth, Tennessee remains considerably poorer than the U.S. average.

In large part, these economic problems have been caused by worldwide economic forces. The low-wage industries that Tennessee traditionally has attracted increasingly are locating overseas. The fast-growing business service industries (computer software, management consulting, accounting, etc.) have bypassed Tennessee because the state attracts a relatively greater number of branch plants than the corporate headquarters that utilize these business services. Perceived problems in Tennessee's educational system and a small high technology base have handicapped the state's efforts to generate high tech jobs.

While no policy could have solved the state's economic problems totally, this report argues that a formally developed economic development strategy could significantly help the state deal with its economic problems. Like most states, Tennessee has no formal strategy for its future economic development. The concept of an economic development strategy is apparently more attractive to academic theorists than political leaders. The development of such a strategy, however, would be politically difficult in Tennessee because of the state's strong geographic divisions.

Finally, this study argues that ongoing evaluation of state economic development efforts is important if these efforts are to be effective. Ongoing evaluation also would encourage long-term planning, countering the tendency of the political incentives in most states, which encourage state leaders to use economic development programs for short-run purposes.

The overall study is divided into three chapters. Chapter 9 provides background on Tennessee's economic development. Chapter 10 describes Tennessee's current economic development policies. Chapter 11 evaluates these policies and suggests needed improvements.

Regional Diversity

All states have regional divisions. Tennessee's divisions are more pronounced than most, resulting in a state that "has been traditionally hard put to develop a single sense of itself."[1] These divisions occur between regions, between urban and rural areas, and between different cities in the state; they are political and cultural as well as economic. Thus, in considering alternative policies, state leaders face the constraint that there is no single Tennessee economy.

The Three Grand Divisions

Tennessee's most important division is geographic: the three "Grand Divisions" of East, Middle, and West Tennessee.[2]

East Tennessee is part of the Appalachian region in terms of geography, economics, politics, and culture. Small backwoods and mountain farmers dominated the area in the pre-Civil War era. East Tennessee was pro-Union during the Civil War and has remained Republican. The region's culture reflects the conservatism and independence of Appalachian mountain people. East Tennessee was the first area of the state to attract significant manufacturing, due to the abundant natural resources in the mountains and the relative difficulty of agriculture in the area. East Tennessee is still the most manufacturing-oriented of the state's regions.

West Tennessee is part of the Mississippi Delta economy and society. The fertile, flat "black bottom" lands of this region traditionally supported a cotton based economy, with Memphis as a key cotton processing and distribution center. With its large slave plantations, West Tennessee was pro-Confederate during the Civil War and remains Democratic. The presence of slavery resulted in a much larger minority population in West Tennessee than in the rest of the state: about one-third black versus 16 percent black for the state overall. West Tennessee is still the most agricultural of the three regions.

Middle Tennessee falls between the extremes of East and West Tennessee. Although slavery was prevalent in this area, the pre-Civil War economy was based more on livestock and grain than on cotton. Like West Tennessee, Middle Tennessee was pro-Confederate during the Civil War and is Democratic today, but, unlike West Tennessee, the Middle Tennessee economy today is based more on manufacturing and services than on agriculture.

The three Grand Divisions are officially recognized in the state constitution, and many state commissions are required to include a certain number of members from each of the Grand Divisions.

Rural Dominance in an Urban State

Overlapping the regional divisions are splits between urban and rural areas in Tennessee. Urban and rural splits are common in many states, but Tennessee is unusual in that rural politicans still maintain political control. Tennessee's population was almost 40 percent rural as of 1980, compared to 26 percent for the United States as a whole.[3] With their numbers growing, urban legislators are challenging formulas for the distribution of state public works money. For example, the 1985 legislative session included an urban-rural fight (won by rural interests) over the distribution to counties of a 3 cent hike in the state gasoline tax.

Tennessee cities are divided by distance, different economic bases, and location near state borders. Table 9-1 gives a thumbnail sketch of the economic base of Tennessee metropolitan areas. As can be seen in the table, Memphis and Nashville are service rather than manufacturing cities: Memphis specializes in

Table 9-1. Distribution of Employment and Location Quotients in Tennessee and U.S. Metropolitan and Nonmetropolitan Areas, 1976

	A. Metropolitan Areas with 0.5–1 Million in Population				
	U.S.	Memphis		Nashville	
	%	%	LQ	%	LQ
Manufacturing	24.3	16.5	.68	19.5	.80
Distribution	10.5	14.0	1.33	11.2	1.07
Corporate Complex	14.6	12.3	.84	12.8	.88
Retail	16.0	16.3	1.02	13.2	.83
Consumer Services	4.0	4.1	1.03	4.6	1.15
Social Overhead	6.6	6.3	.95	7.6	1.15
Government	18.2	20.8	1.14	16.0	.88
TVA	—	0.1	—	0.1	—

	B. Metropolitan Areas with 0.25–0.5 Million in Population						
	U.S.	Chattanooga		Tri-Cities		Knoxville	
	%	%	LQ	%	LQ	%	LQ
Manufacturing	22.5	31.7	1.41	31.4	1.40	25.2	1.12
Distribution	9.4	8.2	.87	8.3	.88	9.2	.88
Corporate Complex	12.4	10.7	.86	5.4	.44	10.7	.86
Retail	17.0	13.1	.77	12.7	.75	13.4	.84
Consumer Services	4.7	3.9	.83	2.5	.53	3.5	.88
Social Overhead	6.3	4.1	.65	4.9	.78	5.5	.83
Government	21.5	17.1	.80	14.4	.67	21.4	1.18
TVA	—	2.1	—	—	—	2.1	—

	C. Nonmetropolitan Areas and Metropolitan Areas with Less than 0.25 Million in Population					
	U.S.	Tennessee Valley Nonmetropolitan		Clarksville/ Hopkinsville	
	%	%	LQ	%	LQ
Manufacturing	26.0	31.7	1.22	13.2	.51
Distribution	8.7	5.7	.66	4.7	.54
Corporate Complex	8.7	4.1	.47	3.8	.44
Retail	16.9	9.4	.56	9.9	.59
Consumer Services	4.0	2.6	.65	1.9	.48
Social Overhead	5.9	2.6	.44	1.9	.32
Government	23.1	14.7	.64	50.4	2.18
TVA	—	—	—	—	—

Note: The distribution category consists of the census classifications of wholesale trade and transportation/communication/public utilities. The corporate complex category consists of corporate headquarters, finance/insurance/real estate, and business services. Social overhead consists of medical and educational services. These categories were originally developed in T. Stanback, *Services, the New Economy* (Montclair, N.J.: Allanheld, Osmun, 1981).

The % column gives the percentage of employment in the geographic area in the various industrial categories: manufacturing, distribution, etc. The location quotient (LQ) for an industry in a local area is simply the ratio of the local area's percentage in that industry to the national percentage. Location quotients greater than 1 imply an area is relatively specialized in that industry. For example, the Memphis LQ of 1.33 for distribution implies that Memphis has 33% more employment in distribution than if its employment share in distribution was at the national average for cities the size of Memphis.

Source: R. Gilmer, A. Pulsipher, and R. Mack, "Job Creation in the Tennessee Valley: Part 2—Problems in the Service Sector," Working Paper, Tennessee Valley Authority, Chief Economist Staff.

distribution; Nashville is strong in education and health services. Knoxville, Chattanooga, and the Tri-Cities are manufacturing oriented; Clarksville is dominated by a large military base.

Economic differences among cities occur in all states, but Tennessee cities are separated psychologically because the large distances between cities place them in different media markets. Nashville's media, for example, give more coverage to events in southern Kentucky than to events in Memphis or Knoxville. The Memphis, Chattanooga, Tri-Cities, and Clarksville metropolitan areas all extend into surrounding states. Residents and businessmen in these border cities naturally have their attention drawn outward to the economies and politics of their neighbors rather than to the rest of the state of Tennessee. An interesting fact that symbolizes the state's geographic diversity is that the Tri-Cities are closer by air to portions of Canada than to Memphis.

Income and Growth Disparities

Another division in the state arises from the disparity among different areas of both the level and growth rate of average income. The major cities are close to or above the national average in per capita income.[4] In rural Tennessee, the situation is quite different. Ten rural counties (out of a total of ninety-five in the state) have per capita incomes less than one-half the national average, while an additional forty counties have per capita income between one-half and two-thirds the national average. Many of these rural counties are remote from interstate highways and urban amenities; they offer little to potential industry except low wages and hard workers.

Current growth patterns are accentuating these disparities between metropolitan and nonmetropolitan Tennessee, and between Nashville and the rest of the state. Table 9-2 shows employment growth rates for different areas in Tennessee since the 1979 business cycle peak. Nashville and the Tri-Cities have been booming; Knoxville and Memphis have enjoyed moderate growth; while Chattanooga and the nonmetropolitan areas have lagged behind the United States

Table 9-2. Percentage Growth in Nonagricultural Employment in U.S. and Local Areas in Tennessee, 1979–85

	% Growth
United States	8.8
Tennessee	4.7
Nashville Metropolitan Area	17.2
Tri-Cities Metropolitan Area	11.1
Memphis Metropolitan Area	6.1
Knoxville Metropolitan Area	5.7
Chattanooga Metropolitan Area	.8
Remainder of Tennessee	3.4

Source: Tennessee Department of Employment Security.

and the rest of Tennessee. As a result of slow employment growth, unemployment in fifty Tennessee counties (forty-four of which lie in nonmetropolitan areas) was above 10 percent in 1986, compared to a national average of 7.0 percent and a state average of 8 percent.

The Challenge to State Economic Policy

Tennessee's diversity makes it difficult to take unified state action on any issue, particularly if the action appears to favor one area of the state over another. In interviews for this study, regional resentments were frequently expressed. For example, one Memphis leader claimed that the state Department of Economic and Community Development steered industrial prospects away from Memphis:

> Memphis gets poor representation from the state. The last couple of commissioners [of ECD] have been from Middle Tennessee. The state's site reports to prospects always list percent black for old black Memphis, but you never see percent hillbilly listed for clean white Knoxville.

Several business and political leaders in Middle and West Tennessee expressed resentment at the perceived focus of the state-sponsored Tennessee Technology Foundation on the Oak Ridge-Knoxville "Technology Corridor" in East Tennessee. This regional division contrasts with North Carolina's successful approach to high technology, the Research Triangle project that began in the 1950s. According to one observer, Ezra Vogel, the key to the success of the Research Triangle was the unified effort of North Carolina business and political leaders.

> North Carolinians, with no single large urban area, centered their philanthropy on the state. . . . The great unifier was the University of North Carolina. In many states the elites were divided among several universities, but even after Duke University was built in the 1930s, those who aspired to state leadership, whether business, political, or academic, overwhelmingly went to the University of North Carolina. Most of the people active in the development of the Triangle . . . had studied there. . . . A student leader at the university, Luther Hodges, was to draw on these relationships when he became governor and helped launch the Research Triangle.[5]

Tennessee, with all its regional divisions, has no comparable unifier for the elite. The elite groups of Tennessee are split among Vanderbilt, The University of Tennessee, and out of state schools.

In addition to political problems, the several subeconomies within Tennessee make the development of an overall state economic policy a more complex task. The state would be foolish to promote only one particular industry given Tennessee's diversity. It is tempting to abandon any attempt at forging a unified economic policy. Some state policy, however, always will be implicit in the budgetary and regulatory actions taken by the state.

Tennessee Economic History

Tennessee's economic history continues to shape the state's present fortunes. Its agrarian background handicapped the state's industrial growth during the late nineteenth and early twentieth centuries, then helped lead to rapid growth in new manufacturing branch plants from World War II to the early 1970s. The subsequent slowdown of the Tennessee economy in the late 1970s and 1980s is partly attributable to the narrow base of this post-World War II boom. The agrarian tradition also continues to influence Tennessee politics and workplace relationships.

The Agricultural Legacy

Like much of the South, Tennessee was dominated by agriculture prior to the Civil War.[6] Almost no significant manufacturing industries existed in the state during this period, with the exception of some local market oriented industries (flour mills) and a few resource tied industries (iron). In 1860, the entire South had less manufacturing than either Pennsylvania, Massachusetts, or New York.

After the Civil War, agricultural dominance created problems for the southern economy. West Tennessee, like much of the rest of the South, was dominated by cotton, and prices were depressed for much of the latter part of the nineteenth century as world demand for cotton grew slowly and new cotton plantations were opened west of the Mississippi. For other agricultural products, Tennessee and the South faced tough competition from the Midwest.

The lack of a preexisting manufacturing base, in a nation with strong manufacturing centers in the Northeast, limited Tennessee's industrial development options in the post-Civil War period. Tennessee had neither the skilled labor pool nor the manufacturing infrastructure needed to compete effectively with the North in most industries. Tennessee had a comparative advantage only in industries that intensively used resources the South had in abundance, natural resources or unskilled labor. Manufacturing growth in Tennessee during the late nineteenth and early twentieth centuries, therefore, was concentrated in industries such as textiles, lumber, food processing, cottonseed products, and some iron and steel. Despite this growth, Tennessee's manufacturing share remained well below the national average. In 1899, the Tennessee ratio of manufacturing employment to population was 38 percent of the national average. By 1919, this ratio had increased but only to 49 percent of the national average.[7]

Furthermore, this limited industrial growth, which was concentrated in a few low-wage industries, was insufficient to increase Tennessee's per capita income relative to the U.S. average. Tennessee per capita income fell from 80 percent of the national average before the Civil War to around 55 percent of the national average after the war, where it stayed until the beginning of World War II.[8]

There are several explanations for the state's poverty and weak industrial sector during this period. The low-wage industries that located in the South did not advance job skills or encourage a supporting industrial infrastructure. Indeed, these industries had chosen the South because they did not require such skills or infrastructure. Also, continual advances in agricultural productivity helped expand the surplus of unskilled labor in the South, reinforcing the South's relative attractiveness to low-wage, labor intensive industries.

Tennessee's industrialization was vigorously promoted by state boosters. According to one Tennessee historian, "Scarcely had the noise of battle ceased in the Volunteer State when the urban press began a campaign for industry and 'economic carpetbaggers'. . . . Yankees who recently had laid waste to the South were forgiven if they would return with capital and industrial expertise."[9] In the 1920s and 1930s, this boosterism led to widespread subsidization of new industries in the South. For example, many small Tennessee communities provided free buildings to new industries, financed by deductions from employees' salaries.

The economic structures of Tennessee cities and regions that developed during this period persist in modified form to the present day. Memphis developed into a distribution and commercial center in the late nineteenth and early twentieth century, with manufacturing limited to cotton processing industries and lumber; today, Memphis remains a distribution center, particularly for food products. Nashville has always been a financial and publishing center, particularly religious publishing, due to its central location within the South. Today, Nashville maintains its strength in finance, printing and publishing, and in educational institutions founded by religious groups. Knoxville, Chattanooga, and East Tennessee were the earliest areas in Tennessee to develop significant manufacturing, and these areas today remain more manufacturing oriented than the rest of the state.

To some extent, the economic differences among Tennessee's regions today reflect a continuation of the comparative advantages that originally brought about these differences. Memphis, for example, is still a good location for distribution purposes. But these continued differences also show how an area's original economic base encourages economic growth of the same type. For example, Memphis business leaders, oriented towards distribution, have actively supported expansion of the city's transportation infrastructure; since World War II, Memphis's airport has been expanded aggressively.

The Post-World War II Industrialization

Tennessee began to show signs of significant economic progress relative to the rest of the United States during the 1930s and World War II. The creation of the Tennessee Valley Authority in 1933 helped attract electric intensive industries, such as aluminum, to the state. World War II increased the demand for electric intensive products, as well as for all types of labor. But the most dramatic progress took place after World War II, particularly in the 1960s and early 1970s.

Tennessee per capita income rose from 56 percent of the national average in 1939 to 67 percent in 1947 and to 82 percent by 1973, with two-thirds of this last increase taking place from 1962–73. Tennessee's share of nonagricultural U.S. employment also rose dramatically, from 1.55 percent in 1939 to 1.99 percent in 1973.[10] Most of this increase also took place during the 1960s and early 1970s.

Growth in income and employment was accompanied by structual shifts in the Tennessee econony. From a predominantly agricultural state, Tennessee became a predominantly manufacturing state. By 1973, Tennessee's manufacturing/population ratio was 32 percent greater than the national average. In 1947, this ratio had been 24 percent below the national average.

Much of the state's industrial growth took place in the South's traditional low-wage industries: textiles, apparel, leather goods, lumber, and furniture. Particularly after 1960, however, an increasing proportion of Tennessee's economic growth occurred in more sophisticated, higher-wage industries. Between 1959–73, sophisticated manufacturing in Tennessee had an annual growth rate of 10 percent, while low-wage industries grew at an annual rate of 4.7 percent.[11]

Most industrial growth in Tennessee has occurred in branch production facilities rather than headquarters or research facilities. A symbol of this trend is the General Motors decision in 1985 to locate its Saturn Company production facility in Tennessee but to keep Saturn engineering and administration in Michigan. As Table 9-1 showed, every metropolitan area in Tennessee is at least 10 percent below the national average in the proportion of employment in corporate headquarters and related activities.

In retrospect, there are plausible explanations for the post-World War II branch plant boom in Tennessee. Much U.S. manufacturing apparently reached a stage, after the war, in which its production technology became relatively standardized, requiring less skilled labor or close supervision by corporate headquarters. Construction of the interstate highway system and other advances that reduced transportation costs allowed manufacturers to locate outside the nation's existing industrial complexes. In addition, over the years, the South had developed a sufficient industrial infrastructure to support rapid growth in industry.

Given these economic factors, it was inevitable that, at some point, U.S. industry would move southward to utilize the region's cheaper labor. Most observers, however, could not have predicted beforehand the precise timing of this movement. It is not clear why the 1960s were the period of rapid growth rather than a decade or two earlier or later. If state policy makers in 1947 had sought to develop an economic strategy for Tennessee, they probably would not have received accurate intelligence from their economic advisors about the magnitude and timing of Tennessee's economic growth, although the general trend should have been clear.

Since 1973, Tennessee has continued its economic growth, but has slowed down to a rate no faster than that of the rest of the United States. Tennessee per capita income has hovered around 80 percent of the national average. Tennessee's share of nonagricultural employment has declined from 2 percent of the national total to around 1.9 percent. After dropping below the national average for most of the 1970s, Tennessee's unemployment rate has stayed above the nation's since 1979.[12]

The exact time this slowdown began is difficult to determine. A manufacturing dependent state such as Tennessee would be expected to experience a greater cyclical decline than the nation during the 1974–75 recession. Data indicate that, in 1976 and perhaps 1977, Tennessee was recovering normally from the recession, increasing income and reducing unemployment relative to the nation. But sometime between 1977–79, Tennessee's economy began slowing down relative to the national economy by all indicators. This occurred before the beginning of the 1980 recession and is part of a general slowdown in the East South Central states (Tennessee, Kentucky, Alabama, and Mississippi). The East South Central region in 1984 had the highest unemployment rate of the nine U.S. census regions, after ranking third lowest in 1976.[13] A later section of this chapter will discuss features of Tennessee's current economy that have contributed to this slowdown in growth.

The Continuing Rural Character of Tennessee

Today, Tennessee has a predominantly manufacturing economy rather than an agricultural economy. Agriculture is a smaller share of aggregate personal income in Tennessee (1.15 percent in 1983) than in the United States (1.75 percent).[14] But the state's culture is still strongly influenced by rural agricultural tradition.

The Tennessee rural tradition continues for several reasons. First, Tennessee agriculture is still an important source of jobs. Agricultural jobs were 6.3 percent of all Tennessee jobs in 1983, compared to 3.7 percent of all jobs in the U.S. economy as a whole.[15] Four out of five Tennessee farmers work part-time in farming, which is important as a source of extra or seasonal income.

Second, much of Tennessee's manufacturing growth has taken place in rural areas. In 1985, manufacturing employment in twenty-three of Tennessee's seventy-two nonmetropolitan counties was greater than one-third of total county employment. In the United States as a whole, manufacturing employment in 1985 was less than 20 percent of total employment.[16] Industries particularly attracted to Tennessee's rural areas include apparel, footwear, and auto parts. Rural manufacturing growth explains why Tennessee remains 40 percent rural in population, versus only 26 percent for the United States as a whole, even though Tennessee no longer specializes in agriculture.

Third, most of Tennessee's population is two generations or less removed from the farm. Thus, even the urban population of the state retains many rural attitudes and cultural patterns.

Rural tradition has important implications for Tennessee's politics and economy. Politically, Tennessee has a strong strain of rural conservatism: anti-big government, taxation, and regulation. Traditionally, Tennessee has not supported education strongly. Accompanying this conservatism is a rural populist tradition marked by suspicion of businessmen's ulterior motives. While low incomes and high unemployment have encouraged a friendly attitude towards new business, popular pressure against big subsidies for new business remains.

The state's rural tradition has its most important effect on attitudes towards work and employee-employer relationships. In an interview for this study, one executive who had managed plants in both the South and North made the following comments:

> The basic attitude towards work is different in the South. Workers in the North are not as flexible as workers in the South, even in a non-union plant. I attribute this to years of "fat living" in the North. The northern attitude is "you owe me a paycheck, and if I decide to work, that's my decision." ... It takes longer to get workers trained in the South. You also have to overcome some fears about machinery if all they've done is plucked chickens before. But once they're trained, our company figures that labor productivity is 15 percent greater in the South compared to the North.[17]

Another Tennessee plant manager made similar comments:

> In the Northeast there's a lot more argument about working too hard than there is in the South. I think this probably comes from the [South's] agrarian background. It's hard work ... to earn a living from the ground. And a lot of the industry that has been here has been sweatshop industry.

This rural tradition also affects employer-employee relationships. One business leader commented that "people in commercial leadership in the South feel more of a moral obligation to employees than in the Northeast."

Tennessee's Current Economy

Describing a complex state economy requires a variety of perspectives. This section of the study first examines the quantitative evidence on Tennessee's industrial strengths and weaknesses. The focus then turns to the strengths and weaknesses in Tennessee's economy that are perceived by Tennessee's leaders. Finally, the study uses shift-share analysis to analyze the causes of recent trends in Tennessee's economic growth and what they portend for the future.

The Structure of Tennessee's Economy

Table 9-3 shows the percentage of Tennessee personal income in 1983 in various industries. The U.S. shares are shown for comparison. For each industry, the table also shows the location quotient, or the ratio of the industry's share in Tennessee earnings to its share in the U.S. economy. Location quotients greater than 1 indicate that the industry is relatively concentrated in Tennessee; for example, the 2.78 figure for apparel indicates that Tennessee apparel earnings were 178 percent greater than if apparel had the same share in Tennessee as in the nation. Table 9-4 presents analogous statistics for relative Tennessee and U.S. employment in different industries.

These two tables lead to several conclusions about Tennessee's current economic structure. Tennessee manufacturing is concentrated largely in nondurable goods, with 77 percent greater income from this area than the national average. The University of Tennessee's Center for Business and Economic Research, however, projects that the Tennessee economy will become concentrated more in durable goods relative to the nation over the next ten years. This projection was made before GM's announcement of the Saturn plant.

Table 9-3. Distribution of Tennessee and U.S. Earnings Across Industries, and Tennessee Location Quotient for Each Industry, 1983

	% of U.S. Earnings in Industry	% of Tenn. Earnings in Industry	Tenn. Location Quotient
Agriculture	1.75	1.15	.66
Mining	1.66	.58	.35
Construction	5.30	4.78	.90
Manufacturing	23.78	29.07	1.22
Nondurables	8.94	15.81	1.77
Food	1.86	2.38	1.28
Textiles	.63	1.14	1.82
Apparel	.76	2.12	2.78
Paper	.95	1.32	1.39
Printing	1.46	1.51	1.03
Chemicals	1.71	5.00	2.93
Petroleum	.49	.09	.18
Tobacco	.12	.13	1.06
Rubber	.81	1.53	1.88
Leather	.15	.59	3.93
Durables	14.84	13.26	.89
Lumber	.66	.82	1.24
Furniture	.40	.98	2.45
Primary Metals	1.37	1.29	.94
Fabricated Metals	1.76	1.86	1.06
Nonelectrical Machinery	2.89	2.16	.75
Electrical Equipment	2.67	2.20	.82
Transportation Equipment (except cars)	1.68	.97	.58
Cars	1.38	.99	.72
Stone/Clay/Glass	.73	.94	1.29
Instruments	.95	.54	.57
Misc. Manufacturing	.36	.52	1.43
Transportation/Communication/Utilities	7.79	7.23	.93
Trucking and Warehousing	1.65	2.58	1.56
Utilities	1.52	.42	.28
All Other Transportation	4.62	4.23	.92
Wholesale Trade	6.69	6.95	1.04
Retail Trade	9.62	9.99	1.04
Finance/Insurance/Real Estate	6.39	5.23	.82
Services	20.08	18.64	.93
Business Services	3.53	2.54	.72
Health	6.93	7.78	1.12
Legal	1.63	1.41	.87
Educational	.97	.81	.83
Social	.58	.30	.52
Other Services	6.44	5.80	.97
Government	16.97	16.39	.97
Federal Civilian	3.86	4.99	1.29
Military	1.78	.86	.48
State and Local	11.34	10.53	.93

Source: U.S. Department of Commerce, Regional Economic Information System.

Table 9-4. Distribution of Tennessee and U.S. Employment Across Industries, and Tennessee Location Quotient for Each Industry, 1983

	% of U.S. Employment in Industry	% of Tenn. Employment in Industry	Tenn. Location Quotient
Agriculture	3.65	6.27	1.72
Mining	.89	.36	.40
Construction	3.67	3.29	.90
Manufacturing	17.25	22.45	1.30
Nondurables	7.21	12.61	1.75
Food	1.51	1.75	1.16
Textiles	.70	1.19	1.70
Apparel	1.09	3.08	2.82
Paper	.62	.80	1.30
Printing	1.22	1.26	1.03
Chemicals	.98	2.62	2.67
Petroleum	.18	.04	.20
Tobacco	.06	.08	1.27
Rubber	.67	1.08	1.61
Leather	.19	.72	3.76
Durables	10.04	9.84	.98
Lumber	.61	.83	1.36
Furniture	.42	1.03	2.46
Primary Metals	.78	.70	.89
Fabricated Metals	1.28	1.36	1.06
Nonelectrical Machinery	1.90	1.51	.79
Electrical Equipment	1.89	1.75	.93
Transportation Equipment (except cars)	.93	.54	.58
Cars	.70	.61	.88
Stone/Clay/Glass	.53	.61	1.14
Instruments	.65	.42	.64
Misc. Manufacturing	.35	.49	1.39
Transportation/Communication/Utilities	4.66	4.04	.87
Trucking and Warehousing	1.14	1.56	1.37
Utilities	.82	.22	.27
All Other Transportation	2.70	2.26	.84
Wholesale Trade	4.95	5.04	1.02
Retail Trade	14.64	13.46	.92
Finance/Insurance/Real Estate	5.27	3.96	.75
Services	19.75	17.18	.87
Business Services	3.32	2.44	.74
Health	5.62	5.34	.95
Legal	.57	.31	.55
Educational	1.24	.96	.77
Social	1.08	.54	.50
Other Services	7.92	7.59	.96
Government	17.50	16.20	.93
Federal Civilian	2.76	3.05	1.10
Military	2.48	1.46	.59
State and Local	12.26	11.70	.95
Nonfarm Proprietors	7.22	7.41	1.03

Source: U.S. Department of Commerce, Regional Economic Information System.

The Tennessee economy continues to be strong in apparel, textiles, and related industries. The table tends to understate this concentration. Much of the Tennessee chemical industry involves the production of synthetic fibers. The apparel industry, while fifth among manufacturing industries in earnings, is the leading industry in employment; this difference arises from the relatively low wages in the apparel industry. Tennessee also continues to be relatively concentrated in other traditional low-wage industries, such as leather goods, lumber, and furniture.

The Tennessee economy is relatively underdeveloped in business services (consulting, computer software, engineering services, etc.) and, to a lesser extent, in financial services.[18] As discussed later in this chapter, such underdevelopment is probably caused by Tennessee's relatively low share of corporate headquarters.

As mentioned earlier, even though agriculture is less important as a source of income in Tennessee than in the United States, agriculture is more important in Tennessee as a source of jobs.

Although Tables 9-3 and 9-4 are revealing, the use of relatively aggregated industrial categories is misleading in several respects.[19] First, the Tennessee economy is tied to the auto industry more than is apparent in the tables. Much of Tennessee's rubber industry produces tires. Tennessee also employs significant numbers in auto glass production, classified in the stone/clay/glass industry, and in producing auto filters and carburetors in the nonelectrical machinery industry.

Second, the Tennessee economy is tied more to construction than the tables indicate. A third of the Tennessee electrical equipment industry produces household appliances, a greater proportion than the national average, and appliance purchases rise when more new homes are being constructed. Forty percent of the Tennessee fabricated metals industry produces structural components for buildings. And many of TVA's employees are in construction, although they are classified under federal civilian employment.

Third, the location quotient just above one for wholesale trade for the entire state does not show Memphis' specialization in wholesale trade, particularly wholesale trade of farm products.

Finally, the tables show that Tennessee's overall government share is near the national average. But this average reflects Tennessee's greater than average share in the federal civilian sector due to TVA and a considerably smaller share of the military.

Perceived Economic Strengths

In interviews, Tennessee business and political leaders perceived a number of factors that contributed to the state's economic development strengths. These perceptions may not be completely accurate. But discussing perceptions is helpful because it allows a consideration of economic factors that, while difficult to quantify, may nonetheless be real. Furthermore, in economic development, perceptions are often as important as reality.

Greater Work Ethic and Lower Unionization. Almost all Tennessee leaders feel that the work ethic of the Tennessee labor force and the state's traditional employer-employee relations are major advantages in attracting new industry. This work ethic can be put either in a positive or negative light. Some contend that southern workers are less lazy than northern workers. Others claim that the strong work ethic makes poor rural Southerners more vulnerable to exploitation. Both views are stereotypes that are partly true in some circumstances.

Although the rural southern work ethic attracts business above and beyond low unionization, the two are linked culturally. The same worker attitudes that lead to flexibility in responding to management also lead to less enthusiasm for unionization. According to several corporate managers, Tennessee's lower unionization is a significant attraction for new branch plants. This finding from this study's interviews is confirmed by a recent University of Tennessee survey of new plants that chose a Tennessee site. "Less union influence" and "right to work laws" were the second and third most frequently mentioned "essential factors" (of twenty-one possible factors) in a plant's decision about the general region in which to locate.[20]

Tennessee is not especially nonunionized compared to some other southern states. Manufacturing was 15.8 percent unionized in Tennessee in 1984, compared to a national average of 21 percent.[21] A company for which unionization was a prime location factor would prefer North Carolina (5 percent unionized), South Carolina (3.8 percent), or Mississippi (8.7 percent). Tennessee, however, is less unionized than Kentucky (27 percent) or Alabama (20.1 percent) and is comparable to Georgia or Arkansas. Furthermore, business leaders feel that Tennessee's right to work law makes unions easier to live with. As one plant manager said, "With right to work, we're unionized but the union has less than half the workers as members. The threat of being thrown out makes the union more reasonable."

An important question is whether Tennessee's work ethic encourages the growth of technologically sophisticated industries, not just low-wage, labor-intensive industries. For example, can the southern work ethic replicate Japan's much publicized labor-management cooperation? Governor Alexander and other state officials often mention cultural similarities between Tennessee and Japan as a key to Tennessee's attractiveness to Japanese firms. This argument appears farfetched, yet Tennessee leaders point to similar attitudes toward work and workplace relationships in two societies with strong traditional rural cultures.

Tennessee's work ethic and lower unionization has apparently been important to Federal Express, headquartered in Memphis and a leader in the rapidly changing small packages air freight industry. According to Robert Sigafoos,

> The Protestant work ethic prevails in the Bible Belt Locale [Memphis] where about half of the company's 13,000 employees reside. Their daily work philosophy coincides perfectly with that expressed by Fred Smith [founder of Federal Express]. . . . Smith would not have succeeded if Federal Express's headquarters initially had been located in New York, or Cleveland, or Pittsburgh, or Philadelphia, or Los Angeles. [Federal Express] management is convinced that if the

company is to maintain its competitive lead, it must demand greater employee efficiency. . . . Flexibility is needed in order to survive. [This] would be seriously impeded if the unions got control.[22]

Low Wages. Although the wage gap between Tennessee and the rest of the United States has narrowed somewhat in recent years, in 1984, average manufacturing wages in Tennessee were still 15 percent below the national average.[23] Statistics on average wages can be misleading, since they do not control for differences in labor productivity among the states, but, as discussed earlier, Tennessee's lower wages may be accompanied by higher productivity in some types of labor.

Central Location. State and local officials in Tennessee publicize the state's central location, with easy access to markets in the South, Midwest, and East. Nashville economic developers, for example, hand out maps with concentric circles showing that 50 percent of the U.S. population lies within 600 miles of Nashville.

Tennessee clearly has some market access advantages over states such as Minnesota, Maine, or Texas. Market access alone, however, cannot explain why a plant might choose Tennessee over other similarly situated states. One plant location decision maker said that his company considered sites within a 200 mile radius of Nashville, the geographic center of the company's customers. This circle of sites included parts of Indiana, Illinois, Kentucky, Ohio, Georgia, Alabama, Mississippi, Arkansas, and Missouri.

Good Transportation Network. Tennessee's good transportation network complements its central location. A number of major interstate highways crisscross the state. Memphis is a regional hub for several airlines, the national hub for Federal Express, and has good access to rail, road, and river transportation. Nashville became a regional hub for American Airlines in early 1986, and many Nashville business leaders believe that this will have a major effect on the city's economic growth.

Tennessee's transportation network should be further strengthened by the major road construction program proposed by Governor Alexander and passed by the legislature in early 1986. Chapter 10 discusses this program further.

Technical Talent at Oak Ridge. Due to the Oak Ridge National Laboratory and the University of Tennessee's nearby main campus at Knoxville, the Oak Ridge/Knoxville area has over 2000 residents with Ph.D.s, almost 5000 engineers, and 1200 computer-related personnel. Historically, the National Laboratory's research effort has focused on nuclear energy, hardly a growth area in the U.S. economy today. But the Oak Ridge/Knoxville area has strengths in other research areas, many of which are spin-offs from nuclear energy research. Research on building safer nuclear reactors at Oak Ridge attracted and trained experts on instruments to detect impurities in materials. Other research strengths at Oak Ridge are computer software and high temperature materials, and plant tissue culture at UT-Knoxville. Later sections of this report discuss Tennessee's efforts to promote economic growth using this research base.

Entrepreneurial Climate of Nashville. The Nashville metropolitan area is by far the most rapidly growing area in Tennessee. A number of Tennessee leaders observed that Nashville has a good "entrepreneurial climate," in contrast with the rest of the state. According to one business leader from East Tennessee, "We would have had the equivalent of a Silicon Valley in Tennessee if Oak Ridge had been located near Nashville."

Interviews for this study revealed several possible explanations for Nashville's greater entrepreneurial climate. First, historically, Nashville has been strong in a number of industries that are dominated by small businesses, such as printing and music. This small business concentration makes Nashville banks somewhat more familiar with small business problems and more aggressive in their lending practices.

Second, Nashville is the wealthiest area of the state. More capital is available in Nashville for speculative investments.

Third, Nashville has a greater number of entrepreneurial role models. The success of one entrepreneur or venture capitalist leads to attempts by others and greater interest in entrepreneurial activities by potential investors. One such role model in Nashville is Jack Massey, a venture capitalist who helped start Kentucky Fried Chicken, Hospital Corporation of America, and the Winner's Corporation.

Finally, cultural attitudes toward entrepreneurship are more favorable in Nashville. According to one Middle Tennessee business leader,

> Middle Tennessee is a very entrepreneurial area. East Tennessee natives are a very conservative lot of people. The out of staters at Oak Ridge and TVA don't seem to change it. Memphis is not entrepreneurial either, perhaps because historically it has depended on cotton. . . . A plantation economy doesn't lead to entrepreneurship.

Business Climate. Business and political leaders frequently mentioned a friendly attitude toward business by the state government as a state strength.

Perceived Economic Problems

Tennessee political and business leaders also perceive a number of problems within the Tennessee economy. It should be noted that even a mistaken perception can be a problem for industrial recruitment and economic development.

Foreign Competition and Tennessee's Low-Wage Unskilled Industries. Almost all Tennessee leaders agree that foreign competition is damaging low-wage Tennessee industries, such as footwear, textiles, and apparel. According to one executive in an unskilled labor intensive industry, "We just can't offset relationships of 5 or 10 to 1 in labor rates [between the United States and foreign countries] in our type of industry."

Table 9-5 shows TVA statistics on industry trends in the Tennessee Valley region. The TVA region includes all ninety-five counties of Tennessee plus seventy-five counties in surrounding states, so trends in Tennessee and those in the

Table 9-5. Sources of New Manufacturing Jobs in the Tennessee Valley: Historical Trends and Predictions

Time Period	Total Manufacturing	Low Wage	High Tech	Construction Sensitive	Electricity Sensitive
1960–69	26,823	8,509	9,803	7,900	4,004
1969–73	23,495	8,478	8,332	7,190	−828
1973–79	6,115	−3,290	5,167	2,992	610
1979–98 (predicted)	4,699	60	2,255	308	−123

Note: All figures are in jobs per year. Low-wage industry includes apparel, textiles, lumber, furniture, and leather; high tech industry includes instruments, electrical and nonelectrical machinery, rubber and plastics, and chemicals; construction sensitive industry is lumber, furniture, and stone/clay/glass; electricity sensitive industry is chemicals and primary metals. Because of overlapping definitions and omitted industries, the total of listed industrial categories does not equal total manufacturing.

Source: Tennessee Valley Authority, Chief Economist Staff, *Economic Outlook,* July 1984, Table 16, page 57.

TVA region will be quite similar. According to these figures, between 1969–73 and 1973–79, growth in low-wage industry jobs dropped from 8478 per year to −3290. This 11,768 drop in jobs created per year explained two-thirds of the total drop in manufacturing jobs created between the 1973–79 and 1969–73 periods.

In the future, low-wage industries in Tennessee are likely to face continued problems, given the availability of unskilled labor in developing countries and the growth of world trade. The most optimistic forecasts for low-wage industries in Tennessee are those by TVA economists, who believe that the "benefits of [high technology] will be spread [to] low-wage industries such as apparel and textiles," thus increasing the competitiveness of U.S. locations.[24] But even TVA's optimistic forecast is that low-wage employment in Tennessee will stay at the same level for the next fifteen years. If these technological improvements do not occur, these industries could decline drastically in Tennessee. The likely decline or stagnation of low-wage industries need not pose a severe problem for Tennessee, if a sufficient number of jobs in other industries can be created and if workers and communities dependent on low-wage industries can adjust to economic change.

Perceptions of a Poor Tennessee Educational System. Virtually all Tennessee leaders mentioned the quality of the Tennessee educational system as an economic development problem. According to one private sector leader, "Our major drawback is we have a very undereducated work force. It's both a black and white problem, although anti-intellectualism is probably more of a problem in [predominantly white] East Tennessee than in West Tennessee." According to a current state official, "a lot of our communities just can't support a very sophisticated plant."

In contrast, interviews indicated that executives who had located new plants in Tennessee did not perceive education to be a problem. This view is confirmed in the recent University of Tennessee survey of new Tennessee plants. The quality of local schools was the eighteenth most considered factor (out of thirty-three factors) in choosing the final site. These findings do not necessarily contradict the views of state leaders. Interviews indicate that Tennessee currently attracts plants with low educational requirements. Education may still be a problem if state leaders wish to attract more sophisticated industry.

The perceived problems in Tennessee education extend to the state university system as well as to primary and secondary schools. According to one former state official, "UT has been a real problem in exploiting the research advantage we have at Oak Ridge, although some positive changes may now be taking place."

Hillbilly Image. Many state officials felt that the state's national image hampers industrial recruitment. One state official said, "[Northerners] think of Tennessee as hillbillies and country music. They think Tennessee must be the pits."

The image problem has two components. First, the hillbilly image exaggerates concerns about the availability of skilled labor. "Finding a skilled labor force can sometimes be a genuine problem in Tennessee, but it's not nearly as bad as the image," said one state official.

Second, the hillbilly image leads to concerns about the quality of life in Tennessee. According to one northeastern company that decided against locating in Nashville,

> The country-western image of the city was not appealing to [Easterners] and was hard to overcome. . . . Employees would probably not have believed an audio-visual presentation or a brochure on the superior qualities of Nashville, and it was simply not possible to have all employees visit the city to experience the same positive reaction as that experienced by the visiting [site selection] team.

Increasing Industrial Energy Prices. At one time, TVA provided low-cost energy that attracted electricity intensive industries. TVA industrial electricity is no longer particularly cheap relative to the rest of the United States. This change occurred because regional demand for energy outgrew the supply of cheap hydro power. Ninety percent of TVA power now comes from coal or nuclear energy. Furthermore, the legislation that created TVA requires that the cost advantages of hydropower generation go to residential consumers.

As a result, many of the electricity intensive plants in Tennessee have become "swing plants," operating only when the economy is strong enough to make electricity prices cost effective. According to TVA, many of Tennessee's aluminum facilities now "open only when [aluminum] prices are high and close when economic conditions are poor."[25]

Relative Weakness in Regional or National Corporate Headquarters. Recent TVA research suggests that Tennessee's underdevelopment in the business service and financial service industries is due to the small presence of corporate headquarters in the state.[26] This underdevelopment of business and financial services is worrisome, because over one-third of new U.S. jobs between 1979–84 were generated by these industries.

Tennessee's low proportion of business services cannot be explained by the state's lack of large cities, in which corporate headquarters and business and financial services tend to locate. As shown in Table 9-1, when compared to U.S. cities of similar size, Tennessee cities are weak in what TVA calls "corporate complex" activities: headquarters operations and business and financial services.

Reliance on Interest Sensitive, Cyclical Industries. Tennessee is already more sensitive than the nation to business cycles and high interest rates due to the concentration of manufacturing, particularly construction related and auto related industries, in the state. The 1984 *Economic Report to the Governor,* by the University of Tennessee's Center for Business and Economic Research, predicted that Tennessee will become more concentrated in durable goods manufacturing over the next decade and expressed concern over this increasing vulnerability to economic cycles.[27]

Perceived Lack of Venture Capital and Support for Entrepreneurs. Opinion widely differs over the availability of venture capital in Tennessee. Bankers and venture capitalists, particularly in Middle Tennessee, believe plenty of venture capital is available for sound ideas. Political and business leaders in East and West Tennessee perceive greater problems with venture capital, particularly seed capital for initial start ups. Many of these same observers, however, feel that an even greater problem is the inability of most entrepreneurs to formulate a good business plan.

The Tennessee Tax Structure: Strength or Problem?

Tennessee's overall tax burden is relatively low. According to the U.S. Advisory Commission on Intergovernmental Relations, Tennessee's state and local governments collect 15 percent less in total tax revenue than would be collected with the "average" state's tax rates.[28] Tennessee has no personal income tax, which distinguishes the state from its neighbors, all of which have a personal income tax.

Tennessee taxes on business income property, while slightly lower than the national average, are above those of most of its southern neighbors. ACIR figures indicate that Tennessee corporate income taxes are 7 percent below the national average, compared with 15 percent below for Arkansas, 24 percent below for North Carolina and Kentucky, 29 percent below for Alabama, 35 percent below for Mississippi, and 42 percent below for Virginians.[29]

Tennessee officially sets the assessment to market value ratio higher for business property than for residential property. Business property tax rates average about 1.1 percent of the market value of real property, which is slightly above rates in Virginia and Arkansas, 50 percent higher than North Carolina's, and about twice rates in Georgia, Alabama, and Mississippi.[30]

This Tennessee tax structure is not attractive to capital intensive industries compared to that of other southern states. In some cases, such as Nissan and the Saturn plant, local governments provide property tax abatements to capital intensive companies. The lack of a personal income tax, however, may help attract high tech industries that need to attract engineers and other professionals.

Because most high tech industries are not capital intensive, they are less concerned about taxes on property or profits.

One consequence of the absence of a personal income tax is a high sales tax. As of 1987, the sales tax rate in most Tennessee jurisdictions was 7.75 percent, one of the highest rates in the country. Because the sales tax exempts many services, the sales tax base has tended to grow slowly as the U.S. economy becomes more service oriented, resulting in frequent pressure to raise tax rates to keep pace with increasing public service demands. Tax reform efforts have been blocked by the reluctance of political leaders to consider a state personal income tax.

In sum, while Tennessee's low personal taxes and low overall taxes may attract some industries, higher taxes on capital and the uncertain nature of the state's future tax system presents problems for Tennessee's economic development.

A Shift-Share Analysis of Tennessee's Economy

To further analyze Tennessee's economic problems and to explore why Tennessee's relative growth halted in the 1970s, a shift-share analysis of Tennessee's economy was performed for three time periods: 1959–73, 1973–79, and 1979–83.

Shift-share analysis divides economic growth in a region into three components: a portion that would occur if the region had the same mix of industries as the national average and those industries all grew at the average national rate; a portion due to the region's different mix or share of high and low growth industries from the national average (the "share" component); a portion due to differences between the regional growth rate for industries and the national growth rate for these industries (the "competitive shift" component). This division is purely algebraic in nature and cannot prove causation. The analysis in this study uses real personal earnings as the measure of economic activity, because a longer time series is available for industry data on personal earnings than for industry data on employment. Table 9-6 presents a summary of these three components for the three time periods. Several conclusions can be reached from this table.

Table 9-6. Decomposition of Tennessee Real Earnings Growth into National Component, Share Component, and Shift Component

	Average Tenn. Growth per Year	Growth if Identical to U.S.	"Share" Effect	"Shift" Effect	Total Tenn. Effect
1959–73	480	367	−3	116	113
1973–79	393	322	−22	92	70
1979–83	−61	7	−16	−53	−69

Note: All figures are in millions of 1972 dollars and are averages per year of the change between the beginning and end of each time period.

Source of Personal Earnings Data: U.S. Department of Commerce, Regional Economic Information System. Deflator used is the consumption price deflator used in calculating the real consumption portion of GNP. The source for this deflator is the *1985 Economic Report of the President* (Washington, D.C.: Government Printing Office; 1985).

First, a majority of the changes in Tennessee growth can be attributed to national growth trends, particularly in the recent recession. Of the $87 million decline in annual Tennessee real income growth between 1959–73 and 1973–79, $45 million can be attributed to a decline in national growth. Of the $454 million decline in annual Tennessee growth between 1973–79 and 1979–83, $305 million can be attributed to a decline in national growth.

Second, Tennessee's industry mix generally has been unfavorable relative to the nation in all three time periods (the state has above average shares of national low growth industries and below average shares of high growth industries). The magnitude of this "share" effect, however, has never been large relative to other factors.

Third, the growth of Tennessee relative to the nation was extremely strong in the 1959–73 period. All of this relative growth advantage was due to industries growing faster in Tennessee than in the nation.

Fourth, significant declines occurred in both the latter two time periods in this Tennessee growth advantage relative to the nation. Tennessee's relative growth declined by $43 million per year between 1959–73 and 1973–79, and by $139 million per year between 1973–79 and 1979–83. Over this last four year period, real earnings in Tennessee declined significantly, while remaining virtually unchanged in the nation.

Fifth, half of the 1973–79 decline in Tennessee relative growth was due to increasing problems with Tennessee's mix of industries (the "share" effect); the other half was due to a decline in the relative growth rate of industries in Tennessee versus the United States (the "shift" effect). In dollars, of the total $43 million decline, $19 million can be attributed to the share effect, $24 million to the shift effect.

Sixth, the relative Tennessee decline in the 1979–83 period can be attributed totally to a decline in industry growth rates in Tennessee relative to the nation. The industry mix of Tennessee actually became a smaller problem; the "share" effect, however, declined dramatically.

To analyze the reasons for these changes in the "share" effect and "shift" effect, Table 9-7 presents a condensed version of the complete shift-share analysis. The thirty-three industries actually used in the analysis are condensed into ten easier to interpret categories. The following are the principal conclusions from this table.

First, the generally unfavorable industry mix is due primarily to an above average share of slow growing low-wage manufacturing and a below average share of the fast growing business services sector.

Second, the 1973–79 decline in Tennessee industry relative growth was concentrated totally in the private sector. The decline occurred across a very wide range of industries, but was particularly pronounced in higher-wage manufacturing. Increases in federal civilian earnings (mostly TVA construction projects) and state and local government tended to mask the magnitude of the private sector slowdown.

Third, the more recent slowdown in Tennessee's relative growth is due mostly to the government sector. Cutbacks in the federal civilian sector (TVA

Table 9-7. Analysis of Contribution of Various Economic Sectors to Tennessee's Share and Shift Components

Economic Sector	Tennessee Above (+) or Below (−) Average in Share	Share Effect			Shift Effect		
		1959-73	1973-79	1979-83	1959-73	1973-79	1979-83
Private Sector	(−)	−3	−29	−10	114	22	4
Agriculture and Mining	(−)	3	2	12	−23	−5	−18
Manufacturing	(+)	−5	−26	−2	88	15	34
Low-wage	(+)	−8	−21	−14	21	−4	6
Other	(−)	3	−5	12	67	19	28
Services and Trade	(−)	−1	−4	−21	31	−1	0
Business Services	(−)	−1	−4	−13	0	−5	4
Banking	(−)	0	0	−1	2	0	−3
Other Services and Trade	(0)	0	0	−7	29	4	−1
Other Private Sectors	(−)	0	−1	2	18	13	−13
Government	(0)	0	7	−6	2	70	−57
Federal Civilian	(+)	0	−1	1	4	41	−29
Federal Military	(−)	1	7	−6	−6	2	−3
State and Local	(0)	−1	1	−1	4	27	−25
Total		−3	−22	−16	116	92	−53

Note: Share effect for each industry is defined as Tennessee Specialization Differential times (Industry U.S. Growth Rate − Average U.S. Growth Rate). Tennessee specialization differential equals Tennessee real earnings in the industry minus hypothetical real earnings if Tennessee had same share as nation. Hence, share effect is positive if (1) Tennessee has more of industry than average and industry grows faster than average, or (2) Tennessee has less of industry than average and industry grows slower than average and is negative otherwise. This method of defining the share effect is a correction of a method used by Edgar Dunn (Appendix G in vol. I of *The Development of the U.S. Urban System*, Baltimore: Johns Hopkins Press, 1980). It differs from the usual industry share effect, which is defined as Tennessee Real Earnings times (Industry U.S. Growth Rate − Average U.S. Growth Rate). However, both methods add to same total share effect for all industries. The method used here essentially answers the question: How would Tennessee growth have changed if this industry had the same share as the nation, with the Tennessee differential going into an industry with an average growth rate? The usual method answers the question: What would have happened if the industry disappeared for Tennessee and was replaced with an average growth rate industry?

The shift effect used here is simply the usual shift effect: Tennessee Earnings in Industry times (Industry Growth Rate in Tennessee − Industry Growth Rate in U.S.). It answers the question: What difference would it have made if Tennessee had grown at the national average in the industry?

Low-wage manufacturing industries are defined as apparel, textiles, lumber, furniture, and leather.

cancellations of nuclear power plant projects) and state and local government cutbacks have been particularly significant. The manufacturing sector actually improved its performance relative to the nation over that of the 1973–79 period, although it did not approach the performance of the 1959–73 period.

Fourth, both the low-wage manufacturing sector and business services have become greater problems over time. Tennessee's concentration in low-wage manufacturing has become more troublesome as the national growth rate of this sector has deteriorated relative to the average for all industries. Furthermore, after the 1959–73 period, Tennessee growth rates in low-wage manufacturing did not deviate significantly from the national averages in these industries. Tennessee's weakness in business services has become a greater problem, as this industry's growth rate has increased relative to the average for all industries. As mentioned earlier, the weakness in business services is probably caused by the small number of corporate headquarters in Tennessee.

These findings imply that Tennessee will improve its economic performance relative to the nation in the late 1980s and 1990s. Future TVA cutbacks are unlikely to be as large as those of 1979–83, and the state and local government sector will probably stabilize. If manufacturing continues its current strength relative to the nation, other private sector activities, mostly dependent on local demand, also should improve their relative performance from current levels. Relative private sector growth should be above that of the 1970s, while relative government growth would probably be less than that of the 1970s.

The most obvious problem areas are low-wage manufacturing and business services. If low-wage manufacturing declines drastically in the United States, Tennessee probably will not escape the trend. Furthermore, while business and financial services are growing in Tennessee, they are not growing any faster than the rest of the United States. A significant increase in Tennessee's share probably requires the attraction of more corporate headquarters.

The biggest uncertainty in this outlook is Tennessee manufacturing growth relative to the nation. This analysis does not clarify why Tennessee's relative manufacturing growth slowed down in 1973–79 and then improved in 1979–83. Until we understand better the causes of these changing trends, any predictions must be uncertain.

10

Recruitment and Fundamentals: A Description of Tennessee's Economic Development Policies

This chapter describes Tennessee's current approach to economic development policy. The chapter first gives an overall view of Tennessee's policy of "recruitment and fundamentals." The next two sections consider Tennessee programs that are specifically targeted at economic development (such as industrial recruitment), and Tennessee programs that promote economic development by improving services such as schools. Finally, the chapter analyzes the role of various decision makers and interest groups in determining state economic development policy.

Many of Tennessee's current economic development policies reflect the approach of Governor Lamar Alexander, a Republican who served from 1979–87. Governor Ned McWherter, a Democrat, was elected in 1986, but as of early 1987, it was not yet clear what changes McWherter would make in the state's economic development policies. But, as will be made clear in later discussion, the state's political tradition suggests that any changes will be gradual rather than sudden.

Informal Economic Strategy

Like most states, Tennessee has no formal economic development strategy, in the sense that there is no formal process that leads to the adoption of a written, explicit strategy. Tennessee does have an implicit strategy with two components: recruitment and improving basic public services.

Tennessee's recruitment strategy aims to attract manufacturing branch plants, headquarters, and distribution facilities. Tennessee does not aim its recruitment efforts at particular industries and does not try to encourage companies to locate in particular geographic areas. Over half of the state's $7 million annual budget for economic development goes to industrial recruitment.[31] Other Tennessee economic development programs promote high technology, small and existing business, and exports, but these relatively new initiatives lose out in both budget and political attention to the recruitment of new industry.

This branch plant strategy has been accompanied by Governor Alexander's personal strategy of focusing on a few fundamentals. Alexander believed the key fundamentals were improvements in basic public infrastructure: "My plan for addressing the needs has been better schools, better roads, clean water, healthy children, and a competitive environment." While branch plants were important in his view, improving the overall environment for all types of business was more important. Recruiting branch plants was important in affirming what Alexander called a "national verdict" that Tennessee has a good economic environment. Thus, in Alexander's view, most of his major new initiatives (the Better Schools program, the Safe Growth effort, the 1986 proposal for road improvements) were really economic development programs of the most important kind. The proposal and coordinating of these programs stemmed from Alexander's own personal vision rather than a formal planning process.

There are several reasons why Tennessee's economic development strategy is implicit and informally developed rather than explicit and formally developed. First, during the Alexander administration, the governor preferred his personal, intuitive plans for state development to a formal planning process, according to several observers close to him.

Second, a more explicit policy might arouse intrastate rivalries. According to one local official, "The state has to be extremely sensitive to competition among the cities."

Third, given the state's diversity, an overall economic development strategy for Tennessee may not be feasible, according to some state officials. These officials argue that economic development strategies are more feasible at the community level.

Fourth, the State Planning Office is relatively weak. The office recently has had two primary activities: running a state data center and organizing "Homecoming '86," a community heritage celebration.

Fifth, the Research Division of the state Department of Economic and Community Development (ECD) has neither the charter nor the resources to do long-range planning. This office currently focuses on research support for industrial recruitment: information packets for prospects, lists of possible prospects to contact, etc.

Finally, the Industrial and Agricultural Development Commission, which is supposed to oversee ECD, plays a passive role. The commission includes the governor, the speakers of the state house and senate, and twelve other members.

According to one observer, "The commission just receives reports and approves the ECD budget."

There are additional reasons why the state's explicit economic development efforts have focused on "smokestack chasing." One reason involves the political benefits of this strategy. According to one state official, "ECD is the department which makes the governor look good."

A second reason is that recruiting new branch plants is a relatively straightforward activity compared to other economic development policies. State officials are more uncertain about how to help small business or existing business. Programs with these goals are relatively new all over the United States, involve a large universe of potential clients, and offer less tangible measures of success. While it is easy to recommend that a state should broaden its economic development efforts beyond branch plant recruitment, it is not clear that we currently understand how the government can assist other forms of economic development. There is merit in focusing on goals that one can accomplish, as Tennessee focuses on recruiting new branch plants.

Formal Economic Development Programs

Most of the state's formal economic development programs are coordinated within the Department of Economic and Community Development (ECD), and so this section focuses on ECD. In addition to industrial recruitment, ECD provides services to existing business, helps local communities with economic development, and along with the Tennessee Technology Foundation, helps promote high technology.

History and Organization of ECD

Tennessee state economic development efforts began in 1945 with the establishment of an Industrial Development Division of the State Planning Commission. In subsequent years, the economic development function was shuffled among various departments and state offices. In 1972, the present Department of Economic and Community Development (ECD) was established. Although ECD's primary development efforts are directed at industrial recruitment, ECD was in part established to broaden the state's economic development efforts beyond industrial recruiting. Figure 10-1 shows an organizational chart of ECD. The Energy Office and the Office of Local Planning Assistance are not as closely related as the other offices to economic development, and will not be considered further in this chapter.

Industrial Recruitment

Tennessee's techniques for recruiting new branch plants are similar to those used by most states. First, the state advertises in national and international media such as the *Wall Street Journal* and *Business Week*. The goal of this

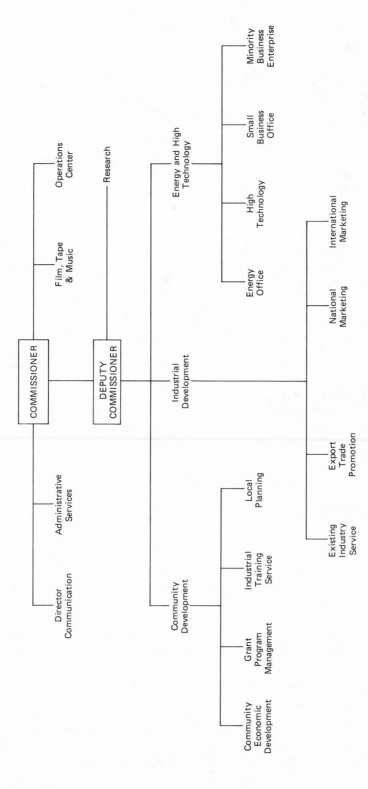

Figure 10-1. Organizational Chart, Tennessee Department of Economic & Community Development

advertising is to create a favorable image of Tennessee for corporate officials making location decisions. The state spends about one-half million dollars a year on advertising, about average for a state its size.

Second, state officials make frequent recruiting trips to cities in the United States and overseas. Twelve to fourteen national trips and eight to ten international trips are made per year. Following the Saturn plant announcement, ECD officials announced plans to significantly step up the volume of recruiting trips over the next few years. On most national trips, state officials attempt to make about seventy-five calls on corporations headquartered in the city visited.

Third, companies that plan to open a new plant (industrial prospects) are provided with information on Tennessee and on possible Tennessee sites. Officials provide a prospect with information on about ten to fifteen possible sites in Tennessee, and the prospect, if interested, will narrow the list down to five to seven sites. The state's goal is to get prospects to visit Tennessee. "If the prospect visits the state, we figure we have a 1 in 3 chance of getting him," said one ECD official.

Fourth, if needed, the governor will personally contact the chief corporate officials of companies considering Tennessee.

One difference between the recruiting efforts of Tennessee and other states is that the state does not maintain any overseas offices, not even in Japan, where Tennessee's overseas recruiting efforts have been most successful. In the past state officials considered opening overseas offices but decided these offices would be too expensive and ineffective.

Perhaps the most important difference in recruitment efforts between Tennessee and other states is that Tennessee avoids heavy subsidies for new plants, particularly subsidies provided with state money. The state offers no special corporate tax breaks for new plants; no state funded loan programs, loan guarantees, or interest subsidies; no free land or buildings. Local governments usually are not encouraged by state law or policy to provide property tax abatements. According to one state official, "If a company wants super tax breaks, we suggest they might want to go down to Mississippi or Alabama."

The two state funded subsidies that do exist are Industrial Training Service (ITS) funds and the provision of access roads. ITS pays for short-term (about six weeks average) training of Tennesseans employed in new plants, and sometimes for significant plant expansions. State vocational-technical schools usually provide much of the training; company supervisors sometimes may do some training (in which case the company is reimbursed by the state), or ITS itself may provide training. Training expenditures average about $300 per trainee. ITS is essentially a politically acceptable vehicle for providing small grants to new branch plants, with the grants tied to the number of Tennesseans employed. ITS tries to target its assistance to new branch plants that offer higher-wage jobs. The annual ITS budget varies from $1.5–4 million. Each year, ITS assists about thirty to fifty new branches and twenty to thirty expansions, with about 8000 Tennesseans receiving training.

Industrial training programs by now have become almost universal among states. Tennessee is similar to other southern states in having few strings attached to the ITS program in terms of eligibility for the training and the type of training and in providing full funding for training. Some northern states provide only a partial share of training costs and have more requirements attached.

The provision of industrial access roads, connecting major new plants with nearby interstates, is also a common practice of state governments. The two most prominent examples in Tennessee are the Nissan and Saturn plants; in both cases the state provided access roads that cost millions of dollars to construct. Whether this should be viewed as a "subsidy" is questionable. The access roads can be considered part of the standard package of public services that corporations receive for their taxes. It is not clear, however, that smaller companies receive the same level of pub..c services; while smaller companies get roads, they do not get new road networks tailored specifically to their site requirements.

Other Tennessee subsidies are funded by the federal government and local governments. Local governments aggressively make use of industrial development bonds (IDBs), whose implicit interest subsidy is provided by the federal tax exemption for municipal bonds. Local governments sometimes also will provide some type of property tax abatement for property acquired or built using an IDB; under Tennessee state law, this is the only legal method for local governments to provide property tax abatements. The state also uses about 40 percent of its federally funded "Small Cities" Community Development Block Grant program to provide below market interest rate loans of up to $500,000 to new companies locating in small cities and rural areas.

Tennessee officials give several reasons when asked why the state avoids large subsidies for new branch plants. First, officials feel Tennessee can compete for new industry without subsidies. "We already have a low tax burden and a good geographic location," said one state official. A second reason is that a poor, low-tax state such as Tennessee cannot afford extensive subsidies. A third reason is the feeling that such subsidies could hurt as much as help by antagonizing existing industry. "Good corporations like the approach of equity—it means you're not going to give my competition a bigger carrot," argued one Tennessee economic developer. Finally, there is Tennessee's tradition of rural populism. Several state leaders said, in virtually the same words, that, "Tennessee's philosophy is that industry should pay its own way."

Issues about Tennessee's Techniques
of Industrial Recruitment

Controversy surrounds three principal issues concerning Tennessee's current marketing techniques. First, there is disagreement about the organization of recruiting trips. The prospects visited in a given city include Fortune 1000 companies, previous calls, companies with plants in Tennessee, and companies that have made inquiries to ECD. Usually about seventy-five prospects are targeted in a particular city. Most calls are made "cold." Letters are sent informing prospects that Tennessee officials will be visiting on a particular day, but appointments are not arranged. During the trip, ECD teams attempt to see the real estate or planning officer for prospect companies. Their goal is to see as many companies as possible.

To some observers, this approach seems inefficient. A number of those interviewed complained that recruiting trips they were on (ECD teams often take along local officials and other state officials) seemed disorganized: "Half the folks we called on weren't there; another quarter didn't want to see us," complained one observer. Several observers suggested that ECD should target fewer companies, identifying those most likely to expand, and try to set up good appointments beforehand, using Tennessee corporate officials as contacts if necessary. This would allow for more thorough research beforehand on the companies. One corporate real estate officer said that most state and local government officials expected him to solve their problems; he would prefer an explanation of how that particular state could solve his company's problems. Many of these comments on targeting prospects echo those made in a 1984 audit of the department by the State Comptroller's office.

ECD officials feel that these criticisms reflect a lack of understanding of the realities of industrial recruitment. They argue that recruiting should not target only those companies likely to expand soon. The aim is to build up a personal working relationship and trust with key corporate officials. ECD officials point out that Nissan, which located a plant at Smyrna in 1980, first had contact with the state in the early 1970s. "The audit didn't recognize that a lot of recruiting is very long-run missionary work," said one ECD official. Furthermore, spending a great deal of time targeting prospects and setting up appointments would restrict the number of calls that could be made. According to one official, "You have two possible strategies. One is to spend a lot of time on research, and only talk to a few prospects. The second is to skip the research and knock on a lot of doors. We've chosen the second strategy." These ECD responses could be argued to be contradictory in that personal relationships with key corporate officials are less likely to develop by just knocking on doors. As of early 1987, there were some signs that criticisms of ECD recruiting trips were beginning to affect ECD policy. ECD officials said that some recent recruiting trips only focused on a few industries, and involved more preset appointments than "cold calls."

Second, some observers expressed concern that ECD didn't extend enough recruiting assistance to the larger urban areas in Tennessee. ECD officials admitted this was probably true, arguing, "The metro[politan] areas don't need help as much. The big cities in Tennessee usually organize their own recruiting trips, maybe with a state person along. Also, with our personnel, we couldn't keep on top of what's going on in the metro areas very well." A related issue is whether the state should more actively recruit service industries. According to one ECD official, "We don't deal with service industries as much because the cities can handle them." This perception of the cities' capabilities was not shared by all observers, including some industrial recruiters for cities.

A final issue is the lack of extensive state subsidies for new branch plants. ECD officials expressed fear that Tennessee would soon be forced by competitive pressures to enter the subsidy race. As one ECD official put it, "It's becoming more difficult to compete with other states that give subsidies. If IDBs are phased out, we'll definitely have to reconsider the subsidy issue." Although IDBs have not been phased out yet, recent federal tax laws have placed increasingly severe limitations on the amounts per capita of such bonds that can be issued in each state, so Tennessee may soon have to confront the subsidy issue.

A possible precursor of the future was the Nissan branch plant decision in 1979. Nissan received over $7 million in ITS money, much of it to fly some of its workers to Japan for training. The state spent over $11 million to redo the highways and access roads near the Nissan site. Local governments agreed to reduce the normal property taxes for the Nissan plant to the estimated cost of services plus $500,000 per year. Reportedly, this last decision came as the race for Nissan narrowed down to Tennessee and Georgia, and Nissan began commenting that its property taxes would be much lower in Georgia. One observer familiar with the Nissan situation argues that, "The state should really have a policy on subsidies, not just do them on a case by case basis."

Services to Existing Business

In addition to the Industrial Training Service, ECD operates several other offices that provide services to existing businesses in Tennessee. The primary role of the *Existing Industry Services* (EIS) office is to act as an ombudsman for Tennessee businesses in their dealings with federal, state, and local government. The target group for this office is all Tennessee manufacturers with more than twenty-five employees. EIS field staff make a special effort to contact officials personally at all new branch plants in this group. Examples of EIS assistance include helping a company work out its water pollution problems with federal environment officials, helping a firm appeal its state-assigned unemployment insurance tax rate and obtain a lower rate, and encouraging local and state officials to work out a sewer hookup problem that had prevented the construction of new housing for some key employees of a Tennessee company. EIS also runs a "Product Match" program in which the office attempts to find Tennessee suppliers for other companies in Tennessee. EIS services are provided through five field representatives located around the state. The office deliberately keeps a low profile, which might explain why some local officials do not know exactly what EIS does. According to one former state official, a key rationale for EIS is that "new prospects will talk to existing industry, so you need to keep them happy."

The *Export Office* provides information and marketing assistance to Tennessee companies interested in exporting to foreign countries. According to ECD officials, the office has, since its 1978 inception, contacted most potential exporters in the state either personally or through regular seminars on the basics of exporting. The office now focuses its attention on the companies with the greatest export potential. The export office has a financial specialist who helps Tennessee exporters deal with the Export-Import Bank and the Foreign Credit Insurance program. The office also leads Tennessee trade missions overseas and helps Tennessee exporters with trade fairs. According to ECD officials, the Export Office staff of four and budget of $150,000 is about average for southeastern states, but does not compare with some of the larger states, such as New York.

The *Small Business Office* has a small staff, with only two professionals. The office attempts to provide information to new and small businesses on state license, tax and regulatory requirements, federal and private sources of capital, and business advice. Information is provided by phone and letter, through a 108-page "Guide to Doing Business in Tennessee," and through informational services and conferences cosponsored with groups such as the Small Business Administration and TVA. The office also attempts to monitor state legislation relevant to small business.

The *Office of Minority Business Enterprise* (OMBE) provides additional assistance to minority businesses in Tennessee. With greater resources than the Small Business Office, OMBE is able to go beyond simple information and referral and actually help minority businesses put together a detailed financial plan. Most of Tennessee's minority businesses are in construction related industries, so special assistance is focused on that sector. OMBE is notified via a computer network of all major private and federal construction bid opportunities, along with the construction specifications. A software package assists minority contractors in calculating costs in preparing their bids.

As mentioned earlier, these industry services have a lower priority for the state than industrial recruitment. One reason for this, in addition to the political factors mentioned earlier, is the serious technical problem of determining how to deliver and evaluate these services. For example, one ECD observer stated, "What do you do with 79,000 small businesses in Tennessee and a three or four person staff?" These services also lack the tangible measures of success available to industrial recruitment efforts. There is no readily available timely data on state exports, small business starts, or plant closings. ECD has not seriously attempted alternative methods of measuring the effectiveness of these services. The result is that the ECD Commissioner's main source of information about these offices' performance consists of each office's self-evaluation.

Community Development

The Community Development (CD) Division within ECD began as the state agency charged with coordinating the federal Appalachian Regional Commission programs in the state. Started in 1965, ARC provides funds for highways, infrastructure, and other needs in Appalachia, a region that includes fifty counties in East and Middle Tennessee. Following federal criteria, the state recommends grant recipients and administers the grants. ARC funding has been reduced to around $15 million a year in Tennessee.

Throughout the 1970s, the CD Division remained largely separate from the rest of ECD. In 1979, however, the division was drawn into ECD's overall development efforts by the Alexander administration. Alexander's first ECD Commissioner, Jim Cotham, directed the Community Development Division to come up with ways to integrate local community development programs with the rest of ECD.

This initiative evolved into the current program of "Community Economic Development Preparedness." The rationale for this program is that local communities are crucial to successful industrial recruiting because, as many officials said in interviews, "local communities make the sale, not the state." The program is limited to communities under 25,000 in population. ECD staff provide an array of technical assistance to these communities, including help in organizing a local Chamber of Commerce or other development group, information on what other rural communities have done in economic development, assistance in developing an economic development plan, and advice on appropriate land for industrial development. The most politically potent portion of the program, however, is the Three-Star Certification. Communities that have shown that they are "ready for industrial expansion," as judged by an outside review team, are given the Governor's Three Star Award. This award process provides publicity for the governor and local political leaders, and puts political pressure on local communities to organize their economic development efforts better.

The CD Division also administers a low-interest industrial loan program to industrial prospects using federal "Small Cities" Community Development Block Grant (CDBG) funds. This program began in 1982 after the federal government allowed states to take over this portion of the CDBG program from the Department of Housing and Urban Development (HUD). Tennessee has chosen to use 40 percent of these CDBG funds for industrial loans. This represents a major shift from HUD's priority of housing rehabilitation. The industrial loan program provides another link between the CD Division and the rest of ECD.

Despite this greater integration of the CD Division with the rest of ECD, ECD and state government officials are still uncertain about what role community development should play in the state's economic development program. The state's community development efforts focus on assistance to the poorer rural communities. Many of these rural communities are experiencing economic distress due to plant closings. Many of these communities, remote from highways and urban amenities, will find it extremely difficult to attract industry no matter what their degree of "preparedness." Some state officials argue that the Three Star program is deceptive because it may contribute to unrealistic expectations.

The key issue is whether the state should be doing anything more to help distressed rural communities. Advocates of the present policy argue that "we should sell what we can sell," but they admit this policy does not solve the employment problems of older rural workers affected by plant closings. A small departure from the current policy was made in 1986, when the legislature appropriated $5 million to set up the Tennessee Economic Development Corporation, which would make loans and invest seed capital in businesses in economically distressed areas of Tennessee.

High Tech

State and local officials are promoting several high technology initiatives at both the state and local levels. Within ECD, the small (one or two person staff) High

Technology Office serves as a catalyst, helping organize local high technology efforts and encouraging greater awareness of high technology by Tennessee's industrial recruiters.

The Tennessee Technology Foundation (TTF), an entity separate from ECD, provides the major state commitment to high technology. Although nominally a statewide organization, TTF is located in and focuses its efforts on the Tennessee Technology Corridor in the Oak Ridge-Knoxville area. State resources supporting the project include: a $2 million endowment to pay for TTF staff; plans to complete the Pellissippi Parkway from Oak Ridge to the Knoxville airport, the "corridor" along which high tech firms are supposed to cluster; and the construction of a new campus for the State Technical Institute at Knoxville. The Technology Foundation staff is helping plan the industrial zoning for the corridor, provide assistance to potential high technology entrepreneurs, and publicize the corridor concept.

The origins of the Technology Corridor provide an interesting example of how economic development policy is made in Tennessee. Reportedly, Governor Alexander was in Knoxville at a meeting on some other topic, and someone suggested that something should be done to bridge the gap between Oak Ridge National Laboratory (ORNL) and the University of Tennessee (UT). This conversation led to Alexander initiating a Technology Corridor task force in 1981. The task force in turn developed the proposal for the Technology Foundation and Corridor, and the Democratic legislative leadership supported the needed appropriations.

Other efforts closely related to the corridor include the Tennessee Innovation Center and the University Venture Capital Center. Both of these efforts were spurred by private venture capital groups. The Innovation Center is a business incubator begun in 1984 by Martin Marietta, which manages ORNL for the Department of Energy (DOE). Martin Marietta's involvement in the center stems from the commitment it made to DOE, when awarded the ORNL contract, to encourage more economic spinoffs from the laboratory. The Innovation Center is modeled on and partly owned by a business incubator in Salt Lake City, Utah. As with most incubators, the Innovation Center provides cheap office space and other support services for entrepreneurs, particularly in developing a business plan. Unlike some incubators, the Innovation Center plans to acquire an equity position in most companies it assists.

The University Venture Capital Center theoretically will serve any inventor in the state, but it will naturally tend to be of particular help at its location near the main UT campus at Knoxville. The center will be jointly run by UT and Venture First, a North Carolina based venture capital firm. The Venture Capital Center will assist entrepreneurs in evaluating their ideas and drawing up plans and will attempt to locate investors for an entrepreneur's project.

A number of other local high tech efforts are underway around the state. A Biomedical Research Zone is planned for Memphis, to capitalize on the UT Medical Center and a number of large hospitals in the Memphis area. Task forces are also looking into high tech possibilities near the Tri-Cities and near the UT Space Institute at Tullahoma. Finally, TVA has earmarked $30 million

in venture capital funds for the TVA region. This investment pool will be managed by Massey Burch, the leading venture capital firm in Nashville. The $30
million is part of Gulf Oil's settlement with TVA from a uranium price fixing
lawsuit.

The limited time these programs have been in operation makes evaluation
impossible. Based on the interviews conducted for this study, however, several
points emerge.

First, Tennessee's high tech efforts will never be regarded as a success by
most Tennessee leaders until a major outside high tech firm locates a substantial
research facility in the state. According to TTF staff, a larger number of small
businesses have started up in the corridor area than in the Research Triangle in
North Carolina, which is home primarily to subsidiaries of large corporations.
That is not enough for many Tennessee leaders. One observer complained that
"the Foundation spends all its time working with small companies. 'Grow your
own' is important, but you need to spend more time going after the big ones."

Second, the state funds devoted to Tennessee's efforts are quite small compared to the expenditures of many other states. TTF's $2 million endowment
cannot compare with the magnitude of other states' high tech programs.

Improving Basic Public Services

Part of Governor Alexander's economic strategy was to improve basic public
services that both promote economic development within the state and attract
business outside the state. Alexander focused on three major public services and
amenities: schools, the environment, and roads.

Better Schools Program

The Better Schools program, introduced by Governor Alexander in 1983 and
passed by the legislature in 1984, is one of the most comprehensive of the recent
state educational reform measures.[32] The program is the major initiative of Governor Alexander's second term. It was one of the first major proposals in the
current educational reform movement that has swept the country, particularly
the South.

The Better Schools program made changes in the Tennessee educational
system from primary and secondary schools through the universities. The overall theme is rewarding excellence in education: More educational funding is tied
to stronger performance on evaluations. The centerpiece of the program is merit
pay for public school teachers. This merit pay is linked to a career ladder for
teachers. A teacher passing the evaluations for a higher level receives a higher
salary and the chance to make even more money if he or she will work during
the summer on special projects, such as training other teachers. A team of
trained evaluators from outside the teacher's school district makes the evaluations. Educational researchers developed the valuation criteria. These research-

ers argue that research in the last ten years enables them to identify the characteristics of effective teaching.

Other less publicized aspects of the Better Schools program include merit pay for principals, the Center of Excellence program, and centralization of authority for vocational-technical programs. An outside team evaluates principals, who can receive state funded salary increases if they meet criteria for effectiveness developed by educational researchers. Center of Excellence grants provide extra funding for special programs at state universities. Finally, administrative authority for post-secondary vocational-technical education was centralized under the State Board of Regents. A 1982 Job Skills Task Force of prominent Tennessee businessmen appointed by Governor Alexander recommended this action. The task force based their centralization recommendation on the perceived success of North Carolina's centrally run voc-tech system.

The origins of the Better Schools program illustrate the personal style of leadership preferred by Governor Alexander. Reportedly, the program originated in conversations between Alexander and Chester Finn, a professor of education at Vanderbilt. Finn, who was once an aide to Senator Moynihan of New York, was named Assistant Secretary of Education for Research at the U.S. Department of Education in 1985. Finn has been widely recognized for some time as one of the leading neoconservative critics of the current administration of public schools. The key point to note is that the program was developed through an ad hoc, informal process, spurred through the personal interest of Governor Alexander, rather than through any regular, formalized planning process.

As one might expect, the Better Schools program was politically controversial. A one cent sales tax increase was needed to fund the program, raising objections from both conservatives opposed to tax increases and liberals who preferred a state income tax. More important, the program faced vigorous opposition from the Tennessee Education Association (TEA), which represents most Tennessee public school teachers. The TEA and most public school teachers have a deep distrust of evaluation. This distrust stems partly from past experience with politically biased evaluations by public school principals who understood little about effective teaching. The vehement opposition from TEA blocked the initial Better Schools package in 1983. Support from most voters and business helped pass the package in 1984. Some younger legislators, both Democratic and Republican, were particularly key to the passage of this package.

Despite the Better Schools program, the state still ranks very low among the states on such measures as spending per public school pupil and average teacher salaries. In the 1983–84 school year, before passage of the program, Tennessee ranked forty-seventh among the fifty states on spending per pupil and forty-third in teacher salaries.[33] The Better Schools program increased state funding for education by 24 percent from 1983–84 to 1984–85.[34] This funding pushed Tennessee's ranking to forty-sixth in spending per pupil and thirty-eighth in teacher salaries, still far behind most states.[35]

Safe Growth

The Alexander administration implemented a number of initiatives in environmental policy.[36] These initiatives generally have won support from environmentalists as well as business leaders. To clean up the state's water, $14 million in state grants and loans have been approved for municipal waste water systems in smaller communities. In addition, the state has decided to enforce water pollution laws equally against both industry and cities, breaking with its previous policy of allowing municipalities greater leeway. Illegal dumping of hazardous wastes has been made a felony. A hazardous waste clean-up fund has been created, financed by state appropriations and a fee on industry. An incentive fund has been set up to reward the first community in Tennessee to accept a hazardous waste facility. Finally, the state has funded a $2 million annual Natural and Cultural Heritage Areas Acquisition Fund to protect unique natural or cultural sites. For a conservative, poor state with low taxes, this environmental activity is surprising.

Three factors explaining this surge of activity emerge from interviews. First, various ad hoc groups appointed by the governor have allowed good communication among different groups. During his first term, Alexander established a Safe Growth Action Team of commissioners and private citizens to make recommendations on environmental issues. A hazardous waste task force also was appointed, with representatives from both the Tennessee Manufacturers Association and the Tennessee Environmental Council.

In Alexander's second term, the Safe Growth team was reorganized into a Safe Growth Cabinet Council, consisting of the governor and the commissioners of cabinet departments concerned with environmental issues. According to one close observer of the cabinet council, "This has been the smallest change with the biggest result. The big benefit is that commissioners get to know each other professionally as well as personally." The environmental policies adopted reflect a broader range of interests. For example, the decision to hold cities to the same waste water standards as industry apparently arose from ECD's input into the Safe Growth Cabinet Council. Furthermore, the personal contact creates better working relationships among the different departments. Commissioners are more likely to phone each other about issues overlapping departments, and the staff members of each department are less likely to perceive other departments as the enemy.

Alexander also continued to appoint ad hoc environmental task forces during his second term. After the initial failure of funding proposals for clean water in 1983, Alexander and the Democratic legislative leadership set up a Select Committee on Clean Water consisting of key legislators and cabinet commissioners. This effort paved the way for the adoption of key water funding proposals in 1984.

A second factor in the state's success has been a small (two person) professional staff that first served the Safe Growth Team and now works for the Safe Growth Cabinet Council. This interdepartmental staff has ensured continuity between the various efforts and has served as a conduit for delivering information from outside environmental consultants to the various task forces, the Action Teams, and the cabinet council.

Finally, state environmental policy has benefited from the personal interest of the governor. Early in his governorship, Alexander made water clean up a high priority. In Alexander's own personal vision for the state, clean water and jobs are closely related, as the Safe Growth name symbolizes. His goal was to avoid the growth problems that have occurred in other states, and that, in turn, have impeded future growth. Tennessee's ad hoc approach to environmental policy reflects Alexander's policy making style. According to one observer, the state's Safe Growth effort is "deliberately not institutionalized. This is the way Alexander wants to conduct policy." At the beginning of Alexander's second term, there was some discussion of reorganizing all the state environmental and resource agencies into one "super agency." Alexander chose not to pursue this kind of reorganization. According to one state official, "He wanted to do something with a short-term payoff. You just can't do reorganization in less than two or three years. Reorganization doesn't necessarily solve the problems anyway."

The 1986 Roads Program

In 1986, Governor Alexander proposed, and the legislature enacted, a major new highway construction program. The program would focus on six new Bicentennial Parkways, costing a total of $870 million, and fifteen other Priority Roads, costing $330 million. In addition, the governor promised to speed up another $1.6 billion in highway construction projects. The program was to be financed by a four cent per gallon increase in the gasoline tax to pay the debt service on the required bonds.

The explicit rationale Alexander presented for the roads program was that it would promote economic development: "It will help the most to bring jobs into Tennessee *right now* if we can tell [industrial prospects] we are building the best state road system in America while they are building their plants."

The roads program was enacted after a vigorous political battle between the legislature and the governor. Legislators expressed concern about the program's financing, about whether the program provides enough assistance to the state's major urban areas and to the most depressed rural areas, the exact timing of the promised speed up of already approved construction projects, whether the four cent per gallon tax increase will be enough to finance all the proposed roads, and whether the program ties the hands of future governors. There was much legislative reluctance to increase the gas tax in an election year, after having increased it three cents in 1985 to pay for road maintenance. Negotiations between the legislature and governor forged an agreement, giving Alexander another triumph, and legislators the roads they wanted.

The Economic Development Policy Process

This section analyzes the roles of different decision makers, groups, and institutions in influencing economic development policy in Tennessee: the governor and legislature, the business community, the labor movement, political parties, and TVA.

The Role of the Governor and Legislature

By both the state constitution and tradition, the governor plays the dominant role in setting state policy. The state constitution gives the governor strong appointment and budgetary powers. The cabinet is appointed by the governor rather than elected. The governor also has a line item veto power on appropriations bills, although the legislature can override the veto with a simple majority.

The Tennessee legislature usually reacts to proposals from the governor or interest groups, and rarely initiates new policies. This reactive role can be attributed both to tradition and to the part-time nature of the legislature.

The legislature is particularly willing to let the governor take the lead on economic development issues. Both the governor and the legislature share favorable attitudes towards new business.

Governor Alexander's Policy-Making Style

Because of the governor's dominance of economic development policy, the process for setting economic development policy in Tennessee largely depends on the governor's policy-making style. Governor Alexander's style was to focus his attention on a few issues and delegate other issues to his commissioners. As one observer close to Alexander put it, "The governor targets a few priorities. Up to Better Schools it was Jobs and Clean Water. He spent a lot of time with the Japanese. He didn't try to talk to everyone in the world."

Governor Alexander believed this focus on a few issues is essential to a governor's success: "If a governor is able to focus, put everything he's got on a specific area, he's certain to get a result, because no one else has that much to throw into it." Critics of Alexander claim this focus caused other problems to worsen due to lack of attention. For example, for the past several years, the state has been in major legal trouble with the federal courts over overcrowded prison conditions.

On issues Alexander got involved in, he was very much his own strategist and planner. Alexander acted as the state's primary intelligence-gathering arm, seeking to intuit trends and how they might affect the state. In Alexander's view, "the governor is the chief see-er of [state] needs, the chief planner." The impetus for the Better School Program, the Tennessee Technology Corridor, Safe Growth, the 1986 Roads Programs, and many other initiatives came personally from Alexander. He was praised in several interviews as being an excellent planner, perceiving how education, clean water, better roads, and jobs all fit together. But if "planning" is taken to mean a formal state planning process, Alexander is not favorably inclined. According to one observer, the explanation of Alexander's preference for his personal plans over formal planning is that "he lets his own enormous abilities lead him astray."

In pursuing his initiatives, the governor often used ad hoc groups and task forces, usually with extensive private sector involvement, to develop his proposals. This approach bypassed existing state institutions. Alexander's task force approach may reflect his greater trust in the private sector than state agencies and an impatience with working through existing agencies. On economic development issues, Alexander initiated the following ad hoc groups: Job Skills Task Force; Technology Corridor Task Force; two Small Business Conferences; Memphis Jobs Conference; West Tennessee Jobs Conference. Business members dominated these groups.

Alexander's delegation of great authority to commissioners gave increased importance to his method of choosing commissioners. In most cases, he brought in businessmen to run state departments, asking only a two year time commitment. As a result, turnover in his cabinet was relatively high. ECD, for example, had three commissioners during Alexander's eight years in office.

Alexander's second term produced one major change in the governor's administrative style: the cabinet councils. In addition to the Cabinet Council on Safe Growth, cabinet councils were established in the areas of jobs, social services, personnel, corrections, and the Saturn project. Each council included the commissioners from the relevant department and was chaired by a commissioner. Alexander expected the personal presence of the commissioners at the cabinet council meetings and frequently attended them himself.

While generally favorable statements were made about the councils, several observers said that most cabinet councils had not met the same success as the Safe Growth Council. In particular, the Jobs Council has not had the policy impact of the Safe Growth Council. While the Jobs Council has debated important issues, such as interstate banking, the Technology Corridor, and adult illiteracy, it has not played as central a role in setting economic development policy as the Safe Growth Council has for environmental policy. This may be due partly to the lack of any permanent staff assigned exclusively to the Jobs Council.

The Political Role of Tennessee Business

Tennessee businessmen as a group have not pushed for any major new initiatives in the state's general economic development policy. One reason for this lack of involvement is that most Tennessee businessmen do not usually focus on the overall interests of the state. When Tennessee businessmen get involved in public interest activities, they usually focus on the interests of their particular community or metropolitan area.

As a result, there is no effective statewide group of public interest oriented businessmen. There is no statewide Chamber of Commerce. Statewide business groups exist, but they focus on the narrowly defined economic interests of their members. The most prominent statewide group, the Tennessee Manufacturers Association, lobbies on issues such as workers' compensation reform, the definition of industrial machinery for a special sales tax exemption, and right to know legislation regarding toxic substances at the workplace. Another statewide group, the Tennessee Taxpayers' Association, traditionally has focused on research on state and local tax issues and has not effectively pursued broader issues. These two groups merged in July 1985, but the new organization has not yet taken any broader perspective on business interests.

The Tennessee Business Roundtable, an organization of business executives formed in 1984, is perceived by some of its members to be the beginning of a public oriented statewide business group. However, the Roundtable got off to an extremely bad start because its charter declared the Roundtable's dedication to a "union free environment" in the public sector. Tennessee unions threatened to withdraw their pension funds from several banks who initially joined the Roundtable, and the banks were forced to drop out. A number of business executives feel the Roundtable has been fatally crippled by its "union busting" image.

A major reason why Tennessee lacks an effective statewide public interest oriented business group is the state's enormous regional diversity. Several observers feel the lack of early statewide banking in Tennessee has also been a factor. Until 1971, Tennessee had only countywide banking. Even today, a number of restrictions remain on statewide banking, and most banks still focus primarily on their home communities. Banks throughout the United States often provide business leadership in broad economic development issues because their economic interests are advanced by general economic growth in their service areas. Because they have been restricted to countywide service areas, Tennessee banks historically have taken a narrow geographic perspective. This tendency has begun to change in the last few years, as Tennessee's major banks become statewide organizations, but as yet these changes have not substantially affected state politics.

Several business leaders argued in interviews that North Carolina has had greater economic success than Tennessee in part because of an effective statewide business organization, Citizens for Business and Industry. This group's success, in turn, is partly attributable to leadership by state banks made possible by early statewide branch banking. According to one Tennessee business leader, "North Carolina banks [have] a sense of statewide responsibility."

The Role of Labor and Other Interest Groups

Labor unions and other interest groups have not played an important role in economic development policy in Tennessee. As with business groups, the Tennessee labor movement exerts its political muscle on issues of more immediate concern to its members, such as workers' compensation.

The labor movement's evaluation of Tennessee economic development policies is mixed. Labor heartily approves of attracting new branch plants but believes that not enough resources have been devoted to preventing plant closings. Lobbying on this issue, however, is not a labor priority. The labor movement perceived the Alexander administration as unsympathetic to labor's concerns. The labor movement may push for greater state activism on the plant closing issue now that Democrat Ned McWherter has been elected governor.

Bipartisan Consensus and Partisan Differences

As mentioned earlier, Alexander's dominance on the economic development issue was reinforced by the pro-business consensus that has traditionally existed within Tennessee. In a relatively poor state such as Tennessee, measures to promote new industry are popular among both Republicans and Democrats. As a result, despite Democratic control of the legislature and Republican control of the governorship through the mid 1980s, the cooperation on economic development issues has been excellent. Both Speaker of the House McWherter (now Governor) and Lieutenant Governor Wilder (Speaker of the Senate) backed Governor Alexander on key economic development issues, such as the funding for the Nissan package and the Tennessee Technology Corridor endowment. They readily promised their support for any state funding that Alexander felt he needed for the Saturn project.

While Wilder and McWherter supported Alexander's leadership in economic development policy, both were more inclined than Alexander towards government intervention in the private market to achieve economic development goals. Wilder supported a number of proposals for state government venture capital pools or state loans to business. McWherter, while running for governor in the 1986 election, was interested in exploring business subsidies aimed at targeting industry in rural and urban areas with high unemployment. McWherter joined Wilder in 1986 in backing state support for venture capital. A small version of this idea, providing $5 million to set up a Tennessee Economic Development Corporation, passed the legislature in 1986. The traditional Democratic-Republican division over government activism is thus evident even in a conservative, pro-business state such as Tennessee. But as lieutenant governor and house speaker, Wilder and McWherter usually did not actively push their policy proposals, instead deferring to Governor Alexander.

TVA's Role

The Tennessee Valley Authority has had a great indirect impact on Tennessee's economic development through its provision of cheap power, flood control, and improved river transportation. Although no comprehensive study has quantified TVA's economic effects, the large increase in electricity intensive industry in the valley after TVA's creation seems presumptive evidence of TVA's impact.

TVA's direct involvement in Tennessee's current economic development efforts is surprisingly small. For some time, TVA has operated an industrial recruitment division that provides information on services to industrial prospects. TVA recently started an existing industry services division that provides free information from TVA experts to businesses considering an expansion. TVA's economics division has produced several excellent studies on the TVA region's economic stagnation since the early 1970s. In general, however, the state government seems to have little awareness or involvement in TVA's economic studies or development programs, and TVA in turn has not attempted to integrate its development efforts with the state's.

TVA's lack of involvement can be traced to two basic tensions built into the original TVA set-up. First, although TVA's original purpose was to help develop the Tennessee Valley area, the U.S. Congress has prevented TVA from actively recruiting new branch plants in the North. In this respect, TVA differs from most power companies, which until quite recently were often more active than state governments in industrial recruitment.

Second, while TVA depends on political support from the region it serves, the TVA Act gave it an independence from state and local governments in the region. This independence is treasured by TVA and resented by local political leaders. TVA is frequently regarded by state leaders as bureaucratic, unresponsive to state priorities, and uncommunicative with the state about its activities.

The lack of strong involvement of TVA in Tennessee's economic development is a great loss to both TVA and Tennessee. TVA could use the extra political support for its non-power programs. A poor state like Tennessee could certainly use the resources and expertise available within TVA.

11

Assessing the Past and Looking Toward the Future

The final chapter on Tennessee details two favorable findings on Tennessee's economic development policies and suggests five policy options for consideration by Tennessee leaders. The concluding section highlights a few important lessons from the Tennessee experience with economic development.

Finding 1: "Smokestack Chasing" Helped Tennessee's Economy— But This Strategy Has Limitations

Industrial Recruitment Works

The prevailing custom in academia is to deride recruitment as "smokestack chasing" that wastes the resources of state governments. The evidence suggests, however, that Tennessee's "smokestack chasing" has had some marginal effect, although the effect is not substantial.

Tennessee clearly has attracted more new branch plants than would be expected for a state its size, particularly Japanese plants. Two data sets support this contention.

The first data set contains information on the new manufacturing branch location decisions of the Fortune 500 companies between 1972–78. This data set was developed by Professor Roger Schmenner of Duke University from Dun

and Bradstreet data. While many other researchers have used Dun and Bradstreet data, Schmenner's series is unique in that it was cross checked with the
companies, resulting in numerous corrections. According to Schmenner's data,
of the 1606 new Fortune 500 branches from 1972–78, Tennessee attracted 75,
or 4.7 percent. This proportion far exceeds Tennessee's share of U.S. population
or employment, which hovers around 2 percent.

The second data set contains information on all the Japanese manufacturing
branch plants in the United States. These data are collected by the Japan Economic Institute of America (JEI), a research organization sponsored by the Japanese government. Between 1970 and the end of 1984, Japanese manufacturers
located ninety-four branch plants with 100 or more employees in the United
States. Of those ninety-four large branches, seven are located in Tennessee, or
7.4 percent of the total. Again, this percentage far exceeds Tennessee's share of
U.S. employment or population, although the actual number of branches
involved is small. Tennessee's success is more impressive when one notes that
California, with the advantage of a West Coast location, captured twenty-five of
these ninety-four Japanese branches. Tennessee thus attracted over 10 percent
of the sixty-nine non-California branch plants.[37]

There are a number of possible reasons for Tennessee's success in attracting
new branches: a strong work ethic and low unionization, central location, and
low wages. Using the Fortune 500 data, Table 11-1 provides quantitative evidence on the relative importance of these factors.[38]

The key policy issue, however, is whether Tennessee's success in attracting
new branch plant locations has any relationship to Tennessee's industrial
recruitment efforts. Quantitative proof of the effects of these recruitment activities is elusive. Three pieces of evidence are consistent with the view that Tennessee's industrial recruitment has had some effect on the margin, although none
of this evidence is conclusive. First, Table 11-1 shows that the state attracted 4.7
percent of all new Fortune 500 branch plants in the United States rather than
the 4.3 percent that would have been predicted by observable characteristics. In
numbers of plants, six of the state's seventy-five new Fortune 500 plants between
1972–78 are unexplained by observed Tennessee characteristics such as wages
and central location. The quality of the state's industrial recruitment relative to
other states is one of several unobserved variables that could explain these extra
branch plants.

Second, shift-share analysis showed that Tennessee's manufacturing growth
relative to the nation was significantly better in the 1979–83 period than in the
1973–79 period. This improvement coincided with Governor Alexander's
increases in ECD's recruitment budget during his first administration.

Finally, interviews were conducted with executives who had considered
locating or had located a branch plant in Tennessee, and most of these executives gave high ratings to Tennessee's industrial recruitment efforts. While none
of these executives believed that state recruitment efforts had affected their location decision, they praised Tennessee recruiters for their speed in coming up
with lists of sites and other information, their candidness in discussing the characteristics of various sites, and the ease of access to top state officials. Tennessee

Table 11-1. Contributions of Various Factors to New Branch Plants Locating in Tennessee

	Percent
Percentage of new Fortune 500 branches that would be *predicted* to locate in Tennessee, if Tennessee were identical to U.S. in most characteristics	3.2
Actual Percentage	4.7
Difference Between Actual and Predicted	1.5
Part of Difference Due to	
Lower Wage Rates	.5
Greater Road Density	.4
Lower Unionization	.3
Location	.1
Lower Taxes	.1
Other Observable Variables	− .3
Total Due to Observable Variables	1.1
Part of Difference Not Explainable by Observable Variables	.4

Note: These calculations are based on an econometric model that estimates how different state characteristics affected the probability of Fortune 500 branches being located in the state during the 1972–78 period. The predicted figure of 3.2 percent allows Tennessee to differ from the U.S. in land area, population, and existing manufacturing, but imagines that Tennessee is identical to U.S. in all other observable variables.

Source: T. Bartik, "Business Location Decisions in the United States: Estimates of the Effects of Unionization, Taxes, and Other Characteristics of States," *Journal of Business and Economic Statistics,* 3, no. 1 (January 1985).

was not always ranked as the best state in its recruitment efforts, but it was considered one of the better states by most of those interviewed.

There are a number of plausible reasons why state recruitment efforts would affect location decisions. Corporate officials often want to locate a new branch and get it going within a very short-term period, sometimes, according to one ECD official, within four months. The state that can most quickly provide accurate comprehensive information on a number of suitable sites has an edge. Easy access to high state officials reassures prospects that red tape will not unduly delay the project.

Given the relatively small Tennessee budget for industrial recruiting, only a very small marginal effect is needed to justify the industrial recruiting effort. Even if Tennessee's recruiting truly makes a difference for only three or four plants a year, many state political leaders would believe the approximately $4 million spent on recruitment is a good investment.

Reasons for Tennessee's Success with Japan

Similar factors help account for Tennessee's success with Japanese branch plants as for Tennessee's general success with branch plants. But several special factors were also mentioned in interviews.

First, the Japanese are very concerned about the work place relationships in their new American plants. The traditional rural work ethic and low unionization seem to be more important for Japanese corporations than for American corporations.

Second, Tennessee was one of the earliest states to pursue Japanese branch plants, in the mid-1970s. Tennessee was not alone—Georgia also was involved early on—but Tennessee's early start gave the state an advantage over most other states.

Third, Tennessee officials feel they were more sensitive to the Japanese style of doing business than were officials from other states. According to Tennessee officials, Japanese companies are much more thorough and patient than American companies in making location decisions and put more of an emphasis on developing personal relationships between key corporate and state officials. According to one Tennessee official, "We've taken time to study the Japanese. They're very thorough. They may make 100 trips in for one plant. . . . You have to be patient with the Japanese. You can have an hour of small talk with a Japanese executive, while it's three to five minutes for an American executive." Other states, suggested Tennessee officials, may have stumbled with the Japanese by going for the "quick sale."

Fourth, Tennessee's early successes with some Japanese companies helped interest other Japanese companies. Japanese corporate officials, unfamiliar with the United States, relied on the existing Japanese branch plants for information, and the reports from Tennessee were usually favorable.

Finally, Governor Alexander's skill at personal relationships with the Japanese was considered important by many Tennessee officials. "The Japanese have tremendous respect for Governor Alexander" said one official. Another observer commented that "Lamar is as much interested in style as content. He's compatible with the Japanese. Protocol is a big deal with them."

Why General Motors' Saturn Plant Is Being Located in Tennessee

The recent Saturn plant announcement, while an enormous plus for Tennessee, does not represent a triumph of any special Tennessee recruiting technique. Rather, the Saturn plant decision was determined by fundamental factors of economics and corporate strategy. An analysis of the Saturn plant decision must be speculative because of the reticence of both GM and the state on the decision. Nonetheless, a number of key factors seem to have been involved in the decision.

First, Saturn president William Hoglund has stated publicly the importance of Tennessee's central location and the resulting access to markets. Hoglund specifically has mentioned the shift in U.S. population to the South and West as a factor making Tennessee more central in market access today than it was in the past.

Second, Tennessee's work ethic, right to work law, and general attitude towards unions probably was a factor. Even though workers in the Saturn plant will be represented by the UAW, with many of the workers hired from laid-off GM employees in the North, the plant is supposed to set a new course in U.S. labor-management relations, hallmarked by greater cooperation and flexibility. The general cultural atmosphere in Tennessee will support such a relationship. The Saturn workers hired from Tennessee will have the traditional southern work ethic. Many of the laid-off GM workers who apply for jobs at the plant probably will have come from the South originally.

Third, Tennessee's lower wages may also be a factor. Although the Saturn plant will pay close to regular union scale wages, GM will face lower costs because of the lower wages paid by its suppliers. For a project designed to eliminate the $2000 per car cost advantage of the Japanese, this will be important.[39]

Fourth, the symbolism of putting the new plant near the Nissan plant may be part of GM's corporate strategy. GM seems determined to convince the American public that Saturn will be a totally new type of American car, with the quality and cost effectiveness of the imports. The Saturn site search has brought tremendously favorable publicity to the project. A recent poll showed that 41 percent of the American public is aware of the Saturn car. The location near Nissan symbolically makes the new car a competitive equal of Nissan's small cars.

Fifth, if the UAW was given any role in the decision, the location near Nissan would have advantages for the union. Tennessee labor movement officials make it clear that they expect some day to organize the nonunion Nissan plant. Labor officials welcome the UAW-organized Saturn plant as a spur to organizing Nissan.

Finally, GM probably knew before the location decision was made that the Saturn plant would receive subsidies similar to the Nissan project. Immediately after the announcement, both GM and the state referred to Tennessee's traditional policy of providing industrial training, highway access, and other public works for major plants such as Saturn. Within a few days, the State Revenue Commissioner said that a property tax reduction would probably be worked out by local governments with Saturn, as it was with Nissan. Since then, a significant property tax abatement has been negotiated with GM, plans for a state funded access road have been announced, and an additional $21 million in state training funds for the Saturn project has been discussed. Governor Alexander said in an interview that, while no specific deals were made before Saturn was announced, the state had told GM that "it's our job to provide job training and roads and water."

State recruiting efforts for the Saturn plant did not differ in basic methodology from the recruitment of any other branch plant, although the Saturn project was treated with special care by ECD. Governor Alexander spoke several times with Roger Smith, chairman of GM, and Hoglund, head of Saturn, during the course of the competition. ECD regularly provided information on the state and sites to GM, hand-delivering each packet of information to Detroit. One would not expect Tennessee's provision of information to be crucial with a corporation as large as GM, which clearly has the resources to gather information quickly without extensive assistance from the states. Tennessee recruiting efforts may have helped symbolize to GM the state's generally favorable attitude towards new business and the Saturn project.

One key point is that Tennessee offered relatively few financial incentives for the Saturn plant compared to other states. A study by Professor James Papke of Purdue University indicates that Tennessee was not the lowest tax state for Saturn.[40] Of the fifteen states that were seriously considered by GM for the Saturn plant, Tennessee was only the sixth lowest in taxes. The property tax abatements, access roads, and industrial training given to Saturn by Tennessee were more than matched by the multimillion dollar offers of other states.

Limitations of Tennessee's Branch Plant Strategy

Although Tennessee's branch plant strategy has met with success, it has two limitations.

First, the attraction of new branch plants has not prevented the recent stagnation in Tennessee growth. The new branch plants have been counterbalanced by problems in other sectors of the Tennessee economy. Furthermore, the new branch plants locating in the United States, increasingly have become limited in number and size, as U.S. industry moves overseas and the domestic economy shifts toward services and small business. As one Tennessee official put it, "The golden days of industry leaving the North and moving south are over."

Second, as TVA studies have indicated, a branch plant oriented economy also is an economy weak in business services. Tennessee's share of the growth in this dynamic sector is below average.

Is State "Smokestack Chasing" in the National Interest?

Even if they agreed that "smokestack chasing" attracted branch plants, most academics would argue that its general practice by state governments is not good for the nation. The customary argument is that smokestack chasing is a zero-sum game from a national perspective: Tennessee's gain is some other state's loss.

While there is some truth to this argument, it fails to recognize the full implications of state competition for all groups in society. The zero-sum argument ignores the other "players" who are affected by competition, most importantly, consumers. The general process of competition leads to better goods and service provision for consumers at minimum cost. As states provide subsidies and extra services to attract business, the benefits to business will eventually be passed on to consumers. Furthermore, the process of competition could result in state and local business taxes that approximate the marginal costs of state and local public services to business. In turn, product prices will approximate the marginal costs of all resources used in producing the product, including state and local public services.

Despite some possible efficiency advantages to state competition for business, this competition creates difficulties for state and local efforts to redistribute income away from business and toward state residents, in particular low-income residents. Attempts to redistribute income away from business will fail if businesses change their location decisions in response. But this problem is inherent in a federal system that allows mobility. If one believes in a federal system with capital and labor mobility, then redistribution will have to remain primarily a national function rather than a state and local one. This is an old public finance truism that appears in a new form in the debate over state competition for business.

Finding 2: Governor Alexander Has Been an Effective Salesman for the State

Interviews with a wide range of Tennessee leaders revealed virtually universal agreement that Governor Alexander's personal salesmanship has attracted business to the state. "Alexander's the best governor we've ever had for economic development," commented one Democratic leader.

A new plant may last for twenty, thirty, or more years. It is not immediately obvious why a business executive facing a thirty year decision should care about a governor who will be out of office in a few years. Business leaders interviewed suggested two reasons. First, in an uncertain world, companies may use the current political leadership of the state as an indicator of the future political climate.

Second, most problems with branch plants arise during the initial siting or the few years immediately afterwards. During the initial phase, permits have to be obtained and tax and regulatory issues settled. These issues may recur during the first few years as the plant expands before settling down. The responsiveness of state political leadership during this critical period is more important than the expected responsiveness of leadership twenty years hence.

Still, the effect of a governor's salesmanship on business location must be kept in perspective. The effect is likely to occur only on the margin for a few new plants. Some of Tennessee's first Japanese investments were achieved while Ray Blanton was governor. Blanton recently completed a prison term for peddling state liquor licenses. Interviews with close observers suggested that Governor Blanton was a poor salesman for the state. Incompetent gubernatorial salesmanship does not cripple a state's industrial recruitment and excellent gubernatorial salesmanship does not cause an economic boom.

Policy Option 1: Tennessee Should Consider a Formally Created Economic Development Strategy

The Case for a Strategy

A state economic strategy is a coherent array of economic goals, from the very general to the quite specific, and a set of general methods for achieving those goals.

Tennessee's current approach to economic development policy qualifies as a strategy because it has goals—raise family income, attract new branch plants—and general methods for achieving those goals—to aggressively recruit new industry, avoid big subsidies, improve basic infrastructure. The strategy is created informally in that it has evolved over time, and there is no clear way to modify this strategy.

A formally developed economic strategy for Tennessee would only be worth the effort of development if the current strategy were inadequate in some respects. The following are some new approaches that a formal strategy could consider.

Targeting Industry on Recruiting Trips. A formal strategy might consider whether to target specific industries for recruitment. This does not imply that state policy makers have perfect knowledge of the best industries for the state's economy. Recruiting trip resources are limited, and they must be allocated in some way. A number of targeting criteria might be used: a perceived comparative advantage of Tennessee in attracting that type of industry; perceived special benefits to Tennessee of the industry; a belief that a particular type of firm is more likely to be swayed by aggressive recruiting; industries in which Tennessee is weak despite an apparent comparative advantage, such as the instruments industry; industries in which nearby states are stronger than Tennessee for no apparent reason.

Targeting Regions Within Tennessee. A strategy might consider whether to target economic growth to underdeveloped areas in Tennessee, and if so, what criteria to use (unemployment, per capita income). A strategy might also consider what methods of targeting are appropriate for different regions. For example, some poorer areas could attract new industry with tax subsidies and public infrastructure; more remote poor areas probably will not attract industry with any reasonable subsidy but might be considered for special job training and job search aid, or as possible sites for government facilities or state parks.

Review of Tax Structure from an Economic Development Perspective. As one observer put it, "the legislature and governor have never sat down and said 'what do we need to do to be more competitive in taxes.' We just make modifications on a case by case basis." For example, the property tax reductions granted by Tennessee local governments to Nissan, Saturn, and others are indicators of a more general problem with the Tennessee tax structure, relatively high taxes on capital intensive industry. Tennessee might consider whether it wants to attract such industry; whether there is some other type of industry it wants to attract, and if so, what tax changes will help; or whether the state wants a "neutral" business tax system, and if so, how that could be achieved. All these issues could be addressed in the context of a formally created strategy.

A Review of Banking and Insurance Regulation from an Economic Development Perspective. A strategy might consider what type of banking and insurance company regulation, or deregulation, would best advance economic development goals while protecting other public and private interests. A number of observers of small business contend that current banking regulations, which discourage risky loans regardless of the expected return, unnecessarily restrict availability of capital to small businesses even if their business prospects are favorable.[41] Given Tennessee's recent problems with the failure of banks controlled by the Butcher brothers, state officials are unlikely to consider allowing riskier bank lending. Mechanisms can be devised that might encourage sound loans with both higher risk and a high expected return, while protecting depositors and deposit insurance funds. For example, some states have encouraged the formation of high-risk loan pools with the participation of a number of state banks and insurance companies. This allows for some risk sharing among these financial institutions and encourages special state attention to prevent these loan pools from being abused.

Public Sector Infrastructure Support for Particular Types of Economic Activities. A strategy could consider the desirability, given the state's goals and comparative advantages, of public infrastructure projects, such as a network of state assisted small business development centers, a state "seed capital" pool, or joint university-industry research centers.

Better Integration of Transportation Planning into Regional Development. A strategy might consider the extent to which highways should be used as a developmental tool and the way the state's plans fit into overall economic development goals for different regions of the state. While the 1986 Roads Program was rationalized by Governor Alexander as an economic development program, it is not at all clear whether the roads network he proposed best advanced the state's economic development. There is no overall economic development plan into which the roads program fits.

Better Integration of City Economic Development Efforts into Overall State Economic Development. Communication about economic strategies between Tennessee cities and the state is weak. A formally developed strategy might provide a vehicle for such communication, and for discovering what city-state link ups could be helpful. For example, the state might help cities recruit service industries.

The point is not that all of these strategic elements are desirable or even mutually consistent. But, if any are deemed worthy of serious consideration, then a formal strategy becomes more attractive.

One can argue that a formal economic strategy is not needed in Tennessee, because the informal policy process has allowed for new initiatives such as the Better Schools program, the Technology Corridor, and the 1986 Roads Program. These initiatives, however, depend very much on the personal vision of one man, Governor Alexander. While no system can escape some reliance on the personal vision and political priorities of the governor, a formal process for strategy creation might enable these personal visions to emerge sooner. Perhaps the Technology Corridor would have begun closer in time to North Carolina's

Research Triangle if Tennessee had a formal process for considering that option.

Furthermore, a formal strategy might allow the initiation and coordination of important economic development policies that, for one reason or another, are not the current focus of the governor. Perhaps the governor must be, as Alexander argued, the chief planner for the state. If the governor is the only planner, however, issues often slip through the cracks. Also, the economic development process falls apart if the state elects a governor who is not as interested as Alexander in economic development. Finally, a formal strategy process would help determine whether the governor's development priorities are optimal for the state.

Dangers of a Tennessee Strategy

A Tennessee strategy has two principal dangers. First, no strategy conceived as one single direction for the state can work, given the state's diversity. A strategy must be conceived as a set of goals and general approaches that allows for diversity.

Second, even if regional diversity is allowed, some interpret a strategy as implying a rigid industrial policy. Goals, even for a region of a state, can be outstripped quickly by economic change. Nashville's leadership did not intend for the area to become a significant auto production center, but Nissan and Saturn have brought that about. It would have been foolish to block this change. Policy makers should not let strategy be a straitjacket.

A strategy is probably most useful if it recognizes our limited ability to predict the future. No one in Tennessee predicted the branch plant boom of the 1960s or Tennessee's slowdown since 1973. While based on some view of the future, a strategy should be flexible enough that it still will be applicable if predictions are incorrect. For example, despite Oak Ridge's expertise in measuring instruments, the instruments industry has not been very successful in Tennessee. Suppose, to take a purely hypothetical case, that a study indicated that (1) the instruments industry was expected to be a fast growth industry in the United States and (2) improvements in various science departments at the University of Tennessee would help catalyze additional activity in the state's instruments industry. State support for improvements in UT's science capabilities would be a flexible strategy in that such improvements are likely to yield positive benefits even if the predictions of instrument industry growth are overstated. On the other hand, a strategy of special state subsidies for the instruments industry would prove to be a disaster if the predictions were incorrect because of the inflexibility of this type of strategy.

Possible Processes for Strategy Creation

A Tennessee strategy could be developed through several institutions that already exist in the state. One possibility is the Industrial and Agricultural Development Commission, which was created originally to oversee ECD policy. However, a strategy might encourage a wider variety of policies and elicit cooperation from more state agencies, if it were developed by a group both close to the governor and separate from any particular cabinet agency. One such group is the State Planning Office (SPO), which could develop a strategy if its economic development planning capabilities were upgraded and if it were clear that SPO's development planning had the confidence of the governor. Alternatively, the Cabinet Council on Jobs could play a strong role in developing a strategy if provided with its own independent staff and a director close to the governor.

An economic development strategy probably would most appropriately be developed formally on a biannual basis, both soon after a governor begins a new four-year term and midway through the term, to allow response to changing circumstances. The Tennessee legislature could encourage the continual revision of a strategy by requiring the governor to prepare a written, biannual economic development strategy.

Policy Option 2: Tennessee Should Consider Developing a Better Economic Intelligence Gathering Capacity

Tennessee currently has no regular system for analysis of long-term economic development trends. As mentioned in Chapter 10, neither the State Planning Office nor ECD's Research Division does any long-term economic research. UT's Center for Business and Economic Research prepares an annual "Economic Report to the Governor," but the report focuses on short-term business cycle trends.[42]

Professional economic analysis of the Tennessee economy will assist policy makers in making better decisions about Tennessee's economic development strategy. The need for economic analysis is particularly great if a complex, formal economic strategy with specific industrial or regional goals is to be created. Economic analysis may prove helpful even if the economic strategy remains informal, however. The economic analysis may focus policy attention sooner on developing economic trends, and more specifically on key problem areas.

A better intelligence capacity might currently help Tennessee's economic policy in two specific areas. First, better economic analysis might help focus greater attention on Tennessee's weakness in business services, and the implications this has for Tennessee's economic growth. TVA's analysis of the service sector is not known among Tennessee policy makers, and Tennessee's problems in this area were never mentioned by any political leaders or state officials in interviews.

Second, economic analysis of venture capital availability in Tennessee might help in the current debate over the appropriate state role in this area. Rather than discussing venture capital in general, the debate might focus more on seed capital, management advice for entrepreneurs, and state banking regulation, the areas that present the greatest problems.

One suggestion for collecting economic intelligence is to require a biannual economic development report. If it were not deemed cost effective for the state to develop in-house economic expertise, the report could be prepared outside state government. Possible sources for the report include the University of Tennessee, Memphis State University, TVA, and consulting firms such as SRI International and Arthur D. Little. Authorship of the report might be varied periodically to obtain different perspectives. In addition to long-term economic analyses, the report could outline policy options for economic development. Thus, the biannual economic development report could serve as a primary information source for the state's preparation of an economic development strategy.

Policy Option 3: Tennessee Should Explore Better Evaluation Techniques for Its Economic Development Programs

ECD's methods of evaluating its programs are inadequate. The only attempted measure of how well the department is achieving its goals is the Annual Growth Report, which lists new plants and expansions in Tennessee. According to one ECD official, "The Growth Report is the bottom line to legislators and the public." The Growth Report, however, cannot distinguish the marginal contribution of ECD to the growth activity described in the report.

The department's other activities are subject to even less effective methods of evaluation. The Export Promotion, Existing Industry Services, Small Business, and other offices are evaluated only by crude measures such as the number of trade mission trips, the number of contacts with business, and the cost per contact. These are measures of the inputs these offices are using to achieve their goals rather than the progress toward these goals.

Inadequate evaluation at ECD has several serious consequences. First, it provides incentives for ECD staff to maximize what can be measured rather than work toward important program goals that are less tangible. For example, the problem of evaluating the marginal contribution of industrial recruitment causes ECD to make as many recruiting trip calls as possible. A high number of calls is deemed evidence that ECD is working effectively to attract new branch plants.

Second, the lack of evaluation impedes program improvements. For example, with regard to the continuing debate over ECD's recruiting trip tactics, the absence of effective evaluation makes it impossible to tell whether a lot of "cold calls" is a better or worse tactic than fewer calls with appointments. Marketing tactics are continued because that is the way things always have been done.

Third, ECD activities whose effects are harder to see are deemphasized. The efforts of groups like the Export Promotion Office, whose results are not immediately apparent, are weakened politically in the struggle for budget resources and gubernatorial attention. The "smokestack chasing" strategy is irresistible politically because of the "smokestack's" high visibility. The political bias towards a branch plant strategy would be reduced by better measures of all ECD activities.

The most sophisticated and complex econometric techniques are likely to be too imprecise to quantitatively detect the small, marginal impact of ECD programs. An alternative would be to use "low tech" evaluations through careful surveys. An independent organization periodically could survey random samples of select groups, such as existing plant managers in Tennessee, small business in Tennessee, and corporate real estate officers around the country. The surveys could ask for specific evaluations of different ECD activities and offices, a comparison of Tennessee with other states where appropriate, and suggestions for improvements. The surveys must be carefully organized to encourage a high response rate and candid answers. The surveys should address questions such as whether ECD efforts made any difference to the actions taken by the business firm surveyed; for example, whether the recruiting trips had any effect on business location decisions. If the same surveys were administered every year or two to another random sample, the change in responses could be examined to determine ECD's progress over time.[43]

This proposal has a key political problem: Governors and state agencies do not want to hear bad news. A governor has little incentive to announce publicly that his evaluation revealed that the state wasted millions on economic development during his administration. Traditional audit agencies often are perceived as a political tool of either the current administration or its opponents. For example, the 1984 State Audit Report on ECD by the Tennessee State Comptroller, which was critical of ECD, was perceived by many state officials as politically biased because the comptroller was a Democrat. A solution might be to use a truly independent and professional evaluation agency, but it's not clear whether such an independent organization would have any base of political support.

Policy Option 4: The State Should Consider Measures to "Professionalize" ECD

ECD's effectiveness suffered during the Alexander administration because of high personnel turnover. The most serious personnel turnover occurred in the commissioner's office: Three commissioners of ECD served Alexander between 1979 and 1987. The turnover was even more extensive in the department's second-level positions: Seven Assistant Commissioners of Industrial Development (Marketing) served from 1979 to 1987. One ECD staffer had five different supervisors within a two year period.

There are several reasons for this high rate of personnel turnover. First, ECD jobs down to the office director level are not civil service, which allows the legal leeway for high turnover. Second, the high turnover in the commissioner's office, a direct result of Alexander's policy of appointing businessmen as commissioners with only a two year time commitment, generated turnover in the lower ranks.

Third, the top ECD jobs, including the Deputy Commissioner and the Assistant Commissioner for Industrial Development, are considered political jobs and sometimes have been used to reward business supporters. Political appointees often do not last long. According to one source, "They think it's a real plum job. They they discover it's a lot of pressure and hard work and they quit."

Fourth, the salary levels in ECD encourage turnover because they are not competitive with private sector alternatives available to the best ECD staff. ECD staff members frequently are hired away by local Chambers of Commerce and by companies new to Tennessee.

Finally, some ECD jobs, particularly those involving marketing trips, tend by their nature to have a high turnover rate.

Personnel turnover leads to confusion over ECD policy directions, and cynicism and poor morale among ECD's long-term staff members. One observer said that "the attitude [at ECD] is, if you don't like the policy this week, wait around and it will change."

Personnel turnover causes problems in recruiting new industry. Attempts to establish personal relationships with key corporate real estate officers become ineffective if ECD turnover is too high. According to several sources, ECD has avoided more adverse effects of the turnover because a few key recruiting personnel have remained throughout the many different Assistant Commissioners of Industrial Development.

The effectiveness of ECD would probably improve if the department were professionalized. ECD jobs should not be considered political jobs; they should be professional positions with the expectation of a lengthy term of service. Professionalization of ECD positions does not mean they should be classified as civil service, which would probably prove disastrous for ECD jobs that require a quick response and long hours. At the very least, all ECD jobs below the commissioner's level should be depoliticized.

There are several possible objections to this recommendation. First, there is always danger that a professionalized ECD could become more bureaucratic. This objection can be met by careful personnel selection and review.

Second, if salaries in ECD remain low, a professionalized staff might consist of the real "losers," those without private sector options. There is no perfect solution to this problem except the hope that somewhat higher salaries, a well-run department, and the amenities of Nashville will attract sufficient high quality personnel to a reasonably lengthy term of service.

Third, the governor might lose control over economic development policy if he were normally expected to keep all the ECD staff. In Tennessee, however, there is enough consensus over economic development issues that any new governor is unlikely to form a policy that radically differs from existing policy.

Policy Option 5: Business Leaders Should Consider Forming a Statewide Business Organization Devoted to Long-Term Economic Issues

As mentioned, Tennessee has no effective statewide business organization focusing on broad public issues. Such a group could make two important contributions to state economic development policy: independent information and evaluation, and political support for a long-term perspective.

Independent Economic Intelligence Gathering and Program Evaluation

A public oriented business group could provide resources and publicity for efforts to gather information on the long-term economic development of the state and for evaluation of state economic development programs. Such a business organization would not have the same incentive as the state government to want only "good news."

Political Support for Long-Term Development Issues

A statewide organization could also provide support for policies that advance the long-term development of the state. For example, the Better Schools program is only the first step in the reforms needed to improve Tennessee's public schools. Better Schools was passed at the peak of the public's interest in school reform and with the vigorous backing of a popular governor. The next steps in Tennessee school improvement will face more difficult political conditions. A public minded business organization would provide crucial support for continued progress in education.

While a broad based business organization could play a constructive role, the creation of such a group is a difficult challenge in Tennessee. In the past, not enough Tennessee business leaders have been willing to take a statewide perspective or economic development. The Tennessee Business Roundtable was an effort to form such a group, but TBR's disastrous initial confrontation with the AFL-CIO and consequent withdrawal of its banking members have dampened many business leaders' enthusiasm for new statewide business groups.

Conclusion: Lessons from Tennessee's Economic Development

Three lessons from Tennessee's experience with economic development deserve special emphasis. First, the personal leadership of a governor can make a significant difference in a state's economic development. In Tennessee, Governor Alexander's efforts were influential in recruiting new industry, promoting school reform, and developing a state environmental policy.

Second, institutions can make a major difference in how effectively a state addresses economic development problems. Tennessee's Safe Growth Cabinet Council provides a positive example of an institutional innovation that enhances effective policy. On the negative side, Tennessee's lack of a state economic development strategy reflects weaknesses in ECD, the State Planning Office, the Cabinet Council on Jobs, and the organization of the Tennessee business community.

Finally, the lack of any effective evaluation of state economic development policies enormously limits the potential of these programs for enhancing U.S. economic growth. Studies such as this are only imperfect substitutes for ongoing studies that allow for data collection. Given the incentives against self-criticism among states, an ongoing national evaluation (either government or privately sponsored) is essential if we are to really understand what works and what does not work for economic development.

CALIFORNIA

Douglas Henton
Steven A. Waldhorn

with contributions from

Richard Stratton
Theodore Lyman
Joyce Klein

12

The Megastate Economy

From its origins in the 1850s, California's economy has been fueled by entre-preneurs who took advantage of the opportunities that arose and had a belief that they could engineer solutions to the problem at hand. California's capacity for innovation has been the key aspect of every stage of its industrial evolution. It began with efforts to extract resources and control water and it has led to aero-space and microelectronics.

Actions taken by public as well as private institutions in California clearly have made a difference in the economic development of the state. Investments in education, water, and transportation infrastructure had a clear payoff in terms of state economic growth. California's entrepreneurial climate exists in part because of public policy decisions.

However, California has not had an explicit economic development strategy or an overt strategy for promoting entrepreneurship and innovation. Many of the actions critical to economic development were taken for other than eco-nomic reasons. California's master plan for education was guided by a concern for equal access and the need to accommodate a rapidly growing population. Likewise, key infrastructure investments were made to accommodate growth and meet specific regional needs. Only in the past decade have public and pri-vate leaders in California talked explicitly about the need for economic devel-opment strategies. Clearly, forces much larger than state policy drive economic change. State policy, however, can shape the directions of economic change and can make a difference in terms of output at the margin.

Evolution of California's Economy

The economic growth of California since 1850 has been sustained by a series of industrial transformations fueled by innovation and adaptation.[1]

World War II represented a turning point as California made the transition from a resource based economy to an economy based on advanced technology. In contrast to the Midwest, which developed a strong durable goods manufacturing base and expanded it in the postwar period, California largely skipped basic manufacturing in its transition from a resource to a technology based economy.

A Resource Based Economy (1850–1940)

Modern California began as a resource based, extractive economy with the gold rush. At that time, California had very few natural comparative advantages other than its resources. Much of the state had arid, desertlike conditions, there were few people, and reaching eastern markets meant sailing clear around South America.

The gold rush brought people to California. Between 1850–60, the number of California settlers grew from 100,000 to 380,000. Local manufacturing grew to produce items too expensive to import. Through import substitution, major cities were born that would live beyond the gold rush. San Francisco and Sacramento developed as support centers for the gold miners. San Francisco became an important shipping, trading, and financial center.

As population grew, cattle ranching revived and, along with wheat farming, replaced gold mining as the state's major money producer in the 1860s. Because of the terrain, farms and ranches averaged about three times the national average in size. Entrepreneur-farmers developed irrigation systems to bring water to the Sacramento and San Joaquin Valleys. Wheat farming gave impetus to the flour mill branch of the food processing industry. The scarcity of labor stimulated the production of farm machinery.

The key economic event of the late 1800s in California was the development of the railroads. Four merchants who had grown rich supplying gold miners (Leland Stanford, Charles Crocker, Mark Hopkins, and Collis Huntington) built the Southern Pacific Railroad into a dominant economic and political force in California. It owned 11.5 million acres of land in the state, about one-fifth of all private land in California. The opening of the transcontinental railroad in 1869 provided a link for California to eastern markets.

While the railroad promoted farming in the Midwest and hastened the decline of California wheat farming, access to eastern markets for fruits and vegetables ushered in California's modern diversified agriculture. The introduction of the seedless navel orange in the 1870s changed Southern California agriculture swiftly. As wheat and barley gave way to fruits and vegetables, the food processing industry (drying, canning) flourished.

During this time, two factors were critical to the success of California's agriculture: technology and water. The University of California, established in the 1860s as a land grant college, played an important role in bringing science and modern technology to California agriculture. The arid conditions in much of California had forced the adoption of new technologies and new products (e.g., dates, almonds, figs, and Egyptian cotton) in agriculture. By the 1890s, culminating in the work of Luther Burbank, major advances had been made in crops (early biotechnology), followed by advances in farm mechanization (the almond huller, the spray rig). Now, irrigation projects were developed to bring water to the Sacramento and San Joaquin Valleys.

California's first major aqueduct, known as the Panama Canal of the West, was built in the early 1900s and helped to fuel the growth of Los Angeles. That city grew from 100,000 in 1900 to 600,000 in 1920, in large measure due to the availability of water.

The next great surge of the California economy was fueled by oil. As a result of major discoveries in Kern and Los Angeles counties, California became the nation's leading producer of oil by 1900. By 1920, the petroleum industry led the industries in the state, with output valued at $213 million.

The oil and water development of the turn of the century generated a number of important spin-off industries including construction companies, which later would play a major role in the creation of the state's transportation infrastructure, and tool makers, who would help build the aerospace industry. A financial network grew up in the state to support the rapid growth.

Although natural resources supported the most important industries in California until 1940, the economy began to diversify around the turn of the century. By 1925, the state was producing iron and steel, locks, ships, pumps, paints, varnishes, and numerous other items that required advanced technology and manufacturing processes. By that year, the state was fully integrated into the nation's economy. Transportation and communication to the Midwest and East were fast and efficient. From this time on, new economic growth in the state could be supported for the most part by something other than the exploitation and processing of natural resources.

World War II and the Cold War: The Great Divide (1940–60)

World War II changed everything about the California economy. It helped transform a resource based economy into an advanced technology economy. The state became a center of military activity for all of the armed services. California's ports were the major funnel for men and materials flowing into the Pacific theater. Large-scale aircraft production developed in Southern California and ship building in Northern California. Between 1940–44, over $800 million was invested in some 500 new industrial plants in Southern California. At its peak, in 1943, the manufacturing work force in the state was more than two and one-half times as large as in 1940. Between 1940–50, industrial production in California went up 53 percent and total personal income rose by 240 percent. Over-all, these investments helped to build the essential infrastructure for the state's future industrial dominance.

At the end of the war, many of the 7 million servicemen who had passed through California during the war decided to stay on. While there was a slow-down following the war, the businesses that had grown during the war continued to invest in new technologies and develop new products, such as jets, missiles, radar, and lasers. Technologies developed for the military would eventually spawn whole new products for civilian use.

Following the Korean War, which stimulated the California economy as World War II had, defense oriented industries continued to grow as new weapons technologies developed. California's aircraft industry, which by the 1950s had evolved into the aerospace industry, pioneered the development of inter-continental ballistic missiles. In 1957, the launching of Sputnik expanded and broadened the significance of nonmilitary space development and again California was able to lead the way. In that year, aerospace firms employed over 270,000 Californians.

Throughout this period, defense spending helped to promote advanced technology development, especially in the aerospace industry. At the same time, the application of these technologies to commercial use was beginning to increase, leading the way to the next phase of California's industrial evolution.

An Advanced Technology Economy (1960–Today)

In the 1960s, California made the transition from dominance by defense ori-ented aerospace to a more diversified, technology based economy that began to serve commercial markets. Between 1960–65, aerospace employment growth accounted for only 22 percent of the total growth for all manufacturing indus-tries. While aerospace still accounted for over 34 percent of all manufacturing employment in 1965, the state's technology manufacturing base was broadening.

California's shift away from military based economic development was made possible by the invention of the integrated circuit in 1959. The first inte-grated circuit was put into production in 1960 by Fairchild Semiconductor, in an area south of San Francisco that has since become known as Silicon Valley. In 1962, the government purchased 100 percent of the integrated circuits pro-duced in the United States. Government purchases had dropped to 36 percent in 1969 and 10 percent in 1978.

The invention, in 1969, of the microprocessor launched the next round of growth. Between 1972–82, the first 30 or so chipmaking firms grew to over 3000 firms, which by then were offering a wide variety of high technology products and services for commercial markets. The key point is that while defense pro-curement played an important role in the birth of Silicon Valley, the transition to commercial markets in the 1960s and 1970s sustained that growth.

Aerospace has continued to rely heavily on defense and NASA spending. In 1980, over 44 percent of all NASA contracts and over 25 percent of all defense contracts were awarded to California firms. Between 1969–71, reductions in the defense budget caused major cutbacks in the aerospace industry, creating layoffs of engineers and technicians and financial difficulties for many firms. Some firms, such as Hughes, continued to diversify into other commercial technology areas. However, during the recent 1979–85 defense buildup, aerospace industries have grown and have become even more dependent on federal spending; several firms have withdrawn from commercial aviation.

By the 1970s, California had become an advanced technology based economy. The largest growth in jobs and output occurred in the technology manufacturing and aerospace sectors. By 1973, California surpassed New York as the state with the highest average hourly value added by manufacturing. The use of semiconductors in microcomputers helped to stimulate a boom in the development of personal computers, led by Apple Computer. Much of the growth in technology based business in the 1970s came from new, small enterprises. Between 1975–79, new business formations in California increased by two and one-half times the national average. By 1980, high technology manufacturing maintained over 3700 business facilities with a total payroll of $6 billion and 23 percent of the state's total manufacturing labor force. This sector, which includes computers, computer services, instruments, communication equipment, and electronic components, accounted for over one-third of the state's manufacturing exports in 1980.

By 1980, a series of regional agglomeration economies had evolved. Silicon Valley had become a center of high technology innovation involving a network of producers, suppliers, service industries, venture capitalists, and lawyers. In Southern California, regional agglomerations emerged around the aerospace industry. Agglomerations were emerging in the San Diego area around biotechnology and biomedical research, with the University of California at San Diego as a hub. Regional agglomerations also developed in the Central Valley around increasingly "high tech" agriculture involving suppliers, processors, and growers.[2]

The new advanced technology economy of California[3] in the 1980s is characterized by the following:

- *Advanced technology in industry*—By the end of the 1970s, California had the world's greatest concentration of high technology industry, the highest industry spending in R & D, and over 30 percent of the nation's scientists and engineers. Technology had become a driving force in both the creation of new products and the transformation of older industries such as agriculture.
- *Services in support of industry*—While over 70 percent of California's jobs are in non-goods producing occupations (the largest in the nation), most of the growth in services is in areas like communications, finance, and business services, which are linked to industry. The growth of personal services, in fact, has declined.
- *Increasing interdependence*—The growth of advanced technologies leads to increased interdependence among firms, groups, and individuals in regional agglomerations.
- *Rapid change and innovation*—Product markets and new technologies change rapidly, placing a premium on innovation and adaptability by advanced technology firms.

• *Knowledge and education*—California has been the leader in public higher education, receives the most federal funds for R & D, and leads the nation in the creation and use of new knowledge. Industry in the state employs more professional and technical workers than the national average.

California Economy Today

The California economy has experienced five great surges fueled by driving industries: mining, agriculture, oil, aerospace, and microelectronics. Each surge has brought a major transformation of the economy and has stimulated new regional economic dynamics. Except for gold mining, each major industry created by these surges has remained and has continued to change and grow. Will there be another great surge, and if so, what will it be?

Impending Maturity or Another Transformation?

There has been a growing concern in California that its economy is reaching a state of maturity that could lead to stagnation or decline. The rapid growth rates of the 1960s and early 1970s have not been sustained. The annual growth rate (in constant dollars) of the California gross state product declined from 5 percent between 1950–60 to 4.3 percent between 1960–70 and dropped to 3.8 percent between 1970–80. *The Economist* noted, in a 1984 review of the California economy, "the state may soon have to settle for the increasingly modest growth typical of a mature economy. Some see a turning away from wealth creation to political brokerage that organized interest groups in older economies tend to occupy themselves with."[4]

The rapid population growth of the 1950s and early 1960s prompted a rethinking of the growth mentality. Ronald Reagan ran for governor in 1966 against the rapid growth in government services that had accompanied population growth. Frustration with the growth of government came to a head with the passage of Proposition 13 in 1978. Jerry Brown ran for governor on an explicit "era of limits" platform. An increasing concern for the impact of growth on the environment and quality of life began to dominate public policy discussions in the 1970s. This concern, expressed by an increasing number of environmental groups, was translated into laws and regulations affecting future growth.

An Economic Profile

The national recession of 1981–82 hit California hard, causing a 3.8 percent decrease in manufacturing employment. In 1982, over 4000 businesses closed and 1.3 million workers were unemployed. During that year, the only gains in manufacturing employment were in microelectronics. In 1983 and 1984, the California economy came back strongly. In 1983, real gross state product grew by 3.9 percent, and in 1984 it grew by 8.8 percent. Unemployment dropped from 9.7 percent in 1983 to 7.7 percent in 1984.

The recovery was led by aerospace and high technology manufacturing. An estimated 20 percent of the state's employment growth in 1984 was in aerospace, electronics, and defense related activities. Southern California's aerospace industry clearly has benefited from the growth in defense spending since 1979. Total federal defense spending in California was up 8 percent in 1984, and employment in aerospace grew by 5 percent. There is a concern that the growing dependence of California's aerospace industry on defense spending may create problems (similar to those of the early 1970s and post-Vietnam War slowdowns) as the growth of the defense budget slows down.

The high technology manufacturing industry, while continuing to grow in 1984, has been experiencing significant restructuring and increasing foreign competition. In early 1985, overcapacity and slowdown in demand began a shakeout in the computer industry. The semiconductor industry faced increasing foreign competition as the Japanese gained more than 60 percent of the market for 64K RAM memory chips. This has promoted the first efforts at protectionism on the part of the previously free trade oriented electronics industry, as chip makers filed antidumping petitions, a possible sign of industry maturity. Agriculture did not join the recovery as product sales and prices generally remain depressed. The strong U.S. dollar caused California's exports to fall from $4 billion in 1981 to under $3 billion in 1984.

Leading the nation, California's economy began its structural shift toward services in the 1940s. By 1950, more than 58 percent of total nonagricultural employment was accounted for by four major service sectors: wholesale and retail trade; finance, insurance, and real estate; services; and government. By 1980, the same four sectors employed more than 69 percent of the total. However, while the annual rate of growth of manufacturing employment declined from 5.7 percent in 1950–60 to 1.7 percent in 1960–70, the rate increased to 2.6 percent in 1970–80. This reflects the growth of high technology manufacturing in the 1970s. It is important to note also the multiplier effect that high technology manufacturing has had on the growth of service and support industries in California. Every dollar of output in high tech manufacturing generates more than a dollar of income in services and support.

Since the early 1970s, California has been experiencing a rapid restructuring in its basic manufacturing industries. In 1972, 64 percent of manufacturing workers were employed in basic industries while 36 percent were employed in high technology industries. By 1983, 56 percent were employed in basic industry and 43.9 percent in high technology. Mature industries such as auto, steel, rubber, and lumber experienced plant shutdowns and layoffs. During 1980–84, over 700 plant closures resulted in over 12,000 jobs lost in California.

Table 12-1 provides a profile of the current structure of the California economy based on a comparison of earnings in California industry vis a vis the United States as a whole. For each industry, the table also shows the location quotient, or the ratio of California's share of industry earnings to those of the U.S. industry as a whole. Location quotients greater than 1 indicate that an industry is relatively heavily concentrated in California.

Table 12-1 indicates that, compared to the U.S. average, California personal

Table 12-1. Distribution of California and U.S. Earnings Across Industries, and California Location Quotient for Each Industry, 1983

	% of U.S. Earnings in Industry	% of Calif. Earnings in Industry	Calif. Location Quotient
Agriculture	1.79	0.42	0.23
Mining	1.66	0.73	0.46
Construction	5.30	4.80	0.91
Manufacturing	23.78	22.09	0.93
Nondurable Goods	8.94	6.14	.69
Food	1.86	1.79	0.96
Textiles	0.63	0.10	0.16
Apparel	0.76	0.58	0.76
Paper	0.95	0.43	0.45
Printing	1.46	1.27	0.87
Chemicals	1.71	0.73	0.43
Petroleum	0.49	0.66	1.35
Rubber/Plastics	0.81	0.53	0.65
Leather	0.15	0.05	0.33
Durable goods	14.84	15.95	1.07
Primary Metals	1.37	0.56	0.41
Fabricated Metals	1.76	1.43	0.41
Nonelectrical Machinery	2.89	2.70	0.93
Electrical Equipment	2.67	4.48	1.68
Transportation Equipment	1.68	3.44	2.05
Motor Vehicles	1.38	0.34	0.25
Stone/Clay/Glass	0.73	0.54	0.74
Instruments	0.95	1.21	1.27
Miscellaneous	0.36	0.37	1.03
Transportation/Communication/ Public Utilities	7.79	7.18	0.92
Trucking and Warehousing	1.65	1.31	0.80
Communications	2.37	2.59	1.09
Utilities	1.51	1.11	0.74
Wholesale Trade	6.69	6.40	0.96
Retail Trade	9.62	9.96	1.04
Finance/Insurance/Real Estate	6.29	6.34	0.99
Banking	1.75	9.96	1.04
Services	20.08	22.58	1.13
Business Services	3.53	4.80	1.36
Health Services	6.93	6.70	0.97
Legal Services	1.63	1.65	1.01
Education Services	0.97	0.85	0.88
Social Services	0.58	0.54	0.93
Government	16.97	17.08	1.01
Federal Civilian	3.86	3.46	0.90
Federal Military	1.78	2.37	1.33
State and Local	11.34	11.25	0.99

income earnings are more highly concentrated in transportation equipment (primarily aerospace), electrical equipment, petroleum, instruments, communications, banking, business services, legal services, and federal military. California earnings are less concentrated in nondurable goods manufacturing, metals, and motor vehicles.

A shift-share analysis of the California economy provides further evidence of the degree to which the state has become dependent on high technology for its economic growth. In this analysis, economic growth is divided into three components: a portion that would occur if the state had the same mix of industries as the national average and those industries grew at the same rate as the national average; a portion due to the region's different mix or share of high and low growth industries from the national average (the "share" component); and a portion due to the differences between regional growth rate for the industry and the national growth rate for these industries (the "shift" component). Table 12-2 shows the results of a shift-share analysis of various California industries. It reveals that nearly all of California's growth has resulted from its favorable mix of industries (the share effect), particularly within durable goods manufacturing, such industries as electrical equipment, transportation equipment (mostly aerospace), and instruments. These high growth industries are more heavily represented in California than in other states. The growth rate for non-

Table 12-2. Analysis of Contribution of Various Economic Sectors to California's Share and Shift Components (in Millions of 1972 Dollars, Losses in Parentheses)

Sector	Share Effect			Shift Effect		
	1959–73	1973–79	1979–83	1959–73	1973–79	1979–83
Farm	(844)	1055	732	(19)	297	(101)
Nonfarm	1477	7485	4176	16	252	(3)
Agricultural Services	83	77	26	90	63	10
Mining	15	(134)	154	(78)	(373)	(24)
Manufacturing	(539)	2206	3318	(1085)	(520)	403
Nondurable	211	695	267	(820)	(260)	67
Durable	(979)	1428	3230	(31)	(178)	188
Electric Equipment	546	399	1034	144	90	64
Transportation Equipment	(899)	281	350	422	363	25
Instruments	70	379	215	(83)	(57)	15
Finance/Insurance/Real Estate	179	985	(571)	44	75	89
Banking	71	(384)	730	(17)	11	(100)
Services	388	2062	(98)	967	576	624
Business Services	196	442	(74)	317	400	368
Government	112	(3646)	2813	1410	716	240
Federal Civilian	31	(141)	117	47	6	(4)
Federal Military	80	(580)	782	217	(137)	(7)
State and Local	181	82	(535)	966	(198)	45
Total	631	8969	4908	(2)	126	0

durable goods manufacturing was lower than the national average for all industries. Tables 12-1 and 12-2 reveal a state economy that shifted from traditional manufacturing to high technology manufacturing and benefited from that shift throughout the 1973–83 period, relative to the United States as a whole.

While business services continue to grow in California, their relationship to high technology manufacturing has become more clear. Increasingly, it has become recognized that growth of services in California is linked to the growth in manufacturing, with as much as 25 percent of services tightly linked to manufacturing as suppliers and service supports.

Current Concerns About the California Economy

In 1985, a number of concerns surfaced about the California economy. Although a return to growth followed the 1981–82 recession, each of the major driving sectors (high-technology manufacturing, aerospace, and high-tech agriculture) experienced some difficulties. Computers have been going through a shakeout, semiconductors increasingly have been threatened by Japanese imports, aerospace is vulnerable to slower growth in the defense budget, and agriculture has been hurt by declining exports. Beyond these immediate problems, more basic concerns emerged about the competitiveness of industries and the impending maturity of the California economy. These include the following:

• *Foreign and domestic competition*—Increasingly, foreign competitors are finding they can compete with products made in California both on cost and quality. Many of these competitors have copied technology developed by California firms. In addition, other states are making investments in technology and education to compete with California.

• *Rising cost of doing business*—California has increasingly found firms deciding not to locate in the state or moving out because they find the cost of doing business too high relative to other places either in the United States or off shore. These costs range from the cost of land and utilities to the impact of regulations and taxes.

• *Declining quality of life*—One of California's greatest attractions has been its high quality of life. It now faces the challenge of preserving its natural environment in the face of rapid growth and making the necessary investment to maintain high quality transportation, parks, and public facilities. Between 1950 and the early 1970s, California invested in first class infrastructure and public services. Since the late 1970s, California's spending on roads and education has declined relative to other states.

• *Changing demographics*—Immigration and aging are changing the demographics of California. Hispanics and Asians are the fastest growing population groups.[5] One in five Californians is Hispanic and Hispanics will be the majority within a few decades. As the postwar baby boom ages, there are fewer native-born entrants into the labor force; many new entrants speak English as a second language or speak no English at all. The changing composition of the labor force presents employment and training challenges for California's economic future.

• *Housing costs*—Housing costs in California are the highest in the nation and have begun to act as a constraint on recruitment of personnel. These high costs are a result of both limited availability of land and public policy decisions concerning land use and zoning.

• *Water availability and quality*—California's continued economic growth has always depended on the ability to engineer solutions to its basic water problem. In recent years, the state has not been able to reach consensus on how to get more water to the southern part of the state. In addition, toxic substances from agriculture and industrial chemicals present an increasing threat to the quality of the state's water supply. A 1985 state report estimated that the cost of cleaning up the current toxic waste problem in California could be $40 billion over the next decade.[6]

• *Uneven growth*—While economic growth has been rapid in Silicon Valley and the Los Angeles basin, some regions of the state, such as the northern timber area and parts of the central valley, have not prospered because agriculture and forest products have not shared in the overall growth. Since 1969, the percentage of persons below the poverty level has grown steadily.

These concerns present a challenge to California as it searches for its future sources of economic growth. As in the past, California has been able to overcome problems through innovation and adaptation. Will it continue?

Explanations for California's Growth

One reason for California's growth has been the presence of entrepreneurs who were willing and able to take advantage of opportunities at hand and create new products and industries that met the demands of growing markets both within and outside the state.

A number of external and internal factors helped to create the opportunities that entrepreneurs took advantage of in building new industries through innovation. This section examines some of the causes of California's growth and the role that public and private institutions in the state played in shaping those causes.

Some primary external causes (or factors outside the direct influence of California itself) appear to be America's frontier tradition, the western tilt of population, the state's natural climate, World War II and the defense build-up, the development of microelectronics technology and the growth of computer technology, and the rise of Pacific basin trade. Each of these factors beyond California's control helped to fuel the growth of California's economy by either attracting people and capital to the state (enhancing supply/capacity) or by creating new markets (stimulating demand). These external factors, together with macroeconomic policy (determined by the federal government through monetary and fiscal policy), international trade patterns (determined in part by exchange rates, tariff, and nontariff policies) set basic parameters for growth in the state. California's economic growth was constrained when macroeconomic policies brought about a recession through high interest rates in 1981–82 or when the high value of the dollar reduced the export of California agricultural or electronics products in 1982–85.

Within these critical parameters, a number of internal factors, under the control of the state, historically, have exerted some influence on the shape and degree of economic growth in California. The evolution of industry in the state suggests two key factors: *state investments in infrastructure and education* and the *state's entrepreneurial climate.* Both appear to be the product of a series of state level actions and decisions, not always made for the explicit purpose of economic development, but still having the result of creating an environment for growth. The following section explores these critical internal factors.

California helped to create its economic comparative advantage by making critical investments in the capacity of the state to create wealth. Two key investment areas that represent this dramatically are physical infrastructure and education.

Investments in Infrastructure

California's investments in infrastructure go back to its early development with the railroad development of the late 1800s followed by the construction of the first set of aqueducts in the 1900s and the major dams and water projects of the 1930s, culminating in the construction of Boulder (now Hoover) Dam, which brought water and power to Southern California.

California's modern infrastructure building began during the postwar administration of Governor Earl Warren. During World War II, as the aircraft and other defense industries expanded in the state and filled the state treasury with tax revenues, Warren refused to enact tax cuts and instead placed all excess receipts into reserve funds. At the end of the war, the huge surplus was invested in the construction of schools, colleges, prisons, hospitals, and water projects. As Neal Peirce and Jerry Hagstrom point out in their *Book of America,* "Rarely has a politician showed such foresight. Without Warren's hoarding of the pot of gold in the 1940s, California might not have been able to make the quantum jump in services indispensable to accommodating its fantastic postwar population inflow."[7]

The highwater mark of infrastructure building occurred between 1958–66, during the administration of Pat Brown. During this time of rapid population growth, Brown promoted the construction of 1000 of California's 1650 miles of freeways, three new university campuses, six state colleges, and a $1.75 billion water project. At the same time that Nelson Rockefeller was promoting massive public works projects in New York, Pat Brown was acting as the "master builder" in California. During Pat Brown's administration, the state's expenditures doubled and the number of state government employees grew by 50 percent.

Pat Brown's philosophy of growth and infrastructure building is captured in this passage written in 1965:

> Growth is the trademark of the Twentieth Century California. Economic growth, which is so fundamental to our hopes for continued progress, can be achieved only by the best efforts of industry, labor, government, and the academic community. . . . Let me review some of the programs of the state govern-

ment which contribute directly to our economic growth. Leading the list is *education*. The state is pouring more than $1 billion into the local school systems every year to provide the best education anywhere in the nation. We make available free college and university training to every qualified student at an annual cost of $466 million. We are now in the process of doubling in ten short years the higher education facilities it took two generations to build. The *California Water Project* is another example of the state's contribution to a sound economy. Without this project, Southern California's growth would have been forced to level off within the next ten years. . . . I regard this as the most significant physical accomplishment of my administration. . . . *Highway construction* is another example of prudent investment by the state of California. This is the only state in the nation where products travel to their markets over the best available highways without the producers paying one cent in tolls.[8]

After Pat Brown, however, the voters of California expressed much less support for growth as a goal of public policy. Concern about the rapid increase in the size of government (and taxes) to provide these expanded public services helped bring Ronald Reagan to office in 1966. The 1969 oil spill off the Santa Barbara coast and concern about the quality of San Francisco Bay helped create an activist environmental movement in California that attempted to slow major infrastructure projects, including highway and water systems. Expressing concern about the impact of growth on environment and society, Jerry Brown rejected his father's growth approach with his explicit call for an "era of limits" in 1974. Thus, California's major infrastructure building phase came to an end.

A 1963 analysis of public capital investment in California between 1950–61 prepared for the state development plan program points out the high degree of investment in infrastructure in the decade of the 1950s, even prior to the full impact of the Brown years. The study points out that

during the period of 1950–1961, total public capital investment increased by a factor of 3.1, while the California population increased from 10 million to 16 million or a factor of 1.6. Since the cost of construction index went from 100 to 135, it might be conjectured that, if capital investment were related only to total population, it would have increased by a factor of 1.6; if this factor is raised to reflect price changes, the corrected factor would be 2.16.[9]

Clearly, during the postwar period, California was investing in public capital faster than its population was growing, thus creating increasing benefits for the future.

Since the late 1960s, California, like most of the nation, has not continued to invest at levels that would even maintain the current infrastructure. While California spent 2.4 percent of its gross state product on infrastructure in 1970–71, it spent only 1.8 percent in 1981–82. The 1984 report of the governor's Infrastructure Review Task Force found approximately $29 billion in deferred maintenance needs and $49 billion in new infrastructure construction needs.[10]

While California, like much of the nation, neglected its investment in basic infrastructure during the 1970s, it has begun to address the problem in the 1980s. Governor George Deukmejian has made this issue a major element of his administration by promoting a new five year, $13 billion transportation program that will repair and improve existing roads and produce 135 miles of new freeways. This represents the first major increase in transportation construction in ten years.

Investment in Education

A major element in California's ability to promote innovation and exploit science and technology has been the development of its colleges and universities.[11] Since its founding in 1868, the University of California has played an important role in the economy of the state, first as a leading center of agricultural research and later as a center of research in science and technology. Unlike eastern schools, which focused more on humanities, California's schools concentrated on science and engineering, fields critical to the state's future economic growth.

Edward Dennison, in his pioneering work on the *Sources of Economic Growth in the United States,* indicated that the greatest source of growth has been investment in education and in research and development. Nearly one-half of past economic growth could be explained by these two sources.[12]

The size of the California investment in higher education, both public and private, surpasses that of any other state. In 1981, it spent $7.9 billion, or 12 percent of the national total, on both public and private higher education out of a national total of $64 billion. More students come to California than to any other state, and California retains a higher proportion of its residents for higher education study than any other state.[13] In 1984, the California Postsecondary Education Commission published a report showing the economic impact of the state's investment in higher education. The report states that for the 1981–82 fiscal year, California colleges and universities had a direct economic impact of $28.3 billion out of a gross state product of $360 billion, or 8 percent of GSP. This figure represents the direct impact of purchases, wages, and contracts. It was arrived at using rather modest multipliers ranging from 2.37 to 2.78 for the respective segments. The report states that

> it did not include such factors as the additional wealth produced by the new knowledge they created, the added income generated by graduates and nongraduates, the enhancement of student skills and talents, or the social and cultural contributions of higher education that, while impossible to quantify, also enriched the quality of life in this State.[14]

California Master Plan for Higher Education

Higher education policy in California is housed in a 1960 document called the "Master Plan for Higher Education." This document specifies the obligations of the state to support opportunities for postsecondary education among its citizens, the state institutions that will provide postsecondary opportunities, the functions of each institution, and the means by which these functions will be coordinated.

The foundations of the master plan were laid in the mid-1940s, when the University of California consisted of four campuses: Berkeley, Los Angeles, Davis, and Santa Barbara. The California State University was not yet formed, but its antecedent, the seven state colleges coordinated by the State Board of Education, included Arcata, Chico, Fresno, San Diego, San Francisco, San Jose, and San Luis Obispo. The board also had loose responsibility for the coordination of the state's fifty-five "junior colleges." Because there was no clear functional division among these institutions to help guide their management, there was little to prevent the leadership of any single institution from lobbying independently in Sacramento for budget, facilities, and equipment. To fill this administrative vacuum, the Liaison Committee of the Regents of the University of California and the California State Board of Education was formed in 1945. This committee was charged with promoting mutual cooperation among the institutions.

Two years later, with the support of the legislature, the liaison committee undertook a survey of the needs of higher education with the intent to make recommendations to the legislature in 1948. The study team consisted of three distinguished educators, led by George Strayer of Columbia University. Their report established many key principles upon which higher education has been built since. Three of its recommendations are important from an economic standpoint.

First, it recommended a functional distinction among the University of California, the state colleges, and the junior colleges. Implicit in this distinction was a de facto manpower plan that since has become more explicit. In essence, the junior colleges were to offer the first two years of instruction and, thus, were responsible for offering technical curricula that culminated in the associate degree or a certificate. The state colleges were to offer baccalaureate and masters degrees and were responsible for offering occupational curricula consistent with these levels of teaching. The university was to concentrate on graduate and professional education and research. Recent data on age differentials among different segments of the state's education system demonstrate the different functions each segment serves. In 1981, the average age of students in the three segments of California public higher education was 23.0 years for students at the University of California, 25.6 years for students in the California State University, and 30.4 years for students in the California Community Colleges. The community colleges are serving an older population that seeks reeducation, retraining, and continuing learning opportunities.[15]

Second, by reserving research and the granting of the doctorates to the university, the study team established a de facto research policy for California. Research became an important part of state educational policy. Its economic implications were to be felt later.

Third, it recommended a plan by which new regional campuses would be built in place of expanding existing campuses beyond their capacities. This principle since has grown into a public system of 134 campuses placed in communities throughout California, each with its own community ties to industry.

The 1960 Master Plan

Between the years 1950–60, total higher education enrollment increased from 240,000 to 497,000 with 8 of the 9 UC campuses established, 14 of the 19 state college campuses established, and 60 of the 106 community colleges established. In 1960, the legislature established a Master Plan Survey Team to establish strategic policies to guide future growth.

In response to the massive growth in higher education and the growing need to assure educational access for all Californians, the Master Plan Survey Team proposed the Master Plan for California Higher Education. This plan also had three components significant to economic development.

First, the plan extended the concept of functional distinction established in the Strayer Report, creating functional specialization among the state's higher education institutions. The plan specifically enumerated these functions so as to prevent the institutions from competing for high-cost programs, which would have created a cadre of high-cost programs at significantly lesser quality than would otherwise have been possible. For example, it gave responsibility for professional schools, such as law and medicine, to the University of California.

Second, and most important, the plan guaranteed access for a tuition-free college education to every qualified Californian. Every Californian who graduated from high school was guaranteed a right to enroll in a California junior college. The upper one-third of high school graduating classes could enroll in a state college, and the upper one-eighth could enroll in the University of California. Transfer policies based on student performance were recommended, which allowed students to move from one level of institution to another on the basis of merit. This design has been described as holding true to two divergent principles at the same time, namely, egalitarianism and merit.[16]

Third, the plan created an organizational context. The state colleges, which up to this point had significant independence because they were under the management of the State Board of Education, were organized into a segment of higher education known as the California State Colleges (now the California State University). This segment was given a chancellor, who serves as its executive officer, and a board of trustees, which has enjoyed significant business representation since its creation. The junior colleges were redefined as community colleges with responsibility to provide transfer courses for those wanting to go to the university or to a state college, courses in vocational and technical fields, and general or liberal arts courses. The community colleges were also made part of a separate segment with its own chancellor and board of trustees. This segment became the focus of most of the growth that occurred from 1960–70, when the number of community colleges expanded from fifty-five to ninety-one. Finally, a Coordinating Council for Higher Education was established, with responsibility to coordinate the growth of higher education, recommend new policies, and provide faithful implementation of the master plan.

Much of the master plan was implemented: Three new universities and six new state colleges were established. One of the new universities, University of California at San Diego, established in 1965, has become one of the leading research universities in the nation. It receives the second highest amount of federal grants after Berkeley and has had an important economic impact on San Diego, by attracting technical talent to the area and stimulating the growth of new technology industries. Another new university, UC—Irvine has had an important impact on the development of Orange County.

The economic development aspects of the master plan, however, were overshadowed by its importance in opening up access to higher education in California. The number of students enrolled in colleges and universities rose dramatically in the 1960s as a result of the master plan. Remedial changes in the educational establishment were created to adjust ethnic imbalances. For the disadvantaged and the minorities, educational access provided a new avenue of opportunity.

Loss of Consensus

In 1964, the Free Speech Movement at UC—Berkeley destroyed the consensus in California concerning support for higher education. Students, reacting in part to the dehumanizing effect of the growing university, spoke out against bureaucracy and the impact of computer punch card identities. The Free Speech Movement was the beginning of a decade of protest activity that ranged across the nation. The protest broke support for higher education in the mind of the public. The University of California, which had been considering sites for additional campuses, cancelled all further efforts to acquire land. Clark Kerr, president of the University and a key guiding force behind the master plan, became the subject of attacks from the newly elected Governor Ronald Reagan and resigned in 1967.

The period of public questioning of the worth of higher education and the value of university research that followed during the Reagan administration and much of the Jerry Brown administration, seemed to cause policy makers to devalue higher education as an investment with an economic payoff.

Concerns about the competitiveness of California industries both internationally and domestically has helped to stimulate a new found concern for education. One event that helped to spark attention was the loss of the Microelectronics Computer Technology Consortium (MCC) to Austin, Texas. Many observers believe that Texas's greater commitment to its university was one key factor in MCC's decision to locate in Austin rather than California. The MCC decision was followed by two years of significantly increased state funding for all levels of education.

Lessons from California's Experience

California made a massive commitment to its higher education system in 1945–66. Between 1966–80, however, the commitment did not increase significantly. Although the state's higher education system came through that difficult time in surprisingly good shape, California's high quality K–12 educational system, which also received high levels of support in the postwar period, has suffered continually since Proposition 13 reduced local property taxes.

What is most interesting about California's commitment to higher education is that it was motivated by a mix of economic and social objectives. Originally, the university's practical role in agriculture and mining was a key motivating force. Later, the role of the university as a magnet to attract talent was a factor. Just as the university's economic potential was being realized in 1960, the focus of attention shifted to the social concern of equality and access. At that point the economic motivation for investment in education began to lessen. When the students who had gained increased access began to revolt, the taxpayers decided it was no longer worth the investment. It took a growing recognition that California was losing its competitive edge to stimulate a return to the economic interest in education.

Creating an Entrepreneurial Climate

In addition to making critical investments in education and infrastructure, California has successfully created an environment that encourages systematic innovation and entrepreneurship. It accepts diversity and new ideas; it tolerates differences; historically it has adopted the immigrant seeking a second chance (a high proportion of California's entrepreneurs have been immigrants).

Through a combination of factors, California was able to create an entrepreneurial climate that promoted high technology industries in the 1960s and 1970s. This is most clearly demonstrated in the regional agglomerations in the Silicon Valley (around microelectronics), in the Los Angeles basin (around aerospace), and in San Diego (around biotechnology and electronics). These regional agglomerations create self-sustaining clusters of major producers, suppliers, investors, and support services. Roger Miller and Marcel Cote suggest several factors important to the development of such regional technology clusters:

> the presence of incubators—companies or labs, where entrepreneurs can learn their trade and polish their skills before going off on their own; the wide availability of contracts to help start-ups survive their critical early years; and the emergence of success models, which not only stimulate entrepreneurship but also reduce risks for investors, suppliers and bankers who are called upon to assist in new endeavors. In addition to these business conditions, three institutional factors have strongly influenced the dynamism of the clustering process in a region: the availability of state-of-the-art technology, the presence of local venture capitalists and strong community support . . . in building and maintaining the institutions that contribute to the development of a high technology base.[17]

Public policy has an important impact on each of these critical institutional factors. As Miller and Cote point out, the role of government should be "supportive . . . [aimed] mainly at creating a hospitable environment and encouraging state-of-the-art research."[18]

The experiences in two of California's regional agglomerations, Silicon Valley and the Southern California Aerospace complex, illustrate how government, the private sector, financial institutions, and universities have interacted to create an entrepreneurial climate that has stimulated innovation and growth.

Lessons from Silicon Valley

The evolution of Silicon Valley[19] illustrates the complex relationship between private and public actions in the development of an entrepreneurial climate that supports regional clustering of technology. Government played an important role in the growth of Silicon Valley, but not the direct role often assumed. The federal government helped to create initial markets and both the federal and state governments helped provide the necessary educational and technology infrastructure for continued growth. After the initial impetus of defense spending, the commercial market for advanced electronics and internally funded research and development formed the base for Silicon Valley's eventual success. Venture capital also was a key, as was the close working relationship between Stanford University and Silicon Valley electronics firms.

Role of Government

Procurement of microelectronics and support of higher education were by far the most important government activities bearing on the development of Silicon Valley. Government sponsored R & D, the traditional support for new technology, had little impact on the semiconductor industry except in building a research base for future development at the state's universities during and after World War II.

Procurement policy was effective because the government established clear performance needs, rather than detailed design specifications, and paid generously if anyone could meet the requirements. That the government's needs were much the same as consumer needs increased the effectiveness of its procurement policy. In effect, the government paid the high development costs for new devices, which were then sold to both the government and the much larger commercial market.

Educational support by both the federal and state government had the broadest and longest range impact, extending to microprocessing and more recent technologies. Government funds provided fellowships and research project support for nearly all Ph.D. scientists involved in semiconductor development until the mid-1970s. Although university research played a minimal role in basic semiconductor development, without this government support, the new industry would have been starved for personnel because of the high cost of graduate education in the physical sciences.

Most of the successful government activities were strongly influenced by the *style* of the government-industry relationship in the 1950s and 1960s—uniquely cooperative, flexible, and task oriented. Building on the close relationships established during World War II and working in a time of perceived national danger, industry and government acted more as partners than antagonists. Two aspects of this relationship were particularly important: the government's willingness to support new, small companies and its willingness to support unexpected new technologies.

The rapid dissemination of technical information has been important to the electronics industry. Informal communication networks cut across companies and regions. The government supported information sharing by financing conferences and journals and by setting relatively lax security standards. The industry and the military chose to speed development through open exchange of information rather than maintain strict secrecy.

After procurement and education, the key government policy was federal tax expenditure. In the 1950s and 1960s, the federal government set relatively low tax rates for capital gains. These low rates encouraged the development of venture capital funds, which were crucially important to start-ups. Tax rates on capital gains were increased during the 1970s and then, under pressure from business leaders, were again decreased significantly in 1978.

Role of the Private Market

Initially, the private sector proved a reluctant consumer of most early semiconductor technologies. Commercial reluctance to apply new technology led several semiconductor firms to enter retail markets in the 1970s with such products as digital watches and calculators. Nearly all such initial attempts failed. However, despite the slow initial commercial adoption of semiconductors and ICs, a significant commercial market eventually developed and fueled the growth of Silicon Valley. With the invention of the microprocessor from 1969 on, most shipments of ICs went to commercial buyers.

Most innovation responded to commercial markets because such customers could respond to new products much more rapidly than the government. The practice of requiring endless testing and documentation before accepting a component ensured that the government would have older technology. Yet, components sold to the commercial market still needed to be reliable. To achieve adequate reliability, alternative production and testing procedures were found. Therefore, commercial components went through one (low-cost) path and government components through a different (much higher-cost) path.

The large, commercial market that developed after 1969 was the single most important key to the speed of development in semiconductor design and manufacturing technologies. Firms would have invested less in research if the long-run market had been a small, government only market that required much less rapid change in products.

Role of Venture Capital

The availability of risk capital was vital to the development of the semiconductor industry. Most of the major semiconductor developments came out of four new firms financed by venture capital: Fairchild, Intel, Texas Instruments, and Mostek. Large, well-capitalized electronics firms played only a minor role in developing early semiconductor technology.

Financing for these new, small companies came from a variety of sources. Early venture capital came from wealthy individuals (such as Sherman Fairchild of Fairchild Aircraft), venture capital firms (such as Venrock), and other companies (such as Baldwin-United). As early investments paid off, venture capital firms grew to become the dominant funding source for new companies in the valley.

Venture capital success depends largely on three ingredients: risk capital, technically sophisticated investment managers, and a strong market for new stocks. Risk capital generally is available from moderately wealthy individuals. Many venture capital investors are executives in the electronics industry itself. Technically sophisticated investment managers are most often financial experts who have learned the technology. A strong stock market for new issues provides the final profits for the venture capitalist, who generally reinvests in new ventures.

Government policy played a major role in making venture capital available. It allowed the creation of early venture capital firms in the once heavily regulated financial industry and then taxed their profits at low rates. Venture capital is so risky—fewer than 10 percent of investments are highly profitable—that banks have made few venture capital investments until recently.

Role of Stanford University

By almost any account, Stanford University was a key ingredient in Silicon Valley's success. It has played its most important role in training commercially minded engineers. Professor Fred Terman and his protege, John Linvill, recruited the brightest graduate electrical engineers, steered them into stimulating research assistantships, taught them to "think commercial," and, when they were ready, encouraged them to join the existing and newly forming high technology companies in the area. Although some of this pattern was seen at Berkeley in the 1930s and 1940s, neither Berkeley nor other local universities forged symbiotic university-industry linkages Stanford did.

Terman did more than just work closely with his students. He was also instrumental in establishing the first university-based research park. Stanford Industrial Park was established in 1951 on 655 acres of excess endowed land that Stanford was prohibited from selling. The park was designed both to provide revenue and to create jobs for the university's graduates.

Summary of Silicon Valley Experience

In many ways, Silicon Valley may be unique, not to be duplicated again. It grew from an unusual combination of government, private, financial, and university forces coming together at the right time to serve a growing market. However, it is clear from the review of forces shaping the development of Silicon Valley that creating a climate for innovation and entrepreneurship in a regional technology cluster involves supportive government actions to help stimulate technology development and diffusion (largely through its methods of procurement, education, and tax policy), stimulate the availability of risk capital (through tax and regulatory changes), and encourage (or simply allow) greater public-private collaboration in education and research. While government did not plan or create Silicon Valley, and the state government role in this case was limited, the case does show that government can play an important indirect, collaborative role in the development of a high tech "industrial district."

Lessons from Southern California's Aerospace Industry

The development of California's aerospace industry[20] presents an interesting comparison to the growth of Silicon Valley. While the semiconductor industry represents perhaps the prototypical example of how collaborative government policies and private action can help support an entrepreneurial environment, thus setting the stage for an emerging industry, the aerospace industry presents a much more government dominated approach to the growth of regional agglomerations. The heavy involvement of the federal government in all phases of the aerospace industry's development greatly affected the pattern of development in Southern California. While the state's "entrepreneurial environment" influenced the decisions of firms to locate in California, other factors, such as the state's educational policy, the presence of a technically skilled work force, the state's natural climate, and the nature of the industries already in place also played major roles in Southern California's regional agglomeration and eventual domination in the aerospace field. The importance of each of these factors will be discussed.

The Federal Government's Role

Development of U.S. defense capabilities spurred and continues to shape the course of the aerospace industry's growth. No real aircraft industry (the precursor to the aerospace industry) existed prior to World War I.[21] Despite the development of mail transport and commercial aircraft, without government support, the industry came to a virtual standstill between wars.

World War II brought the federal government back as a major force in industry growth. This and later increases in defense spending not only created a sudden surge in demand for aircraft but also affected the way in which both capital expansions and research and development were financed within the industry. Throughout the history of the aircraft (and later the aerospace) industry, government spending in research and development was to be the major force in innovation within both the military and commercial sectors of the industry. Moreover, after the end of World War II, the government tried to maintain the existing capacity for aircraft production in case of another war. It therefore maintained a policy of spreading its contracts among the existing suppliers. The result was a sprawling industry, larger than would be expected if the industry's development had been determined solely by market forces, dependent largely on government spending for subsistence.

Existing Industries

Aside from government spending on research and development, the rapid pace of innovation within the industry also stemmed from its ability to build upon technological breakthroughs in other industries. For example, developments in metallurgy and petroleum were instrumental in the development and wide-spread use of the jet engine; California's strength in the petroleum industry made it an advantageous place for firms to locate and thrive. Much later in the industry's development, the nearby existence of an electronics industry became important.

State Educational Policy

The fact that the state of California made a conscious investment to ensure that its college and university system met the needs of local industry made for a readily available, skilled work force. Today, shortages in the number of skilled workers present a major constraint to the industry's ability to achieve its potential for growth.

Locational Factors

Two factors associated with California's location were instrumental in the decision of aerospace firms to locate there. Southern California's moderate climate cut down on the costs of air conditioning and heating, which could add substantially to production costs. Furthermore, its proximity to both the desert areas to the east and the Pacific Basin region made it an ideal location, since the open spaces and arid climate made the desert an excellent testing ground and proximity to the Pacific was important for strategic reasons during both World War II and the Vietnam War. More recently, proximity to the rapidly growing Pacific basin countries opens up increased trade possibilities.

Summary of Aerospace Experience

The aerospace industry presents an interesting case, because for the most part, after the initial technological breakthroughs of the early pioneers such as the Wright Brothers, most innovation was funded and encouraged by the federal government. Government spending was so important that it affected the degree of competition within, and the structure of, the industry. Although the impact of the federal government meant that the state's role in developing a climate for innovation was much less important initially than for Silicon Valley, the state's early emergence in other key industries and its investment in education were instrumental in allowing the aerospace industry to survive the more intense competition that emerged in the postwar years.

13

Inventing the Future Through
Investment and Innovation

The California experience suggests that state level action can affect economic development. While these actions are often taken for reasons other than economic development (they even can be inadvertent), their impact still is important. Several state government roles have been suggested as actions that can affect the economy.[2] These include

- Providing basic support to the market economy;
- Encouraging entrepreneurship;
- Acting as a selective catalyst;
- Facilitating transition of industries and workers;
- Determining the ground rules for distribution.

In California's case, while the state government has played each of these roles, it acted primarily by supporting the market economy through its investment in infrastructure and education and by helping to create and maintain an environment for innovation and entrepreneurship.

Historically, California has not been an active catalyst for economic development, played a strong role in facilitating transition of industries and workers, or explicitly set the ground rules for distribution among regions, industries, or population groups. For the most part, until the late 1970s, the state's position toward economic development was that maintaining California's basic attractiveness would assure both population and economic growth. The laissez-faire attitude assumed that economic development would be inevitable if California's business climate continued to stay favorable. This approach worked well during the 1950s and 1960s, when the state was making heavy investments in infrastructure and education and maintaining a climate for entrepreneurship at a time when the national economy was growing and new markets were being created.

Concerns about competitiveness in the late 1970s and early 1980s occurred during a period of slower national growth. In part, the problems of competitiveness that surfaced in this period could be ascribed to California's failure to continue to invest in its basic infrastructure and education and to the growing impact of regulations and the rising cost of doing business in the state's entrepreneurial climate.

Slower growth stimulated a search for a more explicit state economic development strategy. The state began to take a more active role in identifying specific economic development opportunities in such areas as technology and tourism. During the recession of the early 1980s, for the first time, the state established programs to help address the retraining and employment transition problems of workers displaced by plant closings in such restructuring industries as auto manufacturing and steel. California officials began to look around at the aggressive economic development and marketing efforts of other states, as well as the active industrial policies of foreign competitors such as Japan.

The Search for a State Economic Development Strategy

A starting point in understanding California's search for a strategy is the ongoing debate over what constitutes a "good business climate." There is general agreement that a state with a good business climate will prosper and grow. Since a major goal of state economic development policy is to create prosperity and growth, a good business climate is an important intermediate goal.

The problem is that there are several different definitions of good business climate. In practical terms, this array is expressed in the continuing confusion over various business climate indexes. For example, the Grant Thornton ranking of states focuses on factors important to manufacturing firms interested in relocating plants, while the *Inc. Magazine* system focuses on factors related to business creation and small business activity. Thus, these index systems create different rankings. To choose two dramatic examples, in 1984, Mississippi was ranked sixth by Grant Thornton and forty-ninth by Inc. In 1982, California was ranked second by Inc. and twenty-sixth by Grant Thornton.

Defining "Good Business Climate"

California (like many other states) appears to have at least two competing definitions of a good business climate:

- *Traditional (negative) definition*—In this view, a good business climate is defined by the *absence* of high taxes, excessive regulations, high labor cost, labor unions, and high utility costs. Businesses are assumed to be cost driven and, thus, will locate and grow in environments that provide the lowest priced inputs (land, labor, capital) and the least interference by government.

  • *Alternative (positive) definition*—In this view, a good business climate is defined by what is *added* to the environment for firms. This includes a skilled work force, accessible technology (often from a state university), capital markets, quality infrastructure, and a network of suppliers. Government has an important role to play in helping to create this type of business climate.

The appropriate type of business climate depends in large measure on the characteristics and specific needs of individual firms. A traditional manufacturing firm in a fairly stable but growing market, with heavy capital investment requirements, a relatively low-wage work force, and a need to produce commodity products at low cost in order to compete will be more interested in the first type of business climate. On the other hand, a high technology firm in a rapidly changing market that invests heavily in its skilled, technical work force and needs a high quality of life to attract and retain its workers would be interested in the second type of business climate.

The Pat Brown Years: Action Without a Strategy

California has experienced some difficulties in reconciling these contrasting views of the business climate. Because California did not have an explicit economic development strategy throughout the 1950s and early 1960s, critical investments in education and infrastructure were made for other reasons, largely to accommodate population growth.

Interestingly, Pat Brown made an unsuccessful attempt to weave together the threads of the different policy initiatives in education, highways, water systems, and natural resources. This effort, the California State Development Plan, which began in 1963 and was completed in 1966, attempted to analyze a wide range of state development issues including population growth, economic development, urbanization, and the environment. While the final report suggested a number of strong measures for growth management and environmental protection, it was not accepted by the incoming Reagan administration or the legislature.[23]

The Reagan Years: No Active Role for Government

During the Reagan years, the traditional good business climate definition was accepted. Governor Reagan had a pro-business approach that favored slowing the growth of government spending and reducing regulations. His 1966 campaign for governor attacked overtaxation, overregulation, and the excessive government spending of the Pat Brown administration. Reagan, in contrast to Pat Brown, believed that the role of government was to "encourage business to take over as many social functions as possible by curtailing government encroachment and by providing a healthy climate for private enterprise.[24]

The Jerry Brown Years: From No Growth to Pro Growth

Jerry Brown, elected in 1974, rejected the growth philosophy of his father, Pat Brown. In *Governor Reagan/Governor Brown,* Hamilton and Biggart point out:

> Where Pat Brown had a New Deal belief in the efficiency of government to cure the problems of California, Reagan feared the power of big government to undermine social relations. Jerry Brown, in contrast to both of them, was not convinced that government has the magnitude of power that his father expressed and that Reagan disliked.[25]

While he expressed concern about the impact of technology on the environment, Jerry Brown took office without a strong view about the business climate; he was more interested in environmental and social issues than purely economic issues. Because of his interest in scaling down the size of government, he proposed cuts in the University of California that were larger than anything proposed by the Reagan administration. Because of his interest in containing growth and preserving the environment, he placed restrictions on the funding of new freeways. Finally, because he did not believe the state needed to actively seek new industry, he abolished California's Department of Commerce.

A turning point in Jerry Brown's economic development perspectives came in 1977, when Dow Chemical Company decided to cancel its plans to construct a $500 million plant in rural Solano County near San Francisco Bay.

Under heavy pressure from business leaders the Brown administration began to drop the "era of limits" philosophy after 1977 and became more active in economic development. This began first through efforts to remold the regulatory process to avoid the (often unnecessary) delays that influenced Dow's decision to cancel its plant. Working more closely with business, especially the high technology entrepreneurs of the microelectronics industries, Brown began to promote a positive view of the business climate whereby business and government would work together in partnership to encourage new innovative industries in order to compete in a global economy.

In 1981, Jerry Brown appointed the California Commission on Industrial Innovation to develop a new industrial strategy for the state. In many ways, this commission, composed of leaders from industry, academia, labor, and the financial community, represents one of California's first explicit attempts to define an economic development strategy.

After analyzing and documenting the challenge of maintaining California's competitiveness through innovation, the commission, in its 1982 report "Winning Technologies: A New Industrial Strategy for California and the Nation," recommended action in the following areas:

- *Investment for innovation* through increasing research and development, and investment capital.
- *Education and job training* through elementary and high school technological literacy, enhanced university engineering and computer science programs, and vocational education for jobs with a future.
- *Workplace and management productivity* through policies aimed at increasing worker participation such as employee stock options.[26]

The commission report reflects the view that government must play a positive role in helping create a business climate that will foster innovation and entrepreneurship. Many of the commission's recommendations were put into practice in California, including new joint university-industry research efforts, such as the Microelectronics Innovation and Computer Research Operation (MICRO) at UC—Berkeley and the increased use of state pension funds for investments in innovative start-up companies. The commission, however, delivered its report at the end of the Brown administration and much of its impact was lost when Brown left office in 1982.

The Deukmejian Years: A Change of Direction

George Deukmejian's philosophy of government was much more similar to that of Ronald Reagan than that of Jerry Brown. Deukmejian believed that government should focus on the "basics," education and highways, and seek to create a good business climate.

To address the state's development problems, Deukmejian appointed an Economic Advisory Task Force in early 1983 to develop a comprehensive strategic plan for economic development and job creation in the state. This task force examined the assets and liabilities of the state as seen through the eyes of 360 professional industry-site selectors across the country plus 600 California business leaders and 50 firms that had recently accepted or rejected California as a plant site.

The report found (1) "an urgent need to correct the prevalent misperception that California is a bad place to do business" and (2) "a clear need to return to investment in the basics if California's physical and educational infrastructure is to accommodate the need for sound economic growth."[27] The survey found that 43 percent of the site selectors felt that California's business climate was poor. California business leaders surveyed suggested what the state might do to make California more attractive to new business and to retain existing business: 44 percent recommended establishing a very positive government attitude toward business and 22 percent recommended reducing the total tax burden on business.

The report recommended the following steps to correct these problems:

   • *Fixing the product* through legislative and regulatory changes (making California's tax structure more competitive and streamlining permit processes); reducing housing costs; assuring adequate transportation, water, and utility infrastructure; and improving the quality of education.
   • *Marketing the product* by communicating the "new" California story; emphasizing that the state is diverse enough to offer the right site to meet almost any business need and meeting the information needs of prospects.
   • *Supporting the sales force* by meshing state and local economic development efforts so they are synergistic and achieving careful coordination of the state's economic development programs with related programs of other agencies.[28]

In addition, the task force recommended special focus on retaining present jobs, helping promising embryo firms, and capitalizing on opportunities offered by growing Pacific Basin commerce.

This strategy plan has guided the efforts of the Deukmejian administration. The administration has reestablished a Department of Commerce to lead the state's new $1.5 million marketing effort, created a new privately funded California Economic Development Corporation composed of business leaders who will help market the state, given priority to increased spending in highway infrastructure and education, and launched a major sales campaign for California. The sales campaign was reflected in a state funded 1985 special supplement in *Business Week,* entitled "California 1985: Taking Off the Gloves."[29]

Contrasting Approaches to State Economic Policy

Pat Brown's building strategy, Reagan's business climate approach, Jerry Brown's innovation strategy, and Deukmejian's marketing strategy provide an interesting contrast concerning the state's role in economic development. Essentially, these approaches represent different paradigms of economic development.[30] In particular, George Deukmejian's approach was concerned more with factors that attract *outside* business to the state, while Jerry Brown's approach was directed more to achieving a combination of factors that foster economic vitality, innovation, and productivity *within* the state. The first approach aims at winning the site-location game, while the second emphasizes the internal expansion of a home grown economy.

Jerry Brown's approach during his second term was to promote the public policy support necessary to help home grown technology firms continue to innovate and compete in the global marketplace. This involved promoting free and fair trade, investing in R & D, enhancing education and training, and promoting worker productivity. Deukmejian's approach was to market the state's assets more effectively, so as to compete with other states for all types of manufacturing and service industries. The Brown approach was targeted to high technology and focused on stimulating innovation, whereas the Deukmejian approach had not been targeted and looked more toward industrial attraction and supporting the basics of infrastructure and education.

In the final analysis, the two approaches represent fundamentally different views of (1) the nature of the competitive problem facing California and (2) what constitutes a good business climate. Brown's approach adopted the positive view of good business climate and, thus, saw the need for an active government role in partnership with industry to help promote a skilled work force, accessible technology, and quality infrastructure. The Deukmejian approach adopted the negative view of good business climate and, thus, saw the need for making the tax and regulatory environment more competitive with those of other states by reducing the cost of doing business in the state.

Institutional Capacity for Economic Development

A wide variety of public and private institutions play influential roles in shaping economic development policies in California. The roles clearly have evolved over time as perceived problems change, new public officials with different philosophies and styles are elected, and new private coalitions form to address emerging issues. The following section examines the roles played by some of those most influential in California economic development. These include

- The governor;
- The legislature;
- State economic development organizations;
- Universities;
- Statewide business organizations;
- Individual firms;
- Local economic development agencies;

The Governor: Changing Philosophies, Styles,
and Constituencies

The philosophy, style, and constituency base of each governor have clearly influenced the changing approaches to economic development in California. Pat Brown was an activist governor with a New Deal/Great Society philosophy and a liberal-labor-minority constituency. Ronald Reagan, a forerunner of the New Right conservative philosophy, did not believe in strong government action. He had the support of the Southern California entrepreneurs, who had made their wealth in oil, aerospace, and movies, as well as that of a middle class skeptical of bigger government and new taxes. Jerry Brown, a forerunner of a neoliberal philosophy (liberal goals without big government), began as an opponent of government bureaucracy but became more activist on economic issues. He developed a constituency from the new high tech entrepreneurs, especially those in Silicon Valley, and from among social activists and environmentalists. Finally, George Deukmejian, a conservative, was skeptical of government action and represented a middle class business constituency. The very different philosophies, styles, and constituencies of these four recent governors are reflected in their approaches to economic development.

Pat Brown saw himself as the "Master Builder" and thus promoted growth of government spending in such areas as education, highways, and water systems to meet the needs of the rapidly growing population. Each issue was addressed largely in a separate, categorical manner by building the necessary constituency groups from a mixture of urban interests (freeways and education), rural interest (water systems and education), and minorities (education and social services) in order to win support in the legislature. Brown's attempt at comprehensive planning for economic development, the California Development Plan was never used.

In contrast to Pat Brown, Ronald Reagan, a new style of citizen politician, kept more aloof from party and interest groups. Again, his philosophy of individualism, free enterprise, and limited government shaped his approach to governing and economic development. Governor Reagan's philosophy was distributed to the members of his administration to guide their daily decision making:[31]

- Keep government as small as possible;

- Solve problems and perform government functions at the lowest level possible;
    - Avoid the creation of additional layers of government;
    - Government should not perform a function that can be effectively performed by the private sector;
    - Promote innovative, creative approaches to government programs;
    - Utilize the skills and experience of the private sector in carrying out government programs;
    - Federal government should communicate and administer its programs through the state government to local government;
    - Government exists to protect us from each other. No government on earth can possibly afford to protect us from ourselves.

Reagan's administration turned to business leaders for assistance. Early in his first term, he appointed a 250 member business task force that conducted an agency by agency review of state government and offered recommendations that would reduce the size of government by 10 percent. While Pat Brown had emphasized the problem solving, issue oriented aspects of government power, Reagan emphasized the management functions for government (how to deliver services more efficiently). Business leaders helped to identify more efficient management methods. Major issues facing the Reagan administration were welfare reform, Medicaid reform, and educational financing reform. Economic development was addressed primarily through efforts to maintain a good business climate, remove unnecessary regulatory constraints, and provide efficient government services.

Jerry Brown was primarily interested in promoting *innovation.* Hamilton and Biggart said:

> Although not impressed by the administrative possibilities of government activity, Brown believed government office to be an important forum for articulating ideas and thought that political organizations could be useful incubators for innovation and social change. Both Reagan and Brown saw government as a process, rather than a set of programs. Reagan, however, believed the significant process to be managerial, while Brown saw it to be the generation and testing of ideas.[32]

While Reagan's primary vehicle for making important changes in state government was a task force, Brown encouraged the proliferation of small organizational units within state government as a means of generating ideas. The Office of Planning and Research, which had never been important during the Reagan years, became a center for special projects and studies. Brown created an Office of Appropriate Technology to promote new, more efficient energy sources, such as solar energy. His Office of Citizen Initiative and Volunteer Action stimulated citizen activity in addressing a range of community issues. He created the California Conservation Corps to employ youth in natural resources and public works projects. Brown hoped to avoid bureaucracy by creating competing organizations, minimizing the distinction between appointed staff members and civil servants, and personalizing his organizational decision-making process, using brainstorming sessions rather than routine cabinet meetings.[33]

Jerry Brown's approach had its limitations. Loose organization in the governor's office was disruptive to routine work. Focusing on one issue at a time held other issues in limbo, and many new ideas were never implemented. In the end, by fighting the system, Brown paralyzed government. Reagan's limited agenda of streamlining government was accommodated by California's professionally sophisticated executive branch. Brown could not institutionalize the process of innovation necessary to sustain his nontraditional approach to government.[34]

George Deukmajian, in many ways, represented a return to the Reagan style and philosophy of government. He believed that government power should be limited. State government should focus on the basics (education and transportation) and on promoting a good business climate. He was much more interested in management than in stimulating innovation and new roles for the state. He had consistently vetoed bills passed by the legislature defining new roles for the state on the grounds that these roles were inappropriate for the state to undertake. Much like Reagan, reflecting both his philosophy and his business constituency, he tried to move government functions toward the local level and toward the private sector. For example, he was a strong supporter of the Job Training Partnership Act, which replaced the Comprehensive Employment Training Act, because it provided a strong private sector role at the state level and the establishment of local private industry councils to determine where training dollars should go. He also responded to the request from business leaders to provide additional funding for highways and education. At the same time, his administration had encouraged a new "partnership" between the private sector and local government in the areas of education and infrastructure.

Legislature: Well Organized but Crisis Oriented

Since the 1960s, California has had one of the strongest, most professional legislatures in the United States. It has been the best paid, best staffed, and one of the most active. By the early 1980s, the California Legislature had a staff numbering over 1700 and a $100 million budget. Staff consultants provided professional support to each of the legislature's committees. A nonpartisan, professional Office of the Legislative Analyst provided impartial analysis of legislative issues. (The Congressional Budget Office was modeled in part on this California office.) In recent years, there has been some public reaction to the growing size of the legislative staff. A successful ballot initiative in 1984 required a rollback in legislative staff and budget.

During Reagan's administration, the legislature often played the role of initiator and innovator of new programs. The California legislature (like most legislative bodies) tended to focus on crises and major issues of the moment and did not look at these issues in a comprehensive, strategic manner in terms of the impact on the state's economic development.

Since 1982, the legislature has attempted to address economic development issues in a somewhat more focused manner, reflecting the growing concern about the competitiveness of California's economy as well as the impact of the 1981–1982 recession on the state. In particular, in 1982, the assembly created a new Committee on Economic Development and New Technologies, which, in turn, has established subcommittees on international trade and investment, rural economic development, and biotechnology. This committee has been active in the areas of trade promotion, unitary tax reform, tourism development, high technology development, and the impact of defense spending on the state's economy. The assembly also created a Committee on Small Business, which is focusing on ways to help stimulate the growth and development of new enterprises in the state. In 1984, the senate established a Select Committee on Long Range Policy Planning, composed of leaders from both parties, to examine industrial competitiveness and suggest public policies to promote economic progress to the year 2000. In 1986, a Joint Committee on Science and Technology was assigned responsibility for carrying out the strategic policies identified by the select committee.

State Economic Development Agencies: Up from Obscurity

Since the Pat Brown administration, California has organized state government around an agency system. Brown found that he could not manage twenty-one separate departments, so he created six "super agencies": health, welfare, and security; public works; public safety; corrections; natural resources; and regulation and licensing. The only department focused on economic development, the Department of Industrial Relations, was under the regulation and licensing agency. Reagan reduced the number of agencies to four: business and transportation, resources, human relations, and agriculture. Most of the licensing functions were placed under business and transportation. Reagan also created a separate Department of Commerce that reported directly to the governor's office and handled business contacts and marketing. By the end of Jerry Brown's administration, there were five agencies: business, transportation, and housing; resources; youth and adult corrections; consumer services; health and welfare. Brown abolished the Department of Commerce but later created a Department of Economic and Business Development within the Business, Transportation, and Housing Agency. Deukmejian renamed that department the California Department of Commerce in 1984, but left it under the Business, Transportation, and Housing Agency.

In general, economic development has not had high organizational visibility in the California state government. In 1971, the legislature created a new economic development agency, the Commission for Economic Development. It consisted of ten members appointed by the governor, three members appointed by the senate rules committee, and three members appointed by the speaker of the assembly; it is chaired by the lieutenant governor. Since 1978, the governor and lieutenant governor have belonged to different political parties, which has limited the impact of this commission. The legislature also created the California State World Trade Commission, in 1983, to promote trade and investment opportunities for the state. It is chaired by the secretary of state (an elected official) and includes the governor, lieutenant governor, and twelve appointees from the private sector. In 1984, George Deukmejian created a new economic development agency, the nonprofit California Economic Development Corporation, to help market the state.

California Department of Commerce. Deukmejian has given the Department of Commerce additional visibility as part of the state's overall marketing campaign. In 1984, its budget was increased from $6.7 million to $14.9 million and its staff was augmented.

The program of the Department of Commerce in 1984 included the following:

• A $5 million advertising program aimed at highlighting the diversity of the state. In addition to attracting industry, its purpose was to encourage Californians to stay home and travel within the state and to import travelers and travel dollars from other states.

• A $1.5 million dollar industrial development program aimed at marketing the state to companies considering expanding or locating in California. This involved an advertising and public relations campaign, increased visibility at trade shows, a direct mail campaign, and development of a computerized site selection database.

• A business development program to help businesses obtain building and occupancy permits, arrange appropriate state financing (including small business loan guarantees and California innovation development loans), and assist prospective firms in site location.

• An Office of Small Business Development to provide management counsel, technical assistance, and loan guarantees to small businesses.

• An Office of Local Development to help local communities diversify and strengthen their economies and provide jobs.

The department's special attention to tourism was based on the belief that it is an important job-creating industry, which had been slipping because of competition from other states. The state's $28 billion a year tourism industry generated more than 500,000 jobs and $1.3 billion in state and local taxes. However, California's share of the nation's travel market had not increased since 1979. Additional areas of focus of the department had been retaining the movie business (while the number of movies produced in 1983 went up 28 percent, the number of movies shot in California dropped from sixty-three to fifty-six) and promoting trade and investment with the Pacific Basin. Governor Deukmejian announced a plan to open overseas offices in Tokyo and London to promote trade and direct investment by foreign firms in California. In addition, in his 1985 State of the State Address, the governor announced a Rural Renaissance program to help improve the economic vitality of small communities in agricultural areas. The program included $5 million to promote agricultural exports, $7 million to help rural counties market their investment opportunities, and a $30 million rural economic development fund to finance the public projects needed to win major business expansions.

California Commission for Economic Development. The duties of the commission were to make recommendations on legislation affecting economic development in the state, consider programs of other states relating to economic development, and confer with government officials and representatives of business and industry for promotion of economic development. It made an annual report to the governor and legislature. In 1984, it held meetings focused on reviewing the implementation of the state's enterprise zone legislation, examining regional economic development strategies in other states, and reviewing infrastructure financing alternatives. Task forces produced reports on the costs to the state's economy of toxic waste clean up and on the feminization of poverty. The commission also examined trade and tourism issues.

California State World Trade Commission. This commission had three principal objectives: to influence public policy as it affected the state's ability to trade internationally and attract foreign investment, to create demand overseas for California exports and to promote the state's investment and tourism attractions, and to tap the export potential of the state's medium and small business, which were unaware that their goods could find markets overseas. California established a $2 million Export Financing Program to provide working capital loan guarantees to small business.

California Economic Development Corporation. In 1984, Governor Deukmejian established the California Economic Development Corporation (CEDC) to assist in attracting and retaining both international and domestic industrial and commercial investment. CEDC advised the governor on economic policy, recommended methods to improve communications between California's public and private sectors regarding the state's business and employment climate, and raised funds from the private sector for investment promotion. The corporation was composed of top level business and civic leaders who acted as "ambassadors" to firms interested in the state, providing business to business contact.

Recently, CEDC appointed a Pacific Rim Task Force to promote trade and investment with that region. Working with the Department of Commerce and the State World Trade Commission, the CEDC examined opportunities in the Pacific basin, reviewed current activities in this area, and suggested a future strategy. The task force was composed of seventeen prominent private and public sector leaders

CEDC represented an unusual public-private innovation in economic development. It was a nonprofit, private corporation funded by the private sector, but its members are appointed by the governor. Its role was primarily to promote a better image of the state and provide business to business contact. Unlike many state economic development corporations (e.g., Indiana's Corporation for Innovation Development), it did not attempt to provide new financing mechanisms (seed money, venture capital funds for loan guarantees). It had a small staff and relied primarily on corporate voluntary action to achieve its impact.

Universities: Sources of Wealth

California's colleges and universities have played an important role in economic development. The three levels of the public system—research universities, state universities, and community colleges—serve a number of different functions, ranging from manpower development to research and technical assistance.

Research, Development, and Technology Utilization. Continuing the tradition begun when the University of California was a land grant college serving agriculture, most California universities operate significant technology transfer programs that seek to take discoveries made in the laboratory to the point of application. Stanford University operates the Center for Integrated Systems, a program that examines problems of large-scale circuit integration and artificial intelligence. Stanford, the University of California, MIT, and six companies operate a Center for Biotechnology research. The University of California runs the Microelectronics Innovation and Computer Research Opportunities Program (MICRO), which in 1982 sponsored fifty-one separate microelectronics research programs on six UC campuses. The project was funded in the amount of $4.8 million from the state and from the sponsorship of thirty-three different companies.

Assistance to Business Management and Entrepreneurs. Most of the university schools of business and engineering have some organized way of coordinating the expertise of their faculties with the business and community needs of their local regions. Each California State University business school has someone assigned to coordinate consulting or the teaching of special courses, such as workshops and on-site courses. The business schools of Stanford University and the University of Southern California have programs for entrepreneurs. The California State University systemwide office manages a University Services Program to coordinate the consulting services of all CSU faculty in response to special requests from business and government. The University of Southern California has an Urban University Center, funded by the U.S. Economic Development Administration, which concentrates on using the resources of USC for new business development and the operation of training programs. Many universities and some community colleges, such as Cabrillo College, operate small business assistance centers, where new businesses can secure business planning assistance and learn about sources of new capital.

Industrial Development. There is a strong economic relationship between universities and their surrounding communities. In 1951, Stanford University converted 655 acres of its excess land into an industrial-research park that employs 27,000 people. San Diego took a parcel of land for which it had no purpose and gave it to the University of California for a science intensive campus. It then zoned a surrounding area for a research-industrial park, which now houses a new and significant economy. The Irvine Company of Orange County, California sold Irvine Ranch land to the university for the UC—Irvine campus, then created a master plan for a community with new housing, new industry, and new community and recreational services.

Economic Analysis and Information. Some California universities sponsor economic and business research centers which present industry analyses to the public. One of the most important of these centers is the economic analysis and forecasting service of the UCLA Graduate School of Business.

Case Example of the University's Role in Economic Development. The impact of a public university on economic development is illustrated by the case of University of California at San Diego. The relationship between UCSD and San Diego business is similar to that of Stanford and the Silicon Valley. UCSD began as the Scripps Institute of Oceanography and was expanded to a campus of the university system in the late 1950s and early 1960s, as part of the master plan. The campus, which is the largest employer in the San Diego area outside of the military and the fourth largest university contractor for federally sponsored research in the nation, actively seeks to improve its relationship with its business community. Its extension division surveys business annually to discover emerging new technologies that it needs to incorporate into its curriculum. The division operates a microwave television link between the university and subscriber companies, to deliver university courses to the place of business.

As a result of this sensitivity to its environment, UCSD is developing a new school focusing its research and instruction on the Pacific Basin. This area of the world is becoming a major buyer of California products and is a major exporter of goods to the United States. The school is establishing programs dedicated to understanding the Pacific's cultures, languages, businesses, and its relationship with the larger world.

Statewide Business Organizations: The Big Four

Several major statewide business organizations play an important role in economic development in California. Each has a different composition, style of operation, and set of objectives. Some appear more interested in promoting the traditional view of good business climate, which focuses primarily on lowering the cost of doing business in the state. Others promote the new view of good business climate, which focuses on educating a skilled work force and creating a high quality infrastructure. Four major groups are

- California Chamber of Commerce
- California Manufacturers Association
- California Taxpayers Association
- California Roundtable.

California Chamber of Commerce. This organization represents all types of business in the state and works closely with local chambers of commerce. It acts primarily as a state level lobbying and advocacy organization, employing forty-six full-time staff members organized into four major lobbying groups (agriculture; industry, transportation, and energy; insurance and employee benefits, resources; and taxation/regulatory, consumer and legal affairs), and six special service groups (education, legislative services, legislative action, communications, California chamber services, and membership).

In general, the chamber's focus has been on improving the business climate in California by containing costs and excessive government regulation. It has devoted special effort in recent years, however, to improving the quality of primary and secondary education in the state. For example, a special project, called

Business and Education Together, has provided assistance to local chambers on building partnerships in education.

California Manufacturers Association. The California Manufacturers Association (CMA) represents the interests of manufacturers in the states. This organization, like the California chamber, is an influential lobbying group in Sacramento. Because it represents most of the large industries, CMA has considerable clout on key industry issues.

CMA operates through a group of policy committees composed of over 2000 volunteer members. Current committees focus on energy, environmental quality, human resources, transportation, workers' compensation, health and safety, unemployment insurance, taxation, and government relations. As a member driven organization, the CMA uses these committees to define issues and design and execute its lobbying efforts.

In general, CMA also focuses on maintaining a positive business climate in the state. More than the chamber, however, it has actively sought specific improvements in issues of importance to California industry, particularly human resources and transportation. For example, CMA is a participant in the state's innovative Employment Training Panel program, which uses unemployment insurance to retrain displaced workers or workers threatened by displacement. CMA acts as one of the brokers for the program, helping to match industry funds with panel training funds.

California Taxpayers Association. The California Taxpayers Association (Cal-Tax) is a nonpartisan, nonprofit corporation founded in 1926 to promote efficiency in government through research, advocacy, and public communication. It is supported primarily by large corporations and its board is composed of major business leaders in the state. Unlike the Chamber of Commerce and the CMA, Cal-Tax conducts substantial research on issues of interest to business, ranging from state and local tax policies, to public employee benefit costs, and education and infrastructure spending.

In general, Cal-Tax has been an advocate for both tax reform and critical investment in the state's basic infrastructure. Historically, it has not been an advocate of "tax cutting" (it was not a proponent of Proposition 13) but rather, has promoted more effective and efficient taxation and spending. Since 1981, Cal-Tax has sponsored research, publications, and conferences on the state's infrastructure needs. It has suggested new methods for financing infrastructure in the state. Cal-Tax also has promoted education reform and recently completed an analysis of the implementation of the state's education reform bill passed in 1983.

Cal-Tax staff members maintain that the perception of the business climate in California depends on the requirements of specific companies. Many companies look at spending on education and infrastructure and expanding markets in a state as well as tax levels and labor costs in deciding to locate or expand. On this basis, comparing California to other states solely on its level of taxes and labor cost may be misleading.[35]

California Roundtable. The California Roundtable is a statewide organization of CEOs from eighty-eight major corporations in the state. Modeled along the lines of the national Business Roundtable, it serves as a forum for top business leaders to identify key issues of interest to business and develop new solutions. The Roundtable addresses issues that affect businesses in a variety of different industries. To address these issues, it established CEO study committees, which are supported by senior executives from each company. The study committee reviews or commissions research on the issue and suggested actions by either government or business.

In 1980, the Roundtable identified educational improvement as a high priority for meeting the state's critical personnel needs. A Task Force on Jobs and Education was formed, which soon recognized that the declining test scores and deterioration of basic skills of entry level workers were a result of problems with the K–12 school system (kindergarten, primary and secondary education). On tests of basic skills, California students fell below the national average in reading, writing, and math.

In 1982, the Roundtable commissioned a major independent study of the state's education problems and the ways that business could help improve student performance. The study recommended specific steps for raising education standards, upgrading technical education, reforming school finance, and increasing community and business involvement in schools (through loaned expertise and business-school partnerships). The Roundtable used the report to conduct a public information campaign to raise awareness and communicate to public officials.

A new superintendent of public instruction, elected on back to basics platform, advocated many of the reforms suggested by the Roundtable. After an intense effort in the legislature, the superintendent, with the support of business, linked an $850 million spending increase to reforms that improved graduation standards, lengthened classroom hours, required competency tests for teachers, and established a "master teacher" program, which involves a modified merit pay system.[36]

In education reform, the Roundtable helped to identify an issue critical to maintaining the competitiveness of industry in the state, developed solutions, and mobilized support for action in the legislature. The Roundtable currently has addressed issues related to technical education, especially at the community college level. It also has been working on math and science education in cooperation with an education group, called the California Round Table on Educational Opportunity.

Individual Firms: Public-Private Partnerships

In addition to their involvement in business organizations at the state level, individual firms in California have played important roles on specific economic development issues. While the firms are too numerous to mention, some examples of work by specific firms provide insight into the range of activities.

- *ARCO* has been especially active in promoting public-private partnerships in education and economic development both at the state and national level. It cosponsored, with the U.S. Conference of Mayors, a series of conferences across the country on partnership. In California, it has been active in education partnerships in Los Angeles and economic development partnership in Carson, California. It also has supported tourism and marketing (including printing and distribution of 4 million California brochures), cosponsored billboards, and printed the official state tourism map.
- *Chevron* led a major Business Leadership Task Force in San Francisco, which has addressed training, health care, and child care issues. It also has been active in studying education and aging issues.
- *Bank of America* has been active on the issues of education and child care. Bank of America, along with Chevron, established the California Education Fund to reward innovative teaching.
- *First Interstate Bank* has been active in education and training programs and issues related to Hispanics. It sponsored several conferences on Hispanics in California.
- *Hewlett-Packard* has focused on supporting engineering education and is active in promoting new approaches to industrial competitiveness. Its CEO chaired the President's Commission on Industrial Competitiveness.
- *American Medical International* has been working in a public-private partnership with Irvine Medical Center and the University of California at Irvine to create a world class community-teaching medical center in Orange County.
- *Kaiser Aluminum* has led the redevelopment of Oakland and established education and training programs for minorities in that city.
- *Pacific Telesis* (the holding company of the regional Bell spinoff) has actively supported education and training and provided management assistance for the Mayor's Fiscal Advisory Committee in San Francisco, a model local public-private partnership effort.

There are many other examples of involvement by individual firms. What is especially interesting about these partnership efforts is the success of the firms in addressing community issues while meeting business objectives (i.e., the need for a trained work force, containment of rising health benefit costs, increasing productivity, and the retention of working parents).

Local Economic Development Agencies: New Roles

From the 1950s through the early 1970s, local and state government did not focus explicitly on attracting and retaining business and jobs. Their underlying belief was that California's basic attractiveness was sufficiently powerful as long as government took care of the basics: education, infrastructure, high quality public services. That view began to change in the late 1970s and early 1980s, because of a concern that California was losing out to other states and had lost its image as a good place to do business.

By the 1970s, most counties and many larger city governments had established economic development activities aimed at advertising the locality's business advantages and helping businesses to locate in the city or county. Many local governments continue to work closely with their local chamber of commerce on this basic marketing activity.

Since the early 1980s, several counties and cities, including Oakland, Fresno County, and San Diego County have established more elaborate economic development agencies, either as part of the government or as separate nonprofit corporations that actively recruit business, provide subsidized loans to new and existing businesses, and help to break through red tape.

An organization of economic development professionals, the California Association for Local Economic Development, formed to provide training and technical assistance at the local level and to advocate for local issues at the state level. In 1983, the County Supervisors Association of California (CSAC) formed a Commission on Public-Private Partnerships, composed of private sector and public sector leaders, which made local economic development a major priority. It has helped stimulate local partnerships in economic development and infrastructure financing.

Overall, local governments have become much more active and aggressive in their efforts to attract, grow, and retain businesses. Some local economic development agencies focus almost entirely on attracting new businesses, while others focus on assisting the start up of new small businesses and the retention of existing firms. Whether these local efforts actually add to the overall wealth and economic growth of the state or merely redistribute firms and jobs within the state is uncertain.

Process of State Economic Development: Lessons and Insights

The process making state economic development policy in California traditionally can be characterized by what Charles Lindbolm called *disjointed incrementalism.*[37] The state is so big and so diverse, with so many public and private leaders having different industry and regional agendas, that policy making for economic development is never smooth or easy.

Until the Jerry Brown and Deukmejian administrations, the state did not even attempt to formalize an explicit economic development strategy. While competing views of the business climate guided actions, economic development consisted primarily of the actions taken by the state to support the market economy: investments in education and infrastructure and the creation of an entrepreneurial climate.

Jerry Brown's innovation commission, Deukmejian's economic development strategy task force, education reform, infrastructure investment, and the unitary tax provide important insights into the process of developing an economic strategy. A common framework defining the agenda, building support, key decision points, implementation, and evaluation will be used in analyzing these efforts.

California Commission on Industrial Innovation

The commission's agenda was defined through discussions among Jerry Brown's administration officials and leaders of the high technology industry in California. There was a growing perception of the competitive threat that the high tech industry faced as a result of trade, capital, and human resource policies in the United States. The commission represented a cross-section of industry, education, and labor leaders interested in technology issues. The commission became a mechanism for both identifying recommendations and building support among the business community for Brown's efforts in these areas. While some of its recommendations were implemented, the major thrust of the commission's report was lost when Brown left office in 1983. Because the commission operated outside the legislature and the bureaucracy, it did not leave a strong legacy.

Economic Advisory Task Force

Having campaigned on a platform of economic development and jobs, Deukmejian appointed a private sector task force to map out a strategy. The composition of this group emphasized medium and small businesses, local chambers of commerce, manufacturing groups, and marketing/site location firms. It decided to address the issue as an "image" problem, surveyed the opinions of site locators and relocating firms, and took a marketing approach. Support from the business community was built through task force advisory committees and active outreach programs. The recommendations of the task force largely were implemented by the legislature in 1984. The creation of the California Economic Development Corporation provided a continuing vehicle for business support.

Education Reform

The California Roundtable helped direct business attention to the issue of declining student performance through its Jobs and Education Task Force report. It mobilized public awareness and, through its work with the new superintendent of education, helped formulate an education reform legislative package. The legislature provided the forum for debating the package, with business on one side and education lobbies on the other. Business was able to prevail in the legislative debate and helped convince the governor to sign the reform bill. The implementation of the bill has been monitored by Cal-Tax, which found most local districts complying with its provisions.

Infrastructure

While a number of specific business groups (including the Santa Clara Manufacturer Groups and the Bay Area Council, representing 300 businesses in the San Francisco Area)[38] helped highlight this issue in the early 1980s, Cal-Tax sponsored the first statewide conference on infrastructure in 1982. A business-labor-local government lobbying organization, Californians for Public Improvements, was formed in 1983 to advocate new financing in this area. The governor and his Business Agency secretary (a former head of Cal-Tax) were receptive to this issue. The governor appointed a task force to recommend solutions. The assembly conducted its own research study. The price tag calculated by both studies was too high for either the governor or the legislature. A proposal to create a state infrastructure bank found some support in the legislature but the governor was not supportive. He successfully proposed increases in the state's highway spending. This issue is still being financed by an array of business and local government interests lobbying in support of increased infrastructure financing at the state level.

Summary of Experience

Each of these examples provides different perspectives on the process of economic development policy in California. In each case, the governor played a central role. Through the Brown commission and Deukmejian task force, the governor initiated action and reached out to build business support. In the education and infrastructure cases, business groups helped place the issue on the public agenda and brought the issue to the attention of the governor and the legislature; the legislature served as the major forum for the debate.

Summing Up: Lessions from California's Experience in Economic Development

Both the evolution of industry in California and the evolution of state economic development suggest a number of implications for the state role in economic policy. These can be summarized as follows:

- California's economy evolved through a series of dramatic industrial transformations, fueled by innovation and adaptation, driven by entrepreneurs seeking new opportunities. Today, California is an advanced technology based economy searching for its next great surge.
- The state's primary role in California's industrial evolution was its investment in education and infrastructure and the creation of an entrepreneurial climate. None of these, however, resulted from an explicit economic development strategy. Instead, they were the result of decisions made for a variety of reasons, which added up to a "good business climate."
- During the 1970s, California retreated from its earlier commitments to educational and infrastructure investment. Concerns about the impact of growth created constraints to the entrepreneurial climate.
- In the late 1970s, concerns about competitiveness, impending industry maturity, and a declining business climate stimulated the search for more explicit state economic development strategies.
- Two alternative approaches to state economic development policy have evolved in California: One focused on stimulating innovation and competitive-

ness in technology based industries, which require skilled workers and technology infrastructure and the other aimed at marketing the assets of the state and enhancing the image of California as a good place to do business, by reducing regulations and government interference.

• A wide variety of public and private institutions were involved in disjointed, incremental economic development policy making. One attempt at comprehensive planning in the 1960s was ignored. Thus, policy has been made through the interplay of commissions, task forces, legislative committees, business coalitions, and individual industry actions.

• The private sector, especially business groups, have become interested and active in economic development policy making. In recent years, they have helped return the focus of state economic development to the basics: education and infrastructure. Today, an emerging coalition of high technology, aerospace, finance, and manufacturing industry leaders are expressing growing concern about issues of competitiveness and increasingly are looking to the state and its universities for solutions to these issues.

While state economic development policy may be ad hoc, contradictory, and at times inadvertent, overall it has been effective. Clearly, within the context of external forces affecting the state's economy, California's historic investments in education and infrastructure and its ability to maintain an attractive climate for entrepreneurship and innovation have helped to sustain its dramatic industrial evolution. The margin contributed by the state appears to be rather large.

The California experience suggests some important insights for state economic development policy making. These include the following:

• *More generic policies aimed at improving the economic environment for all industries appear to have more impact than specific policies targeted at individual industries.* The state's policies toward education, research, and technology through its universities and infrastructure investments made the greatest contributions to economic growth. State policies that attempt to focus on a single industry or type of industry (such as high tech) have been more difficult to formulate and implement than generic policies.

• *States can help create a climate for innovation and entrepreneurship.* This involves removing unnecessary constraints and providing necessary ingredients, such as education, financing, and access to technology.

• *Investments in a state's capacity to create wealth may be a more important goal than focusing on either job creation or industry attraction.* Attention to the number of jobs created or number of industries relocated in the state may miss the underlying strength of the state and its capacity to generate new wealth through innovation and entrepreneurship in both large and small businesses. The important measure may be increased value-added output per capita (an indicator of wealth) not just jobs.

• *Creating a good business climate may involve a two-step process of removing the negatives and adding positives.* The two views of good business climate can be reconciled by this two-step process. First, create a fair and equitable tax system, a flexible regulatory process, and an efficient government. Then, make sure there are skilled workers, access to technology, and risk capital.

The California experience suggests that the key question in economic development no longer is how to attract, retain, and grow industry through low-cost land, labor, or taxes. It has become how to invest in technology, human resources, entrepreneurship, and capital to create a comparative advantage.

The definition of what constitutes a "good business climate" has also changed. California has attempted to create an environment for innovation and entrepreneurship through its investments in an expanded infrastructure of education and technology, transportation and communication, and private-sector risk-capital financing. This effort involves action in both the private sector and the public sector. The key role for the state is in designing its public policies and targeting its public investments to encourage this climate for innovation. In the 1950s and 1960s, California had policies that did this successfully, perhaps inadvertently. In the 1970s, California ended these policies and cut back on its investments as it struggled with the impact of growth and a slower national economy. In the 1980s, California began to return to its earlier formula in a more explicit way. California does not yet have an economic development strategy, but it is searching for one that understands the new view of promoting a dynamic comparative advantage in a competitive environment.

Remi Nadeau, in *California: the New Society,* highlighted the state's role as a bellwether. Possibly this still is true today:[39]

> California, perhaps more than any other state is really a fulfillment of the American Dream.... Through its change and diversity, it is a forcing house of national character. Having left behind the social inhibitions of his hometown, the Californian is a sort of American in the making. What America is becoming, California already is.

ARIZONA

Larry Landry

ARIZONA

Larry Landry

14

Diversifying a Natural Resource-Based Economy

If you were to visit the Old State Capitol in Phoenix, Arizona, a tour guide would show you a huge tile mosaic of the Great Seal of the State of Arizona. Looking carefully at that seal, you would see emblems of copper, cotton, citrus, and cattle. The tour guide would tell you that these four Cs are the main components of the Arizona economy.

Before World War II, Arizona had an essentially resource based economy. Over the past twenty-five years, however, the Arizona economy has undergone enormous changes. Cotton and mining have given way to tourism and high technology manufacturing.

Hence, Arizona's economic base today includes a different set of Cs. These include climate, construction, components, and computers. Arizona's climate is the basis of its tourism industry, which accounts for 18 percent of all nonagricultural employment in the state. The state's component and computer sectors account for nearly 50 percent of Arizona's manufacturing employment. Over 400 advanced technology companies in Arizona are involved in electronics, computers, and aerospace manufacturing as well as communications and research facilities. In total, these companies employ over 80,000 people and account for nearly 50 percent of Arizona manufacturing employment.

Arizona's economic landscape has changed dramatically in a short period of time. This transformation has been accompanied by high employment, rising incomes, and increasing overall growth. Recent statistics tell the story:

- According to the U.S. Department of Labor, Arizona continues to create jobs at a faster pace than any other state in the nation.[1]
- Arizona's labor force and employment grew three times faster than the national average during the 1970s.[2]
- Like employment, personal income grew faster in Arizona than in the United States overall. Total personal income increased 88.3 percent in Arizona between 1970–80, compared to 35.9 percent nationally.[3]
- Arizona is the second fastest growing state in the nation. The state's population grew 53 percent between 1970–80, compared to 11 percent for the U.S. overall. This trend continues.[4]

In each of the four decades since 1940, Arizona's nonagricultural employment grew 50–500 percent faster than U.S. nonagricultural employment. In 1980, Arizona's construction employment was 18 times its 1940 level; manufacturing employment was 17 times greater; service producing industries (trade, finance, insurance, real estate, and government) were 11 times greater; and transportation, communications, and utilities were 4 times greater. Even the state's mining sector, which has undergone a rapid secular decline in recent years, grew 1.5 times over its 1940 level. By comparison, no sector in the nation more than tripled its growth during the last forty years.

The state's one pronounced area of decline has been agriculture. Employment in this sector plummetted from about 17 percent of Arizona's total employment in 1955 to about 3 percent in 1982. That decline follows national trends.[5]

Differential growth rates across economic sectors helps explain the maintenance of Arizona's economic health. As Arizona's mining and agricultural sectors grew smaller, its construction and manufacturing sectors grew larger.

Perhaps the single most important factor in maintaining Arizona's economic stability is the tremendous growth of manufacturing in the state. This growth has been generated by the location of new firms and their subsequent expansion in the state. During the 1981–82 national recession, Arizona out-performed the U.S. economy. The tremendous growth and diversification of the state's manufacturing base during the late 1970s and early 1980s made Arizona's economy less cyclical than during the previous decade. In this period, many high technology companies moved to Arizona. At the same time, existing firms expanded their Arizona operations. These developments mirrored economic growth in the state during the 1940s and 1950s, when the foundations were laid for Arizona's modern economy.

Seeds for a High Technology Future

The rise of manufacturing in Arizona is directly linked to the military. The federal government began directing military spending to Arizona in 1941, when the country began to prepare for World War II. The war years saw the operation of several military installations in Arizona, followed by the establishment of defense industries. In the 1940s, Tucson became a strategic aviation center because of its location on an "all weather" transcontinental route. By 1942, the Phoenix area was home to three army camps and six air bases, as well as a number of defense plants. The area offered the army camps desert training grounds, the air bases' fine flying weather, and the defense plants an inland geographic position protected from possible air attacks.

During the cold war, military installations in Arizona continued to serve the national defense, but the state's war-related industries began to serve civilian as well as military markets. Electronics firms were particularly attracted to Arizona. Absenteeism was low and the state's perpetual sunshine allowed manufacturers to meet production schedules and carry on outdoor tests of products like weapons systems without interruption by adverse weather.

The private sector, and particularly Motorola Inc., played a crucial role in making Phoenix a postwar center of commerce and industry. At the urging of Daniel Noble, a company executive, Motorola decided to locate a new facility in Phoenix early in 1948. The facility was a modern research and development center devoted exclusively to military electronics. Although Motorola was based in Chicago, Phoenix's location (between the national defense oriented supply houses of Albuquerque and Southern California) and its favorable business climate attracted Motorola's attention. In addition, the State College at Tempe (later renamed Arizona State University) offered the potential for the development of high quality engineering programs. The most important factor in Motorola's selection of Phoenix, however, was the city's "outstanding climate and its nationwide reputation as a resort and health center,"[6] which, it was felt, would attract high quality personnel.

The Motorola operation in Phoenix proved successful, and expansion followed. Beginning with a team of five engineers and technicians in a small, 6000 square foot, laboratory, Motorola Inc. has grown into Arizona's largest industrial employer and the leader of the Phoenix-Tucson area's rapidly growing electronics industry.

Motorola's successful experience in Arizona helped attract a myriad of large and small high technology companies to the state. Currently, over 320 high technology firms in Arizona have fifty employees or more. In addition, there are hundreds of smaller high technology companies. High quality labor and good labor relations particularly appealed to these firms.[7]

So far, in this analysis, it appears that economic diversification has been the result of a set of fortuitous circumstances: notably, war and sunshine. To a large extent, Arizona has been lucky; the state's amenable climate prompted many military personnel and other visitors to remain in the state permanently. However, without several important modifications, the climate could have been more of a liability than an asset.

One of these modifications was the "miracle of air conditioning."[8] The mass production of air conditioners in the 1950s and the consequent "age of refrigeration" made Arizona livable in the intense heat of midsummer. It also brought an extended tourist season to the state.

A far more important modification, however, involved measures to ensure an adequate and dependable water supply in the state. Although water depletion in Arizona has outstripped supply renewal since World War II, the state did not have any effective groundwater regulations until 1980.[9] State leaders formulated a dual strategy to ensure sufficient water for sustained growth into the future: a supply strategy to bring water from the Colorado River via the Central Arizona Project and a demand management strategy embodied in the Arizona Ground-water Management Act of 1980.

Water supply will be augmented through the Central Arizona Project (CAP), authorized by Congress in 1968 and currently under construction by the U.S. Bureau of Reclamation. This project will develop delivery systems for the last available surface water in the state. The project will transport an allotted 1.2 million acre/feet of Colorado River water annually from Lake Havasu on Arizona's western border to the central agricultural and metropolitan areas of the state. The project is scheduled to deliver water to the Phoenix area in 1986 and to the Tucson area in 1991.

A second strategy for managing demand was added to the supply augmentation strategy in 1980. The Arizona legislature voted to force the elimination of groundwater overdraft in most areas of the state by 2025. As a result of the Arizona Groundwater Management Act, the Department of Water Resources was given the authority to devise and administer mandatory conservation measures. The goal of "safe yield," or striking a balance between recharge[10] and pumping, is to be reached through a series of five and ten year plans, the first of which was implemented in 1985. Because there are important local differences in water supplies and water uses across the state, four active management areas (AMAs) were identified where groundwater depletion was greatest.[11]

Prior to the 1980 law, the only statutory controls on groundwater were enacted by the 1948 legislature only after Governor Osborn called the legislature into six special sessions and only after an official warning from the Secretary of the Interior that groundwater in Arizona must be subjected to regulation or the Central Arizona Project would not be authorized. The 1948 code was intended to be a stop-gap measure, designed to slow depletion while serving as a foundation for future legislation. It was not seen *then* as a solution to the problem, yet it remained in the statutes relatively unchanged until 1980.[12] It was immediately touted by state economic development leaders as unique in the United States in its far reaching, ambitious approach to groundwater management. The act was used to demonstrate that there was plenty of water for growth and that, "this is the Arizona style of decision making . . . when we have a problem, we get a room and solve it."[13] These modifications to Arizona's natural climate provide the foundation for the state's most recent accomplishments of economic development.

The Role of the State Economic Development Agency

Once Arizona's harsh environment had been tamed and manufacturing interests had established beachhead operations in the state, all the necessary components for a second wave of technology based development were in place.

The primary development arm of the state government is the Office of Economic Planning and Development (OEPAD), formed in 1972 in a deliberate attempt to help the governor formulate both the planning and implementation components of the state's economic policy. To facilitate the recruitment of top professionals, the agency was exempted from civil service hiring and firing criteria. The agency was designed to be "unbureaucratic and responsive."[14]

Prior to the Bruce Babbitt administration (1978), OEPAD was plagued by consistent rumors that it was a dumping ground for political appointees and that its primary development emphasis was on trying, without much success, to stimulate economic development in Arizona's smaller rural communities, generally taken to mean everything outside the Phoenix and Tucson Standard Metropolitan Areas.

In fact, before 1978–79, OEPAD was organized principally to provide small cummunities with technical assistance. The agency emphasized the recruitment of industry to rural areas. Metropolitan area economic professionals met in early 1979 with Governor Babbitt and requested that OEPAD's rural emphasis be balanced with an urban strategy.[15]

Governor Babbitt instituted a change in agency leadership but strongly reasserted his conviction that rural economic development must remain the agency's "highest priority" and that Arizona must strive to "balance economic opportunity" throughout the state and not concentrate its efforts on the two major metropolitan areas. At the same time, he also urged support of urban initiatives such as the Engineering Excellence Center at Arizona State University.

As OEPAD sought to help implement the governor's priorities, it also attempted to incorporate the findings of David Birch's study of the job creation process.[16] Birch, working at MIT, demonstrated that over 50 percent of a state's new jobs would come from new businesses or expansion of existing industries. OEPAD split its development efforts in half, with half its resources directed to out-of-state recruitment and half to encouraging businesses already located in the state. These activities resulted in efforts to determine how state government could help enhance capital formation, extensive research into what type of rural incentive programs could be offered (the answer proved to be none), and retention and expansion of existing state industries. The retention and expansion activities focused on enhancing OEPAD's accessibility and symbolic troubleshooting functions. The state urged local chambers of commerce throughout Arizona to visit local businesses, express appreciation for their importance, and urge them to expand locally. This effort intensified in 1980, when Sperry Flight Systems announced that it was expanding to a major new plant in Albuquerque because Phoenix was too bureaucratic and did not care about local industry. Governor Babbitt conducted a series of plant tours and special issue meetings with the large high technology employers, including Sperry. In 1984, retention/expansion activities of the agency became even more vigorous.

OEPAD directed its furthest reaching efforts to rural economic development. The agency successfully worked to locate several new plants in rural Arizona communities. In these instances, OEPAD provided the necessary technical assistance and coordinated the efforts of local leaders. Despite these successes, the agency shifted its focus from only recruitment toward policy development, in order to improve long-range economic development in rural Arizona.

Agency staff believed that it was unrealistic to expect major technology oriented firms to locate in rural Arizona towns, but that it was realistic to convince suppliers of high technology firms to locate in such areas. OEPAD needed to find out which suppliers would be incorporated most easily into Arizona's high technology sector. After a year of intensive study, the agency published "Opportunities in Arizona for Suppliers of High Technology Manufacturers."[17] The study revealed a current and growing need in Arizona for sixteen different suppliers of high technology production items. Although OEPAD's supplier recruitment efforts have resulted in only one documented case of a high tech supplier locating in a rural community (Casa Grande), the concept of vertical integration became the basis of a later statewide economic development strategy.[18]

OEPAD also perceived that rural Arizona's quality of life gave it an advantage over the state's metropolitan areas. The agency applied for and received a $40,000 Four Corners Grant from the U.S. Department of Commerce, which it used to publish an illustrated book, *The Other Arizona,* that demonstrated how special the people of Arizona were and how superior the quality of life was. This "hyping" became a mainstay of Arizona's state rural strategy. Although OEPAD developed the quality of life issues as a way for small rural communities to compete with Phoenix and Tucson, later OEPAD research showed Phoenix and Tucson's perceived quality of life was a significant force in industrial recruitment and expansion in those areas. Consequently, just as high tech supplier recruitment started as a way to help small rural communities and was later enlarged to include all areas in the state, quality of life promotion also became part of a statewide strategy.

Recognizing the need to both develop an overall strategy and to give practical technical assistance to smaller rural communities, the state sponsored a Rural Development Conference, in September 1979. The conference was successful enough to have become a yearly event, attracting over 200 people to rural areas of Arizona. The conference also serves as a forum for marketing OEPAD's programs throughout the rural communities. The conferences are structured to encourage participation and interaction.

While the state cannot point to dramatic successes as a result of these efforts, the effort to create a statewide development strategy provided a framework within which smaller communities could devise and implement their own economic development strategies. The Rural Development Conferences helped create a climate for success and showed state officials that by bringing the right mixture of people together, changes could be made.

Industrial Recruitment

For many years, industrial recruitment was Arizona's primary economic development goal. Back in the late 1940s, men like Patrick Downey, an executive for the Valley National Bank, and Walter Bimson, president of Valley National

Bank, served as the chief traveling representatives of Phoenix. These men always prepared an extensive dossier on Phoenix, which they presented to the decision-making executives of target firms. Tucson, the other major urban area in the state, also maintained an industrial promotion strategy, although it was not as active as Phoenix's.

The state government really did not become a force in the industrial recruitment process until after 1972, when the Arizona Office of Economic Planning and Development was created. Part of the legislation creating this office charged the agency to, "promote and encourage the location of new business in the state."[19]

Despite this mandate, relative to other states, Arizona has not devoted lavish or extensive resources to industrial recruitment and state promotion. The state offers few tax abatements, tax exemptions, low interest loan programs, or traditional state giveaway programs. As a matter of policy, the state does not offer companies free land, buildings, or access to public facilities. The state has limited its recruitment program primarily to the development of special marketing programs to aid in the competition for new firms and to the provision of information to corporations visiting the state. Even for these limited activities, the available resources have been scarce. Between 1974–84, the state's largest advertising budget was $30,000, compared with $600,000 for Florida and $1 million for New Mexico.

OEPAD also has assisted the efforts of industry associations, chambers of commerce, and other community organizations to attract new plants to the state. These partnerships have particularly involved the organization of annual industrial recruiting trips. Since 1976, a contingent of the Arizona economic development community has made about a dozen "prospecting trips" to companies in other parts of the United States to discuss the advantages of locating in Arizona. The trips are organized principally by the Arizona Association of Industrial Developers (AAID), a group of 300 real estate agents, developers, bankers, and utility representatives; OEPAD and local chambers of commerce act as cosponsors.

At first, the trips were aimed at recruiting all types of firms to Arizona. In the last three years, however, the trips have been targeted to particular industries. The 1984 prospecting trip, for example, focused on suppliers to high technology manufacturers. This focus resulted from OEPAD's 1981 analysis of high technology suppliers in Arizona and the Southwest. As a result of the study's findings, AAID and OEPAD decided to make trips to Boston and New York to attract supplier firms. In 1984–85, the department conducted a similar supplier study for the aerospace industry, and its findings established the emphasis for the 1985 recruitment trip.

On March 17, 1983, Admiral Bobby Inman, chairman of the Microelectronics and Computer Consortium, came to Phoenix for a speaking engagement. During the admiral's stay, he expressed optimism about Arizona's chances to land MCC. One week later, however, when MCC announced the finalist cities—none were in Arizona. The admiral offered two reasons for Arizona's exclusion: The state had not yet developed educational excellence in the engineering and research that MCC needed, and the state did not have the sophistication and cultural resources sufficient to attract the type of professional people the consortium needed.

Arizona leaders were shocked at this rejection. Concern about the loss of MCC was expressed throughout the state. Some businessmen and economic development organizations tried to second guess what types of incentives the state should have offered MCC. Far more people, however, began to discuss the role that quality of life and educational excellence play in economic development. Out of this discussion arose a conviction that if Arizona's goal was to be a high technology state, then Arizona needed to have a better understanding of what was important to high tech firms.

In March 1983, Governor Babbitt asked the OEPAD leadership to put together a policy document describing how all state policies should work toward future economic development. The agency leaders, unsure how to do this, advocated a high technology conference as a way to organize broad community input from business leaders to help formulate an economic policy process. Duke Tully, publisher of *The Arizona Republic* and *The Phoenix Gazette,* agreed to cosponsor the conference. Conference participants were charged with studying issues affecting Arizona's high technology future and formulating a plan to address those issues.

On May 7, 1983, just two months after the MCC decision, about 150 business, finance, education, and government leaders participated in the governor's Symposium on High Technology. These leaders heard from such people as W. C. Norris, chairman and chief executive officer of Control Data Corporation; Belden Daniels, president of the Counsel for Community Development; Gary Tooker, senior vice president and general manager of Motorola, Inc.; and Dr. C. R. Haden, dean of Arizona State University's College of Engineering. These individuals discussed the interlinking roles of education, manpower training, venture capital, and industry-university research partnerships in attracting and fostering high technology industries. Then, in small work sessions, symposium participants developed recommendations for action in each of these areas. The participants decided that, after further research into the specifics of the recommendations, a follow-up conference, the Symposium on Arizona's Investment Portfolio, in fall 1983, would discuss a "road map" for Arizona's high tech future.

Everyone leaving the symposium understood that Arizona's "road map" would involve primarily policies and initiatives to enhance Arizona's educational systems, technical training programs, university research, and capital resources. The road map would not address traditional elements of economic development plans, such as improved transportation, water, and sewer systems; increased industry subsidies; and enhanced availability of low-cost labor.

New Directions in Economic Policy

It would be too simplistic to say that the MCC decision spirited Arizona into a new economic policy era. It did jolt the state into realizing that the competition to attract industry (high tech, in particular) is fierce among all fifty states. It also prompted a new look at what factors are important to companies making plant location decisions and initiated an assessment of Arizona's resources in light of these factors. The impact of the MCC decision, however, probably would have been short lived if a group of public and private sector leaders, who for years had promoted education excellence and quality of life, had not seized the MCC publicity to galvanize new initiatives in both of these areas.

Foremost among these leaders were Governor Babbitt, Roland Haden, dean of the ASU Engineering School; and Solly Sollenberger, an Arizona businessman and community activist. While most of the economic development community was devoting resources and energy to prospecting trips and lobbying the legislature for a larger state advertising budget, these individuals had been working to upgrade the graduate programs at the state universities and to improve the quality of Arizona education, in general. They already viewed education reform as an important part of the state's overall economic development strategy.

By the time of the MCC decision, this group had established and secured funding for the Center for Engineering Excellence at Arizona State University. It also had spearheaded passage of legislation creating university research parks in Arizona. Ironically, if not for these efforts, it is doubtful that MCC would ever have considered Arizona as a possible location.

While, on the surface, it would appear to a casual observer that OEPAD was focusing on traditional economic recruiting, in reality, the majority of work was on policy development and programs in what was called internally "the real economic development policy." Under Governor Babbitt's leadership, the policy arm of the agency drove the development side. While working with the traditional private sector economic recruiters on a narrow approach to economic development, OEPAD staff steered Governor Babbitt toward more substantial and comprehensive economic policy development.

Arizona State University Engineering School

The story of the Center for Engineering Excellence begins in 1978, when the principals of several local high technology industries became alarmed by the quality and availability of engineering programs at Arizona State University. This group was led by John Welty of Motorola, Jack Marineck of Garrett AiResearch, Dick Douglas of Honeywell, and George Jude of Sperry Flight Systems. Their concern was generated by the difficulties they encountered in recruiting top-flight engineers. They shared a belief that the ASU Engineering School produced graduates of only moderate ability. Moreover, when these companies were recruiting at top engineering colleges, a recurring question among students centered around the availability of quality graduate education in the Phoenix area. Many candidates believed that an engineer must update his or her professional education every three to five years to be effective in an increasingly technological society.

In 1978, as these concerns began to surface through the Phoenix Chamber of Commerce, Roland Haden was hired as the new dean of ASU's Engineering

School. The high tech leaders helped form a joint advisory committee of local manufacturing and technology based companies and the academic community modeled on the dean's ASU College of Business Advisory Committee, which had been in existence for several years.

The Advisory Council for Engineering Excellence met through the summer of 1978 and, in early fall, requested a meeting with Governor Babbitt. Pursuant to conversations with Pat Haggerty, founder and chairman of Texas Instruments, the governor had become convinced that engineering excellence at the graduate level was critical to high technology development in Arizona. At the meeting, Governor Babbitt charged the group to "think big. I'm not interested in being behind short-term or small-time budget increases; come back to me with a sweeping multiyear program, and I'll support you."[20] Galvanized to action by the governor, the high tech companies, under the leadership of Roland Haden, formed several action committees and designed a five year, $29 million program to dramatically upgrade the quality of engineering programs at ASU. (This program grew to $39 million by the time it was completed.) The project became known as the Engineering Excellence Center.

The program first came on line in late 1978, too late to be included in the University Regents budget recommendations but in time for Governor Babbitt to include the first year of the program in his recommendations to the legislature. Incorporation of the program into the governor's budgetary program was highly unusual, because no other university department had ever asked for an appropriation outside of the regents' budgetary process.

The program was conceived as a public-private partnership, and this proved to be one of its greatest selling points. Approximately two-thirds of its funding would come from public sources and one-third from private sources. The five year plan called for a private sector commitment of $9.5 million. In fact, the private sector surpassed its goal by a factor of approximately two. The Arizona legislature approved funding for the program's first year despite opposition by the legislative staff and the House Appropriations chairman.

The Engineering Excellence Center proved highly successful in obtaining funding during its first five years of operation. Two factors were central to this success. First, leaders of the high tech business community invested a prodigious amount of time working with the legislature. They made it very clear that the program was critical to the future economic growth of Arizona. Second, due to budgetary constraints and changing attitudes toward government that limited other education spending, the time was right for a bold experiment in public-private partnership.

The legislature readily embraced the concept of leveraging private donations with public money. Because leveraging was built into the de facto strategy of the program, the larger high tech companies, such as Motorola, Garrett, and Honeywell, made early contributions to the program and demonstrated a willingness to work with the state government to make the Center of Excellence program a success. This message was delivered by a number of high tech industry representatives, who persistently demanded that the program become an Arizona legislative priority. The Engineering School is now trying to secure approval for a second five year, $57 million plan. Under this plan, about half of the money would come from the state and the rest from private or other sources. The first year funding of this program is on schedule.

Development of the Arizona State University Research Park

The success of the Center for Engineering Excellence, coupled with the emergence of the Phoenix metropolitan area as a location of high technology industry, gave rise to support for the concept of a university research park at ASU.

In 1980, the Advisory Council for Engineering Excellence conducted a series of breakfast meetings during which the group solicited Governor Babbitt's support for the research park idea. The governor's support was critical for two reasons. First, he serves as an ex officio member of the Arizona Board of Regents and, hence, often provides leadership at regent meetings on policy issues. The Board of Regents would have to establish a research park legally in order for it to become operational. Second, for the concept to become a reality, statewide support would have to be secured; the governor would be a key player in generating this support. Because of the intense competition among the three state universities, the development of a park at ASU would depend on clearly demonstrating its benefits to the entire state of Arizona and to the state university system as a whole.

In 1981, Dr. J. Russell Nelson was appointed president of ASU. Apprised of the growing support for a research park, he assigned the responsibility of formulating an initial plan to an ASU vice president, Dr. Frank Sackton. A feasibility study was completed and forwarded to the university administration for review. The completed review was positive. On November 30, 1981, members of the university administration, the Arizona Board of Regents, and business leaders visited the research park at the University of Utah to learn more about research park activity and development.

The momentum continued to build and, in 1982, the university administration appointed an ad hoc committee to analyze the feasibility of developing a park at ASU. President Nelson forwarded the committee's recommendations and other information to the Arizona Board of Regents. The board approved the concept of a research park and authorized the university to go forward with the planning, financing, construction, marketing, and management of the project, although the regents had doubts as to whether the park would benefit the entire state and its three universities and whether the park might lure professors from high tech classrooms to more lucrative nonacademic activities. The regents also were concerned that the park might be perceived as a large real estate project to generate money. Nevertheless, the concept had developed to the point where it could be reduced to legislative language. The ad hoc committee promptly began a national search for a director of the research park.

The Arizona legislature passed the research park enabling legislation during its thirty-sixth session and Governor Babbitt signed House Bill 2413 into law on April 27, 1983, as an emergency measure. The bill became effective immediately upon his signature.

One month earlier, during the legislative session in which the research park bill was being processed, Reginald W. Owens, a practicing city planning consultant, was appointed director at ASU responsible to President Nelson's office for the development of the park.

In July 1983, Owens submitted a 250-page report, *Research Park Analysis and Project Development Recommendations,* to the president of the university and to the Board of Regents. The report recommended the formation of an independent not for profit corporation under contract to the university, as was allowed under H.B. 2413. This entity would be responsible for the planning, design development, management, and marketing of the research park. Owens firmly believed that the creation of a not for profit corporation was crucial to the research park's success. He felt that the corporation would provide some degree of autonomy in the day to day operation of the park and would allow for the institution of a streamlined decision-making process. This autonomy would also make it far easier to recruit firms for the park. If the corporation were not formed, interested firms would have to negotiate with the regents, a cumbersome process. The Board of Regents eventually accepted the idea of a not for profit corporation at its September 1983 meeting. One year later, the Research Park Corporation had successfully negotiated for the 1985 construction of two multitenant buildings, which were completed on schedule.

ASU's Research Park is unique in that it was totally funded by the value of its land. The initial funding for consulting services, the budget of the park office and day to day expenses came from monies generated by crop sales from the land, farmed by the university. The roads, utilities, and other infrastructure were constructed by the local community through the mechanism of a municipal improvement district using tax-free bonds. The district loan payments will be paid from future tenant rents. In the event of an emergency, the land could be subordinated for an interim funding source. Upon completion of the infrastructure, the land value will approach $45 million.[21]

Education Reform

Along with his efforts to enhance Arizona's leadership in engineering, Governor Babbitt initiated proposals to improve higher education across the curriculum. In a speech before the High Technology Conference in May 1983, in which he declared the state's aim of leadership in high technology, Governor Babbitt outlined a three point program:

1. for universities to establish centers of excellence that nurture and support the development of high technology;
2. for universities to take leadership in reestablishing high quality education at the elementary and secondary levels;
3. for Arizona community colleges to take a strong leadership role in vocational and technical education.

To carry out this program, Governor Babbitt began to prepare a legislative agenda full of educational items. In 1983, he appointed three separate task forces to study education reform. The first of these groups was the Governor's Committee on Quality Education chaired by Dr. John Schaefer, former president of the University of Arizona. This task force issued a report in November 1983, *Popular Concerns; Unpopular Choices,* which contained forty-eight recommendations and cautioned that "apathy or inaction will only serve to guarantee mediocrity in our schools." That report led Governor Babbitt to appoint a second task force to study teacher training at Arizona state universities. A third task force was formed to focus on the use of computers in schools. This group developed guidelines for school districts on hardware and software selection, teacher training, and curriculum development that integrates computer utilization.

Together, the recommendations of these three task forces largely formed the basis for the governor's 1984 State of the State address. Governor Babbitt made it clear that his number one legislative priority was educational excellence at all levels. He asked for legislation to extend mandatory school attendance from the eighth grade to the twelfth grade. Accompanying this request was another to extend the school year by two weeks. The most important request in his view, however, was additional funding for teachers' salaries. He asked the legislature to freeze the State School Trust Fund at the fiscal year 1982–83 level and to specify that all income earned above that level be used to supplement teacher salaries and reward outstanding performance.[22]

For universities, the governor recommended full funding for all programs of the Center for Engineering Excellence at ASU and increased funding for programs in agricultural technology, astronomy, electronics, and medicine at the University of Arizona. He strongly believed that the state's commitment to research and development in engineering and electronics should be matched by a similar effort in the biological sciences.

"The place to start," he said, "is our number one health problem—cancer." He asked the legislature to increase the sales tax on cigarettes by one cent per pack to give substantial support to the cancer research and treatment center at the University of Arizona. The revenue would help "put Arizona on a track to the development of a bio-technology economy."[23]

The Arizona legislature was not in total accord with Governor Babbitt. It did enact legislation authorizing compulsory education to age 16 or tenth grade. The legislators even added a few of their own initiatives, such as free textbooks through high school, a student loan program to attract potential math and science teachers, and career ladders for teacher advancement. Nevertheless, the legislature did not support the governor's proposal for using the State School Trust Fund for teachers' salaries nor his proposal for a cigarette tax for cancer research. However, the legislature earmarked some property taxes for cancer research.

Educational reform initiatives continued into 1985. Governor Babbitt focused attention on early childhood education, asking for $3.5 million to improve the quality of programs in kindergarten through third grade. Once again, however, the real education battle centered on the governor's push for increased teacher salaries.

On March 14, 1985, the governor delivered a special message to the legislature, "on the urgent issue of teacher salaries."[24] In that message, he proposed a specific plan to raise overall spending on teacher salaries by 10 percent. This plan called for increasing direct state aid to school districts by

> 1. enacting a concurrent resolution that would refer to the voters two amendments of Article 9, Section 21 of the Arizona Constitution, designed to raise the state aggregate expenditure limit by 5 percent each year and exempt the revenues of the state land trust from the aggregate expenditure limit;
> 2. enacting legislation, effective in 1987, to remove the land trust from the state aid formula and devote the entire proceeds of that trust to a fund specifically designed to supplement teachers' salaries;
> 3. financing an additional $25 million per year for teachers' salaries by renewing and earmarking the soon to expire eight cent federal cigarette tax for that purpose.

The governor might not have been successful had he not been able to hold hostage a transportation funding package that was very important to the legislature. As a result, Babbitt gave his approval to a half-cent sales tax increase to fund a multibillion dollar freeway construction program. In exchange, the legislature passed Babbitt's proposals to increase teacher salaries.

A Comprehensive Economic Development Strategy

Governor Babbitt's involvement with educational reform legislation, high technology conferences, and university research budget wars led him to conclude that the state could not continue to pursue its economic future in piecemeal fashion. Arizona needed a much more comprehensive and analytical strategy for economic growth.

The High Technology Symposium and the follow-up Symposium on Arizona's Investment Portfolio, held in 1983, provided the opportunity to develop a comprehensive state economic development strategy with the participation of the business and education communities. At the Investment Symposium, Governor Babbitt promised a published strategy, based on the results of the two conferences, within sixty days. "Arizona Horizons: A Strategy for Future Economic Growth" was actually presented on April 16, 1984, by the governor during a breakfast in Phoenix and a luncheon in Tucson with business, education, and government leaders who had participated in the two symposiums. The document was printed by *The Arizona Republic* and *The Phoenix Gazette*.

"Arizona Horizons" identified four major long-term economic development goals:

> • to promote the growth of diversified high technology industry in Arizona;
> • to encourage the creation, expansion, and retention of new small business firms;
> • to ensure that the optimal economic potential of all areas of the state is recognized and supported;
> • to ensure that the citizens of Arizona are educated for a knowledge intensive future economy.

The report also sets forth recommendations for specific actions and programs in the areas of research and development, capital availability, entrepreneurial and small business support, and education and personnel training. In addition, the report made several general recommendations to enhance the overall economic climate in the state.

For the most part, "Arizona Horizons" simply integrated the policies and programs the state had been pursuing for several years under Governor Babbitt's leadership: educational reform, greater university research budgets, and increased business-university partnerships. However, it suggested major new directions for the state. One of these proved to be controversial in its implementation. This was a new emphasis on the growth and expansion of new small businesses within Arizona. Although committing more resources to support business start-ups was clearly conducive to furthering research and development and technological innovation, some felt such an emphasis was contrary to the state's traditional primary economic strategy, industrial recruitment.

Entrepreneurship and New Enterprise Development

With the publication of "Arizona Horizons," OEPAD became a strong advocate of committing more resources to increasing new business start-ups. The agency believed, on the basis of David Birch's research and other studies, that the key to long-term economic prosperity and the creation of new and better jobs for Arizona citizens lay with strategies designed to help individual investors and entrepreneurs start new businesses and to help existing firms in the state expand and thrive.

Not all economic development leaders in Arizona were of the same mind as OEPAD. Organizations that strongly supported industrial recruitment, like AAID and some chambers of commerce, resisted this new focus. They viewed it as an abandonment of out of state recruitment. OEPAD recognized that a new constituency had to be built in the state for this element of overall economic development strategy.

The process of constituency building started with the formation of the governor's Task Force on Innovation. Governor Babbitt supported a redirected focus toward enterprise development. He was familiar with the recent studies concerning the job generation and innovation powers of small business, and he was concerned that Arizona's economic strongholds would not diversify beyond high technology manufacturing plants to research and development headquarters and new spin-off businesses. The Innovation Task Force was composed of government, industry, education, and financial leaders and was staffed by OEPAD. It was charged with assessing Arizona's entrepreneurial climate and making recommendations to the governor regarding statewide efforts for promoting and supporting businesses developed by entrepreneurs.

The task force concluded that the entrepreneurial climate definitely could be improved in Arizona. It recommended the creation of the Arizona Innovation Consortium to bring together universities, the private sector, and state policy makers to achieve goals outlined by the task force. These goals included compiling an inventory of the public and private resources and services available to entrepreneurs, disseminating information, and providing referral to entrepreneurs to enable them to find the resources they need; encouraging the educational community to present timely and current programs needed by the entrepreneurial community; conducting policy analysis and constituency building on issues affecting the entrepreneurial climate; and promoting public awareness of the importance of entrepreneurship and new business development.

Governor Babbitt established the Arizona Innovation Consortium in February 1985. Its members included several successful Arizona entrepreneurs; presidents of three banks; directors of the two Entrepreneurial Centers at Arizona universities; the deans of the College of Business at Arizona State University, the University of Arizona, the Northern Arizona University; key legislators; representatives of the venture capital industry; and the executive director of OEPAD.

The consortium was not the only organization focusing on entrepreneurship to emerge in Arizona in recent years. In 1984, Centers for Entrepreneurship were established at both Arizona State University and the University of Arizona with large endowments from two Arizona entrepreneurs. In addition to offering educational courses in entrepreneurship, these centers conduct research on the entrepreneurship phenomenon and promote interaction between the corporate and academic communities. Also, in 1984, the ASU College of Business formed the New Venture Development Council, composed of fifty founders of growth oriented companies located in Arizona, to serve as a network within which entrepreneurs share ideas and information and generally provide psychological support for each other. The council also offers seminars on topics crucial to the survival of a new firm and recommends programs that ASU could provide for entrepreneurs and fledgling companies. Roland Haden, dean of the ASU Engineering School, along with several local venture capitalists, organized a nonprofit organization, the Arizona Research and Development Corporation, to provide seed capital to entrepreneurs. In Tucson, a partnership was formed with local business people, chambers of commerce, and the city to create a small business incubator.

The concept of enhancing the entrepreneurial climate clearly has taken hold in Arizona. In addition to the emergence of these organizations and programs in the last several years, venture capital fairs, awards banquets to honor Arizona entrepreneurs, and special newsletters for entrepreneurs have proliferated. Furthermore, in 1984 the legislature appropriated about $130,000 for OEPAD to create a new business development program, to assist start-ups and entrepreneurs. In 1986 the Arizona Department of Commerce conducted a statewide conference on new enterprise development and published a guidebook for business start-ups in Arizona.

By no means has this activity reduced recruitment efforts. There appears to be a growing understanding that the state economic development strategy is multifold and that a choice need not be made between industrial recruitment and new business growth. Instead, the focus of policy making is on how best to strengthen the existing industrial base with a combination of recruiting efforts and strategies to increase the creation of new businesses and to improve the survival and expansion rates of existing firms.

In the future, the balancing of these two goals, plus others like rural economic development, will be the job of the newly formed Department of Commerce. On July 1, 1985, the governor's Office of Economic Planning and Development became the Arizona Department of Commerce. The legislature wanted this change for two reasons: to remove the organization overseeing state economic development from the governor's office; and to relegate the function of economic development to the status of a major state department. With this change, the legislature is expected to be more supportive of the department and more attentive to economic development issues in the future.

Conclusion

Arizona has experienced tremendous economic prosperity in the last several decades. Much of this growth resulted from factors such as climate, natural resources, technological inventions (such as air conditioning), defense procurement, and decisions of major corporations, which are beyond the control of the state. Some part of the prosperity, however, results from efforts by the state to direct its economy toward high growth.

Through the late 1970s, the state's economic development strategy entailed little more than friendliness and a favorable tax climate, in order to attract industry. Overall prosperity precluded the need for a more aggressive role by government. Issues that threatened growth were dealt with on a piecemeal basis with no attempt at long-term planning.

Increased involvement on the part of the state in the early 1980s derived from the growing realization that government could play an affirmative role in support of economic development, especially by providing "basics" such as highways and education, a strong research base, a capacity to transfer technology from the laboratory to the work place, and an enlightened labor force. Hence, when the state began to play a role in economic development during the Babbitt administration, its efforts were directed towards fundamentals and away from the more gimmicky approaches like advertising budgets and tax incentives.

Also during the Babbitt administration, the state first went through the process of developing a comprehensive economic development strategy. This helped focus on specific actions that would make Arizona attractive to the modern, high technology economy. After analyzing the ingredients of the technology industry, the state focused its efforts on university research, industry-university research partnerships, technology transfer, an enlightened labor force, entrepreneurs, and environmental and cultural assets. The MCC incident demonstrated that investments in these areas could have tremendous payoffs in the future. If the state had not invested in the Center for Engineering Excellence and planted seeds for a university park several years earlier, Arizona probably would not have even been considered in the initial bidding for MCC.

The assumption underlying the state's most recent investment in its entrepreneurial climate is that existing industry will not automatically provide the growth the state needs and that, therefore, new businesses must be formed and existing companies must be induced to develop new products and do business more aggressively. Simply trying to attract a company from another state will not provide enough real economic development. Arizona continues to operate on the assumption that improved technical and scientific education is the best means to develop the state for success in future industries.

INDIANA

Charles R. Warren

15

New Institutions
for Economic Strategy

Indiana dramatically illustrates the increased activism of state governments in economic development. In the short space of five years, 1981–86, Indiana transformed itself from a passive, reactive, noninterventionist economic bystander into an aggressive, sophisticated participant active in shaping its economy. This transformation resulted from the radical change in the way the state's public and private sector leaders view the role of state government.

During this period, the Indiana General Assembly under the leadership of Governor Robert Orr and Lieutenant Governor John Mutz enacted over seventy separate bills for economic development. New job training, industrial incentives, and assistance programs were established and several quasi-public, nonprofit, and for-profit institutions were organized to help refine and implement a recently completed strategic plan, "In Step With The Future." The Indiana Department of Commerce was bolstered by budget increases and reorganized to emphasize business expansion and retention. Perhaps of greatest significance was the recent creation, in June 1985, of an apparently unique, statewide public-private partnership organization, the Indiana Economic Development Council, led by a sixty-eight member board of directors, composed of representatives from business, industry, labor, the universities, and government, with a mandate to plan strategically, coordinate, and evaluate the state's economic development activities.

The dramatic role reversal in the Indiana state government, from passivism

271

to activism, can be accounted for by a combination of national forces that affected most states and local forces specific to Indiana:

> 1. The cumulative impact of the 1974–75, 1978–79, 1980, and 1981–82 economic downturns or recessions and their severity among the states of the Great Lakes region;
> 2. The reduced role of the federal government in domestic assistance programs, and a recognition that state government responsibilities necessarily must increase;
> 3. A bipartisan consensus among Indiana's public and private leadership that a more active state role was required;
> 4. Most important, the leadership of the governor and the lieutenant governor in making economic growth the number one priority on the political agenda and setting conditions conducive to the implementation of new initiatives.

This case study describes Indiana's economic development activities during these five years. To understand how far the state had come, one must first look backward to the social, political, and economic conditions that characterized the state, particularly in the 1960s and 1970s.

Historical Background

Neal Peirce and Jerry Hagstrom, in their *Book of America,* describe Indiana this way:

> Indiana is in many ways a microcosm of what America once was. Here one finds people clannish, patriotic, protective of property, suspicious of government. Hoosiers take perverse pride in letting someone else be first. They view with skepticism outsider's newfangled ideas infiltrating the heart of the heartland.[1]

Although they admit that "a metamorphosis in latter-day Indiana" is underway, much of their characterization remains accurate.

Hoosiers have traditionally been wary of government and exhibit a decided preference for low taxes and minimal public services. Their antigovernment feelings are demonstrated by the fact that Indiana has one of the lowest number of state employees per capita of any state in the nation and is ranked forty-third out of the fifty states in state/local taxes per capita ($584, compared with a national average of $740).[2] State government salaries are considered to be very low compared to private sector standards and attracting qualified professionals is a perennial problem.

The Republican Party has controlled the executive and legislative branches of state government continuously since 1969, and both U.S. Senators are Republican. But substantial areas of the state are heavily Democratic and pro-labor, though not necessarily pro-liberal. Political activities are based on a well-developed patronage system.

Although Indiana began with a rural, agriculture based economy, only 1 percent of its workforce is now in farm related occupations. Indiana today is basically a manufacturing state, with just over one-fourth of its workers employed in those industries, primarily steel and auto related.

This shift from agriculture to manufacturing has been of central importance to Indiana's economy. Donald Carmony argues that "the evolution of manufacturing has been the principal factor in changing the economic base of the state since the Civil War and especially since the advent of the twentieth century."[3] In the nineteenth century, Indiana manufacturing was closely tied to agriculture, but by the early 1900s, "the important Hoosier industries were iron and steel, railroad cars, foundry and machine-shop products, glass, carriages and wagons, furniture and clothing."[4] Indiana became an important pioneer in the automobile industry with over 200 brands of cars made in the state at one time or another. This has been an important historical legacy, and while Indiana is not now listed as an "auto-producing" state, the production of automobile component parts is a major part of the economy. Today, General Motors is the state's leading employer with 50,000 workers.[5]

During and immediately after World War II, Indiana enjoyed economic prosperity. From 1940–50, its total employment increased by 31.3 percent, compared to a national average of 24.5 percent.[6] During this period, most of Indiana's growth was attributed to increases in durable goods manufacturing, especially metal industries, machinery, and transportation equipment.[7] By 1950, the number of jobs in manufacturing exceeded the national average—a fact still true today.

The next two decades were marked by ups and downs in Indiana's economic fortunes. From 1950–60, employment growth was less than half the national rate (4 percent compared to 9.3 percent).[8] Between 1960–70, however, employment in Indiana increased at the same rate as the rest of the country and 327,000 jobs were added.

The 1970s were marked by complacency and optimism. "As late as 1978, the Indiana Department of Commerce was making hopeful forecasts about the state's economy: "Indiana's economy seems to be advancing and will continue to do so."[9] Nonetheless, Indiana's employment failed to keep pace with national growth once more. From 1970–80, Indiana again experienced job gains at only half the national average (13 percent compared to 25 percent).[10]

Key Trends Affecting Indiana's Economy

The Dominance of Manufacturing

Peirce and Hagstrom's comment that "Indiana is a microcosm of what America once was" aptly describes Indiana's economic base today. Just as the United States was once an industrial giant, Indiana remains a manufacturing state. Nonetheless, as a part of the national economy, Indiana remains subject to national economic trends. The most significant trend affecting the economy of Indiana is the transformation of the larger U.S. economy from manufacturing to services, as has been documented by Eli Ginzberg:

> Today employment in services in the United States is approaching the same 70 percent that were bound to the soil a century and a half ago. Only 32 percent of the labor force are still engaged in the production of goods (mostly in manufacturing) and a mere 3 percent are employed in agriculture.[11]

In light of the nature of employment growth in the national economy, it is not surprising that Indiana's employment growth has been sluggish: "Of all new jobs added to the economy from 1969 to 1976, 90 percent were in services."[12] Indiana has experienced substantial growth in the service sector, but those gains have been offset by the employment losses in manufacturing.

There is little doubt that Indiana has suffered a long-term decline beyond the effects of any cyclical economic downturn. The numbers, across an array of indicators, provide clear evidence and some insights into the reasons for Indiana's poorer performance relative to other states.[13]

> 1. Population growth, 1970–80: 5.7 percent, only half the national rate;
> 2. Per capita personal income, 1984: $10,567 against a national average of $11,675; ranks 34 out of 50 states;
> 3. Percent manufacturing employment, 1982: 24.9 compared to a national average of 21.2 percent.
> 4. Percent unionization (nonagricultural labor force): 30.4 compared to national average of 22.2 percent;
> 5. Average hourly manufacturing wages, 1982: $9.79 compared to a national average of $8.50; Indiana ranks eighth highest among the states in this category;
> 6. Educational attainment levels: Indiana ranks thirty-third among the states in percent of population with a high school degree, and forty-seventh lowest in percent of population with one to three years of college and with four or more years of college.

These statistics and rankings can be attributed directly to the dominance of manufacturing, especially steel and autos, in Indiana's economy. (Indiana is the number one steel producing state in the United States.) Indiana's manufacturing sector has a high hourly wage and is heavily unionized, compared to the nation but not to the Great Lakes region. The state experiences persistent population decline and a "brain drain" due to out-migration, which partly reflects the lack of economic opportunities in the state. Its lower standing in per capita income can be attributed to the blue-collar character of its work force and the current substitution of lower paying jobs in the service sector for higher paying manufacturing jobs.

Table 15-1 shows the changing composition of Indiana's work force during the period 1970–82. The table clearly indicates that changes in the composition of the national labor force are reflected in Indiana, although to differing degrees. During the period from 1970–82, Indiana lost 122,915 manufacturing jobs, a loss that was almost made up by a gain of 110,297 jobs in the service sector.

Table 15-1. 1970 and 1982 Employment in Indiana by Industry with Percent Change by Sector

Sector	1970	1982	% Change 1970–82
Total Employment	2,197,737	2,366,885	+7.7
Agricultural Services, Forestry, Fisheries	3,087	6,526	+111.4
Mining	7,063	10,291	+45.7
Construction	83,636	76,699	−8.3
Manufacturing	711,401	588,486	−17.3
Transportation, Public Utilities	102,882	104,193	+1.3
Wholesale Trade	77,375	101,636	+31.4
Retail Trade	302,345	356,571	+17.9
Finance, Insurance, Real Estate	77,690	101,838	+31.1
Services	266,406	376,703	+41.4
Government	307,358	350,299	+20.9

Source: INDIRS, Indianan Information Retrieval System, A data base of the School of Business, Indiana University, Bloomington.

Large percentage gains were also experienced in the agriculture and mining sectors, but on top of a very small base. Admittedly, 1982 data do not reflect the recoveries of the manufacturing and construction sectors that occurred in 1983–86. More recent data for the manufacturing sector alone show that by June 1984, employment had risen to 629,600 but by June 1986 had declined again to 602,900.[14] There is little doubt that Indiana lost a substantial number of jobs in its most important economic sector.

Education and Economic Development

The continuing low level of educational attainment of Indiana residents is a major concern of the state's public and private leaders. By most national standards, Indiana ranks very low; its educational achievement ranking is comparable to such traditionally impoverished states as Mississippi and Alabama. Improving the quality of education was a major priority of Governor Orr. Indiana increased spending for education to the point where, in 1986, it consumed approximately half of the state's general fund expenditures, one of the highest proportions among the states. Yet, Indiana still ranked thirty-ninth among the fifty states in annual average expenditure per pupil.

On the other side of the coin, a lack of jobs for graduating professionals resulted in a "brain drain," especially evident in the case of engineers. Although Purdue University is one of the premier engineering schools in the country, "Indiana ranks fourth in the total number of undergraduate and graduate engineering students enrolled in institutes of higher education."[15] While many engineers earn their degrees in Indiana, few remain in the state. Indiana has 2.45

percent of the U.S. population but only 1.81 percent of the nation's scientists and engineers.[16]

While part of the problem was due to the loss of educated residents, the past availability of high-paying factory jobs also decreased the incentive for some to attend college. As one elected state official put it, "Why should these kids go to college? They can graduate from high school on Friday, buy a new car over the weekend, and go to work on the assembly line on Monday."

Strengths and Weaknesses of Indiana's Economy

During its 1983–84 strategic planning project, the state asked the consulting firm of A. D. Little to identify Indiana's major strengths and weaknesses. The firm pinpointed ten factors:[17]

Strengths:
1. Central location;
2. Available, diverse mix of skilled labor;
3. Diversified economic base;
4. Business climate perceived favorable to other Midwest states;
5. Low energy costs.

Weaknesses:
1. Perception of poor labor-management relations;
2. High prevailing wage rates;
3. Negative perception of quality of life;
4. "Guilt by association" with rest of Midwest;
5. Uncertainty regarding future impact of environmental regulations on cost of energy.

Indiana lost more time to work stoppages (strikes) than any of the other forty-nine states, with a resulting decrease in the productivity rate of its workers.[18] Indiana does not have a right to work law, but there has been a recent decline in the percent of unionization. Most observers also agree that labor-management relations have improved and that union leaders are less confrontational and more cooperative.

The state has a central location and a good transportation system, with twelve interstate highways. Its location is advantageous geographically, especially for the Great Lakes region, but may be less so demographically: General Motors' decision to locate its Saturn plant near Nashville, Tennessee, was made partly because Nashville is "within a day's drive of 75 percent of the nation's consumers."[19]

Low energy costs are attributed to an abundance of high sulphur coal within the state; however, the acid rain issue has raised uncertainty over future energy rates. Customers in Indiana would face electric rate increases of 28–43 percent, if forced to meet acid rain legislation pollution control levels now being considered by Congress.[20] This problem is common to all the states in the Great Lakes region, and those states are considered to be Indiana's major economic competitors.

Former Economic Development Strategy of the State

Before 1980, Indiana's approach to economic development was clear and simple: maintain a low tax rate and stable tax structure. Tax relief was considered the most important action the state could take to boost the economy. One of the most significant accomplishments of Governor Otis Bowen, who served from 1973–80, was enactment of a legislative package of statewide property tax relief in 1973.

Between 1962–80, property taxes as a percentage of combined state and local taxes dropped from 56 to 33 percent.[21] This trend considerably enhanced Indiana's comparative tax advantage and significantly reduced the tax burden on industry.

In the mid-1970s, industrial and business incentives were created primarily through revisions to the state tax code. A property tax abatement law for blighted areas was enacted in 1977. Indiana was one of the first states to provide tax credits for energy conservation. Tax credits were allowed for housing and business rehabilitation, and tax increment financing was passed in 1977, largely to assist Eli Lilly and Company, a major pharmaceutical firm and one of Indianapolis' largest employers.

Aside from tax relief and incentives, the role of state government was minimal. According to the chairman of the Indiana House Ways and Means Committee, "an economic development focus within state government was nonexistent. There was little or no government intervention in business decisions."

The director of the Commerce Department's new Division of Business Expansion described the state's posture in similar terms: "We were more reactive than proactive. The philosophy was that we were not going to compete for industry. The state's leaders did not believe in industry incentives. Their attitude was that someone has to pay for them."

Under this philosophy of restraint, the Department of Commerce concentrated its activities on modestly funded promotion and advertising, and technical assistance to local governments to help them devise their own economic development strategies. The only significant program operated by the department was industrial development loans to communities for infrastructure projects.

The Department of Commerce has a somewhat peculiar place in Indiana state government. It reports to the lieutenant governor, who serves as executive director of the department. In the past, the governor and lieutenant governor were elected separately and could be from different political parties. They now run as a team, which at least ensures that they are of the same party. The success of the Commerce Department and the lieutenant governor's leadership depends strongly on his or her relationship with the governor. The governor in 1986, Robert Orr, served as lieutenant governor under his predecessor. Governor Orr had numerous ideas and ambitions for strengthening the state role in economic development, but he lacked the necessary gubernatorial support to bring them to fruition. Governor Orr supports fully the economic development activities of Lieutenant Governor Mutz.

The Development of a New Strategy

Indiana's past efforts at economic development could hardly be called strategic, nor could it be said realistically that the state had a strategy for economic growth. Although a Pollyanna attitude still prevails to some extent among Hoosiers, the state's leaders now recognize that Indiana has gone and continues to go through a significant economic transformation. There also is a widely shared consensus that collective action by leaders in the public and private sectors is essential to preserve the economic vitality of the state's citizens and the fiscal integrity of its government.

Because of this new awareness, Indiana now has an economic development strategy, but as Brian Bosworth, president of the Indiana Economic Development Council, made clear, "The state's strategic plan is not comprehensive but is a process of picking and choosing the key elements with the greatest impact." Indiana's strategy is composed of several elements that together provide a strategic framework for action. The strategy is new and changing but is based on three primary components:

> 1. The leadership and policy goals of Governor Orr and Lieutenant Governor Mutz;
> 2. "The Orr-Mutz Economic Development Package, Phases I–V;"
> 3. An ongoing strategic planning process based on the initial study, "In Step with the Future . . .: Indiana's Strategic Economic Development Plan."

Leadership

The development of an economic strategy could not have happened without the successful and acknowledged leadership of the state's chief executives. Governor Orr set the tone and provided support and encouragement for an active state role. Lieutenant Governor Mutz provided direction, ideas, and energy to the strategy process. To be sure, other key actors played essential roles and deserve much of the credit. However, there was unanimity among those interviewed that John Mutz was the primary driving force behind Indiana's economic development strategy. A legislative leader commented that most of the economic development bills were passed because Lieutenant Governor Mutz wanted them and vouched for their need. The legislature had confidence in Mutz and his competence. Ideas for new legislative programs were said to have come from the Department of Commerce headed by Mutz. A senior bureaucrat in the Department of Commerce pointed out that when Mutz took over, the entire philosophy of the agency changed: "The message was: 'Get as creative as you can.'"

The Orr-Mutz Package

The "Orr-Mutz Economic Development Package," issued in July 1985, was an agenda of legislative programs for economic development enacted or amended since 1981. It is also a rhetorical, promotional document designed to catalog state resources and impress the business community with the state's seriousness about striving to be a good place in which to do business. The brochure lists a mix of programs related to industrial assistance. Some of the legislation simply refines existing programs that preceded the Orr-Mutz administration; others are more symbolic than substantive. One example is the provision of a "windbreak" tax credit to landowners who plant trees for soil conservation.

The Strategic Plan

"In Step With The Future" is the published report of a joint state chamber of commerce and Indiana state government strategic planning process, begun in early 1983 and completed in May 1984.

Impetus for the development of a strategic plan came from the Indiana state chamber of commerce and its president, John Hillenbrand. The state chamber had become increasingly concerned about the sharp declines in business activity during the recessions of 1980–82. It also was disenchanted with the performance of the Department of Commerce and the absence of any significant industrial incentives from state government. It felt that the commerce department had become too political, lacked continuity and professional experience, and spent too much time "reinventing the wheel." The chamber's dissatisfaction coincided with John Mutz's ambitions to move the Department of Commerce into a more active role.

John Hillenbrand's leadership ensured that the process would be bipartisan and effectively would bridge the public and private sectors. Hillenbrand had the full confidence of the business community. He was the Democratic nominee for governor in 1980 and ran against the Orr-Mutz ticket. His campaign, and that of his successful opponents, stressed the need for a more active economic development policy. Hillenbrand was chairman of the Executive Planning Committee, which directed the preparation of the strategic plan: In 1986, he served on the executive committee of the Indiana Economic development council and was chairman of one of its seven policy committees.

Several public hearings were held around the state during the strategic planning process to secure a diversity of views; yet, the resulting plan essentially was the work of a small group of leaders, experts, and consultants. There was no significant involvement on the part of the state legislature in its development. Apparently, only the economic development cognoscenti were even aware of its existence. A legislator doubted if "90 percent of the state legislators knew about it."

In some respects, the strategic plan report constituted a wish list of forty-nine vaguely worded programs or activities that, at times, were little more than exhortations to work harder and do better. There was a tendency among those aware of the strategic plan to either grant it too much or too little importance. Yet, "In Step With The Future" made a significant contribution to the development of the state's economic strategy for several reasons.

First, the process brought together the key actors involved in economic development, and, thus, helped spawn the statewide public-private partnership that still exists.

Second, it produced a tremendous amount of research and analysis of the problems and the potential of the state's economy. Over 100 background and technical papers and reports were commissioned or collected during the process. Reports were prepared by staff of the state chamber; faculty members of Indiana, Ball State, and Purdue Universities; commerce department employees; A. D. Little consultants; and businesspersons. The result for the state was a much clearer picture of the changes in the Indiana economy and a strong factual basis on which to develop proposals.

Third, the involvement of key representatives from industry, banking, labor, and the state universities along with the background research produced a clear consensus, at least among those who participated, that aggressive, constructive action was required. In other words, the process of preparing a strategic plan was a major step in breaking down the complacency and optimism about future growth that had retarded the search for new initiatives.

Fourth, the strategic plan process and the report served as an important source of ideas for new policies and program initiatives. Outside experts were brought in to explain what other state governments were doing. For example, Indiana's Community Business Credit Corporation, which now provides banks a credit pool for risk reduction, was proposed by an out of state consultant hired to study the problem of venture capital.

The strategic plan was an analytical and political springboard for the more inclusive and sophisticated strategy process that followed.

The Design of New Approaches and Organizations to Implement the Strategy

Indiana's economic development strategy rests upon an innovative approach to organizational design and a calculation about the future of the national economy and the state's potential within it. Organizationally, it relies upon a complex set of public and private instrumentalities that can bring together the advantages and resources of each sector. The strategy also presumes a high level of consensus and stability among the state's political and business leaders. The strategy is based on the following beliefs or assumptions:

1. Further economic growth will be generated from the state's existing industrial base;
2. Manufacturing of durable goods will continue to be the mainstay of the state's economic activity;
3. Technological advances and new product development are keys to continued growth, but narrowly defined strategies to bring in "high tech" industries are unrealistic;
4. While a shift to greater employment in the service sector may be inevitable, public policies to encourage that shift are unnecessary and politically unacceptable.

There is a consensus behind the state's strategy that Indiana is a manufacturing state and for the foreseeable future, will continue to be so. The manufacturing sector requires assistance and special attention to remain competitive, nationally and globally. If growth in manufacturing can be promoted, growth in the service sector will proceed on its own.

Indiana chose to implement its economic strategy by creating a network of public agencies, quasi-public corporations, and private organizations and associations. This public-private partnership design effectively blurs the distinctions between the two sectors. The structure of the network is illustrated in Figure 15-1.

The Indiana Economic Development Council

The Indiana Economic Development Council (IEDC) is clearly viewed as the most important, overarching organization in the network. It is a private, non-profit corporation with a sixty-eight member board of directors, all of whom are appointed by the governor, who is chairman of the board. The lieutenant governor serves as the council's chief executive officer.

The IEDC has three major responsibilities: (1) strategic planning—to update, revise, and manage the state's strategic planning process; (2) coordina-

Figure 15-1. Organizational Structure of Indiana's Strategy

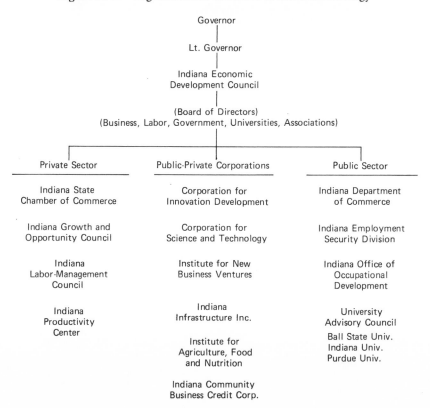

tion and new program development—to serve as a "birthing agent" for new programs or institutions and to ensure consistent implementation of both public and private economic development activities; (3) evaluation—to determine the costs and benefits of existing programs and suggest modifications or eliminations.

While IEDC appears to be the manager of economic development activities, its key participants describe it more as a central guidance system, which is not consumed by day to day operations but instead looks to the future needs of the state. Since it is a new organization, its actual role still is being determined. IEDC was incorporated in April 1985 and held its first organizational meeting on June 6, 1985. IEDC is funded by an appropriation of $200,000 from the state and $100,000 from the Indiana State Chamber of Commerce.

The substantive mission of IEDC derives directly from the "In Step With The Future" strategic plan. Seven key objectives define the responsibilities of its committees:

> 1. Business Climate/Business Assistance: including taxes, regulations, and quality of life;
> 2. Education and training;
> 3. Energy: supply, distribution, and financing;
> 4. Infrastructure: investment strategies;
> 5. Technology: productivity enhancement, transfer, and innovation;
> 6. Productivity: issues affecting managers and workers;
> 7. Finance and capital formation.

This agenda and division of work address the major problems and trends identified during the strategic planning process as directly relevant to the strengths and weaknesses of Indiana's economy.

In summary, the IEDC serves as the umbrella, coordinative body that provides private sector input into public policy formulation and a structured interaction between state government officials and the leaders of those key associations and institutions with an interest in economic issues.

Private Sector

The Indiana State Chamber of Commerce and its Growth and Opportunity Council play central roles in the implementation of the state's strategy. Aside from being the key initiator and proponent of the strategic plan and a funder of the IEDC, the state chamber operates a number of activities designed to aid economic development.

The state chamber's Growth and Opportunity Council manages the Indiana Small Business Council, which is both an advocate and a source of technical assistance. Under a Small Business Administration grant, the GOC has established sixteen local development centers to provide management and technological assistance. GOC also operates a construction advisory group, an Indiana Technology Referral Network, and an Economic Development WATS line. The state chamber also provides assistance to local chambers, local development agencies, and existing industries around the state.

The Indiana Labor-Management Council (ILMC) is linked directly to the Growth and Opportunities Council and is responsible for strengthening work force productivity and labor-management relations. It serves as a technical advisor to existing plants, an information clearinghouse, and an innovator of productivity methods. In 1985, the legislature appropriated $500,000 to fund productivity improvement programs.

Public-Private Corporations

Indiana's legislature has chartered several corporations since 1981 to address specific issues identified in the strategy. The most important ones are the Corporation for Innovation Development (CID), the Corporation for Science and Technology (CST), and the Institute for New Business Ventures (INBV). Together they provide a tripartite approach to new business development.

Chartered in 1981, CID was the first economic development corporation created in Indiana and the first of its type among the states. CID "is a privately owned venture capital investment company which was founded with the objective of making equity oriented direct investments in Indiana businesses."[22] Its chartering legislation provided a 30 percent tax credit to CID investors, which raised a $10 million fund for the corporation to invest. CID's purpose was to overcome the lack of seed and venture capital in Indiana and to provide a vehicle to attract and leverage other sources of investment funds. It invested $4 million by 1986 and attracted over $20 million from out of state investors. In addition to its role as an investor, CID provides technical, managerial, and marketing assistance to the firms it supports. Profits from its investments plus other sources, such as Small Business Investment Corporations, provided a pool of over $60 million in risk capital for Indiana businesses.

The Corporation for Science and Technology, created in 1982, is a private, nonprofit corporation funded by the state ($20 million for the 1985–87 biennium). CST has three main functions: (1) advice and counsel to industry on the adoption or availability of new technologies; (2) business advice and counsel on new product and technology development; and (3) funding of new technology development. CST receives royalties from those new products that are successful. As of 1986, it had invested $20 million in approximately thirty projects. CST invests only in firms whose products will be manufactured within Indiana.

The Institute for New Business Ventures, created in 1983, is a private, nonprofit corporation funded by a state appropriation of $850,000 (1985–87). INBV provides training and technical expertise to entrepreneurs exploring new investment opportunities. It sponsors conferences and workshops on business management, investment opportunities, and resources for entrepreneurs. Its educational programs have reached over 900 participants from sixty-four Indiana counties. INBV works closely with local economic development officials and has spawned some local counterparts, such as Ventures Fort Wayne. Among its special projects are an Enterprise Advisory Service, which provides consultation to entrepreneurs free of charge, and the Seed Capital Network, which provides computer matching of new ventures and potential private investors.

CID, CST, and INBV work closely together, often making referrals to one another and collaborating on joint projects. Together, the three provide a unique combination of resources to promote new businesses and aid the modernization and competitiveness of existing companies through venture capital, technology, and expertise. These three corporations, IEDC, the Indiana State Chamber of Commerce, and the Department of Commerce have all been located in the same office building, directly across the street from the state capitol. This strategic move has increased cooperation and coordination among these organizations.

Three other public-private corporations established since the completion of the strategic plan were designed to meet specific problems or needs. Indiana Infrastructure, Inc. (III), a nonprofit corporation, "is in the business of building a knowledge base to aid decision making and to recommend strategies pertaining to Indiana's infrastructure problems and prospects."[23] Essentially a research and advisory body, it plays a key role in developing infrastructure investment strategies for the state. It receives its funding from Purdue University, the Department of Commerce, and private sources. Indiana's universities contribute staffing support and expertise.

The Indiana Institute for Agriculture, Food and Nutrition was created to promote and market Indiana's farm products and to aid in the development of export markets.

The Community Business Credit Corporation (CBCC), a for-profit entity acting under public charter, "provides a pool of credit to the Indiana banking industry in order that, through loan participation in the corporation, member banks may reduce the risk of lending often associated with a new or rapidly growing small business."[24] CBCC is patterned after similar entities in other states and provides another tool to increase available sources of debt and venture capital.

The reliance on private corporations, state sanctioned and/or state supported, to implement and guide the state's strategy represents a novel approach to institutionalizing and actualizing the public-private partnership concept. Their uniqueness derives from the fact that they are not simply publicly chartered, autonomous entities operating in isolation, but that they are an intertwined set of organizations with overlapping membership and joint or common objectives designed to function within an overall strategic framework.

There are several reasons for Indiana's adoption of a public-private organizational design, some of which are obvious and others that reflect conditions specific to the political culture of the state. The financial corporations (CID and CBCC) relied upon state enabling powers or tax credit provisions to get started, but their continued operation depends upon private market conditions and the impetus of profit. The other organizations (IEDC, INBV, CST, III, and the Agriculture Institute) are structured to allow for the joint ownership and participation of leaders from the public and private sectors. As such, they provide links that can help build a consensual basis for action. The private corporations have another strong advantage over government agencies. They can operate in a more flexible, nonbureaucratic manner. Their quasi-government status allows them to combine resources from various sources, including funds and personnel. As private corporations, they can also operate in a nonpolitical environment, which is a very important consideration in a state as highly partisan as Indiana. The president of CST prized their freedom to operate: "we are unbureaucratic, not encumbered by politics, patronage, or state regulations. Our only restriction is that we serve Indiana business to promote economic growth in Indiana."

Two other factors rationalize the use of private corporations: the need for professionalism and the importance of credibility. Indiana state government pays relatively low salaries and most of its senior positions are filled by patronage, which makes it difficult to attract and retain highly qualified and experienced professionals. In addition, the reputation of the Indiana state government works against a direct government role in many economic development functions. Business persons often are suspicious of bureaucrats and unwilling to divulge their problems or needs to a public official. Private sector sponsored and supported activities simply generate more credibility and trust among profit motivated firms and individuals.

Public Sector

Before 1981, the Indiana Department of Commerce was a low-profile, low-budget state agency that was little more than an innocent bystander in economic development matters. By 1985, it had undergone several reorganizations and had been given new responsibilities and programs, a larger budget, a new emphasis, and as a result, a new image.

Indiana's Commerce Department is unique among the states in its placement under the lieutenant governor. State organizational charts depict the economic development agencies as integral divisions of the Office of the Lieutenant Governor (see Figure 15-2). The Lieutenant Governor's Office is made up of four components: (1) the personal, political office headed by an Executive Assistant; (2) an Executive Assistant for Job Training and Services with responsibility for the Indiana Office of Occupational Development and the Employment Security Division, (3) a Deputy Director of Commerce responsible for most of the department's external relations; and (4) a Deputy Director of Commerce for internal programs.

As executive director of the Department of Commerce, commissioner of agriculture, and head of state and federal job training programs, the lieutenant governor clearly is the "person-in-charge" and the preeminent leader of Indiana's economic development strategy.

Much like a federal agency, Indiana's Commerce Department processes loans, makes grants in aid, monitors economic conditions, serves as a broker and clearinghouse, and audits performance. Although it directly manages several major economic development programs, many of the state's development programs operate through external boards or commissions, private organizations, or local community and economic development agencies. The department's major emphasis has been on developing effective working relationships with economic development organizations in the private and quasi-public sectors and at the local level of government.

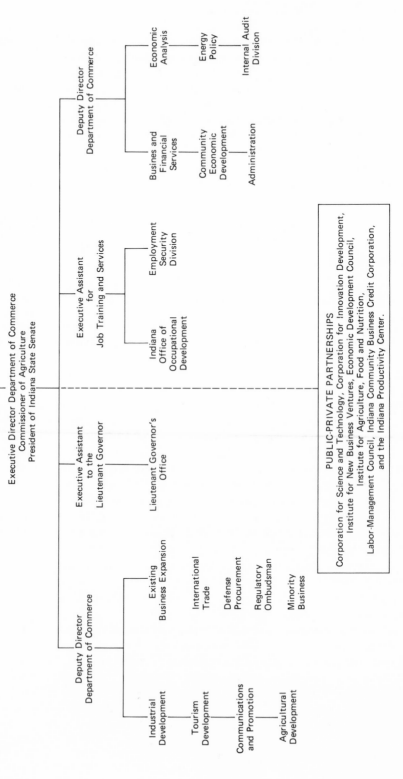

LIEUTENANT GOVERNOR

Executive Director Department of Commerce
Commissioner of Agriculture
President of Indiana State Senate

Deputy Director
Department of Commerce

Industrial Development

Tourism Development

Communications and Promotion

Agricultural Development

Existing Business Expansion

International Trade

Defense Procurement

Regulatory Ombudsman

Minority Business

Executive Assistant to the Lieutenant Governor

Lieutenant Governor's Office

Executive Assistant for Job Training and Services

Indiana Office of Occupational Development

Employment Security Division

Deputy Director
Department of Commerce

Busines and Financial Services

Community Economic Development

Administration

Economic Analysis

Energy Policy

Internal Audit Division

PUBLIC-PRIVATE PARTNERSHIPS

Corporation for Science and Technology, Corporation for Innovation Development, Institute for New Business Ventures, Economic Development Council, Institute for Agriculture, Food and Nutrition, Labor-Management Council, Indiana Community Business Credit Corporation, and the Indiana Productivity Center.

Figure 15-2.

Like most state commerce agencies, Indiana's department engages in activities to attract outside industry, to promote international trade and exports, to promote tourism, as well as extensive advertising and image building.

While the department is opportunistic in its search for economic growth, it cannot be accused of concentrating on "smokestack chasing," which Peirce, Hagstrom, and Steinbach have described as, "each state clawing for jobs at the expense of another."[25] Rather, Indiana has followed the authors' advice to adopt "activist policies which assist expanding in-state firms and aid, in every area from venture capital to technical expertise, the incubation of new enterprises appropriate to local economic strengths and realities."[26]

In late July 1985, Lieutenant Governor Mutz announced the establishment of a new Division of Business Expansion to help clarify the department's priorities:

About 60 percent of our grants to aid new job creation are awarded to Indiana firms, but the perception is that we spend most of our time luring out-of-state companies to Indiana. This new division will sharpen the attention given to the role Indiana firms are playing in our state's economic development. Our message is: We're glad you are here, come grow with us.[27]

The new division works through "account executives" assigned to make regular calls on businesses to explain the services of the department, to determine if firms need help, and to get them assistance. The division also manages programs for export promotion, defense procurement, minority business development, and regulatory assistance.

The newly appointed director of the Division of Business Expansion argues that the department's programs and incentives intentionally are biased toward existing industries and focused on the auto, steel, and durable goods manufacturers. Little attention is devoted to assisting the services sector; however, there have been some exceptions. Insurance and information firms were given state assistance, and their attraction resulted in a thousand new jobs.

No formal machinery exists to coordinate the economic development activities of other departments or agencies in the executive branch. Indiana has not chosen to create an economic development cabinet and does not have a state planning agency. One observer believes that the lack of interagency coordination and long-range planning within the state government is a serious deficiency:

Indiana has no capital structures budget. All capital appropriations are part of the annual or biennial budgetary process which is dominated by election myopia. Coordination of state programs in a central oversight agency was never adequate when the state had an operating "state planning services agency." Today that agency is a shell of no consequence.[28]

Yet, the state officials we interviewed saw few problems in achieving cooperation from other major state agencies on economic development projects. Republican Party control of the state executive branch for over sixteen years produced a consistency in policy that lessens the need for central planning. They cite the fact that economic development was a gubernatorial priority that permeated the entire executive branch. Also, Lieutenant Governor Mutz is respected throughout the state offices and has immediate access to the governor should any interagency disputes or problems arise.

Assessment of Potential Problems

The relative newness of the state's economic development strategy, plus the effect of exogenous factors, particularly the recovery of the national economy, and of the U.S. automobile industry in particular, make it difficult, if not impossible, to show any causal relationship between Indiana's actions and business decisions. However, some anecdotal evidence of the strategy's impact is available.

Despite its loss to Tennessee in the multistate competition for the $5 billion General Motors Saturn plant, Indiana gained substantial new investment from the automobile industry. General Motors decided to locate a new truck assembly plant worth $1.7 billion in Fort Wayne. The state aided that decision by providing funds for highway interchanges and water and sewer construction. In August 1985, GM announced its plan to spend $575 million to modernize its plant in Marion, Indiana. This will provide greater job security for the 3700 employees. The state will spend $3 million to provide job retraining for the GM workers in Marion.[29] In July 1985, Chrysler announced an investment of $350 million to remodel and expand its transmission and castings plants in Kokomo, Indiana. General Motors decided to locate a new research center in Kokomo; a decision attributed, in part, to the state's provision of tax credits for industrial research expenditures.

Two other examples provide evidence of the increasing attractiveness of Indiana to outside industry. Enkei America, Inc., a Japanese firm owned partly by Mitsubishi, in August 1985, decided to build a $12 million wheel plant in Columbus, Indiana. The state furnished Enkei $275,000 for worker retraining and provided the city of Columbus $200,000 for infrastructure improvements at the plant site.[30]

Overall, according to a recent Commerce Department press release, Indiana is one of the most successful states in the country for attracting new business: "In four years, more than 200 firms have come into Indiana. New state programs have helped create or save 46,000 jobs and train more than 10,000 Indiana workers."[31]

It will probably remain difficult for the Indiana Economic Development Council, which is charged with evaluating the state's economic development programs and the priorities among them, to demonstrate the success or failure of specific programs or incentives on a purely cost-benefit basis. The rationale behind a business location or expansion decision simply is too complex to ascribe the result to any single factor. While Indiana now has in place a varied and comprehensive economic development package, on the surface at least, its programs and incentives are comparable to those of other states in its region. Strategies and incentives are essential, but their effect is probably more important in changing perceptions and attitudes about a state, its government, and its business climate. Creating and building an image of a state as "a good place to do business" may be the most important variable that these programs influence.

Despite the mobilization of political support for the new economic development measures, critics point to the small number of jobs created, the lack of entrepreneurs within the state to take advantage of the programs, and to "copy-cat" spending on programs previously adopted by neighboring states. Moreover, while Indiana has successfully devised an economic development strategy, it has yet to achieve a growth rate and prosperity comparable to many other states. The continued loss of jobs in the manufacturing sector, although made up for by gains in nonmanufacturing employment, presents problems for Indiana's long-term strategy, which is based on the continued viability of the durable goods manufacturing sector of its economy. Within the state, there is a prevailing consensus that the United States will continue to make things and that Indiana is a good place for manufacturers. The results of the last few years indicate that, although jobs have been recovered since the last economic downturn, there continues to be a net, permanent loss in manufacturing employment.

National economic growth may continue, and Indiana may receive a disproportionate share of any increase in manufacturing activity that occurs as a result. On the other hand, Indiana may be engaged in a "holding-action" that could be lost in a future national economic recession. Indiana's faith in manufacturing clearly is an attempt to resist or counter trends in the national economy. National trends could be too powerful and pervasive for its strategy to succeed.

Even if the national decline in manufacturing abates, most observers agree that the manufacturing sector is undergoing dramatic changes: from basic products to specialized products, to high value-added products, to a smaller worker/machine ratio, and to the use of more sophisticated, technologically advanced fabricating processes and equipment.[32] These changes could have important ramifications for Indiana's work force. The state's leaders recognize that Indiana's relatively low level of educational attainment must be raised to remain competitive in a more technological economy that requires better educated and more skilled workers.

There is a pressing need for substantial investments in education programs and infrastructure. According to a recent report of Indiana Infrastructure, Inc., $195–554 million more a year must be spent to meet federal waste-water treatment standards by the 1988 deadline.[33] Comparable investments are required for highways and bridges. Indiana enjoys some comparative advantage in the competition for economic growth by virtue of being a low-tax, minimal public services state. Whether the state can maintain that tax advantage while, at the same time, meeting the necessary investment needs in education and infrastructure is questionable. Indiana's transformation from a passive bystander to an active leader in economic development could not have occurred without the continuity and stability of the political leadership it has enjoyed. The strategic plans and new initiatives have received bipartisan support and were noncontroversial. Present indications are that this climate will continue, yet there is a question as to whether the momentum will persist if a substantial change in political leadership takes place or if state's priorities shift.

Indiana has made a dramatic and strategic step in attempting to influence and manage its economic future. Only time will tell whether its efforts are entirely successful. Leadership, an aggressive state role, and a strong public-private partnership may yield the results anticipated. Whatever the outcome, there can be little doubt that Indiana state government is making a positive contribution to the Hoosier economy.

MINNESOTA

Ted Kolderie
William A. Blazar

16

A High Quality Public Sector
as a Strategy for Economic Growth

In Minnesota the state government contributes to the growth and development of the economy mainly by organizing and operating a high quality public sector that maintains and improves the state's productivity and its general quality of life.

Like virtually every state, Minnesota has sponsored a variety of direct economic development programs. These efforts, targeted to particular industries and firms, are promoted by the governor and run mainly by the state's Department of Energy and Economic Development. Although some of these programs have existed for decades, most are relatively new.

It is not likely that these direct efforts have proved critical to the development of Minnesota's economy. Minnesota has never been in a good position to compete with other states using direct inducements. The state lacks the central location that appeals to big firms that manufacture goods for the national market. The state has known for a long time that its success comes mainly from the success of small businesses, nurtured by the state's entrepreneurial climate, which grow into permanent fixtures in the state economy. Moreover, Minnesota recognizes that the state has little control over the powerful forces affecting the state's economy. These forces include both international competition and the national shift to a service based economy.

Rather, the state's economic success has been built on a set of actions that only indirectly affect jobs and investment. These indirect efforts by the state government include providing the private sector with high quality public services

293

and facilities and a supportive framework of public law and regulation; maintaining a policy-making process with a superior capacity to address the problems and opportunities that arise both in its private and in its public systems; and adapting to the forces requiring change. The state has an unusual ability to raise issues in the absence of crisis and resolve problems after thorough (if not speedy) discussion.

The Political Imperative for Productivity

For a variety of historical and geographic reasons, Minnesota has developed a special political culture that treats government and the political process less as an activity through which individuals, families, and interest groups protect and enrich themselves, than as a "commonwealth" in which people come together in order to solve problems. This culture is driven by strategic problems the state has faced throughout its history.

Minnesota is in the very northwestern corner of the northeastern United States, a long way from national markets and from the energy and other resources it needs. It is a large state, thinly populated, and suffers from the costs imposed by great distances. Transportation is expensive; the state maintains the fourth largest road system in America.

The state also has a strong commitment to provide for itself services, institutions, and facilities that are the equal of those in much larger urban areas. Partly, this means public services: universities, schools, and welfare and social services. Partly, it means quasi-public services: orchestras, art galleries, hospitals, and sports that are "major league."

The state's economy, like that of the nation, has been shifting away from the production and processing of natural resources and heavy manufacturing toward white-collar, service jobs. Faced with increasingly national and international markets, Minnesota's growth industries have been technology goods such as computers and, especially, business services (insurance and financial management, consulting, publishing, advertising, health-care services, engineering, and computer software), which are sold for "export."[1]

This type of economic activity, by its nature, is not tied to any particular location and is, therefore, free of resource constraints and high transportation costs. In these areas, therefore, Minnesota can compete with anybody, anywhere.

The state has sought to create the amenities that attract the high-skilled, high-income workers who operate a service based economy: cleanliness, security, good schools, parks, cultural facilities, and social service programs.

State spending on these services has been substantial. In 1984, per capita state and local spending was about $2,600; fifth highest among the states and about 20 percent above the national average.[2] Such high spending catches Minnesota in a strategic dilemma. The services and amenities that attract (and, more important, retain) the technological and business services industries the state wants to develop, unfortunately, also generate costs that can discourage the high-income workers the state needs to run that economy.

This dilemma is complicated further by the social philosophy of the state, which commits Minnesota politically to a progressive tax system. In fact, prior to 1985, the incidence of the state's tax system was the most progressive in the United States. Minnesota was one of those states that went to the income tax rather than to the sales tax in the 1930s. Hence, it did not build its higher education system out of a regressive sales tax on food and clothing. (Even its property tax has become an income related tax.)

Today, Minnesota, therefore, is driven to deal with the *real* costs of its public service system. It is driven to a strategy of good management in its public sector, emphasizing priorities and productivity in its effort to provide the physical facilities and social and cultural institutions it wants for all its people and that represent the inducements it needs for the type of economic growth on which it must now rely.

The Elements of This Strategy

Several elements of the indirect strategy Minnesota has chosen can be identified.

First: There has been a policy of concentrating resources. Minnesota, with 2 percent of the nation's population, does not have many institutions that have grown naturally to a size that permits them to compete on equal terms with similar institutions in older, more populous states. Minnesota, therefore, must deliberately create scale.

This theme runs through Minnesota's history. It is exemplified by the movement that produced the farmer cooperatives, including Farmers Union Grain Terminal Exchange, Farmers Union Central Exchange, and Land O'Lakes, as well as by the effort of the Minneapolis banks in the early 1930s to draw the banks of the region together under holding companies, which today include First Bank System and Norwest Corporation, as a way of building strength.

Minnesota combined its state university and land-grant college and located the combined institution in the biggest city in the state. Until recently the University of Minnesota had the largest single college campus in America. Throughout the expansion in higher education during the 1950s and 1960s, Minnesota kept the advanced-degree programs concentrated in the university.[3] It was research at the university that developed the process for concentrating low-grade iron ores into taconite, thus extending the life of Minnesota's Iron Range. Currently, there is a major effort to focus the university's programs in ways that will be helpful to the state, especially by concentrating more resources on graduate education.

In much the same way, Minnesota "founded" but one city. The state's commerce, government, and educational, cultural, and service institutions are concentrated in the urban region of Minneapolis and St. Paul. Over 2 million people live there; the state's second-largest urban area has fewer than 100,000. The

Twin Cities metropolitan area is as a result one of the nation's major "control points." Minneapolis is a Federal Reserve city and the state is home to the fourth largest concentration of Fortune 1000 corporation headquarters in the country.

Second: The state had a policy of investing in people. The state has made a substantial investment in education at all levels, which produced not only a university of major national rank but also a school system that graduates a higher proportion of the children who enter it than does the school system of any other state. State and local government spends about one-third of its revenues on education. Minnesota ranks fifth in spending per capita on education.

There has been a comparable investment in health care, principally hospitals and medical groups, of which the Mayo Clinic is the best known example. These industries export services by attracting patients from other states. Minnesota spends heavily on the care of the aged: It has a far larger proportion of its elderly in nursing homes, especially "skilled" nursing homes, than does any other state.

In the mid-1940s, when mayor, Hubert Humphrey led the effort to remove the stain on Minneapolis as the most anti-Semitic city in America. Rapidly, this effort broadened to include blacks and other minorities, both in public and in private institutions. In recent years, women have pressed vigorously and effectively for the removal of sex-based discrimination. One of the effects has been to release a major reservoir of talent for the institutions and enterprises located in Minnesota.

The state's emphasis on "human capital" was explicit in the formation of Minnesota Wellspring by Governor Al Quie in 1980. Increasingly, as the state sells management, advise, design, and supercomputers; the "wellspring" of the economy is seen to be human intelligence.

Third: There has been a reliance on the use of system (rather than company specific) incentives and on competition as a stimulus to economic growth and public sector productivity. In 1939, the Minnesota legislature revised tax laws so that business firms would be taxed only on their activity within the state. The revised laws gave businesses a choice of relating this activity to their sales, to their income, or to their property. This policy encouraged the location and retention in Minnesota of corporate headquarters for firms that, even then, were becoming national in their scope.

Businesses are taxed at a relatively low rate of 6 percent on their first $25,000 of taxable income. The nominal rate on income above that level is 12 percent, but the formula for allocating corporate income reduces this for headquarters of companies doing business beyond Minnesota's borders.

Beginning in 1967, as part of a further restructuring of business taxation, computers were among the equipment exempted from taxation, with significant implications for the growth of data processing, software development, and central office activity. At that time, IBM was very nearly the largest taxpayer in Minneapolis.

Pressure remains for two other changes in the system. One would reduce the taxes on the commercial real estate in which the growing services-information sector is housed, which now supplies about a third of the state's property revenue. The other change would reduce unemployment insurance premiums by cutting some benefits.

The state has encouraged competition in both private and public sectors. In the 1920s, the Hennepin County Bar Association ended nepotism in the local law profession and, as a result, made careers in law attractive to talented individuals who did not happen to be the children of law partners.[4]

The Twin Cities area is an "open town." Despite the pleas of local firms for "preference," business firms, nonprofit organizations, and government in the Twin Cities search both in and out of state in their recruiting efforts. A "Buy Minnesota" law, passed during the recession of the early 1980s, was quickly repealed.

The Department of Transportation and the attorney general have moved aggressively to prosecute road contractors for rigging bids. After a start down the road of regulation, the health care policy of the state has turned sharply toward competitive strategies. The legislature in 1984 separated the planning and policy making for transit from its operation. The new Regional Transit Board is contracting more widely for special services to handicapped persons and is moving to test the idea of buying regular-route bus service "by the route." Most recently, the governor has begun turning toward a competitive model for the state's system of public education.

Fourth: Minnesota has made a major, continuing effort to improve the effectiveness of its public sector programs and institutions. The essential prescription for success in business organizations is: Be sensitive to the changing environment and innovate constantly. The same philosophy is being applied to government in an attempt to deal with the real costs of its services and facilities.

There have been efforts, as in the Loaned Executive Program in the 1970s, to transfer particular productivity improvements from the private sector directly to state government. The programs of state government itself, however, are a small part of the public sector in total. Thus, the general thrust of the state's effort has been more strategic. It has taken the form of continuous (legislative) "maintenance" on the public institutions at the local level, where most decisions are made and most money is spent.

Over about a twenty-five year period, the legislature totally rebuilt the system of local government organization and finance, especially that of the Twin Cities metropolitan area, where half the state's population lives.

In 1949, the legislature restructured the municipal code. In 1959, it assumed control of municipal annexation and incorporation, effectively halting the net growth in the number of new municipal jurisdictions. In the early 1960s, county government was modernized and its management strengthened.

In 1967, conscious of the degree to which the economic health of the state depends on the economic, social, and political health of the Twin Cities area, the legislature laid the foundation for what today is arguably the strongest, most innovative system of metropolitan government organization and finance in the country. The Metropolitan Council was made the central manager (though not its operator) for the region's critical infrastructure: airports, transit and highways, housing, parks, and open space. Municipal income taxes were prohibited and local sales taxes tightly controlled. Since 1971, 40 percent of the net growth of the commercial-industrial property tax base has been pooled and shared among all municipalities, increasingly standardizing the business property tax rate.

In the early 1970s, further efforts were made to improve the management of the state government itself. A new Department of Finance was created by consolidating the money management function of the state treasurer, the revenue estimation function of the Tax Department, and the budgeting function of the Department of Administration.

Maintaining the Quality of the Policy Process

A policy and political process that is able to accomplish innovative, nonincremental changes in goverment institutions is itself a major resource and an important element of the state's ability to adapt and to make itself attractive for economic development.

Minnesota has an unusual set of policy institutions, which are exceptional in at least three respects.

First: The state has a considerable ability to raise issues for policy debate. The public sector contributes strongly to this process. Its resources range from a world class university, located in the same community as the seat of government, to the State Planning Agency, which for the past fifteen years has employed a state demographer whose work in sensitizing state officials to the implications of population change has been enormously influential.

Much of the critical work of identifying trends and assigning priorities to issues is done in the private sector. Private institutions are especially important, because setting the policy agenda usually requires asking unpopular questions.

Some of these are questions that public officials are too close to their operations to see. Some are questions that challenge what people inside the institution prefer to take as given. Some questions would simply offend people in influential positions. Raising these questions requires analysts who, at the same time, are close enough to the political process to know what to ask and independent enough of political pressures to be willing to ask them.

The state's newspapers (and, more recently, some television stations) have been an important part of this agenda setting process. So has the changing cast of private, nonprofit issue-study organizations, such as the Citizens League, the Upper Midwest Council, the Minnesota Business Partnership, the Urban Coalition, and the Minnesota Project. So are the privately sponsored forums that focus on the discussion of specific issues: Spring Hill and other conference centers, The Itasca Seminar, the Minnesota Meeting, and countless breakfast, lunch, and dinner clubs.

Business firms themselves play an important part in this process. Along with private foundations, they finance much of this "front-end" research and discussion. Companies and their executives make time for civic affairs. There has been a corporate tradition of inviting public officials in for lunch or using staff meetings for the consideration of public as well as of company or industry issues.

This civic tradition is under some pressure in Minnesota today, but it tends to be reinforced by the practice, quite untypical nationally, for companies to draw their public affairs, community relations, and corporate giving officers not from divisions of the company but from government and the nonprofit sector. Inevitably, given their background, these officers function not only to represent the company to the community but also to explain and interpret the community to the company.

There is a traditional understanding in Minnesota public affairs that, while it is essential to compromise the decisions, it is essential *not* to compromise the proposals.

Minnesota's tendency has been to bring issues and proposals up through its permanent study and discussion institutions rather than to rely on ad hoc studies. This gives the system a built-in capacity to follow a proposal past the point at which the report is issued, through the stage of legislative decision and beyond.

On special commissions, however "blue ribbon," each party at interest in the problem usually seeks and receives a seat: It is difficult, if not impossible, either to raise embarrassing issues or generate nonincremental proposals. Such commissions have a limited appropriation and a limited life, effectively dying at the time they deliver their report.

Of course, there is some use of the "special commission." But the civic tradition remains strong enough that parties not directly interested can legitimately and effectively intervene in the affairs either of a government or of some private industry or profession, without being invited in and without asking permission; raising questions and making proposals and stimulating a community discussion.

Second: Minnesota has a considerable ability to resolve issues. This seems to stem from the use of the dominance of legislative rather than executive bodies at all levels in the decision-making process.

The central role of legislative bodies may result from the relative youth and the short career length of Minnesota legislatures. Young politicians, whose career in the state legislature is not their highest political goal, simply have less at stake personally and less to lose personally from an unpopular decision. In addition, the intricacies of the policy process, the speed at which it sometimes works, and the sheer number of actors involved frequently can offer important opportunities for the sort of dramatic initiative by the legislature that conventional theory usually assumes comes from the executive and its staff.

A legislature, especially when located in the population center of the state, also is more open to the intervention of community and "generalist" groups than is the decision-making process of the executive branch. There tends to be a broader, if sometimes more drawn-out and more heated, examination of proposals and policy options.

During the 1970s, Minnesota systematically changed the system of representation within the structure of boards and commissions that form an important part of the policy process. These changes took the form of dropping the representatives of the interested groups and replacing them with representatives of the general public. The chief engineer of the major electric utility, for example, no longer serves as a member of the agency responsible for pollution control. Presidents of the colleges and universities no longer sit as members of the Higher Education Coordinating Board.

This philosophy was at the heart of the legislature's decision, in 1967, to construct the Twin Cities Metropolitan Council not as a "council of governments," whose members would be sitting officials of the local jurisdictions, but to set up the representation on the one person/one vote principle and to provide that its members be selected by the governor. The system was deliberately built to maximize the ability of the institution to make decisions in situations in which the interests of the different parts of the region conflict.

The Evolution of Direct State Action

Direct action for economic development by the state government is a relatively new phenomenon in Minnesota. Throughout most of the state's history, economic development programs were sponsored and operated by private industry, primarily by the state's railroads, utilities, and larger banks. These companies frequently had economic or industrial development departments. The railroads sought to entice shippers to locate along their own trackage. Local utilities sought firms that would buy gas and/or electric power. The banks recognized that their success depended on a growing community. They led a variety of development initiatives. For example, Minnesota was without a petroleum industry until the First National Bank of St. Paul led an effort to build a refinery at Pine Bend, southeast of St. Paul, tapping off a new pipeline carrying Canadian crude into the midwestern United States.

In the late 1950s, most companies eliminated these economic development departments, as business opportunities outside their traditional service areas became more important. Thereafter, private efforts tended to move through organizations like the chambers of commerce, fed by government projects such as urban renewal, the new domed stadium, and mass transit. The privately organized efforts moved off toward the new areas of economic growth, with the formation of the Minnesota High-Technology Council, the Minnesota Cooperation Office, and the Minnesota Seed Capital Fund, all aimed at nurturing new and smaller high technology companies in a state traditionally specializing in large mainframe computers.

The federal government withdrew from financing the renewal of commercial areas about 1969. Minnesota stepped in with a program of tax increment financing, in 1971. Its cities have since invested heavily in this "self-financing" device: borrowing money to buy land, clear buildings, and install utilities; repaying the loans with the additional tax revenue generated by the new development.

Historically, the Department of Economic Development published business directories, promoted tourism, and sent an occasional trade mission abroad.

But, in the late 1970s, it plunged heavily into direct assistance to particular industries and firms. To help the Iron Range, the state created the Northeast Minnesota Protection Trust Fund in 1977. A Small Business Finance Agency appeared in 1980, "enterprise zones" in 1982, a Minnesota Economic Recovery Fund in 1984, and the Agri-Processing Loan Guarantee Fund in 1985.

The department was reorganized in 1983 into the Department of Energy and Economic Development. DEED took over the Department of Housing and Urban Development's (HUD) Small Cities Development Program and the Small Business Finance Agency. The new department was subsequently authorized to lend up to $60 million for a wide range of projects, including energy development, computer software, tourism, and health care equipment.

The state began targeted tax abatements for research and development (1982), technology transfer (1983), small business equity investment (1983), sales taxes paid on manufacturing equipment (1984) and farm machinery (1985), and approved further tax reductions for taconite (1986). The state's indirect strategy for economic development was overshadowed by this growing and highly visible use of direct strategies.

The Challenge of Politics

The more state government moved to direct strategies, the further the economic development program was drawn into partisan politics. Office seekers attacked incumbents for not doing enough to relieve distress and promote growth. As incumbents, they moved to carry out their promises to "do something." Expectations escalated. The counting game began: The "ins" claimed credit for new jobs; the "outs" contended these claims were inflated. Newspapers tried to sort out the truth: How many jobs *did* this project create? Election after election, legislative session after legislative session, the economic development programs became the focus of controversy.

This trend was intensified by the political realignment in Minnesota that began in 1970 with the election of Democratic-Farmer-Labor (DFL) Governor Wendell Anderson. In 1972, the DFL won control of the state senate, giving it full control of state government for the first time in Minnesota history. The party moved quickly to enact its program, which included improvements in workers' compensation and unemployment compensation benefits, and a big increase in school aid, with higher income and sales tax rates to restore equalization for poorer districts.

This changed political situation required a major readjustment of strategy by the business community. While working successfully through the Independent-Republican party to recapture the governorship in 1978, with the election of former Congressman Al Quie, leaders in the corporate community created the Minnesota Business Partnership, made up of the chief executives of Minnesota's largest firms, to act directly on matters of interest to business with governors of whatever party.

In 1979, there was an effort to roll back parts of the DFL program, which drew the governor and the DFL legislature into a competition to see which could reduce taxes more. Immediately thereafter, the national recession hit the Minnesota budget hard. Already strained by the tax reductions, revenues fell sharply.

In November 1982, an unendorsed DFL candidate, Rudy Perpich, was elected governor. A lieutenant governor under Wendell Anderson, Perpich had served briefly as governor in 1977–78, when Anderson decided to take the U.S. Senate seat vacated by Walter Mondale.

Perpich returned to the capitol in 1983 with new attitudes formed during his four years in private business, with few political obligations, and a new team of officials, many also drawn from the private sector.

The Dilemma of Direct Versus Indirect Action

Through Perpich's four year term, the state expanded its direct development efforts while continuing its indirect strategy.

Direct assistance became increasingly specific to industries and firms. Programs included a World Trade Center, a Convention Center, a horseracing track, a "megamall," tourism proposals, which at one point included a casino on the depressed Iron Range, and a state lottery to aid agriculture. The legislature went along with Governor Perpich's offer of a $1 billion plus package of inducements for the General Motors Saturn plant.

As the 1986 elections approached, the climate for direct action changed dramatically. The Independent-Republicans had won control of the House two years before, and as the session opened, they proposed eliminating the Department of Energy and Economic Development, questioning its effectiveness, charging political favoritism, and proposing to move the development programs to a private, nonprofit corporation.

The department survived. But the future of the direct strategy is in question—not least because of a spectacular controversy early in 1987 over a bill to permit a development agency on the depressed Iron Range to make $24 million available to a cancer-research company that was (as things turned out) in the process of going bankrupt. State policy has shifted. There will be a new program of state grants to local communities, for a broad range of "economic development" activities. The state will withdraw from most of these decisions in general and from loans to businesses in particular. It may, under another new program, begin taking equity positions in the development of particular products or services (rather than in individual firms).

Surrounded by less controversy, the Perpich administration also implemented an indirect strategy, involving measures that restructured and revitalized major state systems, including the tax system. The governor's 1985 budget message itself called for (1) decentralizing responsibility for the delivery of public services, (2) providing competition among the producers of public services; and (3) allowing for choice by the customers.

This theme was offered as a pragmatic response to a practical situation, not as an ideology. Part of it looked toward an increased use of contracting. But, there was no effort to dress this up in the rhetoric of "privatization." It was more a matter of what was done than of what was said. It built very heavily on principles already in use, in efforts to change major systems in private ownership. And, predictably, it attracted far less attention in the media than the governor's initiatives on jobs and the construction of job creating projects.

The Perpich administration set some major policy initiatives in motion.

Workers' Compensation

The state's effort to redesign this program was directed by Steve Keefe, a young chemist at Honeywell who had been elected to the state senate, where he was drawn into the workers' compensation issue and developed some strong and unconventional ideas about both the problem and effective solutions. After leaving the legislature, he chaired a committee of the Citizens League studying the problem, during 1981 and 1982. He returned to state government in 1983, as Perpich's commissioner of labor and industry, to enact his recommended reform program.

At a national meeting of people interested in the future of the public sector in St. Paul, late in 1984, Keefe explained the process of reforming the workers' compensation system.

> We began studying the system, and learned that the benefit level was not the only variable that was driving costs and premiums. We learned that Minnesota had twenty times the amount of permanent disability as Wisconsin. We learned that the litigation rate and the *volume* of disability were more important than the benefit level. We saw the need to redesign the system, to get at the real problems.
>
> We have now changed the system, away from a legal system that spends its energies arguing about who was at fault and toward a medical system that concentrates on getting the injured worker well and back to work.
>
> The [new] law has now been in effect one year. The litigation rate is dropping, from about 15 percent to about 9 percent. And the really new features are still to come into effect. We have open competition in rates: no more regulated rates. The state fund is being underbid by the private market. There are good deals for companies willing to get serious about loss control and willing to shop around.
>
> The general lesson is that, in most cases, we fail to understand how the system really works. We have to get more analytical capability into government and get some independent group involved along with the interest groups. You've got to look at the problem in new ways; yet, also to be practical and to get an agreement. . . . The system is now administered by private firms: we just no longer take the industry's word as to what premium increases are needed. The market now decides that.
>
> We were able to take a different route in 1983, not only because we had a good idea but because we did the political spadework. Also, the general pressure from business for a solution was very influential. The other reason we got the change is just that the legislature knew that labor should not have been opposed, in the interest of the workers. Labor essentially believed the state could get away with doing nothing. No legislator believed that.

Subsequent experience indicated the new system is working. Rates were up in 1986, with the general effort at "recovery" in the insurance business, but discounting was an accepted practice, litigation was down, the duration of claims was shortening, and lost-time was not continuing to develop in the years after settlement of a claim.

After his reelection in 1986, Perpich removed Keefe. The change was generally attributed to pressure from labor, which had never liked the new program. The effect of the change is uncertain. Keefe thought the idea, and the staff assembled to implement it, would survive.

Higher Education

The public colleges and universities in Minnesota traditionally had been funded on the basis of student enrollment. A period of growing enrollment brought more money every year. By the early 1980s, however, the institutions saw declining enrollment ahead, so they began an effort to shift the funding formula from students to programs.

Anticipating this trend, the state's Higher Education Coordinating Board, a single-purpose planning mechanism for the system with members drawn from outside the system, began a study for the legislature on the future funding of post-secondary education. The Board's proposals were enacted in 1983 with strong support from the Department of Finance.

The proposals provided for the determination of the "average per student cost" for each element of the system: the University of Minnesota, the state universities, the community colleges, and the vocational-technical institutes, all separately governed. Student tuition was then raised to one-third of the average cost. Need based aid was provided to cover half of the student's tuition and other costs. The governing boards were given full responsibility to decide between program size and program quality. Funding is based on enrollment choices by students: Revenue flows to the institutions in which the students enroll. The formula, not the appropriation, is determined politically. Finally, the legislature ordered the system to do some long-range planning using this new framework of finance and management. A major proposal in the 1987 legislative session came from the University of Minnesota, which "committed to focus" increasingly on certain key (including graduate) programs, and to defer undergraduate enrollment to other institutions. This would require some change in the financing formula.

Health Care

The pattern of physician practice in multispecialty clinics came early to this part of the country. The famous Mayo Clinic developed in Rochester, Minnesota, in the 1890s.

By the late 1950s, due largely to reporting by the *Minneapolis Tribune's* science-and-medicine reporter, Victor Cohn, about the Kaiser-Permanente prepaid plan on the West Coast, there was a rising level of understanding about the problem of health-care cost and the beginning of a discussion about innovative ways to lower these costs. An effort to develop a prepaid group practice plan had been blocked politically in the 1930s but was unblocked by the state attorney general in the 1950s, and group health plan began to grow.

By the late 1960s, InterStudy, a small research and policy design institute began to argue for fundamental changes in health-care arrangements. In the early 1970s, stimulated by the concerns in the insurance industry, the Upper Midwest Council organized a project that opened the medical system to health maintenance organizations. The council's aim was to provide for competition among HMOs as well as between HMOs and the fee for service system.

Soon after, a large multispecialty, fee for service clinic, urged on strongly by InterStudy, set up a new HMO to solidify its own base of patient care. The employees of General Mills, with the encouragement of company management, became early customers. Other HMOs then appeared. As more and more doctors found *themselves* paying the bills for hospital care, hospital admissions and length of stay began to decline. By the early 1980s, the Twin Cities had become a "medical marketplace."[5]

The health-care policy of the public sector had initially started off in another direction. Minnesota enacted a certificate of need law in 1971, and in the Twin Cities area, the Metropolitan Council began designing a framework of public utility regulation.

By the end of the decade it was clear, however, that the region's seriously overbuilt and underused system was not likely to be reduced by authorizing a public agency to close hospitals. There was a concern, too, that regulation would in time become a "guard dog" preventing free-standing surgical centers or some other innovation from coming into the system. By 1980, the effort at regulation was basically over. Minnesota repealed its certificate of need law and committed itself to competition.

HMOs and the emerging hospital groups quickly became aggressive businesses. In a development not really anticipated, health-care *management* became a growth industry for Minnesota's economy, supplementing the growing industry of health-care technology. Forced by a 1973 state law to operate as non-profit organizations, the HMOs developed separate companies for management, which legally could be for-profit. These quickly discovered that they could expand to manage other HMOs as well and, by 1984, were expanding nationwide. A similar development occurred in hospital management: Twin Cities based companies now manage hospitals throughout the Upper Midwest and in other countries.

In the mid-1980s, the state government began to think of itself as a buyer of health care, which needs to be careful about its costs. Between 1978 and 1983, state expenditures for health care more than doubled, from about $407 million to almost $840 million, while the state general fund grew by a little more than half.[6]

Progress is slow But in 1984 state officials seeking the Saturn plant were surprised, and pleased, to find that Minnesota presented itself positively to General Motors as one of the few states, if not the only state, that had its health-care costs under reasonable control—the cost of health care having long ago become a larger part of the selling price of an automobile than the cost of steel.

Efforts are now under way to deal with Minnesota's very high expenditures (public as well as private) for the care of the aged. The state is seeking some conbination of housing, medical care, food, social services, and recreation as an alternative to the combination offered by nursing homes.

The Public Schools

Recently, the governor has begun applying some of these same principles in an effort to revitalize the state's system of public education. Traditionally good, Minnesota's education system needs a stimulus to further improvement, as other states begin major efforts to raise the quality of their own schools in their strategy to attract high tech and service businesses.

This effort by Governor Perpich hinges on changing the basic system of rewards by introducing new incentives for professional educators to seek out ways to change and improve teaching and management within the schools.

The strategy, therefore, has not turned (as in so many of the southern states) to *requiring* schools, teachers, and students to improve and has not relied entirely on increases in school financing. Instead, it rests on an understanding that the current arrangements set up by the state give the schools no *reason* to change and improve. Nothing links their success to their students' success. The state has in effect assured administrators and teachers that their money will come whether they make changes and improvements or not.

The effort, therefore, is to create a connection between funding and effort. Under Perpich's proposals this would not be done directly, through rewards to schools where test scores are higher but indirectly. Districts would be allowed to accept students from other districts, and students would be allowed to go to districts other than the ones in which they live. Schools would get their students through choice rather than by assignment. Some schools might grow. Others might decline. It would depend on the actions of their boards, administrators, and teachers.

The governor, a former school board member, proposed a program open to public schools only, thus bypassing the thorny issue of private schools and tuition tax credits. His principal supporter in the house was the Independent-Republican majority leader, who added to the bill a feature permitting eleventh and twelfth graders also to enroll in colleges, universities, and post-secondary vocational schools and to earn credit simultaneously toward both high school and college graduation. The major education groups concentrated their opposition on Perpich's plan for interdistrict enrollment and succeeded in knocking it out of the bill. The post-secondary option remained, was enacted, and went into operation beginning with the 1985–86 school year.

Perpich created a "discussion group" of leaders both from the education organizations and from the reform group. Early in 1987 this group agreed, if not on the ultimate vision for the system, on a program of actions by which the idea of expanded opportunities and incentives could be tested. The 1987 legislature seemed likely to extend to students who were definably not doing well or "at risk" an option to move, either to some special learning center or to "regular school" in some other district.

Taxation

Perpich commissioned St. Paul Mayor George Latimer to lead a yearlong effort to design a comprehensive revision of Minnesota's system of taxation. The Latimer Commission's income tax recommendations largely were adopted in 1985. Major property and sales tax reform was held until 1987. In preparation for this effort, the governor named his principal issues staff member, Tom Triplett, commissioner of revenue. "There's not much state government can do to create a healthy jobs climate, but tax policy is one that cuts across everything," Triplett told the *Minneapolis Tribune* on accepting the job.

The Iron Range

Perpich also made quiet efforts to deal with a major soft spot in Minnesota's economy, the taconite industry, which was depressed by the problems of the nation's steel industry. In the years when the Mesabi Range was supplying most of the steel mills of America, Minnesota was able to tax the ore heavily and to export these tax costs to the rest of the nation. In the 1980s, Brazilian ore landed at Chicago was cheaper than Minnesota taconite. The industry began pressing for reductions in its costs: in wage costs, in electric power costs—and in tax costs. In 1986 and 1987 the Legislature did reduce some taxes on the industry and acted to prevent some increases that would otherwise have occurred.

Farming

Since 1983, state officials have been struggling to find a policy response to the growing problems in agriculture. In the boom years, after the Russian wheat deal in 1973, some farmers borrowed heavily and at high rates to expand their operations. When markets shrank, as a result of the wheat embargo and the growth of local food production in Asia, prices fell, land values plummeted, loans were called, and farms were repossessed. As banks failed, bank holding companies based in Minneapolis began selling off their small town banks. A new farm-protest movement arose.

The governor and legislature responded with an interest buydown program in 1984 to lower the cost of rural bank credit, hoping that real relief would come through federal action. When federal relief did not appear, the 1986 legislature was faced again with requests for help from the state. This time it responded with a Minnesota Rural Finance Administration to refinance farm debt and with a program for lender-debtor mediation.

The state's response to the farm crisis represents a policy of adaptation to forces beyond the control of a state government. The change in world food markets is structural, not cyclical. This new adjustment is painful, as always, but not new. Agriculture is declining. It is now Minnesota's second-largest industry, having been passed by health care in the early 1980s.

In all this, the delemma is fairly clear.

The kinds of actions that are tangible and visible, that act directly on jobs and investment, have a real appeal for state officials. They display an evident desire to help people now and, so, are easy to enact. However, they are not fundamental in reshaping the state's economy.

The actions that are truly fundamental unfortunately tend to be intangible and often painful to particular interests in the short run. These fundamental actions make up the indirect strategy.

The indirect strategy can increase productivity when the public sector introduces incentives for organizations and their officials to make changes and improvements. As presently structured, the public sector typically lacks these incentives. Basic improvement in the public sector thus centers around questions of structure and organization, rather than questions of management technique. A state with the ability to adapt its institutional structure is likely to become more productive; and a state that is more productive is likely to make itself more attractive in the race for economic growth.

CONCLUSION

R. Scott Fosler

17

The New Economic Role
of American States

Viewed in a historical context, the recent state economic activism portrayed in these case stud'es is not a departure from American political traditions but very much in keeping with them. The states, as they have done in the past, are responding to practical pressures associated with changing economic circumstance. Their role is more salient now than in the previous half-century, because many contemporary economic challenges are more amenable to public action at the regional and local levels, and because for the moment, the federal government has willingly relinquished its leadership role in domestic policy.

If historical patterns hold true, we can expect a period of further experimentation and shakedown during which the more successful state actions will be sifted from the failures. In time, the states will learn from each other, and a more definable, standard role in economic policy suitable to the new circumstances will take hold among all of them. The key elements of that new role are discernable from the case studies:

- Responsibility for a wide range of actions that affect the economy;
- Strategy to assure those actions will have the most beneficial effect in the context of a changing economic environment;
- Institutional arrangements suitable to the new responsibilities and strategic orientation.

311

The New Economic Agenda

The new state economic agenda encompasses a wide array of purposes that have evolved over the past fifteen years in an ad hoc fashion.

The Goals of State Initiatives

Until the 1970s, the states' primary goal was to *attract* business in order to replace lost jobs and thereby relieve the most overt source of economic pain and political pressure, which is unemployment. Most of the states initiated or accelerated conventional recruitment programs such as financial and tax incentives, advertisement, solicitation, grants for job training, infrastructure improvements, and assistance with site selection.

Soon, however, states realized that jobs were leaving or being eliminated faster than officials could recruit firms to replace them. So a second goal, the *retention* of industry already in the state, was pursued in order to curb the loss of jobs. Measures to keep firms have included cost reduction (e.g., in unemployment insurance, workers' compensation, and taxes), direct subsidies, plant closing legislation, and protectionist legislation (principally lobbied at the federal level). Other measures have been designed to regenerate mature industries through the application of new technology.

Retention, however, also has its limitations. Measures designed to keep jobs can be futile, costly, or even counterproductive. Plant closing legislation, for example, can discourage new business from relocating to the state. Some firms and jobs, moreover, are better not retained, since they can impede the transition to new, more competitive industries and viable jobs.

Consequently, new state programs began to focus on a third goal, the *creation and expansion* of businesses, products, services, and technologies. This has been pursued in part by investing in basic support systems (e.g., education, transportation) and in part through more focused action (e.g., removal of regulatory barriers, promotion of specific technologies, providing seed and risk capital).

All of the states studied have adopted, explicitly or implicitly, a combination of all three goals: attraction, retention, and the creation and expansion of enterprises. Some of their programs, moreover, serve two or more of the goals.

Massachusetts has had little interest in direct recruitment but believes that its efforts to foster the creation and expansion of business will produce an environment attractive to potential out of state investors. Tennessee continues its efforts to recruit manufacturing branch plants but recognizes these as only one of a broader set of initiatives to attract business. Arizona, Minnesota, and Indiana all attempt to recruit firms but stress the importance of education, infrastructure, and quality of life to do so. Michigan claims to have become more selective in its recruitment efforts in order to attract assets, such as venture capital firms, that will aid in the creation and regeneration of enterprise.

The state initiatives, in short, have expanded far beyond the comparatively simple issue of recruitment that governed state economic policy until the 1970s.

They now go to the heart of the *process* by which enterprise is created, expands, innovates to remain competitive, declines, or relocates. That process, state officials have learned, is affected in numerous ways by a wide range of state actions.

The Range of State Economic Actions

The realization that numerous factors in combination can influence private enterprise decisions is inherent in the notion of "climate." "Business climate" traditionally has referred narrowly to business costs, some of which (e.g., unemployment compensation, workers' compensation, taxes, and regulation) are affected by state action. A broader concern with the supporting elements that benefit enterprise (such as education, universities, and good public services) is implied in the notion of "economic climate." The idea of an "entrepreneurial climate" takes elements of both the business and economic climate (costs and supports) and adds a less tangible element of attitude and social culture that encourages innovation, risk-taking, and aggressive business acumen.

In general, the broad range of state actions that affect the economy and are included in various definitions of overall climate can be categorized by seven foundations critical to the process of economic development.

Human Resources. The skill, motivation, cost, and adaptability of the work force is affected by state programs in primary, secondary, vocational, community college, and higher education; job training; employment service, unemployment insurance and workers' compensation; income maintenance and welfare; health and human services; and labor relations (including right to work, collective bargaining, and strike laws).

Physical Infrastructure. The network of facilities required to conduct business and commerce includes infrastructure that is financed, constructed, operated, maintained, or regulated entirely or in part by the state. These include transportation facilities (roads, bridges, mass transit, ports, airports, railroads, etc.), water supply and sanitation, solid waste disposal, communications, energy, and housing.

Natural Resources. States regulate or directly manage key natural resources that either may be the direct basis of business enterprises or indirectly affect business activity by constituting part of the "quality of life" or tourist attractiveness of the state. These include land (both space and soil), water (for supply, industrial use, transportation, seafood, recreation, etc.), air, agriculture, minerals, forests, and wildlife.

Knowledge and Technology. States are major producers and disseminators of knowledge and information and supporters of research and the development of new technology. They finance public universities and research institutions, and they promote links between businesses and knowledge-based institutions in order to encourage the commercialization of research products.

Enterprise Development. State actions directly affect the organization, financing, location, and operation of business enterprises. These include programs designed to encourage the start-up, expansion, and attraction of business through financial and technical assistance, business incubators, research parks, enterprise zones, and export promotion. Included here are the conventionally defined "economic development" activities, which have become far more sophisticated and selectively targeted in some states.

States also directly affect enterprises through regulatory activities that cut across every phase of business activity. Especially important is the regulation of private financial institutions (banks, savings and loans, insurance companies, etc.). States also provide capital directly through seed, risk, and expansion financing mechanisms.

Quality of Life. The general quality of life affects the economy in two principal ways: It is a direct source of business enterprise (e.g., tourism, travel, recreation, leisure); and it is an important factor in attracting and retaining businesses and workers. States affect the quality of life through most of their actions in the other areas but, in general, by providing good public services, directly providing or encouraging the private provision of other desirable public amenities (e.g., hospitals, education institutions, museums, cultural activities, etc.), and assuring an attractive and healthy physical environment.

Fiscal Management. State taxes, fees, and user charges affect both the cost of doing business and the personal expenses of employees. The structure of taxes (i.e., who is taxed, how much, on what basis) can affect business decisions regarding start-up, investment, innovation, expansion, contraction, and relocation. The revenue base also determines the ability of state government to finance activities in the first six categories.

The new economic agenda, in short, is vast and ubiquitous. It reaches into nearly every area of state responsibility and affects the economy of the state generally and individual enterprises more specifically at a multitude of critical points in the economic development process.

The Knowledge Gap

The new agenda poses serious conceptual and empirical question for the state:

- What are the costs and benefits of various actions?
- Which are the most important?
- How can each best be carried out?
- How do various actions relate to one another?
- How do state actions affect the economic development process?

None of these questions can be answered without also addressing the broader context in which actions are taken:

- What is the economic condition of the state?
- What are the prevailing forces affecting the state's economy?

To address these questions requires knowledge in areas that have been unfamiliar in the policy-making experience of state government: for example, market dynamics, the process of entrepreneurship, institutions for human resource development and labor adjustment, changing technology, the role of research and development, the efficiency of capital markets, the evolution of regional economies, and patterns of international trade and investment.

Equally rare, in academic as well as state policy circles, is knowledge about the economic impact of the wide array of state actions. Until recently, most academic work in this field has concentrated on determining the effect of financial incentives and tax structure on the location decisions of firms. A growing number of efforts are underway to evaluate the impact of specific programs and to construct more useful indices to gauge the economic health of states. In addition, practical experience and political challenge have begun to winnow out some programs and promote the refinement of others, even as exprimentation continues with new programs.

For the moment, however, evaluating the impact of the new state initiatives remains difficult. There have been very few attempts to evaluate either the results or the costs of most programs. There are numerous initiatives, and so it is difficult to hold constant for the effects of any one of them and all the more difficult to assess their synergistic impacts. Many of the programs have not been in operation long enough to have had any effect. Data are hard to come by. Evaluative techniques are inadequate to assess the impact of some of the new programs. Nor are most officials eager to cooperate with objective evaluators. Finally, theory that would explain the interaction among the numerous state programs and economic performance is weak at best.

A major task of description, evaluation, and theory building lies ahead.

The Search for a Strategy

In pursuing various parts of the new agenda, the states have laced together programs with varying degrees of forethought and coherence. Over time, however, they have begun to recognize the need to consider their actions in a more systematic fashion. Consequently, they have sought to develop *strategies.*

The essential elements of strategy are (1) *diagnosis* of the state economy and forces affecting it; (2) *vision* that considers and chooses among options to achieve desired ends; and (3) *action* to fulfill the vision. Because the states already do so much that has economic consequences, a strategy can also serve the purpose of identifying actions that are economically damaging and should be curtailed. Because the lack of knowledge and rapid change create uncertainty, strategies also serve as vehicles for weighing risks and monitoring the effects of experimental programs.

Variations in Approaches to Strategy

All seven states have some form of strategy but vary widely in style, assumptions, and priorities. Some have been explicit in diagnosing their circumstances and options, conceiving a vision for the future, and identifying specific actions to be pursued. Explicit strategies range in formality from highly detailed written documents to unwritten principles and purposes that may not be articulated expressly but, nonetheless, guide the actions of influential state leaders. Other states have implicit strategies rooted in the habits and traditions of state institutions. And some have proceeded in an ad hoc manner, siezing opportunities as they arose.

Michigan has developed the most *explicit and formal strategy*. After several years of ad hoc response to growing unemployment that focused on the recruitment and retention of business, in 1984, Governor James Blanchard assembled a group of academicians to think through Michigan's economic condition and devise a strategy that would direct state government actions. The group produced a document, *The Path to Prosperity,* that laid out three long-term options for Michiganders: adapt by creating new ventures, migrate to areas that had greater opportunity, or accept a lower standard of living. These choices were dubbed the "get smart, get out, and get poor" options. The report recommended that the "get smart" option could best be pursued by modernizing the state's base in durable goods manufacturing through the application of up to date technology.

Tennessee has had an *explicit but informal strategy* conceived by the governor. Historically, Tennessee's strategy of recruitment was based on the assumption that the key to economic prosperity was to attract manufacturing branch plants from elsewhere in the United States by promoting Tennessee's comparative advantage in location, low business costs, and low-wage labor force, and by offering selective incentives (in recent years, training grants, access roads, and property tax abatements). That assumption since has been modified. For one thing, the search for manufacturing branch plants now extends beyond the United States and especially to Japan. But more important, the implicit definition of what attracts business was broadened by Governor Lamar Alexander to include strong foundations in education, transportation, and the environment (principally water supply). Improvement in each of these areas was believed to be important not just to attract business but to directly strengthen the economic base of the state as well.

Tennessee leaders never went through a systematic exercise of analyzing the state's economy or writing a formal strategy. But Governor Alexander, in his own mind, had assessed the state's economic needs and identified the major priorities (education, roads, water supply, and recruitment), which he then pursued.

Minnesota, over the years, appears to have pursued an *implicit strategy* of indirectly supporting the private sector with a high quality of life and supporting services to attract and retain valued firms and people and, thereby, also nurture growth from within. This strategy has included the provision of a high level of public services, in part by concentrating resources in such key services as higher education (for example, establishing a single university centered in the St. Paul/ Minneapolis area). In recent years, as economic stress has intensified, the state has relied increasingly on more conventional approaches such as recruitment and direct subsidies. This has created tension with those who favor building on Minnesota's perceived comparative advantage in high quality public services and an attractive quality of life.

California also appeared to have an *implicit strategy* of massive public service investment during the post-World War II expansion. In 1965, Governor Edmund G. (Pat) Brown spoke specifically of the "programs of the state government which contribute directly to our economic growth," among which he included primary, secondary, and higher education, water supply, and highway construction. Brown's principal concern, however, was not so much to promote economic growth as to accommodate the growing population with adequate public services. An effort late in his administration to weave together a comprehensive California State Development Plan was not completed until 1966, the year he left office. It had no perceptible impact.

California generally assumed that its economic growth was inevitable until the Dow Chemical incident in 1977. Thereafter, Governor Jerry Brown embarked on a series of initiatives that included important elements of the new economic agenda. In 1981, he created a California Commission on Industrial Innovation that included representatives from the state's high technology industries, universities, labor, and the financial community. In its 1982 report, "Winning Technologies: A New Industrial Strategy for California and the Nation," the commission recommended high priority attention to investment for innovation, education, job training, and work place and management productivity. While some of the commission's recommendations were implemented, the influence of the report and the philosophy it expressed faded when Brown left office.

Governor George Deukmejian began his administration in 1982 with a more conventional approach to economic development. He appointed an Economic Advisory Task Force that recommended a return to basics: a more competitive tax structure, reduced regulation, lower housing costs, adequate transportation and water supply, and improved education. The task force also recommended a stronger marketing effort by the state to reverse what was perceived to be a negative business image and to compete more effectively with other states in recruiting business. Over time, however, California has added new programs that suggest an implicit strategy of experimentation with a wide range of new approaches.

Arizona provides a clear example of the *ends and means considerations* inherent in any state strategy: Agreement on goals can still leave disagreement over how to achieve them. In the 1970s, there was a consensus that the state needed to diversify its economy beyond its natural resources base in mining and agriculture. However, state leaders differed sharply over the means by which this best could be accomplished. Some favored a conventional emphasis on low taxes and labor costs to attract out of state industry, while others favored strengthening such services as water supply and education. In 1983, Arizona lost the intense competition among the states to attract the newly created Microelectronics Computer Technology Consortium (MCC) because, according to MCC's chairman, the state lacked the caliber of higher education, particularly its university engineering programs, and the cultural amenities required to attract the professional staff the consortium needed. This event helped push the state toward a more broadly conceived economic strategy that stressed the "new basics" of higher education and quality of life. The ends-means consideration then proceeds to the question of how to improve higher education and the quality of life.

Massachusetts' approach has been far more *ad hoc*. When the state faced serious economic problems in the early 1970s, the first instinct of state leaders was to attract industry from other states to replace lost jobs. But, when this approach proved unsuccessful, they shifted their attention to the generation of growth within the state by plugging perceived gaps in capital markets, targeting growth to geographic areas in distress, restructuring taxes, improving work force skills, and supporting new research and development. The broad array of programs to date has not been blended into a clearly articulated strategy. But it is significant that even as the state now enjoys one of the strongest economies in the nation, it apparently is no less eager to find ways of strengthening its economy and building for the future. In perceiving that the state has a continuing economic role and strategic responsibility in good times as well as bad, as much as in the substance of its programs, Massachusetts may have important lessons for other states.

Indiana developed a *strategy based in structure*. In 1984, Indiana produced a written economic strategy, "In Step with the Future," that concluded the state should build on its manufacturing base. Rather than lay out a detailed plan and specific steps to accomplish that goal, however, state leaders decided what they needed was an institutional framework to link key economic organizations, so that specific actions in pursuit of general goals could be pursued as the opportunities arose. For that purpose they created the Indiana Economic Development Council as a loose federation of key public and private organizations with economic impact, to act as an "internal guidance system" for economic strategy.

Similarities in Approach to Strategy

Despite their wide variation, the state strategies have certain features in common. They recognize, implicitly, if not explicitly, that no single action or actions are likely to strengthen a weak economy or sustain a strong one. They all cut across conventional functional lines (e.g., education, capital investment, technology) in both the public and private sectors.

The strategies are "market driven." They do not attempt to supplant private enterprise, which acts according to the dicatates of the market. Each stresses investment in economic foundations and modifications in barriers and supports in order to foster an environment in which enterprise will be created, expanded, retained, and regenerated, as well as attracted to the state.

The strategies also recognize a synergy among factors that shape the economic environment. The "business climate" is defined less narrowly in terms of quantitative indicators that measure the cost of doing business. It tends to be seen more broadly as a composite of factors that determines the conditions in which enterprise can flourish. These include not only factors that affect business directly, such as the availability of capital and technology, but also those that affect the quality of life that can attract and retain employees. Values once seen as separable or even antagonistic are more likely to be seen as capable of synthesis or even mutually supportive. Environmental protection, for example, is as likely to be viewed as an economic asset needed to attract and retain firms and their employees as it is as a barrier to economic growth.

One of the striking similarities is the rhetoric that suggests the states can shape the economic future. In Massachusetts, Governor Dukakis openly adopted a theme of "creating the future." The Michigan case study speaks of "choosing an economic future." The California study speaks of "inventing the future." Gone is the assumption that economic policy is the exclusive realm of the federal government, and that the only role states had to play, if they chose to do anything at all, was to compete among themselves for business. There is no less competition for business; if anything, recruitment efforts are more intense. But many state leaders now believe that the actions they take, or do not take, can significantly affect the extent to which businesses start, grow, innovate, develop and market new products, improve their productivity, develop export markets, contract, decline, relocate, and fold: that is, the *process* of economic development within their states.

The Institutional Challenge

The magnitude of the new economic agenda and the demands of developing and implementing an economic strategy have required major institutional changes. Under the conventional state role, the responsibility for economic development was routinely assigned to a line agency of state government, such as a department of commerce or economic development, whose principal mission was the recruitment of business. In the new role, numerous state agencies are involved, beginning with the top political leaders. The states also have developed more versatile and flexible institutional arrangements that enable them to anticipate change; specialize in new and demanding economic functions; experiment with programs about which there is little knowledge; integrate related programs, institutions, and political values; evaluate the results of their efforts; and make adjustments as warranted by new knowledge and changing circumstance.

The Role of Political Leadership

Because economic strategy involves political choices and programmatic trade-offs across so broad an array of today's foremost public concerns, governors increasingly have played a central role. As political leaders, governors are active in framing issues and building political coalitions to support economic initiatives. As managers of state government, they are key to developing specific programs and coordinating the various agencies of government whose missions bear on the economy.

In responding to the new economic challenge, gubernatorial leadership generally has been driven more by pragmatic considerations than by ideology.

Governors Michael Dukakis in Massachusetts and James Blanchard in Michigan, both Democrats, have been more inclined to experiment with new programs, and establish new institutions than their Republican counterparts, Governor Lamar Alexander of Tennessee and George Deukmejian of California. But this probably reflects differences in the economic conditions of the four states as much as differences in party philosophy. The problems of Massachusetts and Michigan were more severe and of a different nature than those of Tennessee or California. Both Dukakis and Blanchard have won praise from former adversaries associated with business and enmity from allies associated with labor for some of their actions.

When Governor Dukakis was voted out of office after his first term in 1978, his more conservative Democratic successor, Edward King, who later switched to the Republican Party, continued most of Dukakis' programs and added a few more of his own, such as the Bay State Skills Corporation. The one significant policy difference between the two (despite sharper rhetorical contrasts) was King's support of property tax limitations. Dukakis' second term has been something of a synthesis in both sytle and substance of his first term and King's term. Dukakis has adopted a far more accommodating rhetoric and style toward the private sector, in keeping with King's approach, and has continued refining and adding to the programs of his first term which in turn had been maintained and added to by King.

Governor Blanchard's Republican predecessor in Michigan, Willian Milliken, also took an activist approach to the state's economic woes.

While Lamar Alexander of Tennessee focused more on conventional foundations and less on experimental initiatives than his Democratic counterparts in Massachusetts and Michigan, his approach was far more expansive and activist than that taken by his Democratic predecessor, Ray Blanton, who did little more than continue the state's traditional recruitment activities.

Gubernatorial policy in California, by contrast with Massachusetts, Michigan, and Tennessee, has seen wide swings that are more reflective of the partisan ideological differences associated with the national political parties. Governor Pat Brown, a Democrat, was the "master builder" who used the resources of state government liberally to construct roads, schools, water projects, and the university system in his tenure from 1950–66. Brown's political support lay in a broad base of state residents who wanted general public services, in narrower constituencies seeking special services, and in business and labor groups interested in construction contracts. Republican Ronald Reagan capitalized on the public reaction to the growing cost of government and also won business support by promising to curb government intrusion in the private sector.

Governor Jerry Brown came to office in 1974 proclaiming an "era of limits" and tapping the public sentiment that was concerned with values perceived to be threatened by excessive economic growth: quality of life, environmental protection, equity, and personal fulfillment. His abrupt about-face on the economic issue following the Dow Chemical decision in 1977 attested both to long-brewing problems with the state and national economies and to unresolved political tension between the "quality of life" and "economic growth" issues. Brown met with some success when he attempted to synthesize these conflicting forces in his campaign for president in 1980, but it did not help him overcome other political obstacles. While Brown's Republican successor, Governor George Deukmejian, initially adopted a more conventional stance on economic issues, in 1986, he began to take a more activist approach in looking for ways to broadly strengthen the state's economy.

State legislatures have influenced state economic policy through their traditional powers to enact laws, adopt budgets, and set taxes. In general, the legislatures have played a reactive role, but one no less politically important for that.

Historic geographic rivalries and a conservative rural tradition have kept Tennessee's legislature in a largely reactive posture, although this enhanced the leadership potential of a skillful governor like Lamar Alexander. In Massachusetts, most of the creative economic policies and the coalitions that support them were developed outside of the legislature. Many were undertaken directly by executive action. But it was the legislature that hammered out the final political tradeoffs for those new programs that required a legal mandate or substantial appropriations. California's legislature has been among the most aggressive in addressing the new economic concerns, forming task forces, and establishing new committee arrangements that, in some instances, have taken the initiative from the executive branch.

The Organizational Enigma

The organizational challenge has been to strengthen the capacity of individual organizations to perform economically important tasks, while simultaneously accounting for the links among organizations that form parts of broader systems whose overall performance is important to the economy.

Numerous state agencies now are recognized to be economically important. Some of these are traditional entities whose missions generally had not been viewed as having great economic consequence, such as state departments of education, transportation, regulation, etc., universities, and existing quasi-public corporations (such as port authorities). Many new quasi-public organizations have been created in recent years to perform specialized economic tasks, such as providing seed and risk capital, assisting new business formation, promoting exports, and supporting science and technology.

Many attempts have been made to integrate these economically important entities in order to formulate economic strategy, build political consensus, and coordinate programs. Few traditional coordinating devices have proved altogether satisfactory.

One approach has been to place "core economic development programs" in a single agency. These programs generally have included the traditional recruitment activities (subsidies, promotion, solicitation), business financing mechanisms, tourism, community development, training, employment related services, export promotion, business incubators, and industrial parks. Such functions are found in various combinations in departments of economic development, commerce, community development, tourism, etc. This approach has encountered two major problems. On the one hand the core economic development programs are likely to be too sweeping for a single operating agency: they include too many important programs that should receive the priority attention of an agency director. On the other hand, broad as they are, the core programs nonetheless include only a fragment of the economically important programs of state government.

Grouping such functions as business development and training in the same agency has an appealing logic: The people who work to create jobs also can help fill them with trained people. In practice, however, business promoters and trainers often have conflicting agendas. More important, the training programs assigned to economic development departments invariably are just fragments of an extensive system of education and training programs that prepare people for and help them find employment. That system encompasses primary, secondary, vocational, community college, and higher education, a multitude of skill specific training programs, new welfare initiatives that emphasize job placement, financing mechanisms, and private sector training programs. Taken together, this system of human resource programs may be of greater economic importance to the state than the composite of functions included in the typical economic development department. And, the task of improving the overall performance of that system is far broader and more complex than can be addressed by the director of a department of commerce whose daily energies may be consumed in enticing businesses to invest in or not leave the state.

An alternative to putting all economically important functions in a single agency has been to try to better coordinate interagency activities. A common approach has been the establishment of cabinet councils composed of the directors of agencies that affect the economy (e.g., education, transportation, employment, regulation and licensing, environment, finance and budget, agriculture, natural resources, and health). Other approaches have included the establishment of a principal staff office on economic affairs in the office of the governor, assignment of coordinating responsibility to a planning or policy development office in the governor's office, or informal coordination by the governor or a key aide or department head (frequently the director of the principal economic development department).

In Massachusetts, Governor Dukakis used a staff Office of Economic Development to coordinate economic programs. In Michigan, Governor Blanchard established a temporary cabinet council comprised of the economically important operating departments. In Tennessee, Governor Alexander's organizational problem was simplified by the fact that his priorities of roads, schools, and environment corresponded to the missions of traditional operating departments. However, he also found it helpful to assemble task forces to bring together key actors on important issues. For example, he created a "Safe Growth" Cabinet Council consisting of the governor and the commissioners of departments concerned with environmental issues.

No coordinating mechanisms have proved entirely satisfactory. Nor, as Michigan has discovered, does the existence of a clearly articulated strategy assure that it will be pursued by the many people and agencies involved in its implementation, even with the active support of the governor. The next phase in developing the new state economic role no doubt will involve considerable experimentation to deal with such organizational dilemmas.

The Private Sector Connection

The institutional challenge is complicated by the fact that economic concerns transcend conventional public and private sector boundaries.

There has been a proliferation of business organizations attempting to influence state policy. The "private sector" or "business community" has never been as homogeneous as it is frequently perceived to be. But, in recent years, numerous divisions have occurred among private institutions, and a multitude of new associations has been formed. In addition to industry trade associations, business associations have been created to represent manufacturers, small businesses, large corporations, high technology firms, computer firms, software firms, defense related firms, and so on. New and expanding businesses in high technology fields have developed growing political influence in Massachusetts and California to advocate policies compatible with their interests. Large firms in all sectors have increased their own lobbying efforts at the state level.

On the other hand, a centripetal force within the business community has emerged in a number of states in the form of a statewide council or "roundtable" of top business leaders addressing themselves to important economic issues of statewide concern. Private groups have also established partnerships, sometimes with the public sector, to create new institutions to promote technology, expand capital availability, or address other needs that can benefit the economy.

Efforts have also been made by both government and private sector leaders to build consensus and integrate actions among groups in both the public and private sectors and at different levels of government. Most states have made use of broadly based task forces composed of private and public representatives, more narrowly constituted study groups of experts, and various informal groups and relationships centered on the governor or key aides. Governor Alexander's appointment of a hazardous waste task force with representatives from both the Tennessee Manufacturer's Association and the Tennessee Environmental Council is one of numerous examples of links established with the private sector. Massachusetts has been successful in bringing together disparate and often warring groups in associations that have included local community activists, the major universities, financial institutions, labor, businesses, legislative leaders from opposing factions, and executive branch agencies, including the governor.

Indiana's new institutional framework was consciously designed to integrate the expertise and views of various public and private sector groups in the development and execution of economic strategy.

Minnesota has relied heavily on traditional civic institutions to evolve its implicit economic strategy over the years. A few new institutions have been created to deal specifically with economic concerns. Minnesota Wellspring, for example, is an alliance of business, labor, education, and government leaders seeking ways of capitalizing on the state's economic strengths. But, for the most part, the existing civic institutions and traditions appear well suited for dealing with the ubiquitous economic issue and its many links to other public programs and ideas. Key issues confronting Minnesota's civic network today are whether recent state actions of direct intervention will distort and harm rather than promote the economy, and whether Minnesota's traditional process of political compromise will root out or solidify obstacles to economic transition.

The Geographical Imperative

All of the states confront the political and administrative challenge of regional diversity. A single state may encompass parts of two or more economic regions. Such is the case in Tennessee, where the differences among West, Middle, and East Tennessee are so pronounced that they are officially recognized as the three "Grand Divisions" in the state constitution. California's traditional rivalries between the northern and southern parts of the state continue, although the 1986 election also suggested a developing division between the generally more affluent and environmentally conscious coastal populations and the comparatively less well to do and economically distressed communities in the interior. Similar contrasts are found in states where urban economies are thriving while nearby regions dependent on a natural resource or traditional manufacturing base are in distress.

Many economic regions transcend state boundaries. The Boston metropolitan area, for example, reaches well beyond Massachusetts into neighboring New Hampshire, Rhode Island, and Vermont. Still broader regions encompass several states. Leaders in California see common cause (and competition) with Oregon and Washington in developing their Pacific rim advantage.

Recognition of mutual interstate interests had led to extensive contact and new institutional arrangements among the leaders of neighboring states. Massachusetts, for example, belongs to the Conference of New England Governors; Michigan is active in promoting a resurgent Great Lakes coalition; and Tennessee is a member of the Southern Growth Policies Board. Tennessee also is active in the Southeast U.S./Japan Association, which meets in Japan and in the Southeast United States on alternating years. A similar organization has recently been established in Korea.

Economic regions are more than simply the sum of their parts. They are important economic assets in and of themselves. Wealth is generated not just through the solitary actions of manufacturing firms, business services, individual workers, financial institutions, universities, or entrepreneurs but by the interaction and synergy among them. Boston, for example, combines in a single metropolitan area industrial, intellectual, financial, and political assets that seem to provide the synergy that can spark and sustain economic vitality. It is the state capital and the dominant political jurisdiction in the state; it boasts substantial educational, research, and financial institutions; and it is home to many existing manufacturing and service enterprises. Leaders from all sectors interact regularly, often on a social basis. Nashville, Indianapolis, Phoenix, and St. Paul/ Minneapolis are similar in this regard.

No such local concentration of assets or leadership is found in Michigan, where the industrial and financial leadership is in Detroit, the educational and research leadership is in Ann Arbor, home of The University of Michigan, and the government and political leadership is in Lansing, the state capital. State institutions and leadership are even more important in such cases to integrate geographically dispersed assets.

State governments are being drawn more deeply into the governance of metropolitan regions. In part, this is because they have responsibility for key urban functions, such as major traffic arteries, mass transit, health, environmental protection, and education. They also establish the legal, administrative, and fiscal framework in which governments operate. But it is also because metropolitan areas have expanded well beyond traditional local government boundaries and their economies have grown far more complex. Even in the greater Nashville area, which enjoys the advantages of a consolidated city and county government, urban growth has spread beyond the boundaries of consolidated Nashville-Davidson County, creating pressure for increased state government attention. When General Motors chose to locate its new Saturn plant in Spring Hill, Tennessee, in the outer orbit of the Nashville metropolitan area, the government of Nashville-Davidson County had little role to play because the site was well beyond its borders. The Tennessee state government was the only political jurisdiction that could speak for the region as a whole, composed of the fragmented jurisdictions of the municipality of Spring Hill and Maury, Williamson and Nashville-Davidson Counties.

In areas with an even more fragmented pattern of local government, such as the Boston metropolitan area, the state plays a still more important role. In fact, the success of Massachusetts in targeting growth to distressed areas of the Boston region and elsewhere in the state is an example of the influence states can have in shaping regional growth.

One of the greatest institutional challenges to states is to integrate their economic programs in specific geographic regions, assuring, for example, that business incubators, research, product commercialization, financing, training, and export promotion programs are brought together in a practical way in specific locales. To accomplish this will require not only better intergration of programs at the state level but between state and local governments at the sub-state regional level.

Impact of Recent State Actions

What have been the consequences of the various programs, strategies, and institutions developed by the states in the past decade? Because of the difficulties in evaluation noted earlier, the evidence must be carefully weighed in each case.

In Massachusetts, the major economic programs of the first Dukakis administration were not fully underway until 1979, while the state's economy already had begun to improve in the mid-1970s. Ronald Ferguson and Helen Ladd therefore concluded that the state's recent economic programs had no effect on the initial recovery. The claimed successes of the Community Development Finance Corporation, the Technology Development Corporation (both quasi-public organizations), and the Massachusetts Capital Resource Corporation (a private organization established by the insurance industry in exchange for a state tax reduction) would account for no more than .5 percent of statewide employment. The major tax-reduction initiative, Proposition 2½, was not enacted until 1980 and, therefore, had no effect on the initial revival.

Massachusetts' initial economic revival probably can be attributed to its base in microelectronics, high caliber universities, substantial defense contracts, and strong service industries. Businesses performed poorly in Massachusetts between 1967–75 compared with similar industries nationwide, but a more favorable mix of high growth industries along with an improved competitive performance in both slow and high growth industries boosted the state's economy between 1975–83. Between 1975–83, service employment growth (including producer services such as legal, accounting, consulting, advertising, marketing, financial, and information as well as consumer services) was four times greater than all other employment growth in Massachusetts.

Although recent economic initiatives did not cause the initial revival in Massachusetts, Ferguson and Ladd believe some of them—in their direct impact and indirectly by contributing to a more positive economic climate—may have helped sustain or accelerate the momentum once the recovery was underway. Taken together, the various initiatives may have been instrumental in persuading some growing businesses to remain in the state and expand and in helping other businesses to start and grow. They also believe that the institutions and traditions of public-private partnership developed during the stressful years of the early to mid-1970s may have a more enduring value than the programs they were designed to operate.

Ferguson and Ladd found that the geographic targeting initiatives of the Dukakis administration, to revitalize the central cities of older industrial areas, had enjoyed considerable success. While there is no evidence that those efforts increased the net economic benefits to the state as a whole, they brought new economic hope to areas under particular stress and raised the likelihood that, by more effectively marshalling unused or underused economic resources, the overall economic well-being of the state would be improved.

The Michigan economy improved substantially after the recessions of the early 1980s. But, virtually all of the improvement can be explained by broader economic forces, including the national economic recovery, lower interest rates, protection from Japanese car imports, and improvements in the auto industry itself. John Jackson concludes that it is too soon to tell whether the state's actions have had any effect and that it may be a decade or more before a sound judgment can be made. But he believes that state policy is, for the most part, headed in the right direction.

Timothy Bartik concludes that Tennessee's recruitment efforts had a marginal, positive effect on Tennessee's economy to the extent that they were successful in attracting a greater than average share of branch plants for a state of its size. This tends to contradict the prevailing wisdom in the academic literature that recruitment efforts have little effect on business location decisions, but it leaves open the question as to whether the state economy is better off for having attracted those branch plants. Bartik argues further that such competition among states is not necessarily a zero-sum game, as is often maintained in the economics literature, but may provide benefits to consumers by encouraging states to restrain the cost of doing business.

Bartik also surmises that General Motors' decision to locate its new Saturn plant in Tennessee was based on numerous factors aside from any actions or promises made by the state government. In fact, Tennessee's approach to the Saturn competition was noteworthy for the relatively limited financial incentives it offered in comparison with the lavish incentives offered by many other states. The GM decision appears to have been prompted largely by Tennessee's strategic location, its labor force, and the fact that Nissan already had located an automobile plant in the state. Tennessee's success in attracting Nissan and other Japanese manufacturers also appears to have been based on a low key approach that played up the state's apparently inherent attractiveness to Japanese business.

Bartik also concludes that Tennessee initiatives in promoting small and expanding businesses and high technology have been too small to have had any detectable effect and that, while the education and road initiatives look promising, they are too recent in origin to evaluate their effect on the economy.

California's latest economic development efforts are too recent to have had any measurable effect on the state economy, conclude Douglas Henton and Steven Waldhorn. Nonetheless, viewed in the broader historical perspective of California's extraordinary investments in education, transportation, water supply, and general support for its entrepreneurial traditions, the margin that can be contributed by the state, they believe, is substantial.

Ted Kolderie and William Blazar believe Minnesota's implicit strategy of indirectly supporting the private sector has played an important role in the state's historical economic success. Kolderie and Blazar are skeptical about the tendency toward direct financial subsidies to business and are concerned that such approaches will undermine the state's proven if implicit traditional strategy of indirect support. They are more optimistic that new efforts to improve the effectiveness and efficiency of public service systems, in part by encouraging competition among service providers, will strengthen the overall economic environment of the state.

The significant redirection of Indiana's economic strategy occurred only in 1985, but in Charles Warren's judgment, it holds out the prospect for having a positive effect.

Larry Landry attributes most of the economic transformation in Arizona's economy to forces largely external to the state, including defense contracts and the advent of air conditioning, which made the desert environment attractive. But, he credits state actions with having helped to turn those forces to the greatest advantage and position the state to benefit in the future from internal sources of economic growth rather than relying predominantly on attracting firms from outside Arizona.

In sum, there is a general consensus among the case study authors that, historically, while growth was driven by private enterprise responding to market forces, state actions have been critical in providing the foundations without which the private sector could not have functioned. With a few exceptions, there is little evidence that the surge in state economic activism over the past decade or so has had a significant effect in stimulating the economic recovery and growth exhibited in all the states following the recession of the 1980s. The judgment is, however, that changes in state policy probably have contributed to sustaining that growth. None of the authors believes the states will be able to do more than exercise marginal influence on their economies. But all seem to feel that those marginal influences could play a constructive and perhaps decisive role in helping their private sectors and citizens adapt to a changing and more competitive world economy.

The case studies suggest that the institutional changes made thus far in an effort to conceive and implement economic policies, in the long run, may be more significant than some of the policies themselves. In the main, the new insitutional arrangements have increased the capacity of the states to anticipate and assess changing economic conditions and to cope with them in a more flexible and integrated fashion. In the short run, this helps to instill confidence in business leaders and investors. In the long run, states with effective and flexible institutions are more likely to make the successful adjustments required in a volatile, competitive world economy, including the correction of ill-conceived policies that may have been instituted in the first flush of the new economic activism.

National Implications of the New State Role

The success with which the states master their new role will be a factor in determining the success of the national economy. To date, the states probably have benefited from the relative disinterest of the federal government and national media in their innovations. There are many ways the federal government could be of greater help. But, the opportunities for assistance pale before the potential for mischief, should the federal government suddenly begin to intervene in state efforts without sufficient knowledge of the new economic role they are playing.

In time, the aggressive new state policies are likely to create growing tensions among the states and conflicts with federal policies that will require countermeasures or other adjustment by the federal government. The states, for example, increasingly are active in international economic affairs, especially in their efforts to attract foreign investment and promote the export of state goods and services; such activities potentially impinge on federal responsibilities and American treaty obligations.

If historical patterns hold true, the federal government eventually will be tempted to adopt state programs for application to the U.S. economy as a whole.

Just as the New Deal drew heavily on innovations of the states and cities in the early twentieth century, so it is likely the state innovations of the 1970s and 1980s will be adopted in various forms at the national level when the federal government once again takes the policy initiative. There is evidence already that this is beginning to occur with the surge of interest at the national level in competitiveness. Scrutiny will be required to assure that the right lessons have been learned and to guard against the easy assumption that programs appropriate at the state level, therefore, also are appropriate at the national level.

It remains to be seen how the new state approaches will hold up, both economically and politically, during the next national economic downturn. Many of the programs were motivated by economic distress in the 1970s. The recessions of the early 1980s reinforced the states' determination to become active in dealing with their own economic problems. The next downturn may serve to screen out the less durable new programs, although it also may foster others. Part of the state reaction will depend on the federal response to recessionary forces.

States cannot control the powerful forces that are transforming the world economy; nor can they be expected to compensate for inadequacies of the federal government or the private sector. However, they can play a marginal but significant role in promoting a private sector that is innovative, adaptable, and market driven.

The challenge for states in the late 1980s and 1990s will be to develop the institutional capacity and political will to formulate, implement, and continually modify a strategic mix of actions that will prepare their economies to perform effectively in a highly competitive, rapidly changing world. The case studies presented in this volume suggest that states have the potential to meet that challenge.

Development Finance Agencies Created in Massachusetts During the First Dukakis Administration: An Overview of Their Experience

Community Development Finance Corporation

The Community Development Finance Corporation (CDFC), the product of the Wednesday Morning Breakfast Group, was capitalized at the time of the Capital Formation Task Force with a $10 million general obligation bond with which the state purchased the corporation's stock. Through 1982, CDFC's management lacked the proper experience and made several investments without coinvestors that failed dramatically. The executive director commissioned an evaluation in 1982, which, ironically, led the board of directors to replace him with an experienced financier from the Bank of Boston's Small Business Investment Company, who was well known and respected in financial circles. CDFC now finances only early stage investments that are too underdeveloped for traditional institutions and other investments where firms lack sufficient collateral to get the funds they need from primary lenders; CDFC provides the gap financing (usually subordinated loans) that makes up the shortage of collateral or owner's equity required to bring projects within the guidelines for standard bank loans. One-third of the board of directors is from CDCs. By law, each of CDFC's investments must produce local benefits, like jobs or housing, and involve a local community development corporation (CDC). Now, CDFC sometimes is criticized by community development advocates for being financially too conservative.

CDFC's management professes a strong commitment to central city and community based economic development but rejects the view that all community development corporations should develop and operate businesses. Typically, the CDC buys or is granted a financial interest, but the CDC need not, and indeed often should not, play a direct role in the management of the business that receives the investment. Some CDCs have the capacity to develop businesses and CDFC has helped. But most CDCs that lack this capacity concentrate on small scale real estate development and CDFC discourages them from expanding into more complicated business development.

The CDC's role in most non-real estate deals is to introduce the business to CDFC (though CDFC now generates many of its leads through referrals from banks), to negotiate for jobs or other community benefits, to help recruit people to fill those jobs, and if necessary, to serve as an intermediary between the business and the community. The CDFC contract also provides that the sponsoring CDC must be consulted and has veto power over certain changes in a firm's operation, such as relocation. A new loan guarantee program for small business loans (e.g., for $5–10,000) shares with the sponsoring CDC some of the interest earned on funds that CDFC deposits with the lender to ensure the loan.

As of August 1985, CDFC had $7.8 million in investments outstanding on forty projects. Presently, the Massachusetts Legislature has before it a proposal to provide a second round of financing to CDFC including $10 million to be used in the usual manner in conjunction with CDCs and $5 million for projects in cities where CDCs are not active.

Finally, CDFC is helping to structure a large financial package through which CDCs would have a financial interest in redevelopment of the Southwest Corridor in Boston. Through this endeavor, the earliest goal of the Wednesday Morning Breakfast Group, as articulated in 1972, may at last be achieved.

Massachusetts Technology Development Corporation

The Massachusetts Technology Development Corporation (MTDC) undertakes venture capital deals in amounts between $100–250,000. By the end of 1985, its portfolio contained twenty-nine firms in which MTDC had invested a total of $6.5 million. Only five deals had been cashed out, three profitably and two with losses. The annual report for 1985 set cumulative gains over the years on equity investments at $793,000 with cumulative losses on both equity and debt investments of $166,000. Through 1985, the corporation leveraged an average of $5 from coinvestors for each $1 it invested. When subsequent rounds of investment and lending are included, the ratio rises to 10 to 1.

All of MTDC's investments are in early stage high technology firms whose requests for funds have been rejected by other sources. MTDC contacts these other sources to learn their reasons and to gain insights that may aid MTDC in its own assessment. Most of MTDC's investments are part of larger financial packages, where MTDC fills the equity gap financing sought unsuccessfully from other sources. Deals tend not to be at the frontier of technology, but they involve proven advanced technologies applied in innovative ways and often entail a lower expected financial return than would be necessary to satisfy private venture capitalists. Whereas private venture capitalists seek what MTDC's president calls "home run hitters," MTDC's official goals are technology based job creation, economic diversification, and increased entrepreneurship; firms that can hit "singles and doubles" are acceptable. In addition to direct financial participation, MTDC has a Management Assistance and Financial Packaging Program, through which it helps entrepreneurs make contact with and better present themselves to the private investment community. According to the annual report, sixty-two companies used this service in 1985 and, as of the time the report was written, five had achieved "substantial private sector financing."

MTDC has close working relationships with MIT and other institutions that promote the commercialization of technology based products and is an active participant in the MIT Enterprise Forum, where entrepreneurs with technology based ideas present their ideas to potential investors.

Both MTDC and CDFC have had a number of deals "stolen" by the private market, just days before final deal closings. The private risk capital market often rejects small (e.g., $300,000 and less) deals because with the same time and effort it can package larger, more lucrative deals. When MTDC and CDFC do the packaging, deals sometimes become attractive to investors that may formerly have turned them away. It has been suggested that, in addition to packaging, an important reason that deals are taken back by the private market is that MTDC and CDFC now are trusted institutions, with knowledgable staffs, whose judgment increasingly is trusted by the private sector. A few venture capitalists that we spoke with about MTDC agreed. In the meantime, CDFC has begun charging a small up-front fee to cover the cost of packaging.

Massachusetts Industrial Finance Agency

The Massachusetts Industrial Finance Agency (MIFA) was created to be a statewide source for Industrial Revenue Bonds (IRBs) and to house other financing programs including the Massachusetts Industrial Mortgage Insurance Agency (MIMIA). In 1985, the mortgage insurance program insured only six projects involving $1.4 million of investment, and MIFA's 1985 annual report says this represented increased activity. This suggests, as has been alleged in the past, that the program is not aggressively marketed (e.g., see Massachusetts Commission on the Future of Mature Industries, "Final Report"). On the other hand, MIFA's use of the IRB program has been extensive. Between 1978 and the end of 1985, MIFA issued $3.7 billion in IRBs for 2059 projects. In contrast to the apparent underuse of the mortgage insurance program, this volume of IRBs may represent overuse. The federal tax exemption that provides the subsidy in the IRB program gives states little incentive to use IRBs judiciously.

At the same time, Massachusetts' use of the IRB program has not been totally capricious. MIFA cooperates very closely with the Governor's Office of Economic Development in trying to persuade firms to locate in accordance with the state's geographic targeting goals, particularly through the Commercial Area

Revitalization District (CARD) Program. The administration believes that this program, which restricts the use of IRBs for commercial projects to certified CARD districts, has contributed strongly to the movement of many establishments back into central city commercial districts. The validity of this perception is hard to judge. In a MIFA-sponsored survey, 60 percent of CARD project developers said that IRB financing was "a 'most significant' factor in their investment decisions." (MIFA 1985 Annual Report). In 1985, $160 million in IRB financing went into CARD districts for sixty-seven projects. The IRB program, however, has been under attack in Washington and may not survive for many more years.

Facing the threat that the IRB program would be eliminated in 1986, MIFA moved aggressively in 1985 to ensure itself against obsolescence. First, as a founding member of the Council of Industrial Revenue Bond Issuers, MIFA worked to shape and promote tax reform measures that would allow the continued use of tax exempt bonds for economic development. Second, MIFA developed new, stricter guidelines for IRB eligibility, for use in Massachusetts. Third, the agency earmarked $1.5 million of its own funds for a revolving loan fund for the troubled seafood industry; more money for this fund may be forthcoming from the state in 1986. Fourth, the first pool of bonds was sold from a new Guaranteed Loan Program that pools loans to small companies and sells them in the public credit market. The bonds in this first pool totaled $6.8 million, to fund the expansions of six companies. These are only a few of many activities that, taken together, signal that MIFA is vibrant and likely to survive with or without the IRB program.

Massachusetts Capital Resources Corporation

Of the four agencies reviewed in this appendix, only the Massachusetts Capital Resources Corporation (MCRC) is totally owned and operated by the private sector. The $100 million investment fund was pooled by nine insurance companies, after the enabling legislation passed in 1977. The cumulative investment in Massachusetts through fiscal 1984 exceeded $125 million. Insurance company executives, who at first viewed the $100 million as money down the drain in exchange for the insurance industry tax cut, now view MCRC as a success but still consider it ransom for a fair tax break and, therefore, hesitate to promote it as a model for other states. Fifty-one percent of MCRC assets and 60 percent of its deals are with firms from "basic industries," with the remainder in firms that are "technology based"; many are in older industries including shoes, textiles, paper, jewelry, and fish processing. Deals have included a broad range of financial instruments from senior debt to common equity.

MCRC specializes in long-term debt and equity. Roughly 75 percent of its investments take the form of subordinated (effectively unsecured) debt, which according to a recent MCRC annual report, is "not only the most sought after form of capital but also the most difficult to obtain in conventional capital markets." From time to time, as in the case of a 1978 loan for $5 million to the

Wang Corporation, detractors assert that MCRC has done well because it side-stepped the risky investments it was created to handle. (Though Wang appeared well established and large, the firm had a risky capital structure and the Bank of Boston was threatening to foreclose on a major loan.) Foster Aborn, chairman of MCRC's investment committee and a senior vice president in the investment division of the John Hancock Mutual Life Insurance Company, disagrees with the view that MCRC has played it too safe. Aborn argues forcefully that a conventional lender, as he is at John Hancock, for example, would be dismissed from his job if he sponsored deals as poorly collateralized and uncertain as those in the MCRC portfolio. He maintains that MCRC's success reflects some expertise and a good deal of luck.

The development finance agencies just reviewed, MIFA, CDFC, MTDC, and MCRC, are part of a larger state development finance system that includes the Massachusetts Housing Finance Agency, the Massachusetts Government Land Bank, and other technical assistance agencies. Included as well are other state chartered finance agencies that are owned fully by the private sector.

APPENDIX B

California's Next Economic Stage: A Schumpterian Perspective

In many ways, California represents a paradigm of the model of economic development outlined by Joseph Schumpeter.[1] In Schumpeter's view, major revolutionary technologies or events drive an economy through periods of transformation fueled by entrepreneurs. This process of "creative destruction" eliminates old industries and generates new ones. In California, we see these events in the gold rush, the railroads, the discovery of oil, World War II, and the invention of the integrated circuit. Each event brought revolutionary change, created new industries, and provided opportunities for entrepreneurs. Each event destroyed old industries, displacing workers through economic restructuring.

Because of this Schumpeterian process, most efforts to predict the future California economy have come to the basic conclusion that it is not possible to project where future growth will come, largely because it is not possible to anticipate the next technology or industry change. In 1960, a team of SRI researchers prepared a report, "The California Economy, 1947–1980," which projected both population and employment growth.[2] The report was nearly right on population growth. It projected that California's population in 1980 would be 24.7 million and the actual population of the state turned out to be 23.7 million. However, the report could not explain where the jobs would come from to employ the state's expanding labor force. The study examined the state's existing resource based and defense oriented industries and could not find any identifiable large industry that could play the growth generating role played by the defense industries in the 1950s. It predicted that the growth would occur in new industries in the "other manufacturing" categories fueled primarily by import substitution and changes in consumer demand that favor California industries. Without knowing it, they were predicting the rise of the microelectronics industry after 1960 to fuel economic and job growth in California.

In 1966, as part of the preparation of the California State Development Plan, state economists reviewed the past evolution of California's industries and tried to predict the shape of the economy in 1975. They found that

> California's development has been stimulated by a number of distinct and unpredictable surges: Minerals, agriculture, oil, aerospace. . . . The contribution each made to California's development would have been difficult, if not impossible, to predict at the outset of its growth. Each, however, gave way to another phase of development so that policy designed in its context would have become obsolete. *Economic Development policy, then, must be designed to capitalize on the unexpected.* It must be "open ended." This is particularly important because no new "fifth surge" or "industry X" can now be discerned that is capable of providing major growth impetus.[3]

Again, in the 1960 study, "industry X" turned out to be microelectronics. However, the key point is not merely that it was impossible to predict the next driving industry, but that the dynamics of innovation and adaptation in the California economy found the next industry and took advantage of it.

A 1983 California Department of Commerce report on labor force and employment in California in 1990 experienced the same problem of predicting where future job growth will be.[4] By projecting labor demand by existing industries and labor supply, the report found a "mismatch" between supply and demand resulting in a 10 percent unemployment rate in 1990. Because these types of projections indicate what might happen if industry growth remains basically the same, they fail to take into account the possibility of a new growth industry arising in California in the late 1980s.

While neither microelectronics nor aerospace are likely to grow as fast in the future, there are a number of candidates for future growth industries in California: the new "industry X" or sixth surge. A 1982 SRI study for the state, "California's Technological Future: Emerging Economic Opportunities in the 1980s," identified a number of opportunities in communications, automation, new materials, and biotechnology.[5] The state of California is now sponsoring research examining the growth potential for biotechnology, robotics, telecommunications, software, and medical equipment. Clearly, the potential for growth in biotechnology is quite high since California now has over 25 percent of all the biotechnology companies in the United States and leads the nation in Ph.D. graduates in the fields critical to biotechnology (molecular biology, chemistry, biophysics, and genetics). California's large markets for agricultural and medical biotech products should have an important impact on the growth and development of the biotechnology industry within the state.

California also has a strong potential for growth in communications and office and factory automation, as these technologies evolve out of the state's strong base in microelectronics. In addition, it has the potential for advanced materials (e.g., high performance ceramics) and space commercialization evolving from its aerospace industry. Finally, recent breakthroughs in superconductivity provide opportunities for revolutionary applications that could transform California industries.

Which specific industries will be the driving industries of the late 1980s and 1990s will depend on changing markets, new technological breakthroughs, and global competition. Given California's historic capacity for innovation and adaptation, the state should be able to capture its economic share of these new technologies.

APPENDIX C

Economic Development Initiatives in Indiana

This appendix describes some of the more significant economic development programs and incentives that the state now has available to implement its strategy. These programs focus on the areas of attention emphasized by the Executive Planning Committee in "In Step With The Future." Where applicable, the source and amount of funding are listed. State appropriations are for the biennial period 1985–87.

Business Climate and Business Assistance

1. Indiana Main Street Program: designed to aid downtown revitalization of communities under 50,000 through technical assistance and other resources (state aid: $290,000.

2. Industrial and Tourism Promotion Fund: supports the state's advertising, promotion, and "Wander Indiana" campaigns. Its appropriation has been increased from $200,000 in 1981 to $5 million in 1985, mainly to meet the increased competition from other states.

3. Industrial Promotion Matching Program and Tourist Information and Promotion Fund: provides state matching funds to local communities for their own advertising and industrial promotion campaigns ($900,000).

4. Indiana Film Commission: set up after the success of the hit movie *Breaking Away* to promote the production of movies, television shows, and commercials in Indiana ($450,000).

5. Registered Cities and Towns: provides a central data base on Indiana localities for industrial prospects.

Tax Incentives

1. Property Tax Abatement: a local option program enabling a city or county council to declare "economic revitalization areas," where real and personal property taxes on new development and equipment acquisitions may be phased in over five to ten years.

2. Interstate Inventory Tax Exemption: establishes a process whereby business inventories designated for interstate commerce are exempt from property taxes. It is an important step to boost Indiana's potential as a warehousing and distribution center.

3. ACRS: incorporates the federal accelerated cost recovery system into the Indiana tax code and provides greater incentive for capital investment.

4. Repeal of Unitary Tax: forbids the use of the unitary method of taxation in determining the tax liability of foreign multinational corporations in order to encourage new foreign investment, particularly from Japan.

5. Research Expense Credit: provides an income tax credit for business research expenditures.

6. Enterprise Zones: enacted in 1983, it provides special tax exemptions and regulatory relief in up to ten zones in the state.

Job Training

1. Job Training Partnership Act: state enabling legislation qualifies Indiana for over $60 million in federal training and employment funds.

2. Dislocated Workers Training Program: provides $4.8 million in state funds with a federal match for immediate job training and related services for dislocated workers in declining occupations or industries.

3. Training for Profit Program: provides new and expanding industries with funds for additional job training for their employees (state aid: $10 million).

4. Basic Industry Retaining Program: provides financial assistance to Indiana's basic industries (auto, steel, and durable goods) for job retraining (state aid: $10 million).

Infrastructure Investment Strategy

1. Industrial development Grant and Loan Funds: provides infrastructure financing to local communities for new and expanding industry (state grants: of $10.75 million; state loans: $8.75 million).

2. Community Development Block Grant Program: Indiana's use of these

federal funds "focuses primary attention on activities which stimulate job creation and an environment conductive to new business location and expansion." Its $30 million has been allocated among four programs: the Investment Incentive program (business loans), the Industrial Development Infrastructure program, the Community Improvement program, and the Residential Energy Management program.

3. State Investment Incentive Program: provides matching grants for infrastructure projects to communities larger than 50,000 and is designed to leverage private investment, like the federal UDAG program (state aid: $5 million).

4. Economic Development Fund: used for a variety of economic development activities not covered under other programs (state aid: $1 million).

5. Municipal Industrial Development Fund: authorizes cities to establish a special revolving fund to develop and purchase industrial parks.

6. Indiana Bond Bank: established in 1984, provides for a pooling of local bond issues and state issuance of tax exempt revenue bonds.

7. Tax Increment Financing: provides for repayment of revenue bonds by localities from the increased tax revenues that accrue from new development.

Energy Supply, Distribution, and Pricing

1. Indiana Energy Development Board: established in 1980 to promote the use of Indiana's own energy resources and to foster the development of new energy technologies (state aid: $1 million).

2. Indiana Coal Commission: develops new markets for Indiana's high sulphur content coal products.

3. Energy System Tax Credits: provides tax incentives to encourage the installation of alternative energy sources including solar, wind, and resource recovery.

4. Sales tax exemption for energy used in agriculture.

Finance and Capital Formation

1. Banking Law Reform: 1985 legislation provided a major restructuring of state banking laws, primarily to allow multicounty banking and enable interstate bank acquisition.

2. Indiana Employment Development Commission: issues loans and bond guarantees, operates a working capital loan guarantee program, and issues and allocates industrial revenue bond financing.

3. Indiana Agricultural Development Corporation: provides farm loans at below market interest rates through the use of tax exempt bonds.

Notes

Massachusetts

The authors are sincerely grateful to the many Massachusetts officials and citizens who gave generously of their time, knowledge, and insights. To avoid breaching the confidentiality of our conversations and to honor requests for anonymity, we have chosen not to list the names of those interviewed except through isolated references in the body of the paper.

We also wish to thank those who provided helpful comments on an earlier draft, including the Director of the CED project, Scott Fosler, the authors of the companion studies for Michigan, Tennessee, and California, and our colleagues John Yinger and Shelly Metzenbaum. Thanks also go to the many people who loaned us newspaper files, tapes of previous interviews, and other documents, but especially to John Brouder, Samuel Leiken, and Beldon Daniels. Finally, we remain grateful to David "Birny" Birnbaum for his outstanding contributions as a research assistant for this project.

1. The major references for this section are Gene Bylinsky, *The Innovation Millionaires* (New York: Charles Scribner's Sons, 1976); Robert Eisenmenger, *The Dynamics of Growth in New England's Economy, 1870–1964* (Middletown, Conn.: Wesleyan University Press, 1967); Oscar and Mary Handlin, *Commonwealth: A Study of the Role of Government in the American Economy, Massachusetts, 1774–1861* (New York: New York University Press, 1947); Agnes Hannay, *A Chronicle of Industry on the Mill River,* Smith College Studies in History. 21, nos. 1–4, (October 1935–July 1936); Bennett Harrison, "Regional Restructuring and 'Good Business Climates': The Economic Transformation of New England Since World War II," in L. Sawers and W. Tabb, eds., *Sunbelt-Snowbelt: Urban Development and Regional Restructuring* (New York: Oxford University Press,

343

1984); John S. Hekman and John S. Strong, "The Evolution of New England Industry," *New England Economic Review,* (March/April 1981); and Philip P. Shapira, *"The Uneven Economy and the State in Massachusetts"* master thesis, Department of Urban Studies and Planning, Massachusetts Institute of Technology, May, 1979.

2. Hekman and Strong, "Evolution of New England," 36.

3. Handlin and Handlin,, 135–36.

4. Shapira, 28.

5. See Hekman and Strong, "Evolution of New England."

6. See *Report Regarding the Investigation of Causes of Removal from Massachusetts of Corporations Engaged in Textile Manufacturing and Causes of Establishment by Corporations Organized Under Massachusetts Laws of Manufacturing Plants Outside Massachusetts,* Senate Document 267 (1895), cited in Shapira, *Uneven Economy,* 116.

7. *Final Report of the Commission on Interstate Co-operation to the General Court Concerning the Migration of Industrial Establishment from Massachusetts* (Boston: Commonwealth of Massachusetts, 1939). See also, Freeland, Bates, and Lawrence, *A Brief Study of Industrial Massachusetts* (Boston: Massachusetts Industrial Commission, 1931). Both cited in Shapira, *Uneven Economy.*

8. Eisenmenger, *The Dynamics of Growth,* 10.

9. Massachusetts Division of Employment Security, *790 Series,* as shown in *Report of the Governor's Commission on the Future of Mature Industries,* Appendix, June 1984.

10. Bylinsky, *Innovation Millionaires,* 74, 77.

11. See Jane Simon, "Route 128: How It Developed and Why It's Not Likely to Be Duplicated," *New England Business,* 7 (1 July 1985).

12. Nathan Rosenberg, *Perspectives on Technology* (New York: Cambridge University Press, 1976), 20.

13. See R. Eisenmenger, A. Munnell, J. Poskanzer, R. Syron, and S. Weiss, *Options for Fiscal Structure Reform in Massachusetts,* (Boston: Federal Reserve Bank of Boston, March 1975).

14. Per capita income was above the national average despite below average wages, because of higher participation of women in the labor force and a higher share in this state of non wage income.

15. See, for example, the 1985 *Annual Report of the Massachusetts Industrial Finance Agency,* which claims "these programs have contributed enormously to the state's comeback." Also see David Broder, *The Washington Post,* 10 February 1986, p. 1, where he indicates that state policy in Massachusetts is the "secret of both the continuing economic success of Massachusetts and the dramatically altered politics centering on Governor Michael S. Dukakis."

16. See George S. Masnick, "The Demography of New England: Policy Issues for the Balance of this Century," *New England Journal of Public Policy* (Winter/Spring 1985), 22–43.

17. Throughout this section, we use 1983 as the ending year, since that is the most recent year for which complete data are available for the shift-share analysis on which the conclusions are based. The details of the shift-share analysis are reported in Ronald F. Ferguson and Helen F. Ladd, "Economic Performance and Economic Development Policy in Massachusetts," Discussion paper D82-2 of the State-Local Intergovernmental Center of Harvard University, May 1986.

18. Study by Data Resources, Inc., quoted in the *Boston Globe,* 26 January 1986.

19. Massachusetts Division of Employment Security (DES), "Defense Spending and Massachusetts Employment, 1972–1980," 22. DES is currently reexamining the impact of defense spending on the Massachusetts economy but is not yet ready to release its analysis.

20. Ibid, p. 46.

21. See James H. Howell and Linda D. Frankel, "Economic Revitalization and Job Creation in America's Oldest Industrialized Region," unpublished summary of remarks from Public Policy Week conference, (Washington, D.C.: American Enterprise Institute for Public Policy Research, December 2, 1985).

22. *Boston Globe,* 1 July 1984. For more historical details, see Francis Wylie, *M.I.T. in Perspective* (Boston: Little, Brown and Co., 1975).

23. President's Task Force on Private Sector Initiatives, p. 90, and information obtained directly from Venture Economics (company), Wellesley Hills, Mass.

24. Bylinsky, *Innovation Millionaires,* 78.

25. Nancy S. Dorfman, *Massachusetts' High Technology Boom in Perspective: An Investigation of its Dimensions, Causes, and the Role of New Firms,* Center for Policy Alternatives, M.I.T., Report No. CPA82-2, April 1982, p. 108.

26. Nancy S. Dorfman, "Route 128: The Development of a Regional High Technology Economy," *Research Policy,* 12, (1983), 310.

27. See James R. Killian, "Boston, New England,—and the Future," address by the Chairman of the MIT Corporation, made upon receiving the Good Government Award of Crosscup-Pishon Post Number 281, American Legion, 21 January 1960.

28. In this same year, per capita income in Massachusetts exceeded the U.S. average by 6 percent. The explanation for the state's above average income lies in above average labor force participation rates and above average proportions of income from non wage sources. In 1975, 65 percent of the working age population in Massachusetts was in the labor force, in contrast to 61 percent in the nation as a whole. In that same year, non wage income accounted for 30 percent of Massachusetts income but only 28 percent of U.S. income.

29. AFL-CIO, Industrial Union Department, Data Center, "NLRB Elections History," April 12, 1983. Cited in High Tech Research Group, *Massachusetts High Tech: The Promise and the Reality* (P.O. Box 4441001, West Somerville, Mass. 02144, 1984). Also see Bennett Harrison, "Regional Restructuring and 'Good Business Climates': The Economic Transformation of New England Since World War II," in L. Sawers and W. Tabb, eds., *Sunbelt-Snowbelt: Urban Development and Regional Restructuring* (New York: Oxford University Press, 1984), and High Tech Research Group, *Whatever Happened to Job Security? The 1985 Slowdown in the Massachusetts High Tech Industry* (P.O. Box 4441001, West Somerville, Mass. 02144, 1984), for related discussion.

30. See James H. Howell and Linda D. Frankel, *Economic Revitalization;* Nancy S. Dorfman, Massachusetts' High Technology Boom, 94, on the other hand, argues that the role of low wages in high tech is not very important. A definitive answer would require more careful analysis.

31. Massachusetts Division of Employment Security, Commission Calculations, as shown in the *Report of the Governor's Commission on the Future of Mature Industries,* Appendix, June 1984.

32. Ibid., 1981 figures.

33. This section is based on Massachusetts budget documents, interviews, and newspaper articles.

34. See Massachusetts Taxpayers' Foundation, Inc. *State Budget Trends 1972–1981* (Boston), 6.

35. This section is based primarily on interviews and unpublished documents from the Wednesday Morning Breakfast Group, the Task Force on Capital Formation, and the New England Regional Commission. Cases on the Massachusetts High Technology Council (MHTC) from the John F. Kennedy School of Government and the Harvard Business School also were consulted.

36. John F. Kennedy School of Government case on the formation of the MHTC.

37. Numbers from Venture Economics, given in U.S. Congressional Budget Office, *Federal Financial Support for High Technology Industries,* June 1985; Carol Steinbach and Robert Guskind, "High-Risk Ventures Strike Gold with State Government Financing," *National Journal,* no. 38 (22 September 1984): 1767–71.

38. See John Case, "Venture Investing: Opportunities Knock", *INC.,* 6 (March 1984); Council for Northeast Economic Action, with Economics Department of the Bank of Boston, *An Empirical Analysis of Unmet Credit Demand in U.S. Capital Markets,* Report for the Economic Development Administration of the U.S. Department of Commerce, May 1984; James H. Howell, and Diane F. Fulman, "Capital Availability, Capital Cost and Business Development in the Northeastern 'Frostbelt' States," in Peter J. Bearse, ed., *Mobilizing Capital: Program Innovation and the Changing Public/Private Interface in Development Finance* (Westport, Conn.: Greenwood Press, 1982): Joel Kotkin, "Why Smart Companies are Saying No to Venture Capital," *INC.,* 6 (August 1984); Lawrence Litvak and Beldon Daniels, *Innovations in Development Finance* (Washington, D.C., Council of State Planning Agencies, 1979); Sharon Smith, "State Supported Venture Capital Organizations: An Analysis of the Public Policy Implication," John F. Kennedy School of Government, April 1986, unpublished; and Carol Steinbach and Robert Guskind, "High-Risk Ventures Strike Gold With State Government Financing," *National Journal,* no. 38 (22 September 1984), 1767–71.

39. Of course, many deals initially rejected by the private sector eventually get taken. See Albert Bruno and Tyzoon T. Tyebjee, "The Destinies of Rejected Venture Capital Deals," *Sloan Management Review,* 27 (Winter 1986).

40. For example, a state sponsored agency in Alaska failed; see Carol Steinbach and Robert Guskind, "High-Risk Ventures Strike Gold."

41. These numbers do not capture spin-off or "multiplier" effects. It is difficult to gauge what the correct multipliers would be but there is little possibility that they could be large enough to change our conclusions.

42. Presumably, MIFA's assumption here is that the number of commercial jobs the state can support is relatively restricted by the reliance of commercial sales mostly on the incomes of state residents rather than, as with much of manufacturing, on sales outside of the state. Under this view, the Commercial Area Revitalization District (CARD) program that restricts commercial IRBs to certified CARD districts affects mainly the location of commercial jobs as opposed to the number. For a simple explanation of the standard export based model of job growth, see James Heilbrun, *Urban Economics and Public Policy,* 2nd Edition (New York: St. Martin's Press, 1981), Chapter 7. Also, see Roger Vaughan, Robert Pollard, and Barbara Dyer, *The Wealth of States* (Washington, D.C.: Council of State Planning Agencies, 1985) for a related discussion that cautions states against inappropriate uses of this model in designing state policy.

43. See Laura Dowd, *The Employment Impacts of the Industrial Revenue Bond Program in Massachusetts* (Masters diss., Tufts University, May 1985).

44. This section is based on interviews, government reports as cited, newspaper articles, and draws heavily on William M. Capron, *Massachusetts' Urban Strategy: The Dukakis Years* (Washington, D.C.: National Academy of Public Administration, 1980).

45. Of course, the phenomenal growth of the Wang Corporation, now a national leader in office automation, also must be given much credit for the rebirth of Lowell. The state played no direct role in Wang's decision to locate in Lowell.

46. The details of the proposition and its effects are fully described elsewhere. See, for example, Katherine L. Bradbury and Helen F. Ladd, "Proposition 2½: Initial Impacts, Parts I and II," *New England Economic Review* (January/February 1982 and March/April

1982); Helen F. Ladd and Julie Boatright Wilson, "Why Voters Support Tax Limitations: Evidence from Massachusetts' Proposition 2½," *National Tax Journal,* 35, no. 2 (June 1982) 121–48; Helen F. Ladd and Julie Boatright Wilson, "Who Supports Tax Limitations: Evidence from Massachusetts' Proposition 2½," *Journal of Policy Analysis and Management,* 2, no. 2 (Winter 1983) 256–79; and Lawrence E. Suskind, ed., *Proposition 2½: Its Impact on Massachusetts* (Oelgeschlager, Gunn, and Hain, Cambridge, Mass.: 1983).

47. See Helen F. Ladd and Julie Boatright Wilson, "Proposition 2½: Explaining the Vote" in T. Clark, ed., *Research in Urban Policy,* vol. 1 (Greenwich, Conn.: JAI Press, 1985).

48. This section is based on interviews and references cited.

49. See Neville Lee, "The Demand and Supply for Engineers in Massachusetts," Discussion Paper, Economics Department, Bank of Boston, December 1983.

50. See National Science Foundation, "Projected Employment Scenarios Show Possible Shortages in Some Engineering and computer Specialities," Science Resources Studies Highlights, NSF 83–307, 23 February 1983. The article is an appendix in Lee, "The Demand and Supply."

51. Bay State Skills Corporation, *1985 Annual Report.*

52. See David S. Broder, "New Deal-Making Politics: Massachusetts Governor Develops a Machine," *Washington Post,* 10 February 1986; Terence Downing, "Firm Chose Taunton Because of Duke," *Taunton Daily Gazette,* 29 June 1984, p. 1; and Dougald MacDonald, "Gee! How They Won GTE," *New England Business,* 8 (17 March 1986).

53. References for this section include interviews conducted by the authors, published and unpublished documents of the Commission on the Future of Mature Industries, an unpublished paper by Sam Leiken, and tapes of interviews conducted by Leiken as background for his paper.

54. The Product Development Corporation has had a low priority in the Dukakis administration and, to the consternation of strong advocates in the Executive Office of Labor, is not functioning yet.

55. This section based on material prepared by the Department of Administration and Finance, interviews, and newspaper articles.

56. There is widespread confusion in the state about how to view the burden of business taxes. Massachusetts ranks forty-ninth in terms of the approach used by the Advisory Commission on Intergovernmental Relations (ACIR), which measures the share of total taxes with an initial impact on business, but a recent study by William Wheaton, which focuses more appropriately on tax rates, shows that manufacturing firms in Massachusetts pay taxes at rates well above the national average. See William C. Wheaton, "Interstate Differences in the Level of Business Taxation," *National Tax Journal,* 36, no. 1 (March 1983) 83–94.

57. To offset the estimated $35 million annual revenue loss from this part of the proposal, the administration proposed that Massachusetts firms give up 20 percent of the tax savings they were currently enjoying from accelerated depreciation. Though most states decoupled their depreciation rules from the federal rules when the federal government introduced the Accelerated Cost Recovery System (ACRS) in 1981, Massachusetts under Governor King permitted firms to follow the federal code and, hence, reap state as well as federal tax savings.

58. See R. D. Norton, "Industrial Policy and American Renewal," *Journal of Economic Literature* 24, no. 1 (March 1986), for a recent review of central issues in the national industrial policy debate of the 1980s.

59. See an extensive survey of the literature by Karl E. Case, Leslie Papke, and Susan

Koenigsberg, *Taxes and Business Location, Final Report Submitted to New York State Legislature,* December 31, 1984. Also see Roger J. Vaughan, *State Taxation and Economic Development,* (Washington, D.C.: Council of State Planning Agencies, 1979) and the discussion of business costs in the report of the Michigan Task Force for a Long-Term Economic Strategy for Michigan, *The Path to Prosperity: Findings and Recommendations,* November 1984.

60. Of course, at the border between states that have different tax and regulatory structures but access to the same market and imputs, the effects of the differential taxes may be enough to push firms across the border, as from Massachusetts to the lower tax state of New Hampshire. Still, if New Hampshire's lower tax rate was as important as some believe, Massachusetts would not have experienced such a large share of its recent growth in places like the city of Lowell, that are only a short commute from the New Hampshire border. Some entrepreneurs report that Massachusetts' business history and reputation has a symbolic significance that makes them feel like members of a winning team and more than compensates for higher taxes and business costs.

61. Magazine articles that chronicle the struggle between AIM, organized labor, and social welfare advocates can be found dating back to early in the 1920s. Several articles from AIM's magazine *Industry* dating from 1922 are cited in Robert L. Kann and John Brouder, "Social Legislation and the Massachusetts Business Climate: A Political Analysis of the Associated Industries of Massachusetts" (unpublished, September 1976). The oldest trade association in the state, chartered in 1909, is the Boston Chamber of Commerce, but by the mid-1970s, it had become relatively quiet at the state level. Sandra L. Kanter, "Theory of the 'Little' State: Business-Government Relations in the Commonwealth of Massachusetts" (Ph.D. diss., MIT Department of Urban Studies and Planning, January 1981). The "vault," which shares some of its members with the chamber, represented Boston's large financial institutions and exerted considerable power in the fiscal crisis of 1975. An organization of large private employers that called itself *Jobs for Massachusetts* formed in the early 1970s to attract new businesses to the state but abandoned the attempt after it proved futile; JFM still exists and is referred to in this book. The Massachusetts Taxpayers Foundation began in the 1930s, sponsored by large businesses as a fiscal watchdog agency, but it is not generally perceived politically as an activist organization.

62. The economic challenge from Japan was a central topic at a day long conference sponsored in early 1986 by the Harvard Business School and a new organization in the state, called the *International Coordinating Council,* that attracted business and academic people, legislators, and officials from the Executive Offices of Economic Affairs and Labor.

Michigan

This research was supported with a grant to The University of Michigan from the Committee for Economic Development, Washington, D.C. Several people merit special acknowledgment for their assistance. James Kenworthy, William Lukens, and Peter Plastrik were particularly helpful and generous with their time in explaining the story for their respective administrations. Richard Matland made major contributions to the economic history chapter and to the discussions of the debates about workers' compensation costs. I want to thank R. Scott Fosler and the other participants in the project on "Leadership for Dynamic State Economies" for comments on an earlier draft. The opinions expressed here are my own and not the positions of the CED or of the above-mentioned individuals. Any errors are my own creation.

1. Will F. Dunbar, *Michigan: A History of the Wolverine State* (Grand Rapids, Mich.: William B. Eerdmans Publishing Co., 1965), 474–75.

2. Ibid, 484.

3. Much of this history is taken from Peter Eckstein's excellent piece, "The Automobile in Michigan: A Case Study of Regional Development," (unpublished, 1984).

4. Ibid, 9.

5. Ibid, 18.

6. Ibid, 14.

7. For a contrary view see Charles L. Schultze, "Industrial Policy: A Dissent," *The Brookings Review* 2, no. 1 (Fall 1983); and Murray L. Weidenbaum and Michael J. Athey, "What is the Rust Belt's Problem?" in *the Industrial Policy Debate,* ed. C. Johnson (San Francisco: Institute for Contemporary Studies, 1984).

8. Some estimates are that each job or dollar of earnings added to the base economy leads to a total of two or three new jobs or dollars of earnings in the aggregate.

9. D. Ross, P. Courant, P. Eckstein, S. Gleason, J. Jackson, J. Kenworthy, D. Verway, and J. Yinger, *The Path to Prosperity: Findings and Recommendations of the Task Force for a Long-Term Economic Strategy for Michigan* (Lansing: Michigan Department of Commerce, 1984), 14.

10. John E. Jackson, "Economic Change in Michigan: 1978–1984," paper for the Institute for Social Research, Ann Arbor, Mich. (unpublished, 1985).

11. In these data, a birth is any firm new to Michigan during the 1979–84 period. This may be a birth in the conventional sense or it may be an established firm that moved to Michigan from outside the state. Similarly, a failure indicates any firm that quit doing business entirely in Michigan during the same period.

12. Muriel Converse, Ann Thomas, and John Jackson, *Financing Small Manufacturers of Metalworking Machinery and Equipment* (Ann Arbor, Mich.: Institute for Social Research, 1984).

13. This does not mean that state governments played no role in the developmental process. In Michigan, as in many other states, territorial and state governments were significant forces in obtaining and distributing land; in building railroads, canals, and roads; in creating educational systems; and in regulating financial institutions and public utilities. However, in the eighteenth and early nineteenth centuries, these actions were not always taken as part of any explicit development strategy.

14. There are many social reasons related to other policy objectives for state and local governments to fund jobs programs, such as training and income distribution, and to ensure employment of specific subpopulations. However, they do not add to economic growth and development.

15. Regis McKenna, "Sustaining the Innovation Process in America," in Johnson, ed., *The Industrial Policy Debate.*

16. Insurance companies are another source of capital and, in most states, are strongly regulated by state government. They are not geographically restricted in their operations, however; so they do not have a long-term stake in a state's economy.

17. Education at all levels bore a disproportionate share of the budget cuts forced by the recession of the early 1980s. The state constitution mandates a balanced budget. Due to the juxtaposition of the fiscal years for educational institutions (July 1–June 30) and for the state government (October 1–September 30), the state withheld the quarterly educational appropriations in autumn 1981 to balance the state budget, promising to make up the shortfall in the third quarter of the state's next fiscal year (the fourth quarter of the fiscal year for educational organizations), when it was hoped the economy would have recovered. Unfortunately, the economy did not improve, so the additional money was not forthcoming.

18. The single business tax is a value added tax. Michigan does not have a traditional corporate profits tax. The profits tax, which had proved to be too subject to cyclical fluctuations, was replaced by the single business tax in 1975.

19. For an extensive description and evaluation of ITI, see Marietta L. Baba and Stuart L. Hart, "The Industrial Technology Institute: Protrait of a New State Industrial Policy Initiative," in Dennis Gray, Trudy Solomon, and William Hetzner (Eds.), *Strategies and Practices for Technological Innovation* (New York: Elsevier North Holland, 1985).

20. Michigan High Technology Task Force, "History" (unpublished, 1985).

21. An earlier study had recommended more attention to high technology, (see Michigan Economic Action Council, "Toward Growth with Stability" (unpublished 1976, 12–18), but nothing on the scale of the task force and the subsequent research centers had been proposed, let alone implemented.

22. The state treasurer was from Goldman, Sachs in New York and had no previous ties to the state and the Director of Commerce was a Washington, D.C., lawyer whose primary experience was in international trade and whose most recent state connection was as a graduate of The University of Michigan Law School.

23. The department heads were Commerce, Management and Budget, Agriculture, Labor, Licensing and Regulation, Natural Resources, and Transportation and the three officials were the Attorney General, the State Treasurer, and the Superintendent for Public Instruction. The lieutenant governor was an ex-officio member.

24. Timothy L. Hunt, "Michigan Business Tax Costs Relative to the Other Great Lakes States," (Kalamazoo: W. E. Upjohn Institute for Employment Research, 1985).

25. *Detroit News* (9 October 1983).

26. This description also follows that of McKenna, "Sustaining the Innovation Process."

27. The city is taking the same action against the Industrial Technology Institute on similar grounds. This threat has deeply concerned ITI officials and members of the High Technology Task Force.

28. For an extended debate on the subject, see the Hearings before the House Ways and Means Committee on the Tax Reform Act of 1978, a bill that radically altered the capital gains tax explicitly to encourage more venture capital activities.

29. Charles Bartsch, *Reaching for Recovery: New Economic Initiatives in Michigan* (Washington, D.C.: Northeast-Midwest Institute, 1985).

30. Converse et al., *Financing Small Manufacturers.*

31. For a more detailed description of the program's activities, see Bartsch, *Reaching for Recovery.*

32. See Schultze, "Industrial Policy," for an excellent argument against national industrial policies. He makes a strong case for why governments cannot shift and concentrate resources as required for growth.

33. In a speech to The University of Michigan Growth Capital Symposium in April 1986, the State Treasurer cited data showing that Michigan led the nation in the number of business incorporations in 1985.

34. An exceptionally active member of the High Technology Task Force said it would take at least ten years to begin to measure the impact of the institutes they created.

Tennessee

I would like to thank Erwin Hargrove for his review of a preliminary draft of this manuscript and advice on the project. Dan Saks and Mal Getz also provided helpful advice on the project. Jean Bartik, David Gottlieb, Becky Hutto, Deb Wickman, Bill Fox, Mike McGuire, and Charles Cook reviewed a preliminary draft of the manuscript as well, and their comments proved helpful. Useful comments were also received from Bob Holland, Scott Fosler and John Forrer of CED, and the other CED case study authors. Snehalata Huzurbazar performed the calculations for the shift-share analysis in a most capable manner.

Bill Long, the former Commissioner of the Tennessee Department of Economic and Community Development, cooperated actively and fully with the study. I greatly appreciate his willingness to allow this independent review of Tennessee's economic development efforts. I also appreciate Governor Lamar Alexander's willingness to be interviewed for this study.

I would like to thank the sixty-one people interviewed for the study for their time, cooperation, and candidness. Under the ground rules for most of the interviews, I agreed not to quote anyone in a manner that allowed identification.

Finally, I would like to dedicate this study to the memory of Dan Saks, who died of cancer in January 1986. Dan recommended me to CED for this project, and gave me advice on how to organize and conduct this study. Dan's style of policy analysis with both the head and heart, and his courage in facing his illness, will always be an inspiration to me.

1. Neal Peirce and Jerry Hagstron, *The Book of America* (New York: Norton, 1983), 365.

2. This discussion draws on R. Corlew, *Tennessee: A Short History,* 2d ed. (Knoxville: University of Tennessee Press, 1981); the Federal Writers' Project, *Tennessee: A Guide to the State* (New York: Viking, 1939); R. Sigafoos, *Cotton Row to Beale Street* (Memphis: Memphis State Press, 1979); and Peirce and Hagstrom, *Book of America.*

3. Center for Business and Economic Research, University of Tennessee—Knoxville, *Tennessee Statistical Abstract 1987,* (Knoxville, Tenn.: University of Tennessee, 1986) 6.

4. All income information comes from the *Tennessee Statistical Abstract* and the *U.S. Statistical Abstract.*

5. Ezra Vogel, *Comeback* (New York: Simon and Schuster, 1985), 243.

6. See note 2 for a list of sources on Tennessee economic history. Other helpful sources include J. Cobb, *Industrialization and Southern Society* (Lexington: University Press of Kentucky, 1984); and J. Cobb, *The Selling of the South* (Baton Rouge: Louisiana State University, 1982).

7. All figures on manufacturing employment and population are taken from the *Tennessee Statistical Abstract, 1987,* and various editions of the *U.S. Statistical Abstract.*

8. All figures on Tennessee versus United States per capita income are taken from either *Historical Statistics of the United States, State Personal Income 1929–82,* or the *Survey of Current Business,* all published by the U.S. Department of Commerce. Civil War era figures are based on estimated per capita income for the East South Central region and assume that the ratio of Tennessee to East South Central per capita income was the same in 1920 as at the time of the Civil War.

9. Corlew, *A Short History,* 365.

10. All employment figures come from the U.S. Department of Labor, Bureau of Labor Statistics, *Employment, Hours, and Earnings, 1939–1982; Employment, Hours, and Earnings, U.S., 1909–1984,* and various issues of BLS periodical *Employment and Earnings.*

11. "Sophisticated" industries are defined as nonelectrical machinery, electrical

machinery, transportation, and instruments. Low-wage industries are defined as textiles, apparel, leather, lumber, and furniture. All figures are from the U.S. Department of Commerce, Regional Economic Information System.

12. S. Shank, "Changes in Regional Unemployment over the Last Decade," *Monthly Labor Review,* 108 (March 1985).

13. Ibid.

14. U.S. Department of Commerce, Regional Economic Information System.

15. This figure comes from Table 9-4. Similar figures are cited in Patricia Postma, "Diversity and Concentration in the Tennessee Economy" (Center for Business and Economic Research, University of Tennessee at Knoxville, July 1982). I am indebted to this excellent paper for a great deal of detailed information on Tennessee's industrial structure and a good discussion of its history and determinants.

16. Tennessee Department of Employment Security, *Annual Averages: Tennessee Labor Force Estimates, 1981–1985* (n.d.) and *U.S. Statistical Abstract.*

17. It should be mentioned that there is no quantitative evidence supporting this perception of greater worker productivity in the South. But, given the many difficulties in measuring productivity, it seems wise to give some weight to the strongly expressed perceptions of business managers in off the record interviews.

18. This weakness in financial services is relative to the entire nation. Tennessee may not be particularly weak in financial services relative to other southern states. Nashville in particular long has been a strong regional financial center. But, until recently, Tennessee banks have been constrained by state laws restricting branch banking.

19. Again, this discussion draws on the excellent work by Postma.

20. D. Hake, D. Poch, and W. Fox, Center for Business and Economic Research, University of Tennessee, *Business Location Determinants in Tennessee* (Knoxville: University of Tennessee, October 1985).

21. Alexander Grant and Company, *The Sixth Annual Study of General Manufacturing Climates,* 1985.

22. R. Sigafoos, *Absolutely Positively Overnight!* (Memphis: St. Luke's Press, 1983).

23. Alexander Grant and Company, *Manufacturing Climates.*

24. Tennessee Valley Authority, Chief Economist Staff, *Economic Outlook 1984,* 55.

25. Ibid, p. 64.

26. See an excellent series of papers by TVA's economic staff: R. Gilmer, R. Mack, and A. Pulsipher, "Job Creation in the Tennessee Valley: Part 1—Manufacturing in Recession and Recovery" and "Part 2—Problems in the Service Sector," working papers.

27. Center for Business and Economic Research, *An Economic Report to the Governor of the State of Tennessee* (Knoxville: University of Tennessee, 1984).

28. U.S. Advisory Commission on Intergovernmental Relations, *1982 Tax Capacity of the Fifty States* (Washington, D.C.: Author, 1985), 88.

29. Ibid., 36.

30. Author's own calculations, from work in progress on state tax treatment of business property.

31. Figures provided by the Tennessee Department of Economic and Community Development. Two-thirds of the state Industrial Training Service budget was assumed to be devoted to branch plant recruiting, and all of ECD's advertising budget was assumed to be a recruiting tool.

32. This description is based on newspaper accounts and conversations with educational researchers at Peabody College of Vanderbilt University.

33. *1985 U.S. Statistical Abstract,* 947.

34. Finance, Ways and Means Staff, General Assembly of State of Tennessee, *Analysis of Expenditures and Positions and Selected Fiscal Data,* 1985.

35. National Education Association, *Estimates of School Statistics, 1984–85,* (NEA, Washington, D.C., 1985) 36, 40.

36. This description is based on information provided by the Safe Growth Staff and various outside observers of state government.

37. Japan Economic Institute, *Japanese Investment in U.S.* (Washington, D.C.: Author, 1982).

38. According to this table, a state with the land area, population, and manufacturing base of Tennessee would be predicted by the statistical model to attract about 3.2 percent of all the new Fortune 500 branches between 1972–78. Tennessee actually attracted about 4.7 percent, or 1.5 percent greater than predicted. Of this 1.5 percent, about 1.1 percent can be explained by the observable variables. According to the model, most of the difference is due to Tennessee's lower wage rates and unionization and greater density of highways than the mythical average state. A relatively small amount is explained by Tennessee's location and lower taxes; although Tennessee gains from both these factors, many other states also have low taxes and a good location, making Tennessee's gain small relative to the national average.

39. A recent study by this author and others supports the belief that supplier labor costs were a major factor in attracting Saturn. Specifically, the study found that the Nashville area was the lowest cost site of 130 possible sites considered in the model, even though Nashville was not the lowest in transportation costs or state and local taxes. Lower supplier wages appeared to be the key to Nashville's cost advantage in this model. See T. Bartik, C. Becker, S. Lake, and J. Bush, "Saturn and State Economic Development," *Forum for Applied Research and Public Policy,* 2, no. 1 (Spring 1987) 29–40.

40. James Papke, "The Taxation of the Saturn Corporation: Intersite Microanalytic Simulations," CTPS Paper 4, Center for Tax Policy Studies, Purdue University.

41. See, for example, M. Barker, ed., *Financing State and Local Economic Development,* (Durham, N.C.: Duke Press Policy Studies, 1983).

42. The *Economic Report to the Governor* has a useful section on predicted long-term trends but does not really go into as much detail as one would wish for economic development policy purposes. This, of course, is not UT's fault; the state has not requested that UT provide analysis of economic development issues.

43. ECD recently commissioned the UT survey mentioned earlier of companies that recently had chosen to locate in Tennessee, but this survey did not ask for any evaluation of the state's economic development programs. Furthermore, the survey did not include companies that had considered Tennessee but chose other states. These "failures" of state policy are at least as interesting for evaluation purposes as the "successes."

California

The authors wish to acknowledge the assistance of the many past and present California officials who provided useful information and insights in the development of this case study. In particular, we would like to thank Anthony Quinn and Janet Turner of the Office of Research in the California Department of Commerce for their careful review of an early draft. In addition, a seminar sponsored by the Committee for Economic Development in cooperation with the California Economic Development Corporation, a roundtable sponsored by the California Commission for Economic Development, and a review by staff of the California State Legislature provided important contributions to the final product.

We also wish to thank R. Scott Fosler of the Committee for Economic Development for his intelligent guidance of the case study process and the other case study authors for their thoughtful comments on early drafts. Finally, we wish to thank our collaborators at SRI who have contributed their ideas, research and inspiration, either directly or indirectly, to the development of this case study: Ted Lyman, Joyce Klein, Richard Stratton, Tom Chmura, Jim Gollub, and John Melville. The opinions expressed in this case study are those of the authors and do not represent the positions of either CED, SRI, or any of the above mentioned individuals.

1. The section describing the evolution of California industry is based on a number of sources including: Carey McWilliams, *California: The Great Exception* (Santa Barbara, Calif.; Peregrine Smith, 1976); "A View of Economic History in California" in the *California State Development Plan* (Sacramento: California Department of Finance, 1968); Joel Kotkin and Paul Grabowicz, *California INC* (New York: Rawson, Wade, 1982); and "California" in Neal Peirce and Jerry Hagstrom, *Book of America* (New York: W.W. Norton & Co., 1983).

2. Michael Piore and Charles Sabel, *Second Industrial Divide* (New York: Basic Books, 1984) 287.

3. Ted Bradshaw, "Issues for California: The World's Most Advanced Industrial Society," in *Emerging Issues in Public Policy: Research Reports and Essays, 1973–1976* (Berkeley: Institute of Governmental Studies, University of California, 1977).

4. "The Optimists: California Economy Survey," *The Economist* (19 May 1984).

5. Thomas Muller, "The Fourth Wave: California's Newest Immigrants" (Washington, D.C.: The Urban Institute, 1984).

6. "Poisoning Prosperity: The Impact of Toxics on California's Economy" (Sacramento: California Commission for Economic Development, 1985).

7. Peirce and Hagstrom, *Book of America,* 751.

8. Edmund G. Brown, Sr., "A System Engineering Approach to Community Problems: A California Experiment," in *California Future Economic Growth,* edited by Werner Hirsch and Richard Baisden (Los Angeles: UCLA Press, 1965).

9. "Public Capital Investment in California 1950–1961: A Study in Intergovernmental Finance" prepared as a component of the State Development Plan Program by Baxter and Associates (1963), p. 50.

10. Infrastructure Review Task Force, "Infrastructure Report and Recommendations to Governor George Deukemejian" (Sacramento: 1984).

11. The following section is based on research prepared by Richard Stratton.

12. Edward Dennison, *Sources of Economic Growth in the United States,* (New York: Committee for Economic Development, 1962).

13. *Digest of California's Educational Statistics,* p. 146.

14. California Postsecondary Education Commission, "Wealth of Knowledge: Higher Education's Impact on California's Economy" (1982), 3.

15. *Digest,* 60.

16. Interview with Clark Kerr.

17. Roger Miller and Marcel Cote, "Growing the Next Silicon Valley," *Harvard Business Review* (July–August 1985): 115.

18. Ibid., 155.

19. Based on research on Silicon Valley prepared by Theodore Lyman "Silicon Val-

ley: Some Success Factors in the Success Story" (Menlo Park, Calif.: SRI International, 1985).

20. Based on research by Joyce Klein.

21. Herman Stekler, *The Structure and Performance of the Aerospace Industry,* (1965).

22. R. Scott Fosler, "State Economic Strategy: Preliminary Observations," (Committee for Economic Development, Unpublished).

23. Interview with William Spanger, chief consultant to the California State Development Plan, also, *California State Development Plan Program Phase II Report,* (1968).

24. Gary G. Hamilton and Nicole Woolsey Biggart, *Governor Reagan, Governor Brown: A Sociology of Executive Power,* (New York: Columbia University Press, 1984), 184.

25. Hamilton and Biggart, *Governor Reagan/Governor Brown,* 20.

26. "Winning Technologies: A New Industrial Strategy for California and the Nation," (Sacramento: Report of the California Commission on Industrial Innovation, 1982), 11.

27. "Economic Development for California in the Decade of the Eighties," (Sacramento: Report of the Economic Development Advisory Task Force, 1983), 2.

28. Ibid., 23.

29. *Business Week* (10 June 1985); Special Section, 22.

30. R. Scott Fosler, "A Framework of State Economic Options" (Committee for Economic Development, Unpublished 1985), 4.

31. Hamilton and Biggart, *Governor Reagan/Governor Brown,* 185.

32. Ibid., 201.

33. Ibid., 203.

34. Ibid., 213.

35. Interview with Cal-Tax staff members.

36. "California Business and Education Reform," in *Innovations in Industrial Competitiveness at the State Level,* prepared by SRI International with the Assistance of Chemical Bank, for the President's Commission on Industrial Competitiveness, 1984.

37. Charles E. Lindbolm, *Strategy of Decisions* (New York: Macmillan, 1963), 35.

38. "Renewing Our Infrastructure: Workable Ways to Build and Maintain Public Facilities" prepared by Association of Bay Area Governments, Bay Area Council and SRI International, 1983.

39. Remi Nadeau, *California: The New Society,* 1963).

Arizona

This analysis of Arizona could not have been done without the help of many people. I particularly wish to thank Governor Bruce Babbitt and Mary Jo Waits, Chief of Economic Policy, formerly of the Office of Economic Planning and Development and the Department of Commerce. Ms. Waits was particularly valuable in research, writing, and providing special insight into this study. Her critical review of the first draft was of great help to me. Jim Ogsbury, my associate, conducted interviews of key leaders in the community. I also thank Kathleen Becker for her organizational help throughout the study and Virginia Levario for her clerical support.

I must acknowledge Dr. John Hall, Director of the Center for Public Affairs, Arizona State University, for his review of the drafts and his assistance on methodical issues.

I also wish to thank Scott Fosler of CED for editorial assistance and guidance throughout the process.

1. Valley National Bank, "Statistical Abstract" (Phoenix: Valley National Bank, 1986).

2. See 1980 U.S. Census.

3. Ibid.

4. Ibid.

5. The source for these statistics is the Arizona Department of Economic Security, which is the state's official data source.

6. Dan Noble in interview with the *Arizona Republic,* 18 September 1955.

7. The quality and nature of the labor force has always been of high importance to manufacturers. See Noble interview in *Arizona Republic,* as well as "Arizona #1 Study," an unpublished internal document. Also see note 18.

8. Dan Noble interview, *Arizona Republic.*

9. Report of the Groundwater Study Commission, June 1980. (Phoenix: State of Arizona, Department of Water Resources, 1980).

10. *Overdraft* occurs when more water is taken out of the water table than is being replenished. *Recharge* refers to a replenishment strategy whereby water from several sources is put back into the water table.

11. Report of the Groundwater Study Commission, pp. I–4.

12. Ibid.

13. Interview with Governor Bruce Babbitt, September 1984.

14. Interview with Mr. William Turner, who served as head of the study committee that set up the Office of Economic Development, July 1972.

15. The representatives were from APS, First Interstate Bank, and The Arizona Bank. They indicated they also were speaking on behalf of the Arizona Economic Development Consortium (AEDC), Arizona Association of Industrial Development (AAID), and the Phoenix Metropolitan Chamber of Commerce.

16. David Birch, *The Job Creation Process,* (Cambridge: 1979).

17. "Opportunities in Arizona for Suppliers of High Technology Manufacturers," (Phoenix: Office of Economic Planning and Development, December 1981).

18. See Real Estate Research Corporation, *Engineering Trends in Real Estate,* 1984 and National Council for Urban Economic Development, *Competitive Advantage: Framing a Strategy to Support High Tech Growth Firms.* Closer to Arizona, the Governor's Advisory Board of Economic Planning and Development wanted to know how Arizona compared to its competition, so, in spring 1983, OEPAD conducted a survey of 100 firms, 60 of which located in Arizona and 40 of which did not. The results for both those that located in Arizona and those that did not showed that the personnel issues (cost, trainability, availability, productivity, and attitude) were the most important determinant; that quality of life statistically was among the top three and clearly was an important decision-making consideration for those who located in Arizona. Governor Babbitt, in his comments about economic development, felt the quality of life issues have been crucial in Arizona's economic development successes. This report, though unpublished, is called within OEPAD the "Arizona #1 Study," May 1983.

19. See Title 9, Arizona Revised Statutes.

20. The author's notes from the meeting. The author was a participant.

21. Research Park staff memo to the Board of Regents, August 1984.

22. Revenues from sales of state lands (of which Arizona received almost 10 million acres at statehood in 1912) must go into a permanent trust fund, the principal of which

cannot be invaded. Over 90 percent of these revenues are earmarked for education and are held in the School Trust Fund.

23. Governor Bruce Babbitt, "State of the State," January 9, 1984.

24. Message to Arizona Legislature from Governor Bruce Babbitt, March 14, 1985.

Indiana

1. Neal R. Peirce and Jerry Hagstrom, *The Book of America: Inside 50 States Today* (New York: W. W. Norton & Company, 1983), 282.

2. Jerry Hagstrom and Robert Guskind, "Playing the State Ranking Game: A New National Pastime Catches On," *The National Journal* 16, no. 26 (30 June 1984): 1272.

3. Donald F. Carmony, ed., *Indiana: A Self Appraisal* (Bloomington: Indiana University Press, 1966), 68.

4. Ibid.

5. Bill Koening, "State's Car Plants Feed Other Factories," *The Indianapolis Star* (12 August 1985): 1.

6. Indiana Department of Commerce, "An Historical Overview of Indiana's Economy," (Indianapolis: Unpublished, 1982), v.

7. Ibid., vi.

8. Ibid., vii.

9. David A. Reed and Charles A. Sim, "Economic Development in Indiana: Retrospect and Prospect" (Indianapolis: Indiana Department of Commerce, Unpublished, 1982).

10. Indiana Department of Commerce, "Historical Overview," vii.

11. Eli Ginzberg, "The Mechanization of Work," *Scientific American* 247, no. 3, (September 1982): 67.

12. Ibid., 71.

13. See Hagstrom and Guskind, "The State Ranking Game," 1271–72; INDIRS: U.S. Statistical Abstract, 1985.

14. "The Data Bank," *The Indianapolis Star,* (2 September 1986): 25.

15. Executive Planning Committee, *In Step With The Future . . . : Indiana's Strategic Economic Development Plan,* (Indianapolis: Indiana State Chamber of Commerce, 1984), 32.

16. David A. Reed, "An Assessment of Indiana's Educational Attainment Levels" (Indianapolis: Indiana Department of Commerce, Unpublished, 1982), 14.

17. A. D. Little, "Key Factors Affecting Investment Decisions and Indiana's Relative Strengths and Weaknesses in Terms of These Factors," (Indianapolis: Executive Planning Committee Working Paper, Unpublished, 1983).

18. Executive Planning Committee, *In Step With The Future,* 32.

19. Michael A. Lewis and Charlie Cain, "No Fireworks in Winning Plant Bid," *The Indianapolis Star,* (30 July 1985): 21.

20. Executive Planning Committee, *In Step With The Future,* 36.

21. Patrick D. O'Rourke, "Property Taxation," in James A. Papke, *Indiana's Revenue Structure: Major Components and Issues,* Part I, (West Lafayette, Ind.: Purdue University, 1984), 91.

22. Corporation for Innovation Development brochure.

23. Indiana Infrastructure, Inc., brochure.

24. "Orr/Mutz Economic Development Package: Phases I–V," (Indianapolis, Ind.: Office of the Lieutenant Governor, July 1985).

25. Neal R. Peirce, Jerry Hagstrom, and Carol Steinbach, *Economic Development: The Challenge of the 1980s,* (Washington, D.C.: Council of State Planning Agencies, 1983), 8.

26. Ibid.

27. Indiana Department of Commerce, press release, July 29, 1985.

28. Morton J. Marcus, "Indiana's Infrastructure," (Indianapolis: EPC Working Paper, Unpublished, 1983), 5.

29. Bill Koening, "GM to spend $575 Million at Marion Plant," *The Indianapolis Star* (14 August 1985): 27.

30. Bill Koening, "Japanese Firm to Build Wheel Plant in Indiana," *The Indianapolis Star* (21 August 1985): 30.

31. Indiana Department of Commerce press release, July 19, 1985.

32. Interview with Morton J. Marcus, July 22, 1985.

33. Jan Carroll, "$200 Million Annual Waste-Water Funding Urged," *Louisville Courier-Journal* (22 May 1985).

Minnesota

1. Minnesota Department of Energy and Economic Development, "Trends in the Minnesota Economy," in *Minnesota: A Strategy for Economic Development* (St. Paul, Minn.: n.d.), 16–17.

2. Minnesota Taxpayers Association, "How Does Minnesota Compare?" (St. Paul, Minn.: December 1985).

3. Theodore C. Blegen, *Minnesota: A History of the State,* (Minneapolis: University of Minnesota Press, 1963).

4. Conversation with Paul Christopherson.

5. John K. Iglehart, "The Twin Cities Medical Marketplace," *New England Journal of Medicine* 311, no. 5 (August 2, 1984): 343.

Appendix B

1. Joseph Schumpeter, *Capitalism, Socialism, and Democracy* (New York: Harper & Row, 1942).

2. "The California Economy, 1947–1969" (Menlo Park, Calif.: Stanford Research Institute, 1960).

3. California State Development Plan (1968) p. 71.

4. "1990 Labor and Employment in California" (Sacramento, Calif.: California Department of Commerce, 1983).

5. "California's Technological Future: Emerging Economic Opportunities in the 1980s" (Menlo Park, Calif.: SRI International, 1982).

Index